# The Anxious Years

# THE

# ANXIOUS

# YEARS

*America in the
Vietnam-Watergate Era*

# Kim McQuaid

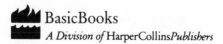 BasicBooks
*A Division of* HarperCollins*Publishers*

Library of Congress Cataloging-in-Publication Data

McQuaid, Kim.
    The anxious years.

    Bibliographical Notes: p. 325.
    Includes index.
    1. United States—Politics and government—1969–1974.
    2. United States—Politics and government—1963–1969.
    3. Vietnamese Conflict, 1962–1975—United States.
    4. Watergate Affair, 1972–1974.  I. Title.
    E855.M39   1989        973.923        88–47907
    ISBN   0–465–00389–3   (cloth)
    ISBN   0–465–00390–7   (paper)

For Panda,

who opened the doors

to love at last.

# CONTENTS

# PREFACE

T HIS BOOK took shape while the author was working in nonsectarian homeless shelters in Belfast, Northern Ireland, over Christmas week, 1985. Its author had taken a vacation from an endowed professorship at University College Dublin in the Irish Republic to face some of the unburied demons of his ancestral land. As he did so, he also began to think more deeply about his native soil. He realized how little he genuinely understood about the recent history of the United States of America: about changes that he had been part of and events that had formed his hopes, fears, and perceptions in very significant ways. He therefore determined, like many an author before him had done, to write the sort of book he wanted to read. One that could make wholes out of the too often kaleidoscopic experiences of his youth.

*The Anxious Years* is history without heroes. It is not a disguised morality play aimed at making one group or another feel better about itself, or allowing any group to rationalize past sins of omission or commission. The book chronicles unhappy events of a tragic time, and does so in a fashion that may better enable readers who grew to adulthood during or after the Vietnam-Watergate era to comprehend the passions and the power struggles that did so much to determine the ideological and institutional contexts out of which they came—or into which they were born.

*The Anxious Years* says what it means. It assumes that history should be taken out of the seminar room and put back in the living room where it belongs. It was written in the belief that the primary responsibility of any chronicler is to the men and women of our own time, and not to the inbred debates of the ostentatiously uninvolved or to the intellectual gymnastics of the academy. The book, therefore, avoids scholarly jargon, assumes no spectacular familiarity with Vietnam and Watergate-related events, and aims at helping to achieve improved awareness of the constant trade-offs between ideals and interests in the real world of politics. History is not made of dead facts we place in the keeping of polysyllabic experts. It is ourselves and what we do or don't do about the issues our past has bequeathed to our future.

It takes no special genius, after all, to determine that the constitutional issues concerning political sabotage and misuse of presidential war powers that surfaced with Watergate are alive and well in the America of the Iran-Contra affair and its aftermath. Richard Milhous Nixon's presidency was destroyed when he overused Guerilla Government techniques developed to strengthen the president's hand in foreign military and diplomatic affairs in domestic politics as well. Ronald Wilson Reagan, meanwhile, turned Guerilla Government into a high art by subverting specific congressional prohibitions against providing large-scale military and "covert action" aid to the *contra* forces in the Nicaraguan civil war, by secretly shipping arms to the theocratic fascists currently in power in Iran, and by making use of a bevy of present and former military officers to do all of this and more. Whatever else the Iran-Contra political and criminal investigations will eventually demonstrate about politics in America, it will not be that benign neglect concerning ongoing constitutional war powers debates is either sensible or feasible.

All authors are necessarily lonely beasts. The two years required to complete this book, however, were made far more pleasant and productive by friends and acquaintances, both foreign and domestic. First, I must thank the faculty and staff of the Department of History at University College Dublin. Their selecting me as Mary Ball Washington Visiting Professor of U.S. History during the academic year 1985–86 gave me wonderful opportunities to write, and to do so in a city that prides itself on its receptivity toward scribblers of many types. Playwrights and drunken poets not least. *A Dhia, Saor Éire.*

Then there are friends who kept me in one piece—or helped put me back together—on occasions too numerous to mention, by reading, for instance, my incessant letters and by responding with ideas of their own. Ideas I have regularly appropriated for my own nefarious purposes. My warm regards, then, to Sid and Helene Amster, Ed Berkowitz and Emily Frank, Rob Citino, Candi and Brian Dunnigan, the late Dave French, Marc Gaynes and Leslie Landis, John and Mary Gray Hughes, Karen Levin, Joel and Margalit Mokyr, Karina and Lou O'Malley, Stan Pozdziak, and Meg Sondey and Bill Hines. I owe them all a very great deal.

Thanks go, too, to students and staff at Lake Erie College. To the students for those occasional shining questions that have kept my mind alive while laboring in the academic trenches, and to the staff for humor that has made the usually humorless folkways of the professoriate much easier to bear. Ellen Tarver of Cleveland worked hard and well typing and retyping my many drafts—and did so, moreover, while managing the transitions to a new job and another beaming baby. At Basic Books, regard and appreciation go to Martin Kessler, and especially to senior editor Steven Fraser and his assistants, first Nancy Peske and then Renée Dye. Special thanks must also be extended to my indomitable project editor, Charles Cavaliere, who set new standards for gonzo creativity. It is inevitable that any author has faith in whatever he writes. But editors have the harder task of weighing intellectual hope and commercial experience. For having faith, I thank them all.

Special appreciation, finally, goes out to my mother, for having the quiet virtues of an educated heart; to my father, for being a man of thought and nature; to my brother, Kevin, for blundering along with me over the years; and to Panda. This one, most of all, is for her.

Dublin, Ireland/Painesville, Ohio
September 1985–June 1988

# The Anxious Years

# PROLOGUE

## *AMERICA THE FORTUNATE*

THE UNITED STATES is a lucky land: endowed, affluent, and geographically protected from non-nuclear threats. Its unusual, universalistic, and ideological nationality reflects this simple and overriding fact. Not for Americans a defining sense of tragedy and loss, not for them the conception of utopia as a blessed past never to be regained. For Americans, utopia is in the future, and achieving this hoped-for state is no farther away than, to paraphrase Henry Kissinger, the intensities of their commitments and energies.[1]

This future-orientation of American life is accentuated by the nation's peculiar and abstract nationality-of-ideas. America is hamburgers and apple pie and science fiction and detective thrillers, to be sure. But these cultural elements—and much else besides—are imports. The United States is a new society that possesses relatively few refinements held in common for centuries or millennia. Instead, to be "American" is to internalize what many commentators have termed a "civil religion," or, to be less pretentious about it, to play by certain political rules of the game. It is these rules, and Americans' willingness to abide by them, that makes them American. The constant reiteration of these abstractions—among which "politics is the art of compromise," "checks and balances," regular elections, peaceful transitions of power, separation of church and state, equal rights and duties among citizens, and the primacy of a legal system based upon historical precedents figure prominently—allows the United States of America to meld a mélange of immigrant and native-born populations together in ways that are impressive (and sometimes confusing) to visitors from other lands. Lands where national identity *is* based upon unique cultures much more than political ideas deemed universal in their application.

America's civil religion, variously identified as "democracy," "liberty," or "freedom," so suffuses our nation that we barely notice it. We who perceive ourselves to be the most practical of people are actually a society of dreamers whose dreams, fortunately for ourselves, are very often held in common. We dream so insistently that it is difficult for Americans to comprehend how other nations can surrender political freedom and go on existing. But authoritarianism, dictatorship, or theocratic fascism *are* the civil religions of many other lands, just as they have been for most of human history. Dictatorship, in Iran, China, or Russia, for example, has often been seen as necessary to preserve the national culture from extinction by foreign enemies. When the dictators get the job done successfully, political freedom is considered a very small price to pay for survival.

Logic like this puzzles Americans, and well it should. History has been kinder to us than it has to most peoples in most places almost all of the time. In this lucky land, catastrophes have been modest, and opportunities for optimism and affluence many. It has been 125 years since Americans buried their own dead on their own battlefields—a handful of small Indian campaigns excepted. It has been equally long since the survival of the nation was directly and immediately at risk.

Lacking most of the grislier elements of national apocalypse, America has been a history of comparatively risk-free security, expansion, victories, and triumphs. Our nation lost far fewer people conquering a continent than French and Spanish kings lost trying to control Belgium and Holland or than Prussian, Austrian, and Russian monarchs lost contesting the ownership of savory chunks of Poland.

Given such a scarcity of catastrophe and threat, a tradition of strong central government has never taken secure root in the United States, and a decentralized political culture based upon individualism and individual rights has flowered accordingly. While most peoples have always been too concerned with the grimmer imperatives of physical and cultural survival to care very much about abstractions like political rights, the United States, at its best, is an embodiment of Enlightenment ideals such as a natural rights–social contract approach to governance. It is ideals, as much as interests, that make Americans tick; that motivate their actions and dreams; that produce their occasional and relatively modest nightmares.

A lucky history and the overarching (and sometimes overweening) idealism that have gone with it have also led Americans to deemphasize history. For all our discussions of national will and national mission, our conceits of ourselves as a great Light unto the Nations and our willingness to universalize the American experience, we tend to ignore our own history and those of other lands.

Here, again, there is method to the madness. History consists of dead facts which often must be forgotten if an ideological nationalism is to work. Immigrants must forget Old Country or Old World habits and examples; Civil War memories should not divide descendants of Unionist, Copperhead, Scalawag, and Confederate; Black, White, Red, Yellow, and Brown should transcend conquests, exploitations, and racisms and seek for political unity within cultural diversity. History, if it does not concentrate upon the evolution and improvement of the civil religion that binds the variety of America together, is a trap, a self-fulfilling tragedy with no way out, James Joyce's Irish tribal nightmare from which he struggled to awake.

Americans have awakened, presuming that they were ever lost in merely historical sleep in the first place. For history is very often perceived tragedy and a sense of loss, as well as an effort, more or less clearly enunciated, to inculcate morality back into an age which historians believe has lost it. The logic that could lead Tacitus to explain, two thousand years ago, that a historian's foremost duty is to record merit and "to confront evil words and deeds with the fear of posterity's denunciations"[2] is largely foreign to the United States. Americans tend to forget both merit and evil, and get on with the present and future-oriented business of life.

They can well afford to. To Americans, a fortunate and untragic people, agreement about procedures and rules is often also deemed a guarantee that the problems to which their civil religion is applied can be solved *quickly*. If only, of course, everybody plays by these same rules.

Civil religion now demonstrates its optimistic, can-do, and future-oriented aspect. It explains, as well, the brash, impatient, and pushy elements of the American character, what many a skeptical reviewer of matters American in foreign parts has termed a kind of endless youthful belief in the *promise* of life.

This aspect of America's nationality induces fury, envy, and wistful shakings of the head by many others exposed to it or dependent upon it. European intellectuals wait for Americans to grow up, to stop acting as if the universe were their oyster and God and the Fates stood at their right hand, and to undergo the chastening experiences that Europe itself sus-

tained throughout the first half of the twentieth century. Our North
American neighbors who inevitably know us best (and sometimes better
than we know ourselves) remark upon the almost Roman arrogance of
Americans, their flypaper culture which imports and then takes credit for
things other nations have developed, and their amazing incomprehension
of the fact that Canada and Mexico are two of the largest and most
economically and intellectually productive nations on Earth.

But, as a bitterly disappointed Mexican dictator once observed during
a drinking bout, his nation was far from God and right next to the United
States. And the United States, for most of the past two centuries, has been
synonymous with economic growth and the political and military authority that flows from it. Culturally and even politically, Mexicans or Canadians may feel almost Greek in their belief that they possess superior com-
prehension of the subtleties of culture and life. But they also know that
they are Greeks living in an age in which the United States has assumed
a Rome-like stature in the practical affairs of the world.

Thus envy enters in. For Americans are "New Romans" in important
aspects. Their major skills are political and technological, as opposed to
artistic and otherwise cultural. As Rome built aqueducts, Americans build
computers. As Rome created and ruled an Empire of Ideas for a thousand
years and more, so Americans universalize their ideology on a global scale.
As Rome received most of its High Culture from Greece and Persia and
other lands, so America imports its versions from around the veritable
globe.

And, again like Rome, America suffers from hubris: a feeling of satisfac-
tion in great powers and great achievements which can induce a sense of
virtue and mission which rises too far above reality, tempts the fates, and
induces disaster. The "sin of pride," the ancient Greeks called such vanity
and the retribution which could follow upon it.

Hubris, alas, is very important in understanding American history in
recent decades. During those years, the bases of U.S. nationality have
taken a beating. Doubts have replaced certainties. Youthful historical innocence, a belief in our exceptional historical status, faith in quick solutions, and conceptions of politics as sets of universalistic principles that can
be applied anywhere and anytime became debatable in a world that had
previously been inhabited by certainties.

Americans, chastened by untoward and unexpected events, had to think
about themselves, learn more about who they were, and better comprehend what differentiated them from the vast majority of other peoples in
the world. Now history became important. Not as a trap, not as an excuse
for past sins of omission or commission, not as a self-pitying wail or a futile

gnashing of teeth. But, instead, as a moral lesson for ourselves and any others who care to learn from it.

Learning lessons is not easy, especially moral lessons. America has long perceived itself as a uniquely moral nation. For "teachers" to admit that they had much to learn was sobering at best.

Knowledge, then, wrenched us. It still does. America the fortunate, at a summit of pride and power, faced unfortunate circumstances, many of its own devising. The stresses and strains that resulted were unpleasant. Fear often substituted for fact, and diatribe or self-pity for reality. The Anxious Years of Vietnam, Watergate, and associated events are, however, the present into which many of us were born, as well as a historical experience with which the rest of us have lived. Understanding these formative events is the aim of what follows here: a plotting of directions from past to present so that what the future may hold will be clearer for us all.

The book is organized in four parts. The first concerns the wrenching events of 1968, the year that formed a generation and the year that devoured a Democratic Party which had led the nation into its second unsuccessful "limited war" on the Asian mainland. Part Two discusses the nature of that war, and it demonstrates how the high-technology Men Out, Machines In strategy that came to be the political golden mean in America after the Tet offensive was politically and militarily disastrous in Vietnam, Cambodia, and Laos. Failing to win a quick war of attrition, the United States chose a policy of mechanized annihilation. It drained the sea to get the enemy fish. Part Three treats the antiwar responses to the Vietnam War, paying particular attention to the New Left. The Movement, I argue, was never as organized, powerful, or leadership-prone as its enemies and its friends supposed; and its weaknesses helped to account for the duration, extent, and destructiveness of the war. Finally, in Part Four, the Nixon administration's overuse of the feral attitudes spawned by Vietnam climaxed in Watergate, a twenty-seven-month legal and political struggle during which a president paid the price for his own and his immediate predecessors' imperial assumptions. Watergate was almost never heroic, but rather one facet of ongoing institutional failure and of constitutional problems left mostly unaddressed. The "system" that "worked" during Watergate was not the one in American civics or political science texts, and efforts to insure that Watergate-style abuses of power never happened again were, accordingly, made very largely passé by the Iran-Contra affair that besmirched Ronald Reagan's presidency.

# PART ONE

# 1968:

# THINGS FALL APART

Duhning the terrible year of 1968, Americans knew their society was
at risk, that even the unifying principles that gave it form were at risk.
Most people were not very articulate about the nature of the threats and
far from agreed about how to resolve them. Still the sense of wrenching
events was widespread. Many affirmed the country was changing from or
changing into something that endangered its power, its coherence, and its
interest, maybe its survival as well. "Things," it was often said, "can't go
on like this."

Indeed they could not. By 1968, American life was characterized by a
climate of crisis and a polarizing sense of unexpected complexity and limits
to the possible. The waves of anger and enervation that followed have
flowed into our own times, as have attempts to resolve issues that became
truly national in scope during the final year of Lyndon Baines Johnson's
plagued presidency.

1968 was a watershed, a year from which people dated things and a focal
point for a "generation." The events of that period set an agenda of debate
that few interested citizens could—or did—ignore. Though change and
transition are constants in human affairs, 1968 was and remains a rip in
time. It was a year in which people were forced to choose and to take

responsibility for their choices; a year in which people learned to hate well—and to love well. Their loves and hatreds are with us still, as embodied history.[1]

Things didn't start out that way. Not quite, and especially not in Vietnam, the hinge on which everything else turned. Success was coming, military and political leaders assured the nation at the start of that year—later than advertised, yes, but truly and without doubt. Light already shone at the end of the tunnel. America's "limited war" of attrition on the mainland of Asia would not end up, as had an earlier anticommunist struggle in Korea, as a frustrating process of risking too much and then having to content itself with the restoration of a status quo ante bellum. In Vietnam, defensive "containment" rather than aggressive "rollback" or "liberation" was the solution. Finely tuned war management would bleed the communists dry, thus demonstrating the United States' resolve to man the frontiers of freedom throughout the wide regions of the world that had been made independent after the retreat of the European empires.

But at the very end of January came the Tet offensive, timed to coincide with Vietnam's lunar New Year—a series of attacks on targets throughout South Vietnam, mounted by an enemy whose days were numbered and whose cause was surely lost.[2]

As the hunted became the hunter, a fault line opened in U.S. politics. The bipartisan political accord that had enabled policymaking elites to wage a limited war in Asia fell apart. Recipes for improving the situation varied, but suspicions grew that the war, as it was then being carried on, was a ticket to nowhere. The American people and their representatives had, somehow, been lied to, perhaps by leaders who had first lied to themselves, perhaps by men whose motives were more manipulative than mistaken. Erring political and military leaders had to "get serious" (i.e., more aggressive) about the war—a view favored by most; or they had to withdraw U.S. combat forces from Southeast Asia gradually or immediately—an opinion held by a growing minority.[3]

The fracturing of the broad political alliance regarding Cold War military policy in Vietnam that followed the Tet offensive delegitimized the "expert" activities that were normally a unifying element of national policy: war. Tet made it appear that the emperors had no clothes, or far fewer than they claimed. It did so precisely when the practicing politicos needed all the legitimacy and divinity that doth hedge kings, commanding generals, members of Congress, bureaucratic barons, and academic entrepreneurs with ambitious miens and attaché cases.

The political nakedness of such leaders after Tet was only partially of their making and only indirectly related to the frustrating realities of the war itself. Vietnam was part of an amalgam of political, economic, and social forces which by early 1968 had acted to produce a sense of flux and emergency in the minds of tens of millions of Americans of all ages, stations, and conditions. Vietnam, race relations, and "permissive" social attitudes were major concerns of the country and those who were leading it. In Vietnam the Most Powerful Nation in the World was obviously falling far behind in its anticommunist schedule. Spectacular and well-televised domestic conflicts had become staple American problems as well. A United States which sought to export its version of society to the rest of the world was having a lot of trouble marketing the product at home. Alarming mixtures of hallucinogenic drugs, cannabis, crime, premarital sex, coddling of legal offenders, uppity kids, foul language, and irreverent and possibly dangerous Black Power advocates sporting Afros, biker glasses, berets, and black leather jackets appeared to millions of the normally faithful to add up to a compelling argument for the immediate restoration of traditional values and behavior.[4]

## The Establishment Feels the Strain

The first to feel popular tremors was the foreign policy elite which had led America into its second "limited war" on Asia's mainland—the sort of people (almost all white, male, and over forty) whose sense of themselves and the world had been forged during the Second World War and the nuclear balance of terror which had followed fast upon it. To such men, the isolationist political and military tradition of prewar decades was an enemy almost as fearsome as communism itself. Between 1942 and 1968, these "national security managers" labored long and hard to lock the United States into a bipartisan foreign policy based upon the twin strategies of internationalism and collective security agreements designed to halt the expansion of revolutionary Marxism around the world. This process of persuasion had its bad moments. Allies grumbled and played hard to get. At home, a unilateralist right wing, afraid of the Big Government that was an inevitable result of global containment and skeptical of foreigners (especially Western European Social Democrats and non-Caucasian peoples, who were outside the pale of their concept of civilization), contended long and hard against everything from military alliances to foreign aid. A weak but vociferous left argued that America was becoming imperialist while trying to enforce a Pax Americana based on the status quo upon the world. In general, however, the national security managers had built well, by a carrot-and-stick process of convincing elected political leaders of the humanitarian and other advantages of containment and collective security where possible, or by scaring them with the spectre of imminent red disaster when they could not.

This foreign policy elite, however, had a fatal flaw. Its members were not, by and large, very representative of or very informed about the nation that they had elected (but almost never been elected) to lead.[5] As Richard J. Barnet has argued, these prosperous, schooled, articulate, concerned, and widely travelled (if also narrow) men were "emigrés in America," strangers in their own land:

> The world in which they moved—the Metropolitan Club, the Council on Foreign Relations, the intimate dinners with ambassadors, newspaper publishers, financiers—bore little more resemblance to the America in which most citizens were struggling to make their lives than the court of Louis XVI bore to revolutionary France. To say that the national security managers were out of touch with the country is an understatement. There was a substantial part of the country [outside of the boundaries of the upper-class suburbs and major cities and prestigious universities of the Northeast and smallish sections of the Midwest] . . . of whose existence they were quite unaware. Their contact with poor people or blacks was limited to the doorman at the Metropolitan Club. The closest they came to seeing hunger in America was when a dinner partner was treated to bad service at a declining French restaurant. They saw themselves as a benevolent aristocracy without obligation to spend time with or on lesser people.[6]

In the wake of Tet, however, a popular revolt against them commenced in earnest. A public that had been convinced of Cold War goals like the preservation of a Free World against the threats of Marxist-Leninist contagion—and which had generally left it up to the national security managers to achieve that goal—splintered and shifted toward two opposite poles: get tough or get out. Vietnam, the latest battleground of the Cold War, ceased to be a Commie turkey shoot or a crusade that didn't require thinking about. Instead, it became a grim race between the opposing side's loss of blood and willpower and the political establishment's loss of internal cohesion and mass political support.[7]

It was all so ironic. Most of the elite were as surprised by Tet as their less data-rich brethren, and for the same reasons. They had thought that America would win in Vietnam, and quickly. Until Tet, almost all ambitious political climbers had loyally supported the war or maintained discreet silence about any doubts. These operators read newspapers and public policy memoranda, to be sure. They listened to briefings, attended high-level meetings and conferences, and read (or wrote) essays for journals of opinion. Some of what they read and heard told them that their optimism was lunatic; that their assumptions about Vietnam amounted to "Crackpot Realism." But like those who preceded and followed them, the national security managers studied less for revelation than for confirmation.[8] They were far more interested in having what they thought they knew affirmed than they were in having it challenged. Their investigations and ritual confabulations in suites over cocktails, therefore, harnessed new facts to old theories. New information, presuming any was let into the system, was tailored to fit old patterns. Eyes tended to glaze over when established arguments (and the careers built upon those same established arguments) were not decisively buttressed; outright challenges to "insiders' " liturgies were ignored.[9]

## The Grass Roots Tremble

Such elite rituals confirming the already known and the already understood came to an end by early February 1968. By then, Tet was well and truly under way. One of every ten of South Vietnam's provincial capitals had been attacked. Anti-aircraft guns had been secretly towed hundreds of miles through "militarily secure" zones and put into action on the approaches to Saigon's main airport. The ancient Vietnamese imperial capital of Hue was in enemy hands. Other highly visible symbolic attacks had been made on a handful of U.S. installations, chiefly a suicide mission aimed at the U.S. embassy in downtown Saigon itself.[10]

Confusion thereupon ran riot in official Washington and in the country at large. Popular levels of perplexity and panic were closely related to levels of ignorance. Like those who were managing U.S. foreign policy, most Americans had rarely thought about the actual events in Vietnam to any appreciable extent. The people knew there was a war going on, but it was far away. In the 1960s, the U.S. economy was glowing. Vietnam demanded sacrifices of relatively few citizens—no increased taxes and no full mobilization of the home front by, for example, calling up the army, navy, air force, or marine reserves. Vietnam was not a war fought by drafting most of the talent, wealth, or energy of the population as a whole, especially that of the wealthier part of that population, as witnessed by wholesale exemptions from military service (e.g., 2-S deferments for all students successfully enrolled in colleges and universities). In such circumstances, all that most people dimly sensed was that the communist enemies hadn't rolled over or run away when America's boys arrived on the scene to finish what the French and the anticommunist Vietnamese hadn't been able to accomplish in the preceding twenty years. During the late autumn of 1967, an administration-orchestrated "progress" campaign had kept most peoples' awareness at near-comatose levels. Everything was all right and the enemy was, indeed, losing fast and steadily. "Gooks" in rice paddies were no match for helicopter gunships, fighters, and bombers, certainly not for B-52s that could rain down explosives from seven miles above. The skeptical, male collegians worrying about how long their 2-S deferments might last, or the friends or relatives of a young man who had come back from Vietnam much quieter than when he left—or not come back at all—were further lulled by weekly "body counts." This bureaucratic arithmetic, which demonstrated that U.S. and South Vietnamese forces combined were killing four, five, or more communists for every man they themselves were losing, was broadcast by all commercial television networks.

It was, then, only a matter of time. The war to stop communism in Asia was being fought by somebody else: small-town hicks, urban low-lifes, and rednecks of various regional persuasions; guys who weren't smart enough to stay out of the army. Those who deemed themselves smarter, and they were many, had little spare time to worry much about the fate of their less fortunate brethren. After all, there was money, good money, to be made selling insurance in Scarsdale, New York, or Kokomo, Indiana. There was money, good money, to be made by getting a degree in chemistry at Harvard, literature at Ohio State, psychology at the University of Chicago, or civil engineering at Cornell. Vietnam was a long way away and there was life to be lived. And, say, didn't that blonde at the next table have great breasts—and an ass that'd knock your eyes out? And wasn't, after all, the mating ritual mostly what it was all about for an eighteen-year-old boy trying to be a man, or for an eighteen-year-old girl trying to be a woman?

No, it wasn't. Not after Tet, it wasn't. For then, as never before, the war "came home" to America. Now, finally, the money, mating rituals, careers, and a whole lot else besides were widely and immediately at risk in a way they had never been before. Increasingly, ill-humored confusion became the order of the day.[11]

## A Leader Hesitates—And Is Lost

Confusion among the leaders, rather than the led, was a different matter entirely. It was less a result of ignorance and subsequent shock than of a chilling knowledge about public events that came, all too belatedly, to public men. In the nation's capital, psychological defeat, "hunkering down," and a loss of the all-important appearance of maintaining political and military initiatives were the major results of the Tet offensive and of what came afterwards.

*The* thing to understand about the political effect of Tet is that it discredited "limited" war-as-usual. The war had to be either accelerated or somehow wound down. The middle ground that President Lyndon Baines Johnson had occupied largely vanished.

Johnson and his Democratic and Republican party allies had to do something decisive. Most Americans wanted them to escalate the fighting and thus resolve what a protégé of Robert McNamara's at the Department of Defense had earlier called the "escalating military stalemate;" deescalation was an alternative increasingly popular among liberal Democrats and some Republicans who were becoming anxious over the thrashing about of a military machine most had called into being in the first place. Or they could withdraw unilaterally, an alternative the radical wing of the antiwar movement had advanced well before Tet.[12]

Johnson, however, hesitated. He selected neither alternative, and so was lost. Politics, most of the time, is theater: theater in which appearances are at least as important as reality. It is a high-variable and low-information environment that is very like a poker game, a game in which a good 90 percent of what usually goes on is impression and bluff. If we use poker as an analogy, LBJ's mistake becomes easier to comprehend. Tet raised the stakes from the two-bit to the fifty-dollar range. But Johnson, who held the cards, didn't put up, didn't shut up, and acted as if the game hadn't, in fact, changed. Instead of acting quickly to resolve the crisis, maintain the initiative, and be decisive (if only by bluffing), Johnson seemed to drift with events. He didn't escalate or decrease the scope of the war; in Peter

Braestrup's words, he "essentially . . . sought to buy time for 'more of the same' . . . He left a big void which others [hawks and doves alike] hastened to fill."[13]

Now began the final act in the tragedy of Lyndon Johnson. Discouraged and sometimes sleepless with worry about the fate of American troops, Johnson was caught on the horns of a dilemma he had labored long—and until then successfully—to avoid. He also faced the dilemma without the assistance of key aides. Secretary of Defense Robert McNamara, in particular, departed on February 29th as Tet sputtered to a close, marking the effective end of the continuum between John F. Kennedy's and Lyndon Baines Johnson's prosecution of the war.[14]

Johnson's dilemma was stark. To escalate the war meant spilling more blood and expending even more treasure. More treasure meant more spending for war *and* correspondingly less for the social welfare programs denominated The Great Society, programs that were just getting off the ground, fiscally and organizationally, in Washington. Lyndon Johnson feared that accelerating the war would kill the Great Society. He was not paranoid. Conservatives who disliked social welfare programs but had been unable to defeat them in Congress were only too willing to use patriotic belt-tightening as a cloak behind which to smother the Great Society in its cradle. Other legislation, including civil rights statutes, faced the same threat.

Johnson's instincts were absolutely correct. Worse, he'd increased the threats facing him. He had pushed a tax cut through Congress on the eve of fully Americanizing the Vietnam War in 1965. It would now be very difficult to go back to ask for a tax increase unless he wrapped himself in the flag and called for all-out war and war taxes.

All-out war, however, was a death knell for domestic social reform. Johnson was hoist on his own petard. Fighting a limited war in Vietnam had allowed for a "guns-and-butter" budget, more war, and more welfare at the same time. This paid rich political dividends for many Democrats who could thereby be liberal in domestic policy and hard-line Cold Warriors in foreign policy. Now Johnson had to choose. If he chose all-out war, as conservative legislators and most of the populace then desired, it could only be at the expense of the social welfare program which Johnson rightly regarded as his finest political achievement.[15]

Johnson failed to choose. He did not escalate the war. But, committed to victory in Vietnam, he did not deescalate either. Instead, he fiddled with the budget, tried to disguise increases in military and social spending, signed a tax increase that was too little and too late, and alienated everybody. The deficit, inflation, and taxes all rose too fast for comfort; the rate of increase of social welfare expenditures was not halted (to the horror of the conservatives) and the rate of increase of war spending was not decreased (to the disgust of the liberals). By insisting upon more of the same, Johnson boxed himself into a corner and became a captive of events.[16]

Now Johnson faced the equivalent in U.S. politics of the death of a thousand cuts, jointly administered by angry Cold Warriors on the right and the restive left wing of his own party. Meanwhile, Kennedyites who had conveniently parted company with him when the war got much rougher than expected engaged in ad hominem abuse at LBJ's expense.

Lyndon Johnson finally regained the political initiative, and in a most unusual way. On the evening of March 31st, following an otherwise unremarkable nationwide address, Johnson called upon Americans to avoid the ugly consequences of divisiveness in a diverse society. Then he announced that, to decrease said divisions, he would neither seek nor accept renomination as president of these United States. LBJ, in other words, resigned office, effective almost immediately.[17]

## *The Doves Move In*

The fox was in the political henhouse now. LBJ's surprise resignation left a void in the center of the Democratic Party's portion of the 1968 presidential race. And one man, by a combination of courage and good luck, was supremely well positioned to capitalize on the resulting opportunity. That man was Eugene J. McCarthy, a U.S. senator from Minnesota and one of the stubbornest political mavericks the upper reaches of U.S. politics had seen in twenty years.

McCarthy, like all people, was and is an irregular cut stone, with many facets to his political personality. In the wake of Tet, two of these facets proved central, visible, and inspiring. The first was a Jeffersonian discontent with the growing concentration of power in the White House, particularly in regard to war and "national security." The second was a Western European–style Christian Democratic instinct that sought to relate the Gospel to society to enable liberals to chart a middle way between a too-selfish and individualist capitalism and a too-collectivist and too-materialist socialism.

McCarthy was a liberal who had little patience with knee-jerk laissez faire or knee-jerk antiradicalism. He also disliked large aggregations of power without countervailing powers to balance them. He feared what would later be called an "Imperial Presidency" which was undermining the power, legitimacy, and self-respect of Congress in general and the United States Senate in particular.[18]

McCarthy knew how the imperial genie had gotten out of the republican bottle. In August 1964, he had joined all but two of his colleagues in the Senate in voting for the Tonkin Gulf Resolution, a legislative blank check that Johnson wanted in order to wage his limited war in Vietnam. McCarthy had agreed to an open-ended war-which-was-not-a-war for which the U.S. Constitution made no provision.[19] Soon enough, however, Minnesota's junior senator had cause to regret his acceptance of legislative legerdemain. Lyndon Johnson engaged in unsavory presidential gunboat diplomacy in the Caribbean in the autumn of 1965. After U.S. Marines assisted in overthrowing the "communist-dominated" left-wing regime of Juan Bosch in the Dominican Republic, Eugene McCarthy began his shift to disenchantment and opposition.

His opposition, however, came late. Eugene McCarthy was a successful political animal, and political animals run risks if they take on sitting presidents of their own party to argue against foreign wars already under way—especially wars they had previously supported. Political bloodletting like this leaves the challenger open to charges of being soft on questions of patriotism, manhood, and party loyalty, and perhaps even of giving aid and comfort to the Marxist-Leninist enemy. Politicos in their right minds do not risk mounting such a political guillotine on the gamble that the axe won't fall. McCarthy hesitated, even after a small group of left-wing Democrats of sometime socialist antecedents started a dump Johnson–stop-the-war movement during the early months of 1967.[20]

Nor was Eugene McCarthy alone. Fellow senators Robert Kennedy, George McGovern, Frank Church, and Vance Hartke all declined to put their heads on a presidential chopping block. Still, McCarthy was less firm in his declinations than the rest. While others said no, Eugene allowed as to how somebody *should* do it, and that he would think about being that somebody.[21] Think about it he did, and for seven long months. Finally, in November 1967, the Minnesota senator announced his challenge to Lyndon Johnson's presidential leadership.

A thundering political silence then ensued. No ambitious Democratic officeholder lined up in support. McGovern, Kennedy, and others sat in purple silence, contemplating future political prospects while McCarthy complained that "They pretend they don't know me . . . They think they can oppose the war without opposing the President and [thereby] keep the [party] organization happy."[22]

McCarthy's complaint struck to the political heart of the matter. He was now doing a great deal more than fighting LBJ; he was also fighting the power barons of the Democratic Party, the thousands of men and women who were tied to Lyndon Baines Johnson by bonds of ideology or electoral interest, or by patronage—the very people who had been handsomely rewarded for winning a landslide victory for LBJ and lots of other Democrats only three years earlier. Lacking support from the leaders of his own party, McCarthy faced the grim choice of building an insurgent movement or dying on the vine.

He would have died on the vine, but for Tet. McCarthy the dark horse had no choice but to seek the nomination of the Democratic Party by running against LBJ in primary elections in those states (a minority) in which nominations had been thrown open to popular, rather than party-organization decision. Moreover, the first primary was in New Hampshire, and the Granite State was tough going for any liberal. No state whose political process would soon enable a reactionary governor to emblazon "Live Free or Die" on its automobile license plates was likely, in 1968 or at any other time, to be soft on communism or the Cold War containment thereof.

Nor was it. Most New Hampshire voters were Republicans. Of the minority who weren't, most who later voted for McCarthy, in mid-March of 1968, were dissatisfied with LBJ and his administration for not being *tough enough* in Vietnam.

McCarthy, however, was the only alternative available to the Democratic Party in the primary election held at the very time that Lyndon Johnson's political credit was badly overdrawn. As a result, McCarthy benefitted from *both* an antiwar (deescalation) *and* a prowar (escalation) protest vote simultaneously. Pollsters later variously estimated that he got three votes from "hawks" for every one or two votes he received from "doves." The combined protest vote gave him 42 percent of the ballots compared to LBJ's 49 percent. More important, it gave him instantaneous visibility on the national television networks that people increasingly depended upon for "news." Within three additional weeks, McCarthy's visibility was further enhanced when Lyndon Johnson withdrew from the presidential contest. The dark horse was suddenly the only horse running.[23]

McCarthy did not have the field to himself for long. Once his candidacy and the events that it fed upon had demonstrated that it was possible to defy Johnson in a conservative state like New Hampshire, flocks of politicians whose discretion had far outrun their valor during the preceding year now discovered messianic qualities in themselves.

Robert Kennedy was first off the mark. Sanctified by the recent martyr-dom of his elder brother and possessing considerable charismatic attributes of his own, Bobby engaged in realpolitik that others could not. Immedi-ately after the New Hampshire primary, Bobby Kennedy announced that he was "reassessing" his earlier decision not to run. It was only one day after McCarthy had vaulted from nowhere into national prominence.[24]

Not content with this turn of the political screw, Kennedy also had an off-the-record meeting with McCarthy the very same day. Significantly, Eugene McCarthy went to see Robert Kennedy, in his brother Ted's Senate office, not vice versa, even though McCarthy was senior to both Kennedys in the Senate and even though he, not Robert Kennedy, had seized the initiative in the first round of the Democratic Party's presidential sweep-stakes.

Robert Kennedy, however, had that divinity which hedges kings—or, in that era of American life, Kennedys. Bobby Kennedy was the beneficiary of massive amounts of political faith from millions of ordinary and not-so-ordinary Americans, people nostalgic about the roseate gleam of an earlier Kennedy presidency that died young and had been replaced by the wheel-ing and dealing of a tired old gladhander from Texas. Bobby Kennedy was seen (and saw himself) as the font of liberal faith in the United States of America. McCarthy's refusal of an invitation from RFK would have been equivalent to a Catholic's refusal of an audience with the pope.

Eugene McCarthy, Irish Catholic that he was, knew a papal summons when he heard one, especially one from another Irish Catholic. Suppress-ing his chagrin at the fact that Kennedy's "reassessment" announcement upstaged him when he needed all of the visibility as a lone hero that the media could give him, Eugene made his pilgrimage unto Bobby.

There McCarthy had the ground taken out from under him in behind-the-scenes fashion. Kennedy, all the standard indirections and nuancings aside, told McCarthy that he now thought himself capable of entering the race and winning the Democratic Party's nomination. McCarthy had made an estimable beginning at great and continuing political risk to himself. Now, however, Eugene would be well advised to vacate the field.

McCarthy, of course, was furious. But fury does not often do when politicians reveal their naked power. The elaborate courtesies of the politi-cal arena were preserved—politics, in its hypocritical aspect, being a very useful substitute for fisticuffs or civil war. Yes, replied McCarthy, Kennedy could certainly enter the race. But he, McCarthy, would not thereupon withdraw; and would instead continue running the race he had already and uniquely begun.[25]

The fat was in the fire. In twenty short minutes, Robert Kennedy had made an enemy of Eugene McCarthy. "Excuse me, but *I'm* cutting in" was the message, and what followed was bruising political battle of the worst order. Kennedy threw his hat into the presidential ring on March 16th. Only three days after his meeting with McCarthy and only four after McCarthy's almost-win in New Hampshire, RFK enthused that what was really at stake, so far as the presidential race of 1968 was concerned, "is not simply the leadership of our party and even our country, it is the right to the moral leadership of this planet."[26]

No one in what was then denominated the political mainstream—publicly, at least—gainsaid the Light Unto The Nations universalisms that matched the most hyperbolic rhetoric of a dead JFK. It was not that sort of year. Not by a long shot.

## The Troubled Rise of the Antiwar Liberals

A "horse race," then, it was. "News" was where the *drama* was, not where the *power* was, and the journalists' interest in the contest between McCarthy and Kennedy helped both. McCarthy's supporters were operating outside of the regular Democratic Party organizations and needed all the help they could get. Meanwhile Kennedy's organization, walking a finer line between being a liberal insurgency and being a moderate pressure group within the party hierarchy itself, was facing furious opposition from lame-duck President Johnson and his supporters.

Both Kennedy and McCarthy, therefore, appealed to the media as well as they were able. Media attention had its negative side, however. The focus upon the two who were challenging the Vietnam War exposed the consummate muddle that characterized most liberal thinking about how to wind down or end the war in Vietnam.

The basic problem was that liberal Democrats had led the nation into the same war that they were now trying to get it out of. John F. Kennedy and Lyndon Johnson had hardly lacked for conservative support in all they had done in Vietnam, nor would the right have protested had they done considerably more. Still, most legislative support and all the presidential pronouncements touting the war had come from the Democrats. The war, therefore, was a Democratic Party problem in the public mind and the Republicans had no desire whatsoever to dispute this view.

The liberal Democrats thus faced the same quandary they'd faced when an earlier bipartisan but limited war in Korea led by Democrats had gone wrong seventeen years earlier. How could they disengage themselves without appearing to have "lost" and without facing the political charge of having become "soft on communism"? Such a Republican charge, translated into electoral terms, could cost many Democrats their political careers.

The problem proved insoluble. Political heavyweights and policy advisors who formulated the strategy gone awry made the same error as Lyndon Johnson had earlier made. They hesitated, and were lost. Some, in particular the Best and Brightest Kennedy appointees, whose expertise Johnson had accepted, respected, and acted upon, resigned their offices and sought refuge from political gales in suites at the Ford Foundation, the World Bank, or in university professorships. Others, especially elected politicians with nowhere to hide, tried to ride out storms by discovering "middle ways" between war and withdrawal. They were, as three perceptive British journalists argued at the time, like "troubled mandarins" with guilty consciences. They were men who, after Tet, turned upon their own creation but who did not know how to kill it before it killed them.[27]

One way, of course, would simply have been to get out, to simply withdraw from direct military involvement in a war that looked less and less winnable without escalations far beyond the half-a-million men and mountains of technology already engaged. Withdrawal, however, was still a "radical" alternative that antiwar liberals wanted to avoid. It was also an alternative opposed by most of the American public (who, be it recalled, then supported *escalation* of the war). The antiwar liberals thus searched for a path between the hammer of the old right and the anvil of the antiwar and antiliberal New Left. Their solution was to replace fighting with talking, espousing a negotiated settlement.[28]

The details varied. A majority of liberals argued, at most, for mutual disengagement: Washington would show its good faith by limiting search-and-destroy operations and by halting the bombing of part or all of North(ern) Vietnam; in return, Hanoi would decrease all rebel military activity. Hanoi should also accept the permanent existence of a separate nation of South Vietnam, one in which its interests might be represented within a coalition government playing by political rules determined by Saigon.

Other liberals offered variations of this talk, not fight theme. The most coherent was a proposal that South(ern) Vietnam be neutralized via the agency of the United Nations or a conference of Asian powers. Central to this left-liberal proposal was a belief in a third force of neutral Buddhists,

Social Democrats, liberals, peasants, city dwellers, and lower-echelon army officers in the south of Vietnam who were equally opposed to the communist puppets of Hanoi and the Washington hirelings of the Saigon regime.

All the rest was expediency. The United States should minimize its losses by withdrawing its forces to defend a few key areas (the enclave strategy); the United States should arrange truly free elections or cease-fires to make the first stage of some dimly conceived settlement possible; the United States should really start talking with Hanoi's leader, Ho Chi Minh; or the United States should carrot-and-stick Hanoi to the bargaining table by a more judicious mix of bombing, search-and-destroy, and peace feelers than any LBJ had been able to devise.[29]

All of this liberal gimcrackery was ingenuous at best. Proposals for negotiated settlements presumed that there were parties in Hanoi or Saigon who were willing to negotiate, or who could be enticed to negotiate, or who could be forced to negotiate, short of measures the liberals had no intention of taking—measures that included bombing Hanoi back to the Stone Age or facing Saigon with an immediate and unilateral withdrawal of American men and assistance. These liberal suggestions further presumed that the United States could somehow talk its way out of a war it had shot its way into without suffering any diminution of political or military stature. Lastly, the liberals, unless they were of a "neutralist" variety, presumed that Vietnamese leaders, north and south, were not fighting a civil war for control of *one* country and, thus, could compromise and agree to dual sovereignty.

Conservatives quite rightly argued that there was a good deal of disguised utopianism in all of this; that the antiwar liberals were now edging away from taking sides in a war they'd helped create; and that liberals were in the self-defeating position of arguing, after Tet, against continued direct military intervention *and* against the communist victory that intervention had been specifically undertaken to avoid. Supplies hadn't been sufficient in 1965, however, and they still weren't enough in 1968. Liberals, as historian Alan Matusow later wrote, were, indeed, "waist-deep in the Big Muddy along with LBJ." And they "were no more certain than [LBJ] was of getting back to shore."[30] What differentiated most antiwar liberals from Lyndon Johnson was this: he had got in, and together with the conservatives, wanted to stay in, because he believed in the Cold War. The antiwar liberals, who had got in and stayed in because of the same belief in the Cold War, now wanted to get out as a matter of sheer political survival. They didn't want to be the next casualties of Vietnam.

A handful of antiwar liberals understood the force of such criticisms especially well. Ironically, none of these politicians was involved in the electoral drama of the 1968 presidential campaign. Ernest Gruening of Alaska and Wayne Morse of Oregon, for example, were the two United States senators who had opposed Vietnam from the start. Neither blinked at the possibility of a unilateral withdrawal without any concessions at all. Both Gruening and Morse, however, were isolates without substantive influence, and they were on their way out of office as a result. They paid the ironic price often charged of people who say the right things at the wrong times.[31]

A third senator, however, used the occasion of his turnaround on Vietnam to produce a critique of the war and the political assumptions which gave rise to it. He did so, moreover, in 1966, well before most of his political fellows—including Robert Kennedy and Eugene McCarthy—became aware of what the future had in store. That senator was William Fulbright of Arkansas, chair of the powerful Foreign Affairs Committee. Fulbright, a southerner whose earlier votes against desegregation and civil rights legislation disqualified him from consideration for the presidency in 1968, was, nevertheless, the one in the Democratic Party who did the most to formulate an ambitious mainstream critique of a limited war gone wrong. Fulbright put himself on record in a book entitled *The Arrogance of Power*. As synthesis, prescription, and self-criticism, it still bears reading.

The basic problem, Fulbright affirmed, was hubris: the "tendency of great nations to equate power with virtue and major responsibilities with a universal mission." The United States had reached a point where its international mission had already outrun its means. Its attempts to control foreign events were getting out of hand. Unless America and American leaders became less prone to think of their nation as "God's chosen saviour of mankind," the United States would begin to waste its vital human and economic energies in a series of ill-advised foreign adventures. These adventures might destroy the domestic bases of national power, wealth, and sociopolitical cohesion, and lead America into an era of weakness, affliction, and disaster. The country was biting off more than it could chew, preachifying about foreign matters it knew little or nothing about, and riding for a fall.

Just in case his cautionary message hadn't soaked in, Fulbright offered specific examples of his central arguments. Vietnam was a prime instance of our arrogance and hubris. There, we were trying to remake a fragile, resistant, and traditional Vietnamese society over in our own image, to "create stability where there is chaos, the will to fight where there is

defeatism, democracy where there is no tradition of it, and honest government where corruption [as Americans define the term] is almost a way of
life." The effort would almost certainly fail.[32]

In Vietnam, furthermore, America was on the horns of a screaming
dilemma. It was fighting a communist movement that was an indigenous
*nationalist* movement as well. "The American view of revolution," Fulbright
continued,

> is . . . shaped by a simple but so far insuperable dilemma: we are
> simultaneously hostile to communism and sympathetic to national-
> ism, and when the two become closely associated, we become frus-
> trated, angry, precipitate, and inconstant. Or, to make the point by
> simple metaphor: loving corn and hating lima beans, we simply cannot
> make up our minds about succotash.[33]

Instead, Americans bombed, bombed, and bombed again while their
leaders protested that only their commitment to freedom and democracy
in South Vietnam led them to do so. At the rate things were going, American anger and frustration at being unable to separate the nationalist–
national-reunification element of Vietnam's insurgency from its commu-
nist-totalitarian, anticapitalist element was leading the United States into
a ridiculous overestimation of the stakes in Vietnam. The war, in fact, was
very fast becoming more a matter of wounded American pride than of
Vietnamese freedom:

> When we talk about the freedom of South Vietnam, we may be thinking
> about how disagreeable it would be [to ourselves and our conception
> of our national mission] to accept any solution short of victory; we
> may be thinking about how our pride would be injured if we settled
> for less than we set out to achieve; we may be thinking about our
> reputation as a great power, fearing that a compromise settlement
> would shame us before the world, marking us as a second-rate people
> with flagging courage and determination.[34]

He asserted such frenzied speculation involving our national status and
determination in the outcome of a struggle in an impoverished country in
Southeast Asia was nonsense. Instead of such prideful drivel, Americans
should simply understand that when nationalist and communist strains
were mixed:

American interests are better served by supporting nationalism than they are in opposing communism, and that when the two are encountered in the same political movement it is in our interest to accept a communist role in the government of the country concerned rather than to undertake the cruel and all but impossible task of suppressing a genuinely nationalist revolution.[35]

In Vietnam, Fulbright went on, we were wreaking havoc rather than trying to arrive at an intelligent peace that should initially entail creating a coalition government in which communists would possess some share of political power.[36]

Here, then, were clear and nonopportunistic views, views which, just as clearly, had become part of the antiwar liberal mainstream in the aftermath of the Tet-related events just described. Now, as Eugene McCarthy and Robert F. Kennedy vaulted to center stage, both issued with varying degrees of intensity precisely the warning—and the solution—that their colleague, Senator Fulbright, had enunciated two years earlier when full-scale Americanization of the Vietnam War was increasing. The question yet remained whether either liberal challenger could resolve the consequences of the Arrogance of Power that had grown to divisive proportions using, *at the furthest extreme*, Fulbright's 1966 proposals for a negotiated settlement and a coalition government.


*Crisis and Charisma*


Few, however, coolly analyzed such policy nuances during the unsettled spring of 1968, for America was increasingly at war with itself. An atmosphere of conflict and crisis polarized political attitudes and turned presidential politicking into a sort of secular religious war. McCarthy's and Kennedy's partisans hated each other. And only four days after Lyndon Johnson's surprising withdrawal from the 1968 presidential race, the United States was rocked by the assassination of Afro-American civil-rights activist Martin Luther King by a hired political assassin in Memphis, Tennessee.

The week that followed King's murder on April 4th was the "long, hot summer" of the riots that took place in the ghettos in 1967 all over again. This time, the rioting was nationwide, and overtly political. The common cause of King's martyrdom unified violent events into a coherent national whole, and not least affected were frightened whites. A Nobel Prize winner had been struck down by the unrepentant forces of racist hatred in the prime of his life.[37] America's chief spokesman for Gandhian nonviolence, interracial accommodation, and integration had had his version of the American dream shattered by a bullet in the brain. The Man of Peace had been killed by war, a continuing civil war over enforcing constitutional guarantees that had been ratified a century earlier.

Civil war analogies were not far from anyone's mind who cared about what Martin Luther King's death symbolized—or could symbolize. Blacks, most particularly, cared. So it was they, above all others, who raged at their fates, present and potential. Over a hundred urban areas erupted or sputtered into violence, and thirty-seven people died. For the first time in American history, an ultra high-technology Situation Room created (right down to its euphemistic title) in the bowels of the White House basement to "crisis manage" the Cold War was also used to plot the course of threatening domestic events. Meanwhile, any crisis manager who cared to could walk outside to see and smell the smoke from burning black neighborhoods, or watch police and armed forces units setting up emergency defense perimeters on and around Capitol Hill. Looking down on it all from a helicopter, just-relieved American Commander in Chief in South Vietnam William C. Westmoreland thought that the fires set by looters and demonstrators "looked considerably more distressing than Saigon during the Tet Offensive." Now, alas, a war was happening to *his* country.[38]

Simultaneously, the war was "coming home" in other ways; ways it had once been wildly radical even to imagine. As sections of Washington burned, New York City was unsettled by escalating demonstrations and do-it-yourself street brawling at Columbia University, located in Morningside Heights, which overlooks some of the country's worst slums. Between April 25th and 30th, a coalition of New Left and Black Power groups, plus nonaffiliated individuals, occupied five university buildings in protest against varied institutional sins which included research and funding links with the CIA and major military contractors, slum landlordism, and lack of regard for local (read: black) community interests and concerns during enlargements of Columbia's campus. On April 30th, after inconclusive posturing and merely academic arbitrations that slowly got nowhere, New York City's police stormed the dissenter-occupied buildings and arrested almost seven hundred people. The collegiate ivory tower became an arena for gloves-off political argument in a fashion that, while hardly abnormal by, for example, French or Mexican standards in 1968, was rare in the United States.[39]

Two days after New York's Finest moved in to resolve what tongue-wagging could not, the scene shifted back to Washington again as a Poor Peoples March on the national capital began. March organizers commenced construction of a not so aptly named Resurrection City on land located between the Washington and Lincoln Memorials.

Here, again, the moment was rich with symbolism. The sit-in by the poor at Resurrection City was intended as a living memorial to Reverend Martin Luther King, who had achieved his apotheosis on the same spot five years earlier while a quarter-million civil-rights marchers cheered his stirring "I Have a Dream" oratory. King's would-be successor Reverend Ralph Abernathy now sought to accent the need to expand civil rights from the political to the *economic* realm (from right to vote and hold office to right to work and be promoted). Abernathy hoped that success in this effort to keep domestic reform initiatives alive in wartime would guarantee his own future as the leader of the overwhelming majority of nonseparatist black people in the United States.

Abernathy failed, however. Resurrection City, once built, sank slowly into the mud of a Washington, D.C. spring. As its varied inhabitants scattered, it was clear that those who spoke for the poor were increasingly deemed passé. Poor = black = waste of time equations became commonplace. Worse, integrationist black leadership weakened at precisely the time when radically different viewpoints reassumed national prominence as George Corley Wallace, Alabama's governor, began the most successful third-party presidential candidacy in American history. Wallace scared blacks to death. Most knew that his little-guy-tired-of-being-kicked-around-by-radical-hippie-egghead-fag-criminal-integrating-unpatriotic-bureaucratic-sons-of-bitches oratory was aimed, in part, at putting Negroes back in the economic and political cotton fields in dead earnest.

Late March to late May of 1968, then, was a dramatic period in U.S. politics. Peace of mind among liberals suffered accordingly. By mid-1968, a sense of crisis was broadcast in the land. So, too, was a widespread desire for heroism and heroes to serve as antidotes to the frustration of American power at home and abroad. Charisma could save what arrogance had begun, or so tens of millions hoped. All presidential contenders, therefore, found it easier to inspire unusual measures of devotion, enthusiasm, and belief. Eugene McCarthy and Robert Kennedy especially benefitted from this condition, for theirs was the most dramatic (and dramatically televised) electoral struggle.

Charisma, however, also has its ugly and self-defeating aspects, especially in a land where politics must be the art of compromise since the checks and balances of federalism mandate compromise. By May, however, it was impossible for the personal-magic-prone McCarthy and Kennedy camps to conceive of allying with one another—even, ironically, for the purpose of common political survival.

## Camelot versus Clean Gene

One fact of American political life now became terribly relevant. The primary battles that the Kennedy and McCarthy forces were fighting were not going to win the nomination for either. Only one-third of the votes at the upcoming Democratic Party convention in Chicago were going to be cast by delegates from states that had primary elections. The other two-thirds were going to come from delegates from the other states where delegates were selected by party leaders and organizers or by restricted electoral gatherings called "caucuses," the outcome of which was decided by the politicos and those few of the faithful who attended. The insurgent "grass roots," in short, were less important in total votes at the convention than the staid and self-protective state and local party organizations— organizations whose leaders were bound to Lyndon Baines Johnson and whichever candidate he supported.[40]

This crucial fact was obscured by the media and the mass equations of drama and power. Kennedy and McCarthy, between them, were racking up 70 to 80 percent of all the Democratic votes cast in the primary states, and thus appeared to most Americans to be the front-runners for the Democratic presidential nomination. Reality, however, was quite otherwise. Even if McCarthy and Kennedy had joined forces from day one, they still would have faced an uphill nomination battle, because LBJ *had* a candidate. That candidate, Vice President Hubert Horatio Humphrey, had been quietly using LBJ's cachet to recruit delegates in the nonprimary states while McCarthy and Kennedy were fighting their supremely public battles of the spring and early summer. Why, then, didn't McCarthy and Kennedy cooperate against the common threat from Johnson and Humphrey? Didn't they know that their battle for antiwar liberal support was internecine, that every dollar or day they devoted to primaries was one less available for capturing or persuading the party hierarchies in the nonprimary states?

They did. And yet, they did not. McCarthy and Kennedy understood that LBJ hated them both and that he was doing everything he could to stop them. Both had done their political arithmetic. Both understood that one protest candidate with all the votes would still have only an outside chance at the nomination unless another Tet-like political chasm opened, or unless the practical, moderate, and prowar Democratic powers could be convinced that continuing "All the Way with LBJ" was political suicide.

Eugene and Bobby understood all this and more, in the long term. Yet, in the short run, each was locked in a battle for political supremacy over the other. In a charismatic year, their charismas were engaged. McCarthy was still outraged at Kennedy's attempt to take over a protest movement he had given initial electoral form. Kennedy's was a battle to recover his moral edge as the leader of the liberal wing of the Democratic Party from "Clean Gene" McCarthy and a bunch of arrivistes and amateurs operating so far outside the party's organizational mainstream that they could convince few except those already converted.

McCarthy's activists cared less about what Kennedy believed or wanted. To the vast majority, especially the college and university students who did much of the dogwork for the McCarthy for President campaign, RFK was a Johnny-come-lately who had thrown away his moral edge by waiting to get into the fight until David Eugene had slain Goliath Lyndon. Bobby Kennedy was part of the problem, not part of the solution. Hadn't he been a key player in brother John's administration when some of the preparatory steps to full-scale Americanization in Vietnam had been made? Hadn't he worked for LBJ as well? Wasn't it other Kennedy Men like "Doctor Strange" (Robert Strange McNamara) who had stage-managed the slaughter? Just where did Robert Kennedy come off saying that he'd seen the light, and should now lead the deescalation-negotiation cause?

Nobody, of course, likes to have their honor impugned, their courage questioned, and their motives subjected to ad hominem abuse. Robert Kennedy certainly didn't. Nor did the upper-echelon politicos who had hitched themselves firmly to this Kennedy's star. The Kennedyites' outrage was only heightened by the fact that the McCarthyites' charges were true. Kennedy *had* waited too long. There were good reasons for delay: personal and familial fears of assassination, for example. But there were also power considerations. Kennedy already had national repute; he had a very good chance to become a mainstream presidential nominee, if he picked the right time and avoided intraparty bloodfests. Kennedy simply had much more to lose and, so, he took five months longer than McCarthy to make his decision.

But by delaying, Kennedy had forfeited his chance to lead the most energetically committed antiwar liberals within the Democratic Party.

Bobby recruited impressive measures of black, Mexican-American, ethnic, and liberal trade-union support, but he never made much of a dent on the collegians. The "brains" stayed with McCarthy; while Kennedy got those, youthful and otherwise, who wanted their visions of Camelot restored. The Kennedy and McCarthy camps kept on fighting, common political survival remained secondary to comparative charisma, and, as Kennedy finally edged out McCarthy in the culminating Democratic primary in California, tragedy struck.

As so often in 1968, the scene could have been crafted by a demented dramatist. On the evening of June 5th, Robert Kennedy addressed a packed assembly of followers. Success was theirs. They had beaten Clean Gene's legions in the largest and last state primary, and could now move on to the convention with that most precious of political commodities: momentum. Kennedy looked like a winner.

Then the White Knight of Camelot was dead. Only seconds after delivering his victory speech, he was sprawled like a broken doll on the kitchen tile floor of the Ambassador Hotel in Los Angeles with several small-calibre pistol bullets in his skull—murdered by an immigrant Jordanian who babbled that RFK was a majority stockholder in a worldwide Zionist–imperialist banking conspiracy.

As Robert Kennedy's life ebbed away in stainless steel surroundings, amid piles of institutional cutlery, American politics began to look like some surrealistic Frankenstein monster. Liberal heroes were dying like flies. Fed-up Americans wondered aloud when "crazies" were going to get shot before they had a chance to shoot. Let Columbia University student James Simon Kunen's stream-of-consciousness remarks summarize the dread that unrolled across the land:

> I am actually writing this at 4 A.M. Wednesday, June 5, and I just heard over the radio that Kennedy has been shot. Again. This is really no novelty, you know, because people get shot every day, and bombed and burned and blown up. But no one cares about that. I mean they don't really mind, because it's a question of flags and things and anyway, people aren't really shot; fire is directed at their positions. And they're not really people; they're troops. There aren't even dead men: only body counts. And the degree of deadness isn't always too bad; sometimes it's light or moderate instead of heavy. We'll all stick it out, don't worry. We'll stick it out because it is a question of honor and thank God we only hear about it once a day [on the TV news], and then it's quickly followed by [an advertisement] by some broad telling you how groovy some gasoline is and how you can get laid

practically as much as you want if you use it. President Johnson's a fool anyway. The old fool's up against the wall. He's practically crazy. Everyone knows that. Even crazy people. Everyone.[41]

Antiwar dissenter Kunen's logic is not the point here; the point is that the second Kennedy assassination in five years rocked the country's emotions like the Martin Luther King murder and the Tet offensive had earlier. On that passionate level upon which societies either live or die, 1968 was a Terrible Year, and it was getting worse, even insane. The war was at the center of the dementia that ensnared the nation. Someone, somehow, had to cut through the web in order to keep the society whole.

Now, in a period of growing alarm, the scene bifurcated. The status quo simply didn't work. An increasingly polarized society looked left and right for solutions.

## Chicago: The Democrats Self-Destruct

It was on the mainstream left that political outcomes most emphatically depended. This mainstream, embodied in the liberal wing of the Democratic Party, utterly failed to resolve any of its outstanding differences at the presidential nominating convention in Chicago. That failure, in turn, set in motion a triumph of conservatism that has continued to the present.

Chicago, by late August 1968, was on edge. The nation's Second City had long prided itself on a decisive, sweaty, and no-nonsense approach to problem solving compared to the effete and elitist East. But as one of America's last big-city "political machine" bosses put up signs for visitors reading "Mayor Richard J. Daley, A Family Man, Welcomes You To A Family Town," all was not well in Chicago or the much bigger political world around it. Second City had bus, cab, telephone, and communication strikes to contend with as the apparatus of modern politics and electronic journalism rolled into town. There were fears of black riots on Chicago's thoroughly segregated South Side, threats which Mayor Daley met by stating that black looters would be shot and black rioters would be shot very dead. Threats of demonstrations by varied antiwar groups existed as well. Daley tried to deal with the latter protest problem by refusing to issue parade permits or to allow demonstrations in municipal parks. He also ringed the Cow Palace in which the Democratic convention was to be held with barbed wire and other obstacles to dissent.[42]

Even the international atmospherics were forbidding. Only a week before the Democrats gathered to select their nominee, Soviet and Warsaw Pact military forces invaded Czechoslovakia and overthrew the reform-minded socialist regime of Alexander Dubcek. Naked *Machtpolitik* of this sort, all too redolent of the crushing of dissent in Hungary in 1956, raised Cold War temperatures, torpedoed the fledgling efforts at nuclear arms control begun by the Johnson administration, and led anxious West European and other allies to ask what the United States had done for them *lately*. Meanwhile LBJ's White House busily floated rumors that new communist offensives in Vietnam were imminent and proclaimed that further weakening of support for the war was impolitic unless party leaders wished to risk facing popular wrath when headlines announced that American boys were being killed in record numbers. "Give 'em an inch and they'll take a mile" was a message being relayed about everything from strikes to the Czech invasion to briefings about the wiles of the enemy—and of the successful U.S. politician.

August 26th to 29th, then, was not a propitious time to be trying to preserve good order and benign behavior within a political party undergoing its worst internal stresses in years. The Democrats were involved in a civil war about the war. The overreaction of the prowar wing of the party in Chicago only worsened the divisions and helped to project an image of the Democrats as losers who could not even make peace on the streets of Chicago or inside the Cow Palace, never mind in Vietnam.

Despite all the rotten atmospherics, it might still have been possible to avoid catastrophe—if the man who had the nomination anyway had only been in a position to compromise about anything. Sadly, he was not.

Hubert Horatio Humphrey was a captive of events and of his own ambition. Although he had all the votes he needed from nonprimary states to get the nomination on the first ballot, he could not mediate anything with the insurgent and popularly selected forces of Kennedy and McCarthy, even though the Democrats needed every semblance of unity they could get. Moreover, Kennedy's and McCarthy's people were *still* at each other's throats, even after RFK's assassination, to the point that the Kennedyites had helped push darker-than-dark-horse Senator George McGovern into the presidential ring only two weeks before the convention in order to have someone to vote for other than Clean Gene.[43]

It might have been so easy. Humphrey could have moved away from Johnson's "What is, is right" approach to a war gone wrong. He could have

made vague noises about speeding up the Peace Talks with enemy representatives that had begun in Paris on May 3rd. He might have incorporated filmy declarations about further negotiations and military deescalations into the Democratic Party platform. All this might-have-been,
however, ignored the reality of who had the power and who didn't. Humphrey knew that many Americans protesting LBJ's policies at the polls
were as anxious to escalate the war as others were to deescalate it. They
were antiwar only to the extent of being opposed to the ways in which the
limited war was being fought. Hubert had no reason to risk alienating
Johnson and many other leaders opposed to deescalation.

Humphrey also was not his own political man. His core of delegates at
the convention, supplied by the remaining Democratic urban machines,
blacks, the white South, and organized labor, had come to him courtesy
of Lyndon Baines Johnson. Johnson, by now anathema to the Kennedy and
McCarthy forces at the convention, did not even appear in Chicago for fear
of generating demonstrations that would only further complicate matters,
but the absentee warlord's presence was nevertheless profound. One move
away from LBJ and Humphrey was a dead duck. Having demonstrated
little vote-getting potential of his own in the four months he had been in
the race, Humphrey, by default, attached his political fortunes to Vietnam
as securely as the president himself.

Humphrey's role was that of the Happy Warrior in an exceedingly
unhappy time, bubbling away about restoring the "politics of happiness,
the politics of purpose, and the politics of joy" to millions who perceived
him as a flatulent fossil of a bygone era. Humphrey's tragedy was that, for
all of his earlier humanitarianism, he was cast, in 1968, as "the champion
of ruffled national complacency."[44] He accepted the assignment.

Happy Warriors like Humphrey, however, had more than an image
problem. They also had a vision problem. They did not understand that
a new post–World War II political generation was edging onto the stage.
This generation, like all youthful aggregations, took the accomplishments
of the past for granted while intently surveying current threats to its
interests and ideals. The Sixties Generation in particular, as it came into
political adulthood after the U.S.-U.S.S.R. brinksmanship of the Cuban
Missile Crisis of 1962, tended toward more intense and polarized political
behavior than its predecessors. Its most politically engaged members were
also moving, by the fall of 1968, toward the emotional view that mainstream political behavior in the United States had become too surrealistic
for comfort. (Vide the quote from James Simon Kunen.) To such eighteen-
to-thirty-year-olds, whatever their political persuasions, politics-as-usual
was looking like a bad joke. So was Hubert Horatio Humphrey.

Most of this was utterly lost on Humphrey and on liberals like him as well as on saurian operators like Chicago's Mayor Daley. Daley, for example, first tried to bootleg the remaining Kennedy, brother Edward, onto the national ticket as vice presidential nominee in the hope that this would garner millions of sympathy votes. After brother Edward quashed that gambit in July, Daley and others hedged their bets on Humphrey by sounding Kennedy out on a presidential bid if the convention became deadlocked. Such hush-hushery even became idealistic, as when Eugene McCarthy made a last-minute bid to withdraw his candidacy before the first ballot to enable Kennedy to unite the antiwar forces at the convention. Kennedy refused out of a mixture of suspicion, dislike, and his need for the support of prowar Democratic leaders for his future presidential prospects.[45]

While all of this convention-eve plotting and counterplotting was going on, most of the assembled political cognoscenti underestimated a crucial variable: the relatively small numbers of delegates and demonstrators on the scene in Chicago who were anxious to manifest public dissent to the all too likely triumph of politics as usual. The beating down of these dissenters by the Chicago police and the party pros doomed the Democrats to political impotence in the presidential race. A breathtaking fifth of the voters abandoned the party they had supported in the previous presidential election.

The details of what went on in Chicago were well reported and well remembered by anyone who had the misfortune to experience them. Lots of heads were cracked in front of television cameras. A minority of those heads belonged to antiwar radicals seeking unilateral, total, and immediate American withdrawal from Vietnam and who wanted a confrontation. Other heads and their owners sat on the stoned shoulders of "cultural revolutionary" Yippies, mocking the institutions, operations, and "hang-ups" of a System they believed to be one big hypocritical mockery of itself. Most, however, belonged to several thousand peaceful demonstrators, McCarthy campaign workers, and spectators unlucky enough to be in the right place at the wrong time—people whose antiwar liberalism consisted in a belief that more should be done—and soon—to deescalate the war via a negotiated settlement route.

The flailing nightsticks and clouds of tear gas, however, obscured such nuances. The Chicago police and Mayor Daley, as well as the Democratic party professionals at the Cow Palace, claimed to be engaged in nothing less than quelling "revolution." Daley defined all demonstrators as enemies of the true, the patriotic, and the beautiful. To him they were enemies to be crushed. As so often in Vietnam, the rule was, "Everybody who isn't with us is against us." Political free-fire zones became the order of the day.[46]

At the Cow Palace, a similar either-or and good-versus-evil view of events held sway, particularly among officeholders and party chiefs. They feared most an antiwar insurgency which, because of grass-roots alliances between the McCarthy, Kennedy, and McGovern delegates on the convention floor, threatened to rend the fabric of party organizations which gave their leaders power, position, and status. Daley and the other anti-insurgency Democrats were fighting for self-preservation, which they equated with the political system they claimed to lead. To fight them was to fight Chicago and America. To protest against them was to get one's head beaten.

The violent absurdity of what followed from these all-too-human equations of self-preservation and patriotism was, by the standards of other nations with less all-pervading civil religions, relatively mild. The public and police riots in Paris circa 1968, for instance, beggared anything in Chicago.

For all that, the shock caused by Chicago was profound. "Welcome to Prague" signs sprouted on lampposts in a scattering of North Side neighborhoods, equating the suppression being meted out by Daley's men with Russian tanks in Czechoslovakia. Although a large majority of Chicago's population made no such comparisons (and, in fact, supported the city's police),[47] all interested citizens of Chicago—and of the nation generally—were appalled by the spectacle of wholesale violence at a major party convention. These were not reassuring sights for people to factor into America's democratic system. For all that, the discussion *had* turned into an argument; the images *were* realities. Journalistic and other bathos was only worsened by the wrenching events that accompanied Hubert Humphrey's name being placed in nomination and voted upon late in the evening of August 28th.

During this most brutal day of a diseased week, the civil war within the Democratic party was paramount and most public. As insurgents vainly protested that Humphrey could not win an election tied to a discredited policy of limited war as usual, their efforts to place a deescalationist-negotiated-settlement plank in the party platform went down to defeat in a closer vote than expected: 1,567 to 1,041. Amidst storms of rhetoric, a few hundred delegates from states where antiwar support for McCarthy and Kennedy was strongest donned black armbands of mourning and began to sing *We Shall Overcome* (someday), the anthem of the civil-rights movement in the South. The analogy thus made, that prowar victors were ruthless rednecks denying liberal antiwar forces *their* elementary political rights, was hardly appreciated, especially by the white delegates from the Old Confederacy who were a key component of the Humphrey-Johnson alliance at the convention.

Counterattacks were inevitable in such a highly charged atmosphere, and they occurred later that same evening. As police broke up televised efforts to stage marches on the convention hall—to chants from the demonstrators that "The Whole World Is Watching!"—brass bands and well-packed visitors' galleries at the Cow Palace put on a show of force for Mayor Daley. Occasional scuffles broke out between McCarthy delegates and ushers who had been told to deny Daley opponents as much access to the floor as possible. Humphrey weighed in on behalf of Chicago's mayor, telling a press conference that the downtown demonstrators were "all programmed" by outside agitators "brought from all over the country." Radical subversion, clearly, was at work.

Humphrey achieved his long-sought nomination just before midnight, and the absurd became the lachrymose. In front of television cameras stationed in his hotel suite, Hubert leapt up, ran over to the TV beaming the news of his victory, and kissed the screen on which was an image of his happy and relieved wife Muriel. Hundreds of thousands of his angry opponents never forgot the image of a gushy man celebrating like a maudlin drunk in his hotel room.[48]

The depth of their anger became clear shortly, when party leaders at the convention tried to celebrate Humphrey's victory with the traditional love feast. To repeated shouts of "No! No! No!" from the convention floor, a diminutive and by now desperate Democratic house majority leader and master of ceremonies, Carl Albert of Oklahoma, brought down his gavel time after time, vainly trilling in a reedy voice that the motion for universal accord was universally carried. Albert et al.'s charade was thrown into the dustbin when party outcast Eugene McCarthy outright refused to play the game; he refused even to come to the Cow Palace for the traditional Good Sport–Clasped Hands of Party Unity media event with Humphrey. The rift between the antiwar and prowar forces was as complete as matters get, short of brawling in the aisles. The next day, Hubert appeared on the convention platforms sans McCarthy (but with McGovern and other team players) and tried to pour oil on deeply troubled waters. We should all love America, and we should all love one another, was the general tenor of his acceptance speech, one which closed with repeated thank-yous to absentee kingmaker Lyndon Johnson.

After a week of bad political theater, Humphrey's paeans to love and understanding were so much bathwater. A great void had opened at the center of the Democratic Party. On both sides of this divide, feuding

Democrats snarled at one another, shrugged their cynical shoulders and hoped for the best or closed their eyes and plied themselves with drink. Hubert Humphrey, meanwhile, ran like a dry creek while trying to avoid discussing the war at all.

The Democrats, for all of Humphrey's efforts at benign neglect, came very close to committing political hara-kiri. They split wide open over the war, with the grass-roots deescalationist–negotiated settlement wing of the party branded as radicals and wreckers. Conservatives, smarting from electoral disaster in the immediately preceding presidential contests made haste to capitalize on events. To this second pole of the polarized politics of 1968 we now turn.

## The Rumblings and Ramblings of the Right

In the cold calculations of many of the powerful, the political bloodletting in Chicago should have relegated the Democrats to infirmity from the start. Republican nominee Richard Nixon and independent challenger George Wallace should have feasted on Democratic misfortune. So they did, temporarily. They should also have gone on to beat the Democrats senseless in November. This they did not. Between September and November 1968, in fact, both Nixon and Wallace bobbled their respective chances to restructure American politics. Their failures, and what flowed from them, helped to delay the complete resurgence of the right wing in the United States for a decade.

First to Richard Nixon, a man who played it safe and almost snatched defeat from the jaws of victory. Then to George Wallace, a man who played it wild and woolly and paid heavily for it.

## Nixon: The Automated Candidate

Richard Nixon had an image problem. "Let's face it," confided one of the Republican candidate's chief media advisers to reporter Joe McGinnis late in the 1968 campaign:

> [A] lot of people think Nixon is dull. Think he's a bore, a pain in the
> ass. They look at him as the kind of kid who always carried a bookbag.
> Who was forty-two years old the day he was born. They figure other
> kids got footballs for Christmas, Nixon got a briefcase and loved it.
> He'd always have his homework done and he'd never let you copy.
> Now you put him on television, you've got a problem right away. He's
> a funny looking guy. He looks like somebody hung him up in a closet
> overnight and he jumps out in the morning with his suit all bunched
> up and starts running around and saying "I want to be President." I
> mean this is how he strikes some people.[49]

He did indeed. Nixon was a cold fish whose woodenness and humorless-
ness had caused problems for him for years. In Richard Nixon's case, the
inevitable privatisms and ambitions of the power seeker were not complemented by the popular wit, savoir faire, and one-of-the-boys gregarious-
ness which are key components of success in American politics. Nixon
lacked the human and humane public touch to the point that a Canadian
university professor, Marshall McLuhan, described Nixon's TV persona
during his unsuccessful presidential contest against John F. Kennedy in
1960 as being like that of a "railway lawyer who signs leases that are not
in the interests of the folks in the little town."[50]

Tricky Dick, his political opponents in America called him. A Uriah
Heep of U.S. power brokering; a guy who always exuded false modesty
and cloying kindness and brittle smiles and who was always and everywhere and continually out for Number One. "Would you," they asked,
"buy a used car from this man?"

So, as millions of confused or angry Democrats thought of Hubert Humphrey as a simpering wimp because he wouldn't say or do anything decisive about the war (either to escalate it, or to end it), Nixon was not
necessarily an improvement. Humphrey was weak, but Nixon, a stronger
character, was dishonest. Between a coward and a crook what was there
to choose?

Nixon was hardly unaware of the hatred, suspicion, and abuse that he
and his persona had engendered during twenty years in public life, nor
were the people who had gathered around him to elect him president of
the United States. To get Nixon nominated and elected, they realized,
required changes in the man, changes in the persona, or both. Nixon had
been around a long time, and had accumulated repute as a has-been and
a loser who had blown his preceding political opportunities. Leaving it to
the candidate to change—or not change—the Inner Man, the Nixon coterie
initially undertook an ambitious effort to revamp his image.

Nixon's people decided on charisma. Nixon must become "larger than life, the stuff of legend," as his main speechwriter put it. Or, as another adviser affirmed, Nixon had to be packaged as "a combination of leading man, God, father, hero, pope, king, with maybe just a touch of the avenging Furies thrown in." Nixon the Has-Been was to be superseded by Nixon the Conquering Hero in a year that badly needed valor, bravery, and gallantry.[51] Nixon's people set out to do precisely this; and, initially, their strategy worked. This fact has been suitably tut-tutted and sneered at and criticized in the years since, as if Nixon and Company let an evil genie out of a bottle and polluted American politics.

The facts are quite otherwise. The image-building strategy the Nixon campaign initially followed was traditional and bipartisan. What was relatively new was that the Nixonians used TV as the major tool in their campaign. Television, which the Democrats had also used with devastating effect in 1964, could massage the masses with imagery that radio, a political technology pioneered by Democrats like FDR and Harry Truman, could not. Nixon merely used new technology for old purposes, and he started off using television better and more thoroughly than it had ever been used by conservatives. This led to howls of partisan outrage and prompt efforts to copy his techniques. Nixon the Has-Been and Also-Ran had his image resuscitated by his media people to the point where he was nominated and then elected mostly on the basis of statements of supreme meaninglessness about war in Vietnam and lawlessness in America—pseudo-profundities that hit escalationist and deescalationist chords simultaneously, applauded the strength of the nation's power and will, and hinted broadly that Nixon possessed a Secret Plan to end the conflict to the benefit of all (just as Nixon's Republican predecessor Dwight David Eisenhower had in the Korean War election of 1952).

It was, however, a very close thing. Nixon even almost failed to be nominated by the party leadership. First, they were often more conservative than he was; second, they were more interested in power than the nuances of Madison Avenue imagery. Nixon's credibility also suffered from an abortive last-minute presidential push from recently elected California Governor Ronald Reagan, whose jeremiads about the imminent destruction of The American Dream at home and abroad were more insistent, consistent, and better delivered to the conservative faithful than Nixon's homogenized waffle.

Reagan was nothing if not frank. His speeches in support of the war and his all-out campaigns against muggers, weirdos, murderers, creeps, drug fiends, and student radicals were good red meat to the party leadership gathered in well-protected convention hotels in Miami Beach. Reagan, in the flesh, had all the charisma that Nixon lacked, and he knew how to use the camera like the Hollywood veteran he was. No cold fish he, but a warm-blooded guy who had done his impressive bit for the Goldwater crusade in 1964. He had subsequently performed the political legwork of talking at endless local and state political fundraising events as compulsively as Richard Nixon: building up the party coffers for forthcoming contests and accumulating political IOUs by the hundreds. If Reagan had declared his candidacy earlier, contested primaries right from the start, and gained a higher-profile national image and more financial backing, he might well have seized the G.O.P. nomination in what was shaping up as a conservative year.

But Reagan did delay and thus gave Nixon his opportunity to win a sequence of uncontested primary victories. More important, Nixon was able to scuttle Reagan by making deals with members of Reagan's own camp—southern Republicans like Strom Thurmond of South Carolina, men who ditched the man they admired for Nixon, a man they needed— needed to avoid another Goldwater debacle, to lessen the threat of another intensive civil-rights push, to protect their political bases from Wallace's third-party threat, and, finally needed to beat off another convention-eve presidential push by much-too-liberal-for-comfort Eastern Establishment Republican Nelson Rockefeller.[52]

Once Nixon had reassured southern conservatives of his intentions, he moved on to protect his political flanks (from Reagan) and theirs (from Wallace) by making deals. He would not be soft on the Commies. He would not cut back on arms spending nor inhibit development of new weapons. He would select a vice presidential running mate (Spiro Agnew of Maryland, it turned out) acceptable to the southern wing of the G.O.P. And he would go as slow as Congress might let him in enforcing civil-rights laws, especially busing and open housing programs. Having done all of this, Nixon surmounted his Ho-Hum, Has-Been, and Second-Best repute with the organizational faithful and achieved a bare majority on the first ballot at the convention.

After his victory of August 7th in Miami, Republican campaign headquarters sprouted in storefronts across the length and breadth of the land. In their windows blossomed posters featuring a smiling Nixon above the official campaign slogan. "This Time Vote," the words read, "As If Your Whole World Depended On It." The slogan nicely caught the sense of alarm, crisis, and threat that characterized the country at the time. Nixon bent that climate of fear to his own political purposes. America's "whole world" was at risk and at stake, and only Richard the Heroic could save it from further shocks like the Chicago Democratic fiasco that occurred barely three weeks after Nixon became the man of the electoral hour.

Such a strategy played well in those vast regions where dwelt the 43 percent of the electorate that eventually voted for the Nixon and Agnew ticket in November. Tens of millions of people believed that their basic assumptions of patriotism, free enterprise, individualism, and governmental minimalism outside of the defense arena were being threatened by avalanches of expensive social-welfare programs, by claims for compensatory economic advancement by blacks and other minorities, and by increasing opposition to U.S. efforts to be the guardian of noncommunist nations all over the globe. Richard Nixon, a man to respect—if never, precisely, to love—presented himself as a leader with the firmness necessary to return the nation to its universal mission-as-usual. Nixon had a strong base of support among a large minority of Americans. He was, however, unable to expand that base significantly beyond the point it reached by September. After getting off to a good start, the Nixon bandwagon ran straight into the sand.

The reason for this was twofold. After September, Nixon stopped making extensive use of TV to refresh his image. He let his "New Nixon" persona harden around him, endlessly repeating media events, canned speeches, and body movements like waggling his fingers in V-for-Victory salutes that made him look like a scarecrow with an advanced case of arthritis. Forgetting that variety is the spice of life—even in advertising— Nixon, together with arrogant yes-men like H. R. (Bob) Haldeman and campaign director John Mitchell, adopted a low-risk campaign strategy that was low-yield as well. Nixon the New became Nixon the Automaton.[53]

Moreover, Nixon proved unable to gain significant support from either Wallace insurgents on the right or moderate-to-conservative Democrats on the left. Wallace supporters were angry and alienated Americans, many of them southern whites, who believed that nobody could possibly be as tough a problem solver as Alabama's own. Wallace, in fact, had drawn millions of them into the electoral arena for the first time in their lives.

With the prowar Democrats, Nixon had a different problem. He could never convince them that he had ceased being a G.O.P. hatchet man—a guy who would smile at them one minute and kick them in the groin the next, the same Dick Nixon who had flayed Democrats of all hues for being Soft on Communism for years. So long as these Democrats had a candidate who did not appear to repudiate Lyndon Johnson's policy of opposing substantial deescalation, they would, and did, vote their party's regular ticket—or, if they *did* think Humphrey was too soft, vote for George Wallace. Not until antiwar "dove" George McGovern gained the Democratic nomination in 1972 in a two-way race in which Wallace couldn't participate because an assassin's bullet had paralyzed him did large numbers of these prowar Democrats decisively back Nixon.

Nixon, then, was sagging by October 1968. He was hanging on to what he already had, but getting nothing more. Humphrey also continued to go nowhere fast. Attention shifted to the third member of the triumvirate of this election year: George Wallace.

## Wallace: Political Protest Personified

Of all the insurgents in an insurgent year, George Corley Wallace of Alabama was far and away the most successful. By early October, in fact, he was a major power on the American political scene. Wallace excited hatred and love, despair and devotion, respect and resentment, and he did so like none of the other presidential aspirants in 1968. He won ten million votes in the most successful independent candidacy in modern U.S. history while Nixon hung on to what he had and Humphrey slouched along until the very end.

George Wallace exuded protest. In the mellifluously combative drawl of his voice and in the bantam rooster stance of his body, he channeled protest and gave it form—the protest of a poor, angry, and Evangelical Protestant South; the protest of lower-class and lower-status whites more generally; immigrants or their children living, say, in Cleveland's West Side. He mobilized people fearful of losing what job and income security they had to blacks who might take away their jobs, undermine the safety of their neighborhoods, or decrease the value of the home that was their largest single investment. These men and women believed, very often correctly, that "limousine liberals" in well-protected suburbs were mandating social changes they expected less well-off whites to pay for.

The protest was profound, and it appalled the affluent "pointy-headed intellectuals" that Wallace so pointedly attacked. So frightened were these analysts that they ignored Wallace for as long as they could. The spectacle of growing White Backlash seemed as menacing to some as the spectacle of racial war throughout a nation where huge internal migrations of blacks had taken place during the preceding twenty years seemed to others.[54]

Neglect, however, would not do. By early October, even the self-consciously intellectual *New York Times* hypothesized that George Wallace might well be running ahead of the humdrum Humphrey. Since in a three-way race Wallace needed only a plurality of the popular vote to win, fears rose that the country was in the midst of a reactionary and "populist" rebellion of prowar, antiblack, and anti-intellectual Yahoos; of Rednecks, Peckerwoods, Hillbillies, Unreconstructed Cowboys, and White Ethnics with odd-sounding East European and other names; of men with hair on their knuckles and eyebrows grown together who were married to women who were overweight and sported bouffant hairdos; of people who weren't schooled or educated and whose idea of a bipartisan discussion was to beat each other up in blue-collar bars after having drunk three too many boilermakers. A spectre of Hard Hat Fascism and a Revolt of the Rednecks took root among the elite. Paranoia is the *mistaken* impression that somebody out there is trying to get you. And, though the threats were overdrawn and mean-spirited, the extent of the Wallaceite challenge was real enough.

A major part of the threat had little to do with popular votes, but with the Electoral College. Electoral votes, not popular votes, decide the results of U.S. presidential elections, a fact that nobody with any claim to political expertise forgot during this period. All Wallace had to do was to deprive Nixon or Humphrey of a majority of the electoral votes (cast, usually, in a winner-take-all, state-by-state vote based on the total number of representatives and senators sent to Washington from each state). Then, Wallace could spoil the election by throwing the eventual decision about who won and who didn't into the House of Representatives for resolution; something which hadn't happened in the United States for almost a century. If the House became the arena, each state delegation would cast but one ballot, the powers of smaller rural states would outweigh the powers of larger industrial ones, and Wallace might be in excellent position to wheel and deal and throw the state votes that he might control to Humphrey or Nixon. The price asked would be power—perhaps Cabinet positions—for Wallace and the political forces he represented.

For these reasons, George Wallace's rise to electoral stardom in the months immediately preceding the 1968 election terrified many Democrats, liberals and conservatives alike. Such concern had practical political consequences. The first was that no strong moves were made by McCarthy's and Kennedy's forces to establish a fourth party to contest the 1968 election by the antiwar liberal left. The price of such dissent, given the Wallace threat, was too high.

Meanwhile, as McCarthy finally quashed fourth-party moves late in September, another powerful set of Democratic players entered the election in earnest. These were trade-union leaders fearful of the effects of Wallace's movement on their bases of organizational power. Established union hierarchies, key legislation, and regulatory accomplishments would all suffer in the event of a conservative victory, especially one that destroyed Democratic control over Congress. The fact that the vast majority of such trade-union leaders had never shown the faintest distaste for the war only made it easier for them to come to the ailing Democrats' aid in their own political interests. Vide longtime AFL-CIO President George Meany, whose "hawk" approach in Vietnam remained ironclad, then and later. The leadership of organized labor, then, used its organizational clout to fight Wallace in the grass roots of industrial America.[55] They launched all-out media campaigns reminding workers that Wallace's Alabama was one of the least-organized, lowest-paid, least-schooled, and most open-shop states in the country.

Meanwhile, another shift of opinion began, as antiwar liberals finally moved over in support of Humphrey. This shift also had nothing to do with love or enduring regard. As late as the final weeks of the campaign, only four in ten McCarthy backers surveyed in one poll said they intended to vote for Humphrey in November. But what these people intended and what most finally did were two different things. Basically, the antiwar liberals voted against rather than for. As election day loomed closer and the threat of Nixon and especially Wallace grew, at least several million Democrats who believed their own party had abandoned them in Chicago moved back into the fold—if only to help elect state, local, and congressional candidates of concern to them.[56]

These combined shifts within segments of organized labor (especially outside the South) and antiwar liberals were made much easier by a series of almost last-minute conservative mistakes which gave political initiative to the hitherto becalmed Democrats.

The Wallace campaign was first to score points against itself. Just as Wallace seemed to be the candidate and spoiler of the hour, his vice presidential running mate, General Curtis LeMay, landed the campaign in political quicksand. Wallace introduced his number-two man to the press on September 10th, 1968, and "Bombs Away" Curt LeMay startled everyone by devoting his brief initial comments as a candidate to issues of nuclear weapons and warfare—"limited nuclear wars," in particular.

LeMay, to do him justice, saw the issues from the perspective of a career military man, an Air Force general only recently retired. He was a person paid to think not about peace and love, but about the grimmer matters of how to kill and how to avoid being killed. Ever since nuclear weapons were invented, arcane debates about how to use them to win wars or preserve the balance of terror had taken place within the military brass and the defense intelligentsia. A main issue in these debates was whether limited nuclear wars could be fought successfully. Could a nuclear power use a few of its weapons to intimidate or defeat opponents without setting off a chain reaction that would produce "all-out" wars, a thermonuclear holocaust on a global scale?

This question was particularly relevant to the resolution of "limited wars" such as the one in Vietnam. Wouldn't it be sensible, some military leaders argued, to beat the "gooks" by using a few nukes to block supply routes (like the "nuclear barrier" General Douglas MacArthur had proposed to halt Chinese movements across the Yalu River during the Korean War) with the intention of breaking up enemy forces, and the "surgical nuclear strike" proposal (made to save the French at Dien Bien Phu in 1954)? Why not call the enemy's bluff by upping the ante and using small nuclear weapons? Especially in a limited war, communist opponents who had nukes (China and Russia) would probably not use them in retaliation in a conflict in which neither was directly engaged. So the hawks in the military establishment had been arguing, long and unavailingly, much to the discomfort of Curtis LeMay, who believed it was possible to fight and win limited nuclear conflicts, especially if the foes America was fighting didn't possess nukes of their own.

Thus, when Curtis LeMay began his maiden press conference by saying "We seem to have a phobia about nuclear weapons," he was thinking as he had often done before as an air force general about "low intensity" nuclear conflict. In making his ideas public, however, LeMay made the worst blunder of his brief political life.[57]

LeMay got folksy about the Bomb, talked about it as if it were just another weapon, one that was "most efficient" to use sometimes. LeMay argued that a lot of propaganda about the horrors of nuclear war and weaponry had obscured common sense. Not only could nuclear weapons be used with great effect, he continued, but dropping a few would not result in an inevitable escalation to Armageddon. America, LeMay implied, was effectively disarming itself through fear. Bombed regions, he went on, speedily recovered. Look at Bikini Atoll in the Pacific, where the United States had exploded nukes for years. The rats there were healthier than ever. There was vegetation, and there were fish in the lagoons. The land crabs were maybe still a bit too "hot" with radiation to eat, but life there hadn't ceased to exist. Far from it.

LeMay's reassuring rhetoric about what he saw as the realities of limited nuclear warfare was a rare political gaffe, even in the frenetic year of 1968. LeMay had forgotten one very essential thing. Most people were not paid to think about war, and war was still, in the public mind, supposed to be fair. It was not, except in the most desperate or self-defensive of circumstances, supposed to involve using thermonuclear weapons which killed every man, woman, child, cat, dog, earthworm, parakeet, and tree in a weapon's "kill radius" before broadcasting death and destruction across wider landscapes. Nuclear war was awful. Besides, it threatened Americans as no Vietcong in a rice paddy ever could or ever had. Limited nuclear war as a possible resolution to the frustrations of Vietnam, therefore, fell very flat. Worse, it led to gales of ridicule which shook the Wallace campaign.[58]

When millions laughed at Curtis LeMay and the "hot" land crabs of Bikini, therefore, they relieved their fears about being asked to think about the unthinkable, to think about weapons that made equations between war and chivalry brutally irrelevant. More important, they also ceased to fear Wallace and started to lampoon him, deriding a man and a movement that they had dreaded. Wallace and LeMay—Bantam Rooster and Mad Bomber—became more amusing than formidable. *"Sieg Heil,* Y'all," one poster put it. For Wallace, who lived off political polarization and could handle others' hatred for him with the skill of an artist, laughter was a heavy burden. Mockery is a surer kiss of political death than hatred or the fear it breeds on.

Richard Nixon, too, had reason to fear mockery in 1968. He was not adept about such matters then or later, however, and so Nixon and Agnew suffered from the same ribaldry that afflicted Wallace and LeMay. Nixon counterattacked Humphrey with a "missile gap" ploy that was a precise copy of one Kennedy had pulled on him in the 1960 elections. But Spiro Agnew's gaffes were more than Nixon could handle. Agnew put his foot squarely in his mouth by becoming too involved in the mudslinging which is part of any vice presidential candidate's political assignment. He tended to discover communist leanings and revolutionary affiliations in nooks and crannies of the Democratic Party, to the point where earlier grudges about Richard Nixon's longstanding political record as a red-baiter were rekindled. Democratic media advisers began centering their fire on Agnew. One widely circulated TV "grabber" announced "Spiro Agnew for Vice President," and followed it up with peals of hysterical laughter, before closing that with a somber printed statement, "This would be serious if it wasn't so funny."[59]

As laughter added to the weakness of the Nixon and Wallace campaigns, Humphrey tried to add to his strengths, such as they were, by cutting the Vietnam millstone from around his neck. His aim was to finally distance himself from Johnson in regard to the war, just enough to convince people that Hubert had the guts to put forth *some* alternative of a deescalationist–negotiated-settlement nature but not enough to alienate the prowar and pro-escalationist forces in the Democratic mainstream. On the same day that Curtis LeMay committed political suicide by waxing too eloquent about limited nuclear war, Humphrey, in a much ballyhooed—and long delayed—speech, stated his change of position on Vietnam.

What Humphrey said changed little or nothing. Listening to him was like observing Canadian humorist Stephen J. Leacock's mythical knight jump on his horse and busily ride off in all directions. Humphrey swam through an ocean of verbal molasses cooked up for him by a committee of speechwriters—strong hawks, pale doves, and the usual assortment of "nonideological" operators—who weasel-worded everything they could. Batteries of dependent clauses fired hither and yon, while Humphrey did his level best to avoid offending anybody whose votes he already had and to attract millions of antiwar liberal votes at the same time.

This long-winded exercise in obfuscation, "coordinated" by one Zbigniew Brzezinski in his role as foreign policy adviser to Humphrey's campaign, should, on logical grounds, have convinced no one of anything. But, by October 1968, there were a lot of Democrats around who were anxious to start believing again in the approach of their party leadership to foreign policy. These voters didn't often think in terms of Fulbright's Arrogance of Power; instead, they hoped that party bosses had finally got the message that Vietnam couldn't keep going on like this. They hoped for the best, or at least the better, in a year that had been chastening to their optimism.

So, even though Humphrey promised, at most, to *consider* the *idea* of some form of negotiated settlement and coalition government *if* the opposition gave back all they had recently won on the battlefields *and* accepted the legitimacy of a South Vietnam and the existing Saigon regime, the Democratic image makers were successful in kidding people (and probably even themselves) that some major breakthrough had been achieved—one that could magically end the civil war which had erupted within the Democratic Party itself in the wake of Tet, the McCarthy and Kennedy movements, and all that went with them.[60]

The resulting Much Ado About Nothing lured most antiwar liberals back into the fold, largely because they now believed that Wallace was a maniac and Nixon was still an unctuous and hypocritical crook. Wallace and Nixon would turn Vietnam into rubble if they got the chance. Humphrey at least promised to consider some alternative.

What followed was a sudden surge by Humphrey, one that pushed Wallace back to the fringes of drama-prone TV media coverage and closed the gap on an overly insulated and programmed Nixon as well. On Election

Day, Humphrey almost won the popular vote, helped along by an election-eve bombing halt of North Vietnam agreed to by LBJ after repeated entreaties from Democrats who well understood the importance of last-minute events. With a majority of only three hundred thousand in a three-way race that brought seventy-one and one-half million people to the polls, Nixon won by one-quarter of 1 percent. On his coattails, moreover, the Republicans gained only five House seats and seven Senate seats. The Democrats still had a majority of fifty-one in the House and fourteen in the Senate. Nixon became the first president-designate in a hundred years whose party did not control at least one of the two houses of the national legislature. "Vote As If Your Whole World Depended On It" had not convinced people that their lives, fortunes, and sacred honor depended all that much on Richard Nixon or the G.O.P.

George Wallace, meanwhile, also had cause for concern. He had won ten million votes but had not been able to spoil the election by denying Nixon a majority in the Electoral College, thus throwing the election into the House. Wallace's strength centered in the Deep South. Union counterattacks kept his vote from organized labor, for instance, to a significant but manageable 16 percent. The great impetus built up in the Wallace campaign had not been well coordinated. Wallace supporters were—and remain—the only third-party partisans in U.S. history *ever* to get their candidate's name on the ballots in all fifty states, but this impressive success was not followed up with an equally impressive organization of local energy and devotion. These energies, accordingly, dissipated. Wallace's remained a personal candidacy and movement, rather than becoming a real political party able to undertake the undramatic, ongoing, and essential grass-roots work that decides what American politics will look like.

## The Climate of Crisis

Nixon had won the presidential race, but the most important results of 1968 were not a matter of who held what office. They had more to do with passions unleashed and moods engendered than with the enumerations of political profit and loss. The year 1968 was a rip in time. It also began the Anxious Years during which much of what had seemed fixed and certain began to appear in flux. A period commenced during which assumptions of an age of steadily expanding American power that had existed since the end of the Second World War were succeeded by the queries, complaints, jeremiads, and ritual cleansings of an era of what Godfrey Hodgson has called "growing doubt, fragmentation, and confusion."[61]

As the terrible year came to a close, the more optimistic citizens could recall that 1968 ended on an upbeat note: the United States put a team of astronauts into orbit around Earth's moon for the first time. In July, as well, the United States had joined the Soviet Union and fifty-eight other nations in signing nonproliferation agreements to take the important first step toward stopping the spread of atomic weapons to those many emerging powers whose welter of regional claims and counterclaims, bolstered with nuclear armaments, would markedly increase the threats of a global holocaust.

Such voices of optimism and hope, however, were often restricted to technical and scientific authorities blithely ignored by the general public or by those deemed politically expert. By December 1968, in fact, the beginnings of trendy "Decline and Fall" or "Fall from Grace" analyses were well and truly under way. America, the argument endlessly went, was like the Rome of the later Caesars—a world power which, having lost its moral force and internal cohesion, was on a collision course with destiny, a course that would lead to disaster unless honesty, spiritual rectitude, and strength (all variously defined) were brought back into a society whose public affairs had emphatically lost all three.

Along with this Decline and Fall–Fall from Grace analysis went an almost instantaneous nostalgia for the leadership of bygone eras, in particular for the presidents of the three decades from 1933 to 1963—the very politicos who had been in power during the era in which the forty-to-sixty-year-old males who formed the bulk of the political and intellectual elite of the nation, circa 1968, had achieved political adulthood and risen to public importance. For not the first or last time, people living in an age of stress began to view their collective history as a glorified reflection of their own personal life cycles. They were past their prime, and so was the country. They were too soon to die, and so was the country. Things just weren't as good as they used to be. What the country needed now, surely, was real leadership once again: Franklin Delano Roosevelt, the brave; "Give 'em Hell" Harry Truman; Crusader for Freedom, Dwight David Eisenhower; Martyred Prince of Liberty and Youth, John Fitzgerald Kennedy; maybe even Government Minimalist, Herbert Hoover.

Unrest and insurgency, meanwhile, was the order of the day. These were the outstanding characteristics of a year in which the opportunistic politicians of the Great American Middle Ground were unable to contain communist insurrection abroad or left-wing and right-wing rumblings and revolts at home. As the "middle" attenuated, the question, for most of the cognoscenti, was whether the nation would lurch right or lurch left. Few, outside of the cautious bureaucracies of the two major political parties, expected that Business As Usual was going to get the job done. Neither Nixon (from caution and contrivance) nor Humphrey (from cowardice) was able to convince the electorate that he was anything more than mediocre. These were the country's "foregone disappointments," to borrow a phrase from three British journalists whose coolheaded and sharp-eyed coverage of the election was a refreshing exception to the reams of perfervid twaddle offered up by Americans themselves that year.[62]

But America lurched nowhere. The liberals were finally scared back into the Humphrey camp by fear of their right-wing counterparts, particularly the Wallaceites. The insurgent Wallaceites, for their part, failed to translate their normally Democratic presidential protest votes into protest votes against other Democratic state, local, and national officeholders elsewhere on their ballots. Wallace the individual did well. But Wallace's millions did not trust the Republicans, and most especially Richard Milhous Nixon, to do anything all that different from the mainstream Democrats.

For all this, in the presidential vote the Democrats did lose at least six or seven million normally Democratic votes to Wallace, especially in the White South. Moreover, an unknown number of very different insurgents, a minority of the antiwar liberals and the New Left groups, stayed home in protest. The combined effect of these two protests damaged the Democrats a great deal more than the Republicans. It gave Nixon the victory—with a smaller proportion of the total vote (43.4 percent) than any president since Woodrow Wilson, fifty-six years earlier.

Now Nixon, who had been handed his shoestring victory by the hara-kiri of his opponents, would see what he could do to "Bring Us Together," as the very war that had done the most to produce his success and his opportunity raged and sputtered. To the story of that far from accidental affray we now turn.

# PART TWO

# VIETNAM, INCORPORATED

## The Cold War Comes to Vietnam

The Vietnam War, in retrospect, remains what it was in life: more an occasion for rationalization and self-justification than an opportunity for understanding. Policy-making elites, in particular, spent much more time and energy defending their wartime positions than they ever spent in choosing them. To comprehend the Anxious Years that that conflict produced, however, ex post facto profundity will not do. We must examine the most important causes of U.S. involvement in the war and also the crucial assumptions which were rarely questioned by leaders or the led.[1]

The most significant single assumption was ideological: the idea of American universalism. This organizing concept of an ideologically defined nation postulates a worldwide application of American ideas and institutions in almost all times, places, and conditions. This belief, almost as alive now as it was twenty years ago, equates America's way of thinking about the world and of the political, economic, and social power relations within it with humanity's progressive evolution. A closely allied assumption, that America embodies and expresses the best that human liberty has yet accomplished, rationalizes the use of U.S. power as a counterweight in the crusade against the forces of Marxist-Leninist darkness. This crusade is cast, like all crusades, in bipolar, those-who-are-not-with-us-are-against-us, terms.

From this overarching idea, and the all-embracing crusade that resulted from it, came others more specifically relevant to Vietnam.

The most important of these ideas was, first, that Vietnam was central to American interests because the major arena of competition between the U.S.-led Free World and the Soviet-organized communist bloc had shifted increasingly toward the Third World during the two decades following the Second World War. Clearly demarcated and stable territorial lines existed in Europe, delineated by the North Atlantic Treaty Organization (NATO) and the Warsaw Pact. In the burgeoning "new nations" of the world, until recently controlled by the European global empires, the boundaries were less well defined. Vietnam therefore, could be regarded as a barometer of the political, economic, and social future of the "developing world" as a whole.

Second, Vietnam was one of the most important flashpoints in this new zone of Cold War contention because it was there that the strategy of advancing communism by means of "wars of national liberation" could be halted. Wars of national liberation began as guerilla wars which chipped away at the frontiers of freedom a little at a time. Unless these "brush fires" of subversion were contained, they might set the whole noncommunist developing world ablaze—to the joy of Marxist-Leninists everywhere, people with all the humanity of a band of Mongol brigands on a bad day.

Third, Vietnam was important because, there, the national liberation efforts of Russia, the spider at the center of the Marxist web, and of China, the second great communist power, were directly involved. As Democratic leader Adlai Stevenson argued in a notably clear and concise statement of the matter, "The period from 1947 to 1962 was largely occupied in fixing the postwar line with the Soviet Union . . . [but we] have no such line with the Chinese."[2] Since the Chinese revolution was in an earlier and more radical stage and they were accordingly backing some of the wilder elements of Third World unrest, it was especially important to fix boundaries over which the Chinese would not move, either acting on their own or as surrogates for Moscow.

The assumption that both major communist powers were attempting imperial expansion there made Vietnam even more of a key bastion of the Cold War. It was, as John Fitzgerald Kennedy called it in a Senate speech in 1956, "the cornerstone of the Free World in Southeast Asia, the keystone in the arch, the finger in the dike." In addition, Vietnam was "a proving ground for democracy in Asia"; "a test of American responsibility and determination"; and a barrier which, if breached, would cost America a great deal of revolutionary harm elsewhere in the region, even around the globe.[3]

Thus Vietnam was perceived as a stopper in the geopolitical bottle. If the communist-dominated guerilla movement which had wrested the northern half of the country from the French between 1945 and 1954 succeeded in gaining control of the southern half as well, an evil genie would be loosed upon the world. Give the communists an inch in Vietnam or any other arena of Third World conflict, and they would take a mile, maybe a thousand miles.

Given conceptual architecture like this—which historians usually speak about as the Munich Analogy, Containment, or the United States as a Policeman of the World—the tactical question, for U.S. policymakers, was how to keep the cork in the bottle in Vietnam and how to prevent the communist genie from removing it. Here, too, American leaders did not lack clear policy directions.

The major principle was that the United States should under no circumstances get itself drawn into another land war in Asia in which China's armed forces were also involved. Korea (1950–54) had established that military maxim. Americans had no business fighting the Chinese in "conventional" (i.e., non-nuclear) wars of attrition. There were too many Chinese to make that feasible. The Korea War had proved too long, too bloody, and too politically disastrous for the Democratic Party and a Democratic president. The thing to do, then, was to use American high technology and nuclear hardware to scare the Chinese off and to insure that the Yellow Hordes stayed home by avoiding a conflict right on China's borders—the sort of fighting, in sum, which had caused the Chinese to invade North Korea after American, South Korean, and United Nations forces had conquered it in the final months of 1950.

Vietnam, therefore, was to be a "limited war" of finely tuned escalations and deescalations aimed at preserving the independence and territorial integrity of southern Vietnam without applying sufficient force to northern Vietnam to bring China into the war. There would be no U.S. sponsorship of a southern invasion of northern territory to reunify the nation under noncommunist auspices, for example. Such ill-considered action might confront American leaders with the grim choice of engaging in nuclear escalation, cutting and running, or having large U.S. military forces bogged down, as in Korea, in a lengthy battle against a second-rate communist power with all the time in the world and oceans of blood to shed in buying it.

How, then, did American policymakers hope to win their limited war? Here, too, the answers were crystal clear.

The first thing was to use American technology and know-how to make the enemy bleed wholesale and continually, to harrass and disrupt and harrass again, to kill more than enough antigovernment insurgents in Vietnam to make it brutally clear that revolution, fought as a war of national liberation or not, simply wasn't going to work—not, that is, at a price that any sane revolutionary would be willing to pay for very long.

Second, while bleeding Marxists to death with military might, a complementary war must be waged and won, a political struggle to "win the hearts and minds" of the Vietnamese people—particularly the masses of the peasantry in the South—without whose support, or at least toleration, the rebel armies could not exist. This hearts-and-minds element of U.S. strategy was based upon economic and technical assistance, public health programs, and efforts at land reform. Improvements in popular security and governmental procedures, such as the suppression of bribery, extortion, and racketeering by South Vietnamese civilian and military officials, were part of this war.

A hearts-and-minds strategy, finally, was as important in America as in Vietnam itself. The limited war in Vietnam had to have a profile and a cost low enough that public opinion on the Home Front (especially as reflected in the U.S. Congress) would stay the course, and not erode as it did in Korea.

Hearts and minds at home were important because public opinion was fragile, a weak reed prey to all sorts of alarms and diversions. The average American knew nothing about foreign policy, or so believed the elite who planned the war. Zero, *nihil,* nothing was what the great unwashed people understood or wanted to understand; it cared more about beer, permanent waves, nail polish, and baseball games. Elected politicians weren't much better. Congressmen in general were suspect: most were not "Profiles in Courage." They lacked the fortitude to stem popular passions and ride out political storms while conducting the long twilight struggle that would determine victory or defeat in the Cold War. The only group with the requisite brains, determination, and tough-mindedness, in fact, was the men of the Brains Trust that John F. Kennedy brought to Washington and Lyndon Johnson kept there: the national security managers of the executive branch of the federal government, men with attaché cases and limousines and drivers and Himalayan self-esteem. Vietnam was to be an expertly managed war at home and abroad, one run by Platonic Guardians who perceived themselves to be the Best and the Brightest of their nation and their era.

So much was clear. Yet, for all the apparent clarity, the specifically Vietnamese elements of the situation remained unaddressed or unresolved, mostly because they were deemed to be relatively unimportant—or irrelevant—to wider Cold War equations of which Vietnam itself was but a small part. These seemingly unimportant questions were of three types: the nature of the revolution in Vietnam; the priorities of the United States in fighting that revolution; and the action America should take if victory proved elusive or even impossible to achieve.

The "nature of the revolution" questions, rarely asked, were several. Was Vietnam's primarily a communist revolution, or primarily a nationalist one, in the hearts and minds of most of the Vietnamese people? This question was central to the United States' ability to defeat that revolution as easily and quickly as its policy elite predicted. Vietnamese nationalists, for instance, might prefer bastards of their own to anticommunist improvements mandated by somebody else. Second, was the Vietnam ordeal a *foreign invasion* of one separate and sovereign nation-state by another nation-state? Or was it, in the minds of most of the participants, northern and southern, a *civil war* taking place within the same society? Was it, if so, a civil war being fought on the issue, not of pro- or anticommunism, but on the issue of whether discontented groups of Vietnamese could register their opposition either to the defeat of the French or the creation of a dictatorship in Hanoi by establishing a secessionist regime, based in Saigon, which would cut the country in half?

The reason questions like these weren't asked was because the U.S. policy elite did not for the most part care how any sort of Vietnamese viewed anything. American leaders thought in terms of convincing the Vietnamese of what Americans knew to be right—or in forcing them to accept it and the political results that flowed from it. And that would be a permanently divided Vietnam whose South would be a firm anticommunist bastion bolstered by American power.

A second type of question-not-asked concerned the United States' priorities in fighting the war. The assumption was that American Omnipotence guaranteed the result. Words about what was foremost were committed to paper, and in the tens of thousands, but they didn't have to be ruminated about unduly. The job would be so easy as to insure that bureaucratic caveats and guidelines never had any real meaning.

Was Vietnam, for example, to be primarily a military war or primarily a political war to win hearts and minds? And, if it was to be as political as military, how technological could American military involvement become without utterly losing track of the first goal in pursuit of the second? Finally, was the war, as a military or political endeavor, primarily a Vietnamese responsibility or primarily an American one—especially in terms of the day-to-day, nuts-and-bolts activities that would translate "freedom," "liberty," and all good things into elements that a peasant in a village could appreciate?

The third type of unaddressed and unresolved questions about Vietnam concerned how to respond to the prospect of failure. What did American leaders intend to do if fortune was not with them, if victory was not as easy or automatic as almost all presumed it would be? What if more and more blood and treasure began to produce less and less in terms of political or military results? Would escalation follow escalation? Or would it perhaps be a good idea to set some limits to the U.S. engagement? Should contingency plans be formulated for such a disengagement? All this would follow the common sense maxim that one who plans only for victories and never for defeats is either a raving optimist or a fool.

Raving optimism and foolishness, however, it was. The Best and the Brightest trapped themselves in a war they could not win—on any limited basis that had any meaning—but which they also could "not afford to lose." Official Washington's bland assurance of victory was followed, all too predictably, by lavish anxieties about possible defeat. Defeat—what to do next if things went badly—had never been conceived of as a possibility by the upper reaches of the foreign-policy elite. Here, truly, was a price tag for the Arrogance of Power.

By early 1968, as we have seen, the widespread sense of social emergency and panic that flowed from these misperceptions and unasked questions was a feverish factor in America's domestic and international affairs. Americans faced a profound shock to their sense of identity and self-esteem, to their view of themselves as citizens of a uniquely favored land that "had never lost a war," and to their belief that they and their leaders had the know-how and know-when to apply U.S. principles quickly, concisely, and compellingly throughout the world.

If any one individual symbolized the dilemma of American power in Vietnam, that man was Robert Strange McNamara, U.S. secretary of defense from 1961 to 1968. As much as it was any single person's, Vietnam was McNamara's War. To understand the nitty-gritty of the conflict, we must first consider the nature of the person whose "operational responsibility" it so emphatically was.

## *The McNamara Fallacies*

Bob McNamara liked numbers. He understood them. His public life before the Vietnam War, in fact, had been spent mostly with numbers. Robert S. McNamara had been, in sequence, an economics major at the University of California, Berkeley; a Harvard Business School M.B.A.; briefly an accountant for Price-Waterhouse; back to Harvard as a professor in the Business School; an officer and a gentleman in the United States Air Force during the Second World War, designing statistical control systems to improve the flow of everything from bomb loads on enemy targets to the personnel manning the planes which delivered them; a Whiz Kid in planning, statistics, and financial analysis at Ford Motor Company after the war; and, in late 1960, the first president of the Ford Motor Company, one of the largest corporations in the United States and the world, who was not a Ford family member. Bob McNamara knew his numbers cold, and he knew what to do with them—to help the Air Force blast Axis cities and supply lines into rubble or to make a great deal of money for the Ford Motor Company.

Bob McNamara of Detroit was the kind of individual who impressed others, especially other big business types with high-level government experience. Bob was just the sort of fellow who could go to Washington and apply sound corporate principles to the business of running the country.

So, at least, thought Robert Lovett, former wartime administrator-in-chief for air power and one of the postwar secretaries of defense under Harry S Truman. When newly elected John Fitzgerald Kennedy sent his headhunters in search of elite corporate talent for the managerial bastions of the New Frontier, Lovett, after turning down the position himself, suggested Bob McNamara of Ford as the sort of man to bring efficiency and order to the largest, most sprawling, and often most contentious bureaucracy in the federal government: the Department of Defense.

Lovett wasn't disappointed. Bob McNamara got on famously at the Pentagon. He got things done, and, in David Halberstam's pithy phrase, projected the image of "the can-do man in the can-do society, in the can-do era."[4] One look at McNamara's pinstripe suits, his rimless actuarial eyeglasses, and his prim businessman's coiffure, and you knew that here was no bleeding-heart liberal with delusions of sainthood. Here stood a tough and no-nonsense business type who knew precisely what he was doing, who expected the numbers to add up, and who expected you to spend your evenings, weekends, and early mornings getting matters right if they didn't.

No sir, Bob McNamara was no pushover, especially not when he had tens and eventually hundreds of billions to spend rearming America at its hour of presidentially identified "maximum danger."[5] To McNamara was delegated the chief responsibility to oversee and understand the largest arms buildup in peacetime U.S. history up to that time, an effort fully equal to anything that Ronald Reagan later essayed. The buildup, during McNamara's seven-year tenure in office, quintupled the numbers of U.S. intercontinental nuclear missiles from 200 to 1,000; launched 41 Polaris-type nuclear-powered submarines carrying 656 rockets with thermonuclear warheads attached; put 600 additional long-range B-52 bombers on the runways; and doubled or more than doubled the numbers of tactical fighter squadrons, combat-ready army divisions, short-range nuclear weapons and delivery systems based in Western Europe, the airlift capacity to get men and materiel from here to there, the specially trained anti-guerilla "counter-insurgency units" such as the Green Berets, and the construction of naval ships.[6]

No, Robert McNamara was no administrative innocent. While he was presiding over the aforementioned production miracle, McNamara was also closing hundreds of redundant or out-of-date military installations over the often vociferous opposition of admirals and generals and U.S. representatives noted for their political wallop. He was applying new systems of program planning, budgeting, and evaluation, and the management and retrieval of computerized data that were later used with only spotty success in many other federal agencies. Last (and most important for our purposes here) Bob McNamara was *the* man with the action in the Vietnam War, the political point man for President Kennedy and, later, President Johnson.

The choice of Robert S. McNamara to do all these things and more was as inevitable as it was just. McNamara expressed the essence of a War Manager: a man who saw conflict—Cold War or otherwise—as an equation to be solved logically and dispassionately by those who knew that force should be coordinated, fine-tuned, and complemented by equally fine-tuned diplomacy. Vietnam, for McNamara, was to be well-controlled and adjusted violence, another version of the Cuban Missile Crisis of October 1962, during which confrontation with communist aggressors would be calculated by judicious and sound escalation to choke off opposition. This strategy did not permit overreaction to threats, it kept military men who couldn't see forests for trees on tight leashes, and it had the best chance of causing the puppet masters of Moscow and Peking to eventually drop the strings holding up their Third World creatures and to desert movements and leaders that were passive tools transmitting Kremlin and Middle Kingdom commands.

McNamara the War Manager, to use another pungent description from David Halberstam, "dominated the action, the play, the terms by which success in Vietnam was determined" in a way that was "intelligent, forceful, courageous, decent, everything, in fact, but wise."[7] McNamara's domination arose, not surprisingly, from his clarity of expression, strength of purpose, and optimism about the war. All this, in turn, was based on the single overriding fact that Bob had the numbers, and the numbers added up.

There was very little messiness, then, in the U.S. secretary of defense's conceptual universe. No babble, guesstimating, or maundering, no qualitative seat-of-the-pants speculation. Bob McNamara, like so many of the bright young men that he brought to the Pentagon, and who also arrived in droves to administer other proliferating programs of the activist Kennedy and Johnson years, were economists by training. They were people who lived in universes of the quantifiable, in worlds of statistics, in realities which could be put on graphs and charts and tables or expressed in percentages. McNamara, as even a sympathetic Washington military journalist wrote of him, "did not really believe . . . [that] all issues could be quantified, just most."[8] "Every quantitative measure we have shows that we are winning this war," McNamara himself stated after his first visit to South Vietnam in April of 1962. These words, which his enemies on the left and the right were to throw back at him ten thousand times, are a requiem for the approach toward war which McNamara embodied.[9]

For McNamara, at base, tried to quantify the unquantifiable. He looked upon the messy and inexact business of political insurrection in Vietnam in the same way that he had viewed his statistical tabulations and specifications for the United States air force twenty years earlier—as a production-destruction problem. It was basically a matter of bomb loads and delivery systems rather than flesh-and-blood human beings who flew the bombers into flak and fighter aircraft, of materiel rather than morale, of mankind rather than men, of quantity and quantification rather than of quality. It was a matter of body counts and kill-ratios, Hamlet Evaluation Systems and "interdiction devices," and all the rest of the "output indicators" that had the power to persuade those who had never fired a shot in a battle or seen a battlefield in the midst of carnage, those who had instead devoted their energies to providing the guns and bombs and butter to the poor devils who knew what it was like to piss in their pants in panic, while hoping that Luck or God or Fate or whatever it was was with them and not with the other poor devils who were shooting at them.

The McNamara Fallacy, public-opinion pollster Daniel Yankelovich concluded sadly in 1972, was a four-part march toward folly:

> The first step is to measure whatever can be easily measured. This is OK as far as it goes. The second step is to disregard that which can't be measured or to give it an arbitrary quantitative value. This is artificial and misleading. The third step is to presume that what can't be measured easily isn't really very important. This is blindness. The fourth step is to say that what can't be easily measured really doesn't exist. This is suicide.[10]

Yet all of the self-defeating artifice mentioned by Yankelovich, and more besides, was practiced by McNamara and McNamara's men, both civilian and military. Shortly before he left the Department of Defense in the latter days of the Tet offensive, McNamara himself had apparently begun to sense the fundamental accuracy of much of what fellow number cruncher Yankelovich would later say. "He would confide to friends," Halberstam reported:

> . . . that if they had only known more about the enemy, more about the society, if there had only been more information, more intelligence about the other side, perhaps it would never have happened; though of course one reason there was so little knowledge about the enemy and the other side was that no one was as forceful as [McNamara] was in blocking its entrance into the debates.[11]

No one, least of all David Halberstam, ever claimed that Bob McNamara, the consummate corporate survivor, did not understand the folkways of prospering in the political bureaucracy. Antiwar Senator Wayne Morse growled at the defense secretary at a congressional hearing in 1966 that he could and did give "brilliant and masterful support of an unsound policy" throughout almost all of his tenure as Pentagon War Manager-in-Chief.[12]

McNamara's Fallacies, it needs repeating, were hardly his alone. He merely illustrated wider trends, trends that were inevitably set into motion in Vietnam as War American Style was undertaken in deadly earnest. There the grim ironies of American perceptions and American power became very grim indeed.

## *High Tech in Vietnam: The Muscle-bound War*

High technology was first used in Vietnam because it was available. Higher and higher levels of technological derring-do were subsequently employed because a muscle-bound military led by civilian and military war managers failed to produce quick victory in a "little war" that became alarmingly and unacceptably big. High technology, finally, became an increasingly popular means whereby U.S. political and military leaders might simultaneously decrease the levels of American casualties and continue to cause enough death and destruction to the enemy to win the conflict. The strategy was "Men out, Machines in." The soldiers had failed because they had been tactically and strategically ill-used by leaders who, all too often, were not leading them at all but who were instead *managing* them while looking upon war as an exercise in destruction engineering and bureaucratic self-advancement.

Lieutenant Colonel Anthony B. Herbert was one of those who smelled a military rat shortly after he arrived in Vietnam early in 1969. A self-described "dumb Lithuanian kid" from a small coal-mining town in Pennsylvania who had gone on to become the most decorated U.S. combat infantryman in the Korean War and to rise through the Army officer ranks without benefit of a West Point imprimatur, Herbert was a nonconformist who had little truck with the Officer and Gentleman guild, what he less than respectfully termed the "West Point Protective Association."

Herbert's faith in American strategy and tactics plummeted for five major reasons. First, there weren't enough "ass in the grass" fighting troops, and there was a surfeit of "support" personnel. Seven of the ten thousand men in Herbert's brigade in Vietnam weren't fighters, but REMs ("rear-echelon motherfuckers"), and he estimated that there were only eight hundred men from his unit out in the field looking for the enemy at any one time. Second, the emphasis was on static defense of overmanned bases rather than on "hot pursuit." This meant that the night (and much of the day besides) "belonged to Charlie" (the Vietcong), and that enemy forces had too much opportunity to attack at will, regroup, and attack again. Third, large U.S. bases were crammed with creature comforts that made men fat in stomach, heart, and head and discouraged combat. Fourth, officers were "covering their asses," not leading their men. They wrote reams of reports and occasionally flew around in helicopters "above the battle" rather than getting down in the thick of things where the action was—and where victories or defeats were decided. Last, officers looked the other way when U.S. or Vietnamese troops tortured or killed civilians and POWs, thus undermining discipline and alienating the populace.[13]

Herbert, the disgruntled infantryman, essentially agreed with Sir Robert Thompson, a British guerilla war expert with some claim to the title, that what was needed in Vietnam was a small elite army, highly mobile, and capable of being deployed and switched to operations anywhere in the country—not a swollen behemoth of an army in which, at the height of the U.S. military buildup in 1968, only 80,000 of a total of 540,000 military personnel in Vietnam were assigned to combat. That force inhabited bases where, by 1971, there existed 90 service clubs, 71 swimming pools, 12 beaches, 160 craft shops, 159 basketball courts, 30 tennis courts, 55 softball diamonds, 85 volleyball courts, 2 bowling alleys, and 337 libraries. Also accessible to them were nickel beer, radio and TV stations, tons of medals, and innumerable Post Exchanges where a guy could buy wonderments like a bottle of Courvoisier brandy for a couple of dollars a fifth.[14]

This gigantic force, moreover, as an angry marine colonel stormed in 1968, was conducting offensive operations which produced contact of any kind with Vietcong guerillas less than 2 percent of the time.[15] This was partly because the men, who were assigned to twelve- or thirteen-month tours of combat duty in Vietnam, were led by an exceedingly numerous array of officers who were rotated around and about the military landscape even faster (in part to more widely distribute "combat experience" and assist possibilities for promotion). A 1968 Defense Department report spoke to this problem when it noted that over half of the battalion commanders commanded their assigned units for less than six months. Meanwhile, more than half of the company commanders were rotated in and out of their units within four months or less. These selfsame captains were usually not even sent on to other direct combat roles, but were instead assigned (two-thirds of them) to staff duties at headquarters before being moved along to another, different job before they left Vietnam at the end of their year in the country.[16]

These critiques about members of the officer corps not generally being in any one place for very long were joined to others that officers, particularly those in the higher ranks, weren't worth much when they *were* around. One particularly eloquent statistic that speaks volumes about the relative lack of direct engagement experienced by American generals is oft cited. Although no less than 110 generals were in Vietnam *in 1968 alone,* only 7 (4 army, 2 air force, 1 marine corps) died in combat during the *entire eight years* that U.S. forces were fighting there. Of these 7, 1 died in a refueling accident, and all but 1 of the rest in helicopters. One American general—1—was killed on the ground after he had landed his helicopter to help an ambushed patrol. Many American officers in lower ranks served bravely and well, but on the upper levels, the story was the same: only 8 battalion commanders died. This compared, for instance, with the one-third of all German generals who died in action in World War II and a German officer corps that, collectively, had a higher percentage of casualties than the men they led.[17]

Statistics like these had concrete human meaning. The ability of any officer to tell any soldiers to do anything and to get them to try their best to do it usually depends upon the respect that those soldiers feel for that officer. That respect often depends on whether that officer is there when the bullets start flying. An officer must bond with his men to lead them and must share their danger, the very danger the officer has ordered them into. This common sense element of military leadership is particularly important when a lot of the soldiers being led don't want to be where they are. By 1969, this was very true in Vietnam. The ranks were restless and they had very good reason to be.

The situation, simply, was that draftees were being used as cannon fodder, while the overwhelming majority of "better material" enlistees were saved for noncombat service. "Enlist and you'll probably go to West Germany. Get drafted, and you're absolutely gonna go to Vietnam!" was a pungent and contemporary comment about how best to stay alive.

Here, again, some stark statistics are in order. In Vietnam itself, about 15 percent of the U.S. forces were "ass in the grass" combat soldiers. By 1970, draftees accounted for 88 percent of the combat infantry, even though enlistees in all services during the Vietnam Era were 8.7 million, four times as numerous as draftees (2.2 million). Losses had a similar pattern. In 1965, 16 percent of the battle deaths were of draftees; by 1969, the percentage had risen to 62 percent. "Only the stupid ones go into the infantry," another bit of folk wisdom had it, "and then they're *really* stupid . . . because they're also dead."[18]

None of this was especially likely to make any member of the infantry's heart frolic, and the infantry have been the ones who have borne the brunt of war since time began. Added to this "negative morale factor" was another factor. The draftees in combat were the least wealthy, least educated, and least occupationally skilled. They averaged between eighteen and nineteen years of age, and they were disproportionately (by a factor of three and sometimes even four) black. Add all of this together, shake lightly, add enemy firepower and the normal human desire for as long and healthy a life as possible, and a sure-fire formula had been arrived at for growing alienation in the military. Of the 2.7 million Americans who served in Vietnam, about half a million received less-than-honorable discharges before their terms of service were completed.

Draftees, especially draftees sent to Vietnam after Tet, were a key factor in this equation of growing unrest. These were the "grunts" who were paying most of the bills in blood and body bags. These were also the men who were the most likely to hate their officers' guts and the most likely to be relatively uninhibited about "fragging," "wasting," or "offing" them, especially if they developed serious doubts about their combat competence.

The doubts that the grunts publicly expressed, and occasionally acted upon with a hand grenade or bullet, were shared by their superiors in rank. Officers who wanted to remain in the military for very long, however, kept their doubt to themselves. As early as 1970, in a confidential survey of 420 officers of above-average record and combat distinction, many described the "typical Vietnam commander" in scathing terms: as "an ambitious, transitory commander—marginally skilled in the complexities of his duties—engulfed in producing statistical results, fearful of personal failure, too busy to talk with or listen to his subordinates, and determined to submit acceptably optimistic results which reflect faultless completion of a variety of tasks at the expense of the sweat and frustration of his subordinates." Even generals expressed a good deal of ex post facto concern about the effects of "careerism" and "ticket punching" (collecting command and other experience purely or largely to secure promotions). In the words of one of their number, Army General Douglas Kinnard, "many leaders made a career out of their own careers rather than a career out of leading their units." Kinnard's mid-1970s poll of fellow army generals with Vietnam experience demonstrated that 37 percent of them agreed with him that such careerism was a "serious problem," 50 percent believed that it was "somewhat of a problem," and only 9 percent stated that it was "no problem."[19]

## Firepower Is the Answer

Given the lousy leadership and lousy morale, something had to happen after the Tet offensive, particularly because the news from the Home Front was only exacerbating the problem. The assassination of Martin Luther

King, George Wallace's candidacy, and burning ghettos caused black troopers to lend more sympathetic ears to others who might remark that "No Vietnamese ever called me Nigger!" (in English, anyway). The antiwar and prowar fracases at the Democratic Convention in Chicago and elsewhere led discontented soldiers generally to start wondering aloud: "Who wants to be the last person to die for a mistake?" All this added up to a political problem. A problem on the Home Front and the War Front alike.

One way for national leaders to try to resolve this problem was to minimize American casualties by maximizing firepower, to replace men with machinery, to substitute technology for blood and guts. The idea, in short, was to use the United States of America's wealth of materiel for the political purpose of sustaining enough public support for the War Managers to allow the war in Vietnam to continue, via the simple expedient of making the conflict considerably lower profile in the mass public mind.

And, so, it was on to hi-tech Vietnam, Incorporated:[20] a strategy which, together with turning the costliest elements of the fighting back to the South Vietnamese military, allowed American mainstream politicians to "get out" (via "deescalation"), but not "bug out" (via "surrender"); to tread the sacred "middle ground" between those too hawkish and those too dovish; to limit the political damage to themselves; to gradually end the full-scale Americanization of the war that had begun after mid-1965; and to return the United States to the stage of indirect involvement (aid, not men) that had existed between 1950 and the Kennedy and Johnson presidencies.

This high-technology technique also became progressively popular because it was more than acceptable to three interested wartime clientèles: the military brass, the civilian War Managers in the Pentagon, and the majority of the electorate. The politicians did what the generals and admirals and technocrats and people all wanted them to do.

The generals' desire for high technology was the easiest to comprehend. It was their professional careers that were most directly and immediately at risk in Vietnam. High technology had been a key element of U.S. military strategy in Vietnam ever since the Arc Light B-52 pattern bombings of suspected jungle hideaways started in June 1965. "The airplane," one air force general had early announced, ex cathedra, "is the equalizer in Southeast Asia." Vietnam War bomb tonnages before Tet already exceeded those dropped on Nazi Germany by U.S. forces. The air strategy, in one memorable bit of postwar Pentagonese, was analogous to "a fire hose, running under full pressure most of the time and pointed with the same intensity at whichever area is allowed, regardless of its relative importance." In Laos, for example, over two million tons of bombs were eventually used, more than Americans had dropped on *all* Asian and European targets throughout all of the Second World War—two-thirds of a ton for every man, woman, and child *in* Laos.[21]

Bombing, on a *"Götterdämmerung* of firepower" scale, was a "hallmark of the U.S. military in Vietnam." It was an equalizer, politically back home not least. More dependence on air power decreased casualties. Even before Tet, it was fast becoming standard practice for American forces to contact the enemy, quickly pull back (when surprise or the opposing forces would let them do so), and call in airplanes and artillery to deliver the punishment.[22]

The post-Tet push for more and more high technology, then, was not anathema to the generals. In fact, it served two self-preservatory purposes. It allowed them to fight on with gusto as manpower was first limited and then gradually reduced. And it also offered the opportunity of snatching at victory and saving their careers from the jaws of going nowhere fast. High technology also presented opportunities to the generals, two of which were identified early by disenchanted Marine Colonel William R. Corson. The first of these concerned appropriations for their services. The second, the "Dr. Strangelove Syndrome,"[23] allowed them to ease around some of the more inconvenient realities of an increasingly unpopular war. High technology meant big spending, so the more technological the service became, the more money it would likely get. The Dr. Strangelove element of the equation allowed, as Corson presciently added, a "mystical belief in depending on the impartiality and preciseness of science to make the basic life-and-death decisions" which was an "abdication of the responsibility of command"—not least in the "political war" for the hearts and minds of the Vietnamese themselves.[24] The generals, then, were securely self-interested in their support for ever more and ever better firepower. What had been an element of U.S. strategy, before Tet, became often the *only* element of American military strategy, after Tet.

Generals, however, are not uniquely selfish. Nor are politicians. Much as the rest of us might like to believe this about Vietnam, the politicians and the brass, in fact, weren't alone. People back home were almost equally parsimonious in their attention to or concern with the wider and more inconvenient questions about technological warfare.

The overwhelming proportion of the American population basically didn't care what happened in Vietnam or anywhere else in Asia, so long as whatever did or didn't happen there didn't redound to their discomfort—psychological or actual. After Tet, however, there was very little of a comforting nature for most Americans to think about in relation to Vietnam. An initial reaction was to back escalation. But once LBJ failed to do that and stuck with limited war as usual, a reaction set in. A "get serious or get out" logic ruled, and steadily increasing numbers of citizens wanted to get out of Vietnam and stop thinking about it at all as fast as possible— in the getting out while not "bugging out" middle-ground style mentioned earlier. This was a very large part of what the liberal deescalation–negotiated-settlement movement within the Democratic Party was all about. This is another way of saying what was said in the 1968 elections. A clear majority, perhaps three-fourths, of the electorate in the latter months of '68 supported neither a unilateral withdrawal (strong "dove") nor a bomb 'em back into the Stone Age (strong "hawk") solution to limited war gone awry. They wanted, instead, to disengage gradually, and "with honor." The South Vietnamese could then go on to win or lose their war, but America would not have lost *her* war in South Vietnam.

A high-technology war was *just* what the doctor ordered for these very numerous and increasingly frustrated Americans, people who, in addition, were increasingly concerned with their *domestic* problems. Via Men Out, Machines In, the United States could wage war in a fashion that could be less and less costly in terms of *American* lives. Megatechnology would demonstrate to the communists that it didn't pay to mess with Uncle Sam. Uncle Sam's people, meanwhile, could go to bed at night knowing that they and their nation were tough and strong, and do so without having to worry so much about whether a lot of their sons were going to die in jungles to buy them their peace of mind. The sons, too, could relax, be as hawkish or doveish as they wanted to be, and not have to pay the bills for *their* views either. High technology was as saleable on Main Street as it was on Capitol Hill or in the ranks of the career military. It made the cannon fodder a *lot* happier.

High technology, finally, was the preferred alternative for our old friends the civilian War Managers of Washington as well. These men had the same selfish interest in high technology as the generals: it might save their careers, perquisites, and sense of self-worth, particularly after Tet made their facile optimism look stupid. Moreover, high technology was a scientific approach to war and, therefore, ideologically congenial to civilians unsettled by the blood-and-guts ambience of old-fashioned officers who did not forget that war is a matter of killing and destroying no matter how abstractly it is done.

These War Managers were (and are) people who live in universes of abstractions, in company with calculations of felicity and econometric models based on data deemed reliable and relevant largely because they *can* be quantified. These were (and are) cold-blooded matters, particularly in a thermonuclear age. Formulations were put together by bright young men who had rarely, if ever, seen a war, and whose appreciation of the mysteries of mass politics was almost equally nil. "They were convinced, not passionate," concludes historian Loren Baritz. "We tried to do in cold blood," LBJ's Secretary of State Dean Rusk recalled later, "what can only be done in hot blood, when sacrifices of this order [of long-continued limited war] are involved."[25]

Hot blood was also a rarity among the "social scientists" who arrived with the war bulging in their briefcases every morning. Theirs was all too often a reality of cost-benefit analyses and mathematical game theory, not a world in which the intricacies of Buddhist politics, local peasant discontent, or the unwillingness of North Vietnamese or Vietcong cadres to perceive the war as an economic or remunerative exercise could be factored into equations. The only rarely quantifiable elements of life were subsumed to the clearer, neater, and dessicated task of trying to discover precisely which combination of military escalations would convince Hanoi that its cost-benefit ratio in continuing the war was too expensive to make rational any more investments of blood, sweat, toil, and tears.

The "kill-ratio" and the "body count" summarized the defense intellectual's world view exactly. Count the numbers of them we kill per day, week, month, or year; and then calculate how many of them we kill for every one they kill of us. When the ratio between the deaths assessed against them and the deaths assessed against us was high enough, victory was at hand—not least because the enemies would be in a position where they could not recruit and train troops as fast as they were being destroyed.

It was all so nice and neat and quantifiable and passionless. It was also very, very irrelevant. Using body counts and kill-ratios alone, the armies of Nazi Germany and Imperial Japan had won their wars against the Soviet Union and China by 1942. "Logically," there was no reason for either invaded nation to continue to pay the awesome costs of keeping the invader at bay.

But war is not logical, modern mass wars most particularly. If one people fights another, the alternative to success can be—and often is—perceived as extinction. So, Russians increasingly hated Germans and Chinese increasingly hated Japanese. Each kill by the enemy only produced a widening circle of enemies. War became more a political act to insure the collective survival of a people than an exercise in applied economic theory, much more. Victory went, eventually, to those who were willing to bleed and pay, and to go right on bleeding and paying and hoping until the other side was exhausted or destroyed.

The numbers and the estimates, then, meant nothing. Two thousand North Vietnamese Army dead here, twelve hundred there. Eight thousand

Vietcong killed during the siege of Hue during the Tet offensive. MIG fighters downed in scores over the skies of North Vietnam—in numbers often inflated, inflated, and inflated again on the assumption that nobody ever kills messengers for bringing good news; and the more of it the better, especially for the messengers.

So, guesstimates became estimates became facts, misleading management tools in a managerial war. Numbers flashed on TV screens once a week, reassuring viewers that attrition was the name of the game and that it was only a matter of time before those being attrited came to their senses and ceased their aggressive foreign invasion (civil wars being spectacularly unresolvable into cost-benefit statistics). Count the bodies and figure that whatever was dead was belligerent as hell. Guerillas don't happen to wear uniforms; women can be guerillas, too, likewise children. Having no guns doesn't mean "civilian"—who knows how many arms the guerillas were able to spirit off? Better be safe than sorry, especially if your commanding officer is looking for a good body count and a good kill-ratio this month. His superior expects it of him and, back in Saigon and Washington, computer banks are busily humming away producing all manner of fashionable econometric nonsense.

Were the civilian War Managers really as insulated and arrogant as they are being presented here? Yes. Were these people fools? No. Did they occasionally realize that what they were doing was absurd? Yes. Did that stop them from carrying on? No. The War Managers had theories, you see, and theories almost always harden into the realities they try to explain.

One technocratic defense intellectual, however, began to realize something of what was going on earlier than his peers. Secretary of Defense Robert Strange McNamara, on whom all the channels of information and misinformation converged, had his first real doubts about the logic behind the operational elements of the war in 1966. These doubts, and what McNamara and others did to resolve them, provided the final impulse necessary to guarantee the triumph of a high-technology, burgeoning firepower, low–U.S. casualty approach. The Electronic Battlefield that resulted was the climax of the Men Out, Machines In strategy for resolving the political and military problems spawned by the messy realities of the Vietnamese war.

## The Electronic Battlefield: The Static Phase

The saga of the Electronic Battlefield began in early 1966. McNamara, dubious about air force claims that more and more bombing of North Vietnam would increasingly slow down the rate of infiltration of arms and men south along the various pathways and roads collectively christened the Ho Chi Minh Trail, authorized a group of M.I.T. and Harvard University scientists with longtime Pentagon and White House connections to begin a feasibility and design study for a static electronic barrier that might accomplish the interdiction job better.

The highly placed scientists were happy to oblige. They, like McNamara, were getting fed up with the Bombs Away! posturings of the Curtis LeMay types within the air force brass. The reasons were both political and strategic (i.e., military).

Politically, the burgeoning bombing was becoming a decided handicap. There was a public relations problem. The image of Goliath B-52s pounding away at Plucky-Little-David peasants in rice paddies was adroitly advertised to the world by Hanoi. The most visible element of the high-technology U.S. war effort got a progressively bad press at home to some extent, and to a far greater extent abroad. More and more reassurances had to be conveyed to West European capitals that American leaders were not going hog-wild, acting stupid, or compromising the U.S. military power protecting various European allies.

Strategically, too, the bombing campaign wasn't paying off. The decentralized, semi-industrial, and agrarian society of northern Vietnam was not the "target-rich environment" of Pentagon Newspeak. Hanoi did not even have to produce the arms its soldiers fought with. It was being given the AK-47s, mortars, recoilless rifles, tanks, planes, surface-to-air missiles, and so forth by the Soviet Union and the Chinese, who were engaged in a military assistance bidding war in which neither communist superpower wanted to appear to be soft on support for wars of national liberation during a period of Great Proletarian Cultural Revolution when comradely relations between Moscow and a spectacularly xenophobic Peking had cooled to arctic levels.

The air force generals, therefore, couldn't blast major industrial complexes to rubble to disarm the Hanoi forces. They were also prohibited from bombing China or Russia, the source of the arms supplies. Vietnam was not worth a third world war. Moreover, they were restricted in their attacks on the Chinese-Vietnam border regions for fear that a badly missed target would give the Westerners-are-all-Devils Chinese Maoists the reason they needed to turn Vietnam into another Korea. The air force was limited, therefore, to trying to destroy weapons already received or already armed and supplied units moving southward from their bases in North Vietnam.

This was unsatisfactory, and not only to the military. But whereas many generals wanted to resolve their frustration by bombing right up to the Chinese border or pulverizing the harbor of Haiphong, even at the risk of sinking Russian vessels unloading there, the scientists, with bureaucratic backing from McNamara, wanted to resolve their bafflement by bombing less. For expanded bombing, they substituted static high technology—a defensive system that came to be known as the McNamara Line.

The McNamara Line was to be an electronic barrier composed of a network of radar, infrared, seismic, magnetic, and acoustic sensors supplemented by hundreds of millions of antipersonnel and antivehicular mines, photo-reconnaissance and patrol aircraft, fighter-bomber and B-52 sorties, and the occasional ground patrol. It was supposed to be an impenetrable wall of firepower in an even higher-technology electronic location-net which would entrap and destroy any enemy units who made the mistake of trying to drive, cycle, run, slither, or creep through it. The line was to extend just below the Demilitarized Zone (DMZ) separating northern from southern Vietnam, and from there—after some argument between scientists and generals—across Laos and on into American-allied Thailand. This "noble idea," said then U.S. Commander-in-Chief in Vietnam General William C. Westmoreland, was to "use advanced technology to spare the troops an onerous offensive task."[26]

The problem, however, according to Westmoreland and other highly placed military strategists, was that the Pentagon scientists with the noble ideas were also a lot too naïve for their own good or anybody else's—too naïve in believing that mostly static machines could do it all. How, the generals queried, were the many components of the scientists' "line" to be defended? Surely, that required men—lots of them—emplaced in fortified combat bases spaced out all along the length of the line or else it would be all too easy for the enemy to break through in force at any one point. He'd suffer for it, but he'd also be gone when air-mobile infantry, artillery, and other forces arrived to finish the job of destruction that the scientists' technology had begun.

No, said generals like Westmoreland, the scientists had the beginnings of a good idea but they'd got the really effective applications of it wrong.

The point was not to construct a static barrier, an Electronic Maginot Line, that the enemy might slip around or through and which would tie down tens of thousands of men. Better to use the scientists' devices as part of a more dynamic and offensive military strategy. The linear barrier fence of the McNamara Line should be replaced with a defense-in-depth to channel enemy movements between the fortified bases Westmoreland was already constructing in the northern border regions of South Vietnam.

Westmoreland proposed a network of strategically sited U.S.-held strongpoints, all bolstered by mines, sensors, and air power: a kind of checkerboard of slaughter to cut down infiltration to manageable levels and, eventually, to win the war. Westmoreland believed his strategy of defense-in-depth would eventually give Hanoi's leaders no choice but to attack key U.S. bases that denied them freedom of movement. Once they did that, they were dead. A Dien Bien Phu in reverse could take place, with U.S. bases like the marine enclave at Khe Sanh serving as the bait to attract an all-out enemy siege and with American air power there to hammer the communists to pieces once they had struck that lure.

Westmoreland's defense-in-depth in the north, as things turned out, didn't work either. North Vietnamese units did not put themselves between hammers and anvils at places like Khe Sanh for long. They did so only, in fact, long enough to distract Westmoreland's and other U.S. leaders' attention away from the countrywide Tet offensive that hit with full force further south at the end of January 1968.

Westmoreland, however, ended up accomplishing one very significant thing by insisting upon using electronic high technology in a nonstatic and non-picket-line way. Even the much overplayed Khe Sanh siege of late 1967 and very early 1968 demonstrated the potential destructiveness of the waves of new equipment that were coming out of the military research and development laboratories at that stage in the conflict. It showed, too, how this Buck Rogers technology could be used in a "360-degree war" without clear battle lines, where the enemy had to be hunted down everywhere all the time. As a chastened William C. Westmoreland left Vietnam after Tet, the dynamic and countrywide military applications of the Electronic Battlefield he had championed were getting under way with a vengeance.

## *The Electronic Battlefield: The Dynamic Phase*

In October 1969, the new chief of staff of the United States Army addressed an annual meeting of high-level military officers in Washington. General William C. Westmoreland started off with well-known bad news. Military leadership remained on trial. Recently initiated military, congressional, and journalistic investigations of the My Lai massacre that had occurred during the latter stages of the Tet offensive weren't helping the status of the officer corps one bit.

This storm, too, would pass, Westmoreland reassured his audience. "Military-industrial-labor-academic-scientific cooperation" was producing a "quiet revolution" in the army, one capable of maintaining U.S. power in a technological age.

American military forces, Westmoreland explained, had started out right in Vietnam: with firepower, personnel, and new tactics of air mobility. For years, however, "we were limited in our ability to locate the enemy. We were not quite a giant without eyes, but the allusion had some validity."

Then, fortunately, high technology improved the giant's vision markedly. By mid-1968, "field experiments" for an "entirely new battlefield concept" were well under way in Vietnam. Instead of just moving, shooting, and communicating, the army was increasingly giving primacy to "intelligence" and "support"—in other words, to finding the enemy force, staying in contact with it all the time, and insuring that, once it was both found and engaged, Americans had the wherewithal to destroy it quickly. "Today," Westmoreland concluded, "machines and technology are permitting an economy of manpower on the battlefield, as indeed they are in the factory. But the future offers even more possibilities for economy." On the "battlefield of the future," in fact, officers could realistically look forward to a "more automated battlefield" in which

> enemy forces will be located, tracked, and targeted almost instantaneously through the use of data links, computer assisted intelligence evaluation, and automated fire control. With first round kill probabilities approaching certainty, and with surveillance devices that can continually track the enemy, the need for large forces to fix the opposition physically will be less important.[27]

"You don't," as another army general, Glenn D. Walker, put it far more informally at about the same time, "fight this fellow [in Vietnam] rifle to rifle . . . You locate him and back away, blow the hell out of him, and then police up."[28]

Neither General Walker nor General Westmoreland was talking through his gold-braided hat. Both—one in the language of the technocrat, the other in the lingo of blood and guts—were summarizing what had become *the* strategic lesson of Vietnam by this point in the war. Buck Rogers was alive and well in Southeast Asia. War was increasingly dynamic, technological, and fought by remote control. And all this dovetailed very nicely with the desires of generals, politicos, the populace, and civilian technocrats alike for a lower-profile war with fewer U.S. casualties.

What resulted from all of this was that the United States military began to depopulate rural Vietnam, Laos, and Cambodia and blow parts of those countries to pieces. Larger and larger swaths of geography were turned into "free-fire zones" in order that a high-technology, low-personnel approach to fighting the Vietnam War could be undertaken. Once a proliferating pantheon of sensors picked up something, it was presumed to be an enemy something. In one well-recorded case, seismic and acoustic sensors recorded jungle thrashings and huffings and snortings which, after they were pulverized by a flight of B-52s guided to their target by a huge computer tracking and targeting base in Thailand, turned out to have been the romantic gymnastics of several tigers during mating season.

The tigers ended up in shreds. So did much else. What had begun as a high-technology war of attrition became a war of annihilation waged over vast regions of the countryside. This transition was not a particularly conscious one, nor was it publicized by the perpetrators. In an apt phrase from eighteenth-century historian of Rome, Edward Gibbon, Americans "endeavored to destroy the country which it had not been in their power to subdue." "Vietnam, Incorporated," British photojournalist Philip Jones Griffiths acidly entitled the strategy. It was a largely unconscious process summarized by an anonymous army major who ordered in artillery and air assaults during the Tet offensive of 1968. "It became necessary," the major said, "to destroy the town in order to save it."[29] It became necessary to destroy rather a lot in order to save it, more and more, in fact. Saving it became equivalent to denying the use of it to the enemy.

Few complaints, logically enough, were heard from American soldiers. There were progressively fewer of those, following the gradual withdrawal of U.S. ground forces, begun with ruffles and flourishes by the Nixon administration in 1969. Those that were there were ambivalent about their status and fearful for *their* lives, as rear guards are wont to be during a withdrawal. Moreover, the high-technology, rural-depopulation approach appeared, to many officers and men, to solve real moral dilemmas. Those concerned the extent to which soldiers should try to mix humanitarianism with survival in a war often fought in the midst of noncombatants or sometimes noncombatant villagers. Many officers and men tended to play this game "safe, not sorry," especially after their units had seen action. It was common for U.S. artillery, for example, to lay down nighttime H&I (harrassment and interdiction) fire against possible enemy movements by blasting areas selected by guess and by golly or simply at random. Yet, for all that, plenty of officers and men spared civilians, or looked upon them as neutral, whenever possible, sometimes at considerable risk to themselves.

Removing all villagers out of areas deemed pro-insurgent, doubtful, risky, or simply inconvenient to defend, meant that difficult trade-offs between compassion and destruction no longer needed to be made so thoroughly, so immediately, or so often. Now killing became long distance; and if "they" were there, "they" deserved what they got.

It began, in increasingly depopulated rural regions, to turn into what the earliest historian of the Electronic Battlefield called "the slick, casual kind of war of the future in which killing would be programmed like a department store billing system."[30]

Others were less pacific in their imagery. Marine Colonel Corson termed what was happening worse than longtime liberal pundit Walter Lippmann's metaphorical "elephant stamping on mosquitoes." Instead, said Corson, the U.S. military response was "an elephant running amok"—via the Electronic Battlefield, as fellow veteran Eric Herter argued during a 1972 investigation by a group of ex-servicemen known as the Vietnam Veterans against the War (V.V.A.W.):

> . . . the people of villages have gone from being [human beings or even] "gooks" and "dinks" to being grid-coordinates, blips on scan screens, dots of light on infrared film. They are never seen, never known, never even hated. The machine functions. The radar blip disappears. No village is destroyed. No humans die. For none existed.

"The technicians who program the computer perform no act of war," another veteran testified at the V.V.A.W. hearings, for

> the man who places the sensor does not see it operate. The man who plots the strike never sees the plane that conducts it. The pilot, navigator, and bombardier do not see the bombs hit. The damage assessor is not in the plane, and all the others who helped mount the raid never participated in it at all.[31]

Finally, as Britisher Griffiths wrote in his searing 1971 photo-essay on the war:

> . . . in keeping with efforts to automate the killing, enlarged "people sniffers" [odor detectors] slung under helicopters have been used. A "positive" reading is intercepted by a second, heavily armed helicopter that follows [the "sensor" chopper] and automatically lets off a barrage of fire at the indicated position. In this way, no human decisions have to be made: a pair of helicopters skim over the countryside, the second raining death whenever the first detects molecules of amino-acid breakdown products, whether from buffalo, Vietcong, or children taking a short cut to school.[32]

For all these occasional protests, the sensors sensed, the bombs rained down, and the American war in Indochina became a grim mixture of weapons testing and proliferating official euphemisms. During the all-out bombing of the Ho Chi Minh Trail from 1969 to 1972, code-named Igloo White, for example, air crews often had no say whatsoever in where and when the explosives they carried were dropped. This activity was electronically automated, controlled by linkups between on-board flight computers and targeting-control computers back at distant bases. As early as 1970, every hitherto relatively low-technology marine division in Vietnam had a SCAMP contingent (Sensor Control and Management Platoon) incorporated within it: 2 officers, 43 enlisted personnel, 720 sensors.

Along with the proliferating technology went proliferating bureaucratic gobbledegook, both military and civilian—emotionless buzzwords, intentionally confusing terminology that characterized so much of the Vietnam Era. Invasion became "incursion"; bombing, "interdiction"; renewed bombing, "protective reaction" (even Westmoreland was amused by this); ambushes, "meeting engagements"; and "search and destroy" missions were rechristened "sweeping operations."[33]

In the end, Vietnam and the Vietnamese became almost irrelevant to the highly automated war that was going on in Vietnam and the surrounding nations. They were blips on radar screens or simply invisible to American soldiers, leaders and people alike. Americans were abusing greatness in the manner that Shakespeare's Brutus identified in *Julius Caesar:* they were disjoining remorse from the exercise of their power.

This separation of act and feeling had powerful effects upon the Vietnamese for whom the war was supposedly being fought. Now, their story must be told.

## "Hearts and Minds": The Scrutable Orientals

Vietnam, as has been said again and again, was a political war. It was a struggle for hearts and minds, and for ideals and interests, more than a matter of battlefield dynamics. Yet, it was precisely here that the American failure in Vietnam was most patent, most important, and most tragic— because of what Americans never learned and because of what they chose to forget. In what follows, we will examine this failure in terms of the Vietnamese populace and the political and military regime of the South.

In Vietnam, the Arrogance of Power was usually also the Ignorance of Power. Arrogance was equivalent to the sheer lack of attention or regard that the overwhelming majority of Americans—at home or abroad, just plain folks or cognoscenti—ever paid to anything Vietnamese.

Start with the Vietnamese language. Languages are not just different ways to say the same things. They are different ways to say *different* things. A word like "naive," for example, is one of the many foreign terms that English has borrowed from a host of languages. Each of these words expresses a reality which, if put into English, would be only partially or indelicately expressed. So, to preserve the distinctiveness of concept, the foreign word has been incorporated into our language to express it. Such borrowings go on all the time, not least during wars.

But not in Vietnam. Not in Vietnam. Vietnamese bequeathed no conceptual bounty to American English. Veterans remember the occasional phrase. But their memories have never, and will never, become part of our common linguistic heritage. America borrowed nothing in Vietnam. Almost no Americans ever bothered to learn Vietnamese in the first place. The language, the embodied expression of Vietnamese hearts and Vietnamese minds, remained, with a few honorable exceptions, a thoroughly closed book to Americans throughout the entire course of this nation's Longest War.

Let none of those whose ideas far exceeded their information be exempted from this charge. Not the Washington insiders at the elite reaches of policy formulation and implementation: these people didn't even bother to learn French, much less Vietnamese. Not the flocks of American reporters who flew in and out of Saigon, completely untutored in Vietnamese, largely unaware of Vietnamese history, culture, or even geography, and prone to send home endless stories about what American diplomats were saying and about what U.S. troops (but almost never Vietnamese or other allied soldiers) were doing in the "drama" of combat. These reporters, though sometimes assisted by a few dozen Vietnamese whose linguistic and journalistic skills allowed them to try to understand what they were unable to understand for themselves, were like the sightless ones in the ancient Hindu parable of the seven blind men and the elephant. Each felt an immediate portion of reality. But, linguistically and otherwise blinded, only the merest handful realized that they weren't seeing the society as a whole. It was, after all, the *American* war in Vietnam that elicited editorial interest and the possibility of promotion.

Nor let us exempt the intellectual guardians of American understanding and virtue back home, the academic devotees of the True and Beautiful and Pragmatic-Political, the men and women who sponsored or produced the grand total of twenty-two dissertations on matters Vietnamese in the fields of modern history, international relations, and political "science" in American universities between 1954 and 1968; years during which a total of 7,615 theses were produced in these same specialties. Let us not forget that, during the most destructive years of the war, there were only two tenured professors in America who spoke Vietnamese. Let us recall to its full Establishment glory and self-delusive grandeur the Council on Foreign Relations in New York, which did not even initiate a research project on Vietnam until 1973. Nor let us exempt the instantaneous geniuses on matters Vietnamese who sprouted up within prowar and antiwar circles like weeds—people who, having read several books, pamphlets, and news-paper articles, could and did tell you all about what the "average Viet-namese" thought about everything, and most especially about the war.[34]

Let us, finally, not exempt the War Manager-in-Chief of the all-out Americanization phase of the war, Robert S. McNamara. He, at a point in early 1964, flew about South Vietnam with General Nguyen Khanh, one of a series of military putschists then in the process of overthrowing one another in their mutually self-defeating efforts to succeed Ngo Dinh Diem in the presidential palace in Saigon. *"Viet Nam Muon Nam!"* McNamara shouted into the microphones at every stop along the way, in an effort to say "Long Live South Vietnam!" in the language of the people and to demonstrate his friendship, respect, and regard for things Vietnamese, including General Khanh.

The secretary of defense tried. He had been "briefed," but the briefing had been too brief. McNamara did not quite comprehend that Vietnamese, like Chinese, is a *tonal* language, one in which the same words, pronounced in different intonations, can mean wildly different things. So, *"Viet Nam Muon Nam!"* McNamara enthused, forgetting that Vietnamese wasn't En-glish. His words came out meaning "The southern duck wants to lie down."[35]

The Vietnamese in the arranged audiences at airports knew better than to laugh outright, and those who didn't were clubbed. So recalled Don Luce, an exceedingly rare American who *was* fluent in Vietnamese. Luce was one of a widely scattered handful of former Peace Corps men, younger foreign service officers, military advisers, and private relief and reconstruction agency workers (often from deeply religious backgrounds) who had been in Vietnam for years. The Don Luces, however, remained suspect, no matter how often they and their language skills were recruited to squire around yet another "fact-finding delegation" on yet another whirlwind tour. Luce, like most of his linguistically adept counterparts, either wasn't "official" at all—Luce spent thirteen years in Vietnam working for the largely pacifist International Voluntary Services (IVS)—or of too low a status within bureaucratic hierarchies. Most were considered too sympathetic to Vietnamese points of view. They had "gone native," as British imperial officials used to put it.

Would that many more Americans had gone native—to the point, at least, of learning Vietnamese. For, mostly by ignoring the language of Vietnam and a great deal more besides, Americans made the worst mistake any party to any war can ever make. They did not endeavor to know their enemy, or their friends either, with the result that the two got confused more or less constantly.

## People as Political Chessmen [36]

Awareness interfered with expertise. Knowing anything much wasn't deemed all that important. Vietnam was a lesser piece—at least initially—in a much wider game of global geopolitical chess. It did not do for the Best and the Brightest to distract themselves by staring too intently or too long at pawns, not when more powerful pieces were at stake. Vietnam, for all the hearts-and-minds rhetoric, remained a pawn. Until the Tet offensive blew the game up in the U.S. players' faces.

It was, moreover, a strange pawn, a society whose mélange of Confucian, Buddhist, Christian, and other folkways was indeed a world away from Judeo-Christian norms. In Vietnam, for instance, astrology influenced everything from the dates of weddings to the days that bureaucrats visited their official charges, from the times that military offensives were scheduled to the number of authors, articles, prefatory words, and especially the date of issuance of the South Vietnamese Constitution of 1967. Whereas, in the 1960s, many better-heeled Americans were using astrology as another tool in the arsenal of sexual selection ("What's *your* sign?"), Vietnamese of all sorts were much more genuinely casting their lives to the rhythms of the stars and the music of the spheres.[37]

Average, or even not so average, Americans boggled at realities like these. They quickly forgot whatever they might have learned in an anthropology course about "cultural relativism": the idea that different societies do the same things in different ways, and that one way is, per se, no better or worse than any other, especially if both ways work well. Relativity, Hell. There was a *war* on. Waiting for the stars to tell you when to attack the enemy was lunatic—especially if you concentrated on the high technology American elements of the war, while ignoring the morale of the South Vietnamese foot soldiers (ARVN) doing most of the fighting and dying after the B-52s and the Phantoms dropped their bomb loads and streaked back to Okinawa or an offshore aircraft carrier.

It was far better, most American experts concluded, for their Vietnamese allies to be shown new and better ways of doing things—the modern American Way of war, government, society, language, and structures and habits of thought. This was the way to get on with the practical matter of winning the war, any war. The United States of America—in an exceedingly selective reading of its own history—had never lost a war. Power was far more important than cultural minutiae like astrology. "Grab 'em by the balls," one bit of American military wisdom had it, "and their hearts and minds will follow."

Not quite, of course. It did not quite follow. Military power was not and is not identical to political power, a lesson that British officers learned in America between 1775 and 1781. By understanding the people of Vietnam as pawns moved by Moscow, Washington, or Peking, the American leaders whose business it was to win the war they had started in 1965 lost the initiative almost as soon as they began. For, as gone-native Don Luce and a fellow IVS relief worker remarked in a book published in 1969, knowing what made the Vietnamese tick—having a concern with the "human spirit," Vietnamese style—was not a luxury or a dependent variable. It was *the* essential element in the war. "[U]nderstanding people," the two IVS men argued, "is the key to successful policy," and "failure to understand them and to respond to their needs [in ways that they can comprehend, appreciate, and absorb] is to fail in one's goals."[38]

This was common sense, surely, a statement of the obvious. But not in Vietnam, where a limited war got very much bigger than expected and did so very fast. The U.S. chess masters knew little about the pawns, and cared less, having forgotten, if they ever knew, that it is pawns which decide the result of the Royal Game in very many instances, especially when one's opponent knows how to use them to devastating effect.

What Americans didn't know about Vietnam is so vast as to defy remembering. The Vietnamese were Asiatic, it was not unusual for U.S. eminences to relate, especially when explaining why the enemy was still fighting and the war still hadn't been won. Their religion and their folkways were different. They didn't have the same love of life or attitude toward life that Americans had. True, they carried with them into battle poems and diaries and pictures of family and sweethearts, as men have done for a thousand years. But the Vietnamese were antlike yellow hordes, banzai charge–kamikaze Japanese whose memory was still vivid in the minds of the Second World War leaders who had led the United States into Vietnam, or "human-wave attack" Chinese infantry from the Korean War of the '50s. The stubborn Vietnamese enemy was a sort of mindless insect lacking morality, discrimination, or reason—fighting to die, while their American opposite numbers were fighting to live.

Bovine misconceptions and cynical self-justifications like this, which equated NVA regulars or Vietcong with hollow-eyed Oriental Death-Worshippers out of a Hollywood film epic, were norms throughout the Vietnam War and remain norms for a majority of Americans now. These norms are only gradually giving way to knowledge as Oriental immigrants of many varieties enter the nation in large numbers for the first time in a hundred years; China has ceased to be terra incognita, and Japan, Incorporated is deemed (often semihysterically) to be America's chief economic and technological competitor on the planet.

## The Army and the Regime

Not all American confusions, however, were as racist or as stupid as these. On less stereotyped levels, people who dealt with the political and military realities of Vietnam every day wondered about the inability of American-style democracy to work in the South, even in Saigon. The nation that the United States had pledged itself to protect as a proving ground for democracy in Asia, was, by the end of the 1960s, a carnival of power grabbing, conspiracy, and counter-conspiracy, in which there appeared to be far more would-be chiefs than dependable and forthright

Indians. "The roles, goals and elements of constituencies of Vietnamese political forces," a disgruntled U.S. commentator with extensive experience with the southern government observed in 1974, "are captured on [American] television and in news photos and clever news items as the minor characters in a Gilbert and Sullivan opera."[39]

But it *was* hard for even the most sympathetic and involved Americans not to laugh, if only to avoid beating their heads against walls in frustration. There were no less than seven coups in the immediate aftermath of the Kennedy-backed putsch that overthrew and murdered President Ngo Dinh Diem in November 1963. Ten successive regimes claimed to hold power in Saigon from that date until June 1965.

An average life span of two months per government over the course of two years was not impressive, especially to the Vietnamese most immediately affected by the political balkanization going on. "Two Vietnamese on a street corner," one standard Vietnamese joke had it, "constitute a political party, while three constitute a party and at least one faction." Or, as another realistically cynical view of the post-Diem era went, "the number of 'parties' at any one time outnumbers the total 'membership' of a majority of the formally declared parties."[40]

Vietnamese politics was often a disaster that *had* happened and kept right on happening. South Vietnam was a weak confederation split along regional, religious, ethnic, and class lines. Warlordism and "local party states-within-the-state" were commonplace. Noncommunist interest groups were generally incapable of forming lasting coalitions which required compromising immediate or not so immediate objectives. No charismatic patriotic leadership counterpointed that provided by the competing Hanoi regime. A rule-ridden and unresponsive civil service was usually more interested in looking after itself than in doing its duty. There was extremely high turnover of ministerial and administrative personnel. Government was restricted, by and large, to an urbanized mandarinate. The South, in Arnold Isaacs' phrase, had a "weak and trembling autocracy" that was "authoritarian enough to be unpopular, democratic enough to be inefficient," and as one of the more effective Saigon leaders, Nguyen Cao Ky, stated after the war, "never learned how to pursue a policy, [but] only the doubtful art of taking measures." The southern regime, moreover, once the cycle of coups was broken by the arrival of the Ky military regime in 1965 and the Nguyen Van Thieu–Ky military regime in 1967, was widely perceived to be a captive creature of the Americans.[41]

Perhaps the best way of visualizing the problem is to think of politics, southern Vietnamese style, as analogous to a bunch of marbles in a very shallow saucer. Every time the marbles (political interest groups) began interacting with each other very strenuously, the danger existed that they would ricochet outside the saucer and the political order would fall apart. The same sort of problem occurred every time the saucer with the marbles within it was given a strong external jolt by, for example, communist insurgents or by the economically, militarily, and politically powerful Americans.

Had the saucer (the political processes and the "rules of the game") of southern Vietnam been stronger, the "civil religion" saucer wouldn't have been a saucer at all. It might have been a deep cup within which interest groups could have collided or coalesced with one another without flying off into outer space or constantly threatening to.

Saigon, however, was not Washington, D.C. The South Vietnamese state was not the American one. Saigon's regime was a smaller version of the Kuomintang government headed by Chiang Kai-Shek in China from 1927 until 1949. It was, as an American officer once remarked, "not a country with an army, but an army with a country."[42] It was a weak military regime fighting a war and trying to ride herd on a disorganized and fragmented polity at the same time. At the top of the regime was an officer corps from wealthy backgrounds who ran the country, when they were not feuding among themselves, and superior to them all was a warlord-in-chief—Chiang in China; Thieu, finally, in Vietnam. Neither man was an inspirational leader. Both were supremely manipulative. Manipulation became a more or less constant necessity of survival in a political landscape populated with feral interest groups only barely held together by bonds of sympathy, self-interest, or even collective political survival. This regime, like Chiang's, faced a better organized and administered communist insurgency and foreign intervention on top of that.

The Kuomintang-Saigon analogy sheds light in another respect, too. Both governments tried to use weakness as a strength in their dealings with America, and both paid the bills for such a strategy. Thieu, like Diem before him, argued, with varying degrees of accuracy or self-interest, that particular American reforms aimed at strengthening popular support for the government were impossible to achieve without massively undermining the regime in the hearts and minds of the Vietnamese economic, political, and military elite. Of land reform, for example, Thieu could say, "Do this, and my enemies will overthrow me. And *then* where will you be?" This logic was persuasive to American politicians worried about being blamed for "Losing Vietnam" by some revivified version of Senator Joseph McCarthy, who had successfully played the "soft on communism" card in the wake of Chiang's loss of China in 1949.[43] Likewise, the argument-from-weakness went, getting rid of, say, corruption among the military

governors of the South wasn't feasible because those fattening off robber-
ies and extortions would simply band together and depose Thieu in conse-
quence. Bad as it was, Saigon's military regime was the best that could be
had in a bad situation. And, besides, Thieu and the other generals were
*our* bastards.

Here, then, was a major irony of the political element of a political war.
The United States, locked into moral and political responsibility for the
fate of all post-Diem governments in Saigon by being an accomplice to
Diem's overthrow in the first place, was often hamstrung in its efforts to
improve the quality of Vietnamese governance. It was hamstrung by its
fears of a far worse communist alternative, one whose existence and
strength was largely due to the comparative weakness, disorganization,
and ineffectiveness of the Saigon regimes themselves.[44]

In trying to replace weakness with strength, the Americans got themselves caught in a vicious cycle. They increasingly moved into vacuums of
policy, to do *for* the Saigon government what it was unwilling or unable
to do for itself. And, as our two previously cited gone-native Americans
all too cogently observed at the time, "The more men the United States
sent, the more Americanized the system became and the less the Vietnamese officials did. And the less they did, the more advisers the United
States sent. 'Let the Americans do it' was a motto we often overheard
Vietnamese saying to one another. 'It's your war, you fight it,' said others."[45]

Popular and official opting out like this only produced more frustration
and "All-right-*I'll*-do-it-then" behavior on the part of the Americans, and
more passivity and *"We're*-not-responsible-for-this" behavior on the part
of the Vietnamese. The result was that a higher and higher U.S. profile
made the war appear, not least to Americans back home, as an *American* war
*in* Vietnam rather than a *Vietnamese* war in which the United States was
playing an allied role. Infinitely worse, it branded the South Vietnamese
regimes as vassals of the foreigners, the Americans. It allowed the Vietnamese man or woman in the street to assume that Americans dominated
the Saigon government and dictated the courses of action that were followed or not followed—thus, of course, making the Americans, in Vietnamese eyes, more and more completely responsible for Vietnam's fate.

Joined to this ennui-inducing element within southern ruling circles was
an action-inducing element among the opposition forces that America had
sent its men and money and guns and electronics to Indochina to destroy.
As Premier Pham Van Dong of Hanoi said of Diem even before Diem's
assassination, any Saigon leader who was weak enough to require increasing American aid would only end up cutting his own throat. He would

produce a Vietnamese nationalist reaction against himself, a descending spiral of weakness-breeding Americanization breeding a patriotic desire to get the foreigners out. "The more unpopular he is, the more American aid he will require to stay in power. And the more American aid he receives, the more he will look like a puppet of the Americans and the less likely he is to win popular support for his side."[46]

Another way of saying what Dong said—and what increasing numbers of Vietnamese felt about Diem and all the Saigon leaders who followed him—was that once the United States began to all-out Americanize the war in mid-1965, the communist forces in what was, until then, a civil war in which both sides were backed by foreign arms, money, advisers, and spies was transformed into one which the communists could and did advertise as a *foreign invasion* on top of a civil war. It was, moreover, a foreign invasion which had been allowed into Vietnam by a secessionist regime in Saigon that was losing the struggle. It was exactly as if Abraham Lincoln had been able to castigate Jefferson Davis for inviting a large British or French army to pull the Confederacy's chestnuts out of the fire for it, thus compounding the sin of trying to destroy the Union by going on to make the United States a European colony once again.

Political logic like this was hard to refute, particularly as higher and higher-profile Americans began doing higher and higher-profile things— from writing psychological warfare pamphlets to setting traffic patterns and placing traffic lights in Saigon, from deciding which Vietnamese villages should be "relocated" (denied to the enemy) for military purposes to trying to restructure Saigon bureaucracies from French to U.S. models, from reforming Vietnamese high schools to advising Vietnamese politicos how to go about the job of implementing a national constitution which looked quite remarkably like the American one.[47]

Apathy and anger became endemic among southern Vietnamese. They lost sight of their own role in determining their own futures—collective or individual, and such profound alienation had unfortunate results. For, as Yugoslav Milovan Djilas argued many years later, the small want to be accounted respectable in the eyes of the great. And when they are not, their stubborn pride can rise to marked heights. Djilas, the communist guerilla leader who had helped win a civil war and fight off foreign invasions during the Second World War, understood the phenomenon.[48]

Had rot like this been restricted to Saigon, however, all might still have been well—or at least a great deal better—for the Cold Warriors back in Washington. The same sort of rot, however, had long since spread to Saigon's army. Apathy, evasion, incompetence, and arrogance bred even more immediately disastrous results there.

## *"Their Lions, Our Rabbits"*[49]

Few disputed that there was lots wrong with the South Vietnamese army, especially if they happened to be in it and had a good listener. Let Arnold R. Isaacs' vignette of a major commanding a paratroop battalion after his unit had just suffered tremendous losses in battle in 1972 stand muster for the thoughts and the feelings of hundreds of thousands of ARVN veterans for whom very few Americans ever cared. Vastly fewer care now.

> He had been a combat officer for nine years, the major said. He had no powerful friends and no money and did not expect ever to sit behind a desk—or be promoted, for that matter, unless a superior was killed or disabled. For anyone used to the American army's system of rotating assignments and scheduled promotions, this business of men serving in combat jobs, for years and years, with no respite, took some getting used to. But that was how the South Vietnamese army worked. Sitting in a field tent and nipping stronger and stronger slugs of brandy, the major spoke on into the evening about the government whose uniform he wore. As he talked, his face hardened in the flickering light of the lantern hanging from the tentpole. It was something far deeper than the combat soldier's dislike of the rear echelon. It was an angry, corroded bitterness that seemed to come from some unreachable depth in his soul. My notes of that evening's talk were lost—washed into illegibility when that notebook was soaked in a rainstorm . . . a day or so later. But I needed no notes to remember the major's summation of his own life. "I do not fight for the government," he said, gesturing at what was left of his battalion—only 150 men or so, fewer than half the number he had led into the battle. "I do not fight for my commanders. I fight only because I am a soldier, because it is my destiny. And I fight for my men. That is all.[50]

The paratroop major was not alone in the fighting, dying, exhaustion, drinking, or in the bitterness that cut to the quick. The army in which he and his men fought year after year (and long after most of the Americans who slighted them had returned home) was a disaster waiting to happen.

The major problems with the ARVN were that the army was trained and organized to fight the wrong kind of war; that its higher-level officer corps was a closed elite that was too often uncaring, inept, or corrupt; that its

soldiers, including its lower-echelon officers, accordingly lacked morale—
or even hope; that the South Vietnamese military was increasingly deni-
grated by Americans who should have known better and acted better; and,
finally, that the ARVN was unable either to protect the peasants or deal
with them in ways that increased their support for the Saigon regime.

The ARVN's structural problems arose from its being created by Americans on American models. When the ARVN was formed after the French
defeat in Indochina in 1954, the Korean War was the dominant experience
in the U.S. military mind. The ARVN, therefore, was organized to respond
to the threat of a cross-DMZ invasion by large, heavily armed, and well-
supplied military forces. A "conventional" army (be it Vietnamese, communist, or Chinese) might strike south with armored columns and infantry
protected by batteries of artillery. Accordingly, the ARVN was organized
into big, high-firepower and road-transportable units of its own. "Training
materials [for the ARVN] were word-for-word translations of American
manuals, without even a paragraph tailored for Vietnamese circumstances."[51]

One result was that the ARVN turned out to be muscle-bound when it
had to face a very different sort of fighting: the hit-and-run guerilla struggle that began in earnest in South Vietnam in 1960–61. Saigon's military
men had lots of trouble reorienting themselves to changed conditions.
Generals, for instance, were reluctant to break up their divisions into small,
lightly armed, formations which could operate without benefit of base
camps and road networks and locate and destroy the enemy while also
protecting widely scattered villages and towns. The ARVN often was like
a man trying to shoot a sparrow with a howitzer: blasting lots of landscape
and lots of people, not bringing down much game, and not being able to
provide lasting security to the peasantry.

The situation never improved much, even as the war became more
conventional, and less guerilla-oriented, in the wake of the destruction of
many Vietcong units during and immediately after the Tet offensive. The
ARVN stayed big and American and expensive, so expensive that the
South Vietnamese economy had not a hope of supporting it in the style
to which it was accustomed. The United States had to pay almost all its
bills for equipment and supply and salary throughout its existence. Once
the war was further Americanized in mid-1965, little changed. The vast
majority of U.S. officers were even more big-battalion and avalanche-of-
firepower oriented than Saigon's military was: U.S. generals were often
extremely suspicious of small, lightly-armed units like the elite Green
Berets, and closely restricted the uses to which these "irregular" forces
were put. (Diminishing numbers of Green Berets, for example, were sent

off to border regions to train Montagnard hill tribesmen to disrupt enemy
infiltration routes.)[52]

Even as late as 1974, after the last U.S. ground and air forces were
withdrawn from the Vietnam War, ARVN commanders were still ammu-
nition-happy, using fifty-six times as much as their communist opponents,
but only about half of what the American commanders had regularly
expended.[53] Saigon's army remained far too dependent upon American
military models and strategies which hadn't won; worse, Saigon's officers
tended to believe secret reassurances provided by U.S. military spokesmen—and the Nixon White House—that high-technology, high-firepower U.S. forces (B-52 bombers operating from nearby bases in Thailand,
for example) would be reintroduced into the war by presidential *diktat* if
the ARVN got into desperate straits.[54]

The ARVN, then, blasted away. So long as the U.S. insurance policy was
there, it could fight a U.S.-style war as, for example, when the ARVN, with
an all-out assist from the American air force, defeated a Korean-style
cross-DMZ invasion mounted by Hanoi during the spring of 1972. Its
commanders, however, remained psychologically and materially dependent upon vast American military largesse, on supplies that could be vastly
increased as the need arose and as C-141 transport aircraft swarmed into
Saigon's airport. Saigon's generals, in a triumph of hope over realism,
further ignored the fact that, by the middle of 1973, President Richard
Milhous Nixon, for all his secret assurances, was less and less able to rescue
himself, much less them. When a congressionally mandated ban on all
further U.S. bombing of Vietnam, Cambodia, and Laos finally went into
effect in Washington in mid-August, the ARVN, left to its own devices,
failed to reorient itself for a much lower-technology and vastly less American war, and suffered accordingly. The end came in early 1975. As always
in such disasters—and as Hanoi's army lunged across the DMZ and toward
Saigon—a handful of ARVN units still somehow fought bravely and well,
commanded, perhaps, by men like our paratroop colonel, struggling because it was their destiny, their responsibility, and their duty to their men.

Our paratroop colonel, however, was not a typical ARVN officer. He and
other fighting officers were rare birds: "Ascetics among whores," one U.S.
marine colonel called them. They were men who spent their careers in the
field rather than in urban billets, and often commanded elite units at the
rank of colonel or below, especially if they had fought against the French
during the 1945–54 phase of the Vietnam War.[55]

The ARVN's commanding heights, unfortunately, contained no former
Vietminh. None. The ARVN's generals, when the Tet offensive blew the
lid off the immediate-salvation-by-America phase of the war, were all

veterans of the French colonial army or men who had been at university or military school in France during the conflict. While to have fought for the French did not by itself make many of these generals unpatriotic (many were Catholics whose aversion to atheistic Marxism was profound), the ARVN hierarchy's patriotism was a selective proposition. The commanders were often more loyal to their caste and class than they were to their country.

It was hard for most upper-echelon ARVN officers *not* to be conscious of caste and class, even if they wished to be otherwise. These officers came from a tiny French-educated elite, recruited overwhelmingly from the old mandarin aristocracy of Vietnam and from the bureaucratic, landowning, and commercial interests that had prospered during the period of French control of Indochina. Education, in such a hierarchical society and equally hierarchical military, was the ticket into the system. A college degree, for instance, was the minimum educational requirement for admission to officer status in the ARVN. Thereafter, connections (whom you knew, not what you knew) got you most of the rest of the way to wherever you were going. American pressure accomplished only a dim beginning of change in the system in 1967, when all of one hundred men from the ranks were promoted. Until then, in an underdeveloped and agrarian country, the peasants and others who made up the vast majority of the ARVN never got to be officers—no matter how long they had been in the army, no matter how good their military record was. Similarly, promotion, once you were an officer, was often made on the basis of who-knew-whom, who-was-related-to-whom, or who-needed-whom-politically. Diffuse bonds of interest groups provided surer paths to success than ability tested under fire.[56]

All bureaucracies and all armies have such folkways. Up-from-the-ranks Col. Anthony Herbert's criticisms about what he and others termed the "West Point Protective Association"[57] weren't misplaced. But the ARVN officer class had more self-defeating exclusivity than most—including that of its communist military opponents. Marxist *political* loyalty was the characteristic of the elite reaches of the Vietcong and the North Vietnam Army officer corps, and promotions from the ranks was a lot more common. Egalitarianism was the operating assumption of a revolutionary army that needed every good officer and man it could possibly get.

The ARVN's officers, meanwhile, remained upper-class urbanites whose attitudes toward the men they led and the people they were supposed to cooperate with and protect were not so much contemptuous as indifferent. This indifference was often bred of sheer ignorance. Whether calculated or accidental, however, indifference, as an American military man noted on the eve of Tet, was "manifest in callousness," in not giving a damn, or in not appearing to in ways that villagers could understand or appreciate. "In a people's war this is suicidal."[58]

It surely was, and the ARVN soldier's morale suffered from that indifference. Even with the best leadership, the South Vietnamese Army grunt had a tough job staying very optimistic for very long. Without it, he became angry, brutalized, and resentful; and he took that anger and sense of despair out—as human beings will—on the people around him.

Here let us recall what Americans too easily forget, or never knew in the first place. An ARVN soldier had a whole lot of nothing compared to his U.S. counterpart. He had a long—and often indefinite—term of service that could keep him in the army for fourteen years or more. He had irregular pay that was sometimes reduced by officers padding their own pockets at his expense. His pay, even when he got it on time and in total, was less and less capable of buying necessities, never mind luxuries, in an economy where inflation averaged 50 percent a year by the late 1960s. He was drafted by a system more riddled with exemptions and favoritisms than the American version was. His family, which often followed him from battle to battle and from camp to camp to look after his needs, often lived in squalid settlements around bases in conditions well below those of the average peasant in a relatively peaceful area. If the ARVN trooper was wounded or disabled, there was almost no "welfare state" at all to fall back on, except the oldest one: his family or what was left of it. Lacking family, he faced the grim realities of begging in the streets. The same insecurities and fears, of course, beset members of his family. A napalm run by a fighter-bomber might go awry, or a mortar round hit his wife's encampment rather than his own.[59]

The ARVN trooper, in addition, was fighting in *his* country. The people surrounding him were not faceless "gooks" and "dinks" or "inscrutable Orientals" to be written off or ignored. They were Vietnamese like himself, human beings whose treacherous, loyal, or disinterested behavior could elicit passionate and immediate responses from a soldier in any society undergoing a civil war. Not for him the technocratic posturings of Americans for whom Vietnam was a place on a map, a place to stay alive for a year before returning back to The World of apple pie, mother, and round-eyed women.

The ARVN's world wasn't ten thousand psychological or actual miles away. It was right where he was fighting and fearing and hoping and dying. In that smaller and more intimate world of loves and hatreds, the trooper very often felt that nobody particularly cared about him. His own officers, who sometimes avoided the inconveniences of the battlefield on weekends or who looked after investments, including whorehouses built to service affluent U.S. officers and men, did not care about him. Neither did the Americans, who were strange enough to start with and who also despised him, took "his" women, lived like kings, bought curios by the trunkful, and viewed him (as the wartime *Newsweek* headline quoted in the title of this section put it) as a rabbit in uniform.

Regarding this latter point, it is well to realize that Americans cast the ARVN in a no-win role and made it a foil for their growing frustration about the war. When "we" won, it was an American victory; when "they" lost, it was the cowardly and incompetent ARVN's fault. Heads I win; tails you lose.

Americans, however, *never* suffered more combat deaths than the ARVN at *any* point in the war. In specific battles, yes; overwise, no. Consider these U.S. figures for average monthly combat deaths for the six years of the conflict during which U.S. forces were most thoroughly engaged in the Vietnam War, a period before Nixon's Vietnamization decreased the average U.S. military losses even further, relative to the Vietnamese losses.

*Average Monthly Combat Deaths*[60]

| Year | U.S. forces | ARVN forces |
|------|-------------|-------------|
| 1965 | 114 | 937 |
| 1966 | 417 | 996 |
| 1967 | 782 | 1,060 |
| 1968 | 1,216 | 2,027 |
| 1969 | 785 | 1,578 |
| 1970 | 352 | 1,782 |

If this demonstrates that the average ARVN trooper was having a high old time while his American opposite number played Davy Crockett out in Injun Country, something is very badly awry with our perception of the war.

Something is and something was. Something which only added to the ARVN's already significant morale problems. Vietnam was mainly a *Vietnamese* war: politically, militarily, and otherwise. But you would never have known that from the way most Americans—leaders or led, in Vietnam or outside it—acted most of the time. And you would never have known it from the way that American news reporters told their fellow citizens what the war was all about. U.S. media reaction to the Tet offensive of 1968 was grimly instructive. When the Tet offensive started, as former war correspondent Peter Braestrup has said, "the South Vietnamese military, to an

American audience, were almost as 'faceless' as the North Vietnamese and the Viet Cong. Rare had been the television or print feature on the ARVN G.I. or officer, the description of the South Vietnamese soldier's life in the field or garrison."[61]

Rare, too, was the coverage during or after Tet, even though Tet attacks were targeted mostly on ARVN units and South Vietnamese installations and even though the ARVN did the bulk of the fighting and dying to beat back the attackers. As always, news about U.S. forces in Vietnam was what journalists believed Americans wanted to hear, so that is what we saw and heard about at great length, to the exclusion of the ARVN: our Vietnamese allies in a Vietnamese war, whose language the reporters rarely understood and whose motivation and behavior fewer tried to comprehend.

The American media were bad enough at giving credit where credit was due, but U.S. military and political leaders generally did no better than journalists in ministering to the morale of the Vietnamese soldier on whose shoulders everything rested. To the Cold Warriors from America, the ARVN were often as invisible or pathetic as Vietnamese as a whole were to the most invincibly ignorant American, the type who said that the trouble with the "Slopes" was that you couldn't tell one of them from another.

Two historical examples can make the point, one military, the other political:

*Vignette the First*
*Scene:* Khe Sanh Combat Base, northern border regions of South Vietnam.
*Time:* Late 1967–early 1968 (Tet offensive buildup period).
*Problem:* U.S. leaders, anxious to create a "Dien Bien Phu in reverse," suddenly discover that there are no *South Vietnamese* units involved in a battle which they are then advertising as being the decisive turning point in the war to date.
*Solution:* To repair the oversight, an elite ARVN formation, the 37th Ranger Battalion, is flown into the Khe Sanh Base.
*New Problem:* The South Vietnamese Rangers, instead of being deployed at some point or points within the defensive lines created by the U.S. marines, are, instead, sent off to trenches located two hundred yards outside the marine perimeter. This positioning is eloquent so far as the expectations of the fighting qualities of these ARVN soldiers are concerned. Word as to what has been done with the Rangers very speedily circulates within ARVN leadership ranks. The effect, predictably, is uniformly bad.[62]

*Vignette the Second*

*Scene:* Washington, D.C., the Pentagon.

*Time:* Early 1969.

*Problem:* The Nixon Administration, having arrived in office determined to substantially decrease U.S. casualty levels in Vietnam by turning over more and more of the ground combat to the ARVN while, at the same time, bolstering them with increased high-technology and air war support, must plan its political strategy to inaugurate the policy shift. Defense Secretary Melvin Laird calls a meeting of the minds at the Pentagon to kick off the project. One of the items on the agenda is what to call the new strategy.

*Solution:* Someone in the group promptly suggests "De-Americanization" as a great way to package the program for maximum political effect.

*New Problem:* General Nguyen Cao Ky, attending the meeting as the representative of the Saigon regime, blows his top. "No! for God's sake," he protests. "That would really prove that you have been fighting the war [instead of assisting the ARVN to fight a Vietnamese struggle]." "The conflict," Ky continues, "is not mainly America's, but mainly South Vietnam's." Ky's unsubtle reminder is belatedly persuasive. The group goes on to settle upon "Vietnamization" as the best name for the Nixon administration program. Ky's morale is not precisely improved by these events.[63]

It is no wonder, then, that men like the previously quoted ARVN paratroop major possessed "an angry, corroded bitterness that seemed to come from some unreachable depth in his soul." It is no surprise that his men had the same feelings, either. They were all the invisible men of the Vietnam War.

## "Pacification" and the Peasantry

Another grim irony of Vietnam was that the one group in Vietnamese society that most often wanted to be invisible was usually not. This group was South Vietnam's peasantry. The Americans, for instance, sought, with decreasing success, to devise more and more indexes of felicity by which the hearts and minds of the peasantry could be measured, gauged, modified, and understood as an increasingly savage war raged all around them.

"Pacification" was the title under which these efforts at maintaining or inculcating loyalty were organized, and it provided further lessons in how not to win a struggle as political as it was military.

Pacification had both military and political aspects, that is, there was a sociopolitical "carrot" and a martial "stick" that, acting together, were to push and pull the populace of South Vietnam toward Saigon and away from Hanoi. The political carrot and the military stick of the pacification program, however, were not well coordinated. The martial element increasingly took precedence over the reconstruction-reform element. Partially, this resulted from the high-technology, wholesale destruction, and no-neutrals-allowed approach of the Americans after the Tet offensive; partially, it was caused by the fact that the Saigon regime was too weak, ill-organized, and conservative either to accomplish the reforms or offer the military protection envisaged in the pacification program.

The failure was crucial. Saigon simply couldn't pacify and protect the country and its people, even after the Americans took over most of the big battles of the war in mid-1967, thus releasing most ARVN divisions for pacification activity. The ARVN couldn't do it even though Saigon's military and political efforts were, by that time, complemented by the presence of a half-million armed militia in the provinces and larger villages, by sixty-person Revolutionary Development Teams meant to be grass-roots counterweights to communist cadres which had been active in such political organizing for years, and by a ragtag collection of People's Self-Defense Forces in the smaller villages and hamlets.

It was all in vain. The ARVN, as we have seen, was not organized into small and flexible units that enabled it to provide permanent security to the peasantry. The same village that was controlled by Saigon's soldiers during the day was often in the hands of the communist-led guerillas at night. Villagers in the middle had little or no choice but to try to survive by walking along the edge of a razor blade, doing whatever was necessary to get along with both sides without getting themselves sliced in half doing it.

It might have been different if the Saigon regime had given most of the peasantry something direct, immediate, and compelling to fight for. But it rarely did. Land reform in that overwhelmingly agrarian country remained a bad joke: long on rhetoric and statistics, but very short on results. As late as 1968, for instance, no less than three-quarters of the farmers in South Vietnam were tenants on property owned by landowners or the government.

Said landowners, the larger ones often absentees living in the larger cities, regularly flouted constitutional limitations restricting annual rents to a maximum of 25 percent of the total annual product. Rates of 50 percent were not unusual, with landlords regularly calling upon unscrupulous province chiefs (all of whom were recruited from the ranks of military officers) for help in enforcing their exactions. Peasant alienation was worsened by the fact that the larger landlords in some regions of South Vietnam were disproportionately "foreign" (i.e., ethnic Chinese) and by the fact that hamlet, village, and district leaders who might have moderated the exactions were, for most of the 1960s, also centrally appointed by Saigon rather than being locally selected in any way, shape, or form.

The result was, as a U.S. Congress subcommittee report concluded in December 1967, that "Land [re]distribution in South Vietnam has been at a virtual standstill since 1962." It stayed that way until a meagre renewal was made in 1970. By that time, the insurgent regime in the South had redistributed five times as much land as Saigon itself had, by the simple procedure of forcibly dividing up estates in areas that it fully or partially controlled. When the Thieu-Ky regime began its all too belated effort, it recognized the obvious fact that hundreds of thousands of Vietnamese peasants already held land seized from landlords who had run away or been assassinated—but it then announced that these peasants could continue to keep these lands only if they provided "appropriate compensation to the former owners." Saigon's initiative, therefore, was unlikely to have cheered the souls of many peasants rightfully skeptical of anything any South Vietnamese regime had ever had to say on the subject of who got what in the countryside, especially, of course, those farmers who had already been given land (at least for the moment) by revolutionaries who hated landlords as much as they themselves did.[64]

The callousness of the Saigon government only exacerbated peasant cynicism. A United States–initiated "defoliation" (vegetation-killing) program, for instance, provided many opportunities for realistic paranoia. Airborne defoliants killed a lot more than jungle, and farmers complained loudly.

An American-funded compensation program was duly created, but angry and hungry farmers who had watched their crops and livestock die made enthusiastic recruits for the throw-the-foreigners-out ranks. Money, alas, did not automatically mean social welfare, especially when Saigon's officials failed to visit defoliant-damaged areas or did not distribute money to the farmers to whom it was supposed to go. Given administrative foul-ups like these, and given the fact that more than a million acres of jungle and cropland were defoliated in 1967 alone, it is not surprising that rumors became rife that some province chiefs were actually requesting unnecessary defoliations in order to pad their pockets even further. Communist propaganda units, accordingly, capitalized upon opportunities provided by defoliation-induced unrest to spread the word that the bad-smelling Americans were spraying killer chemicals everywhere in order to starve the Vietnamese to death and take over their country. Such propaganda often did not strain rural credulity in the slightest, and many affected villagers joined the insurrection in order to fight for the only lives and localities they knew.[65]

Some securely anticommunist Americans realized you couldn't get realistically skeptical farmers to run the risks of fighting against something immediate unless they had something immediately greater to fight for. The guerillas, careful to operate via noncommunist "front" organizations whenever it suited their purposes (which was often), made many of the ideological appeals to anticommunism a murky business for many peasants to even begin to understand. Economic and political reforms in the countryside, however, were different. Agrarians, after all, have never been rabid Marxist-Leninist ideologues anywhere in the world. Intellectuals fight for ideas; farmers fight for land. They were not getting land from Saigon but they were getting it from Saigon's opponents.

Farmers also, however, struggle to make better use of what resources they have, especially when their practical and acquisitive attention is attracted to locally instituted and controlled betterments such as agricultural cooperatives, irrigation systems that can reduce risk and increase yields, or long-term stock and crop improvement programs which can make producers less dependent upon intermediates, government officials, and others who equate urbanity with civilization.

Here, too, efforts were made by isolated Vietnamese and Americans. Much was stonewalled or never got off the ground at all. Some of what did get started was destroyed in the fires of war. What remained was too little and too late. There are many examples of the phenomenon, but let us select one from an unlikely source: the United States Marines.

Marines are supposed to be tough customers, with all of the political sophistication of a bull elephant in rut, but such stereotypes can obscure political nuances in what was a political war. In 1965, a Vietnamese-speaking lieutenant named Paul Ek started an innovative and sometimes even bureaucratically clandestine program: the Combined Action Platoon, or CAP. These CAPs were small groups of volunteer marines who moved into a village or hamlet, worked with its people on simple developmental projects of immediate and perceived benefit, and fought with local militia in a combined, rather than separate, fashion to protect those projects from destruction.*

*Throughout the war, U.S. and South Vietnamese military operations remained overwhelmingly compartmentalized and separate. No joint American–South Vietnam high com-

The idea worked well enough that it was extended to seventy-five hamlets during the next two years. The marine colonel who headed the program, however, argued that CAP succeeded precisely because it did *not* equate winning hearts and minds with gaining support for the South Vietnamese regime. CAP, the colonel wrote before Tet, was one of the very few things that Americans were doing which was not utterly vain, precisely because it helped peasants to resist the encroachments of *both* the Saigon government and the Vietcong. Asking the peasants to fight *for* what Saigon was giving them, or was ever likely to give them, was like trying to build a skyscraper out of marshmallows. The regime was hopeless. The corrupt officials making up that regime were hopeless. The absentee landlords whose interests those officials mainly served were hopeless. The U.S. advisers to those South Vietnamese officials were ignorance and evasion personified. The American military command in Vietnam knew nothing and cared less about fighting a war that was more about minds than materiel.

The only thing to do, the colonel concluded just after he resigned from the service in dismay late in 1967, was for the United States to expand upon small-scale initiatives like the one the marines had begun, ignore Saigon entirely, and create direct alliances of hearts and minds, alliances of interest and regard between the Americans and the peasant multitudes of South Vietnam.[67]

Colonel William Corson's solution is not the point here. Foreign armies are better at enforcing loyalties than they are at fostering them. Corson's argument, however, was a damning indictment of the effectiveness of the regime that Vietnamese and Americans were fighting to preserve and to sell to the peasants at the same time. Colonel Corson, in sentences that Robert F. Kennedy later used, put the overall problem like this:

> The peasant sees that we are supporting a [centrally appointed, unelected] local government structure he knows to be corrupt. So he assumes that we are either stupid or implicated. And he decides that we are not stupid.[68]

The not-stupid Vietnamese, accordingly, often hedged their bets and played for time. Everybody was killing the peasants in order to save them from somebody else. In such an unenviable situation, neutrality, staying out of things, or trying to balance off one side against the other were

---

mand was ever created, and joint operations where U.S. commanders were given command authority over South Vietnamese troops were prohibited, for fear of "puppet" charges. American troops, likewise, did not fight under ARVN command.[66]

sensible policies, good "situation ethics" in a situation where the greatest
ethic was often that which promised the best chance of survival—until,
perhaps, tragedy hit in such a way that there was nothing left to lose by
taking sides.

Here high technology reenters the picture. For, just as it is easy to see
why neutrality, noninvolvement, or balancing-off failed to fit in very well
with the grand ideological assumptions of communist or anticommunist,
or with the if-you're-not-with-me-then-you're-probably-against-me sur-
vivalism of the Vietnamese or American soldier, it also did not fit well
within the American high-technology equation after Tet.

The fundamental problem with hi tech was that it tended to kill wholesale and randomly, while the insurgency it was trying to destroy usually
killed retail and for specific purposes. This posed far from academic problems. The U.S. and ARVN forces often found themselves in a dilemma, one
wherein what was "good" militarily was bad politically, and vice versa.

The sanest military way to get out of the strategic dilemma was to
replace high technology with low technology, to replace machinery with
men, many more men. Inevitably, that meant higher U.S. casualties. This,
as we have seen, was anathema to U.S. politicians and generals, and was
not considered. Precisely the opposite tack was taken by the Johnson
administration and the Nixon administration that followed it. The GIs
were replaced with more and more machines. South Vietnamese military
and political leaders, likewise, preferred to fight a big-battalion, technol-
ogy-intensive war.

The price for Electronic Battlefields and free-fire zones and B-52 bombing raids was that the terror spread by America and Saigon advanced far
beyond any their opponents had ever created.

Some readers with long memories of Vietnam will balk at what is being
said here. They will rightly recall that six thousand people were butchered
by Vietcong units in the old Vietnamese imperial capital of Hue during the
Tet offensive. Others will remember those whose heads they saw displayed on pikes with their testicles stuck in their mouths. True, war is
killing, and guerilla war is terror much of the time. But B-52s also spread
terror, especially when they hit the wrong village, one the flight crews
cannot even see.

The "average Vietnamese," in such a situation, lived in a universe of
terror and counter-terror, and saw themselves as having, at best, a choice
of evils. Illiterate or, at best, semiliterate people in extremely poor countries do not generally spend a great deal of time debating the finer points
of ideology or geopolitics. They expect little and they hope to be left
alone.

To the normal Vietnamese, then, as to normal people in any war since time began, the war was mainly about their survival and the survival of their loved ones. One of Vietnam's leading Buddhist monks put the point well during the Tet offensive, expressing the growing sense of powerlessness and frustration that many Vietnamese of all classes and conditions felt as yet another struggle for control of Vietnam became a very bloody battleground of the Cold War. "Communists," the monk said, "want to save us from colonialism and underdevelopment, and anti-communists want to save us from communism. The problem is that we are not being saved, we are being destroyed. Now we want to be saved from salvation."[69]

The Vietnamese especially wanted to be saved from high-technology salvation. "Our friends," two Vietnamese-speaking Americans wrote just after Tet, "would note that at least the Viet Cong terrorism was planned and directed at specific individuals or for specific propaganda reasons. But the Americans and the Saigon government bombings are so random, and mistakes are so often made, that death becomes arbitrary and senseless."[70]

Just as death became arbitrary, life became profoundly disorganized for millions of Vietnamese shocked and disconcerted by being uprooted from traditional lives, customs, and folkways. A primary reason for neutrality, noninvolvement, and playing both sides of the fence by villagers, after all, was to avoid having to leave the only communities and livelihoods they knew. For example, peasants in a society suffused with Confucian "ancestor worship" wanted to avoid abandoning the graves of those ancestors, graves that might have been dotting the landscape around them for three hundred years, or for five hundred—for more generations, in any event, than most could remember.[71]

High technology, however, pushed peasants off the land in the millions, not least because Tet made *all* Vietnamese suspect. As Peter Braestrup put it, "the South Vietnamese, faceless to most Americans, offered a convenient scapegoat for the Tet surprise—and the war's frustrations."[72]

After Tet, accordingly, there were fewer and fewer neutrals. The effort, under way even before Tet, to depopulate many rural areas in order to deny those areas to the enemy was speeded up. A trendy academic belief was pressed into service to rationalize it all. Forced urbanization, the argument went, would modernize southern Vietnam quickly, and insurgencies based largely in the countryside would wither on the vine. Or, put another way, rural depopulation would solve the prickly problem of locating the enemy "fish" in the "sea"—by the simple expedient of draining the human sea and leaving Vietcong guerillas and North Vietnamese army regulars naked to the full force of a war of high-technology annihilation.

It sounded so neat and clinical, but it was Crackpot Realism. "It is a mistake," the ARVN colonel in charge of training political workers for use in the countryside told Don Luce and John Sommer in 1968, "to move the people off their hallowed land. This is a political war and it must be fought by trained counterguerillas and political cadres, not by massive, impersonal free-strike zone bombings from the air. If we move the people from the land, we will surely lose their support; they will resent us."[73]

Colonel Nguyen Be's caveats, alas, made no difference. The political and social aspects of the struggle were downplayed in Washington and Saigon, and the destruction of traditional values and mores consequent upon removal after removal created resentment, confusion, disruption, and despair which undermined the whole pacification effort.

The scale of the evacuations and removals was massive. Between 1965 and 1972, three to five million Vietnamese or more became refugees in their own land. This was between a quarter and a third of the total populace of the South. The Tet-related fighting alone produced perhaps six hundred thousand new refugees. These refugees, initially those fleeing the rebels and later those fleeing ever more destructive air attacks, swelled into the cities. Saigon's population jumped from three hundred thousand to three million in just ten years. By 1972, probably half of the South's population lived in cities composed, all too largely, of slums, and whose inflated economies were based largely on the American-financed war.[74]

But all was well and getting better, or so the statistics said. So the press releases from a host of official sources said, in the crippling terminology of euphemism, hypocrisy, evasion, self-delusion, and sociologese—in the language, for example, of the Hamlet Evaluation System (HES) put into operation by McNamara's Department of Defense, in cooperation with the CIA, in January 1967.

This HES was the body count and the kill-ratio all over again, pseudo-profundity personified and nonsense masquerading as hard-eyed information. The idea was to blanket the 44 provinces, 250 districts, 2,300 villages, and 13,000 hamlets of southern Vietnam regularly with brief questionnaires regarding the status of pacification in both its security and development aspects. Each U.S. district adviser was to rank the condition of each village and hamlet in his area. South Vietnamese personnel were to go into the villages and hamlets collecting data for the estimates of the U.S. adviser. Estimates were then computerized, tabulated, and analyzed, becoming the basis for monthly pacification statements that went to Washington via a Civil Operation and Revolutionary Development Support (CORDS) office created as an adjunct to the U.S. military command in Vietnam.

The Hamlet Evaluation System, predictably, got more sophisticated over time. Percentages and estimates objectifying progress or lack of progress in the various parts of Vietnam festooned the bureaucratic and media landscape. Meanwhile, the Vietnamese who gathered the numbers for the Americans to crunch often were not visiting risky areas at all, and they spent only thirty minutes to an hour in each of the villages they did visit each month. In the middle of a civil war, Americans tried to measure the intangibles of political loyalty and opinion like public-opinion pollsters estimate election results back home, where people have not witnessed hostilities on their own soil for a hundred years.[75]

It was nonsense, sheer nonsense, as artillery general Douglas Kinnard admitted when recounting a conversation he had in 1970 with a disgruntled U.S. embassy official in Saigon. This bureaucrat told Kinnard

> that the gaps between HES numbers and actual conditions in the provinces had reached ludicrous proportions. He pointed out that although the [latest monthly] report showed that the 111 Corps [military operations] area, which I was in, contained five provinces controlled 100 per cent by the central government, there were three in which neither one of us could drive safely if unescorted. He was right.[76]

Indeed he was. For all the technocratic enterprise that created mountains of statistics and batteries of computers and endless progress estimates, it was "garbage in, garbage out."

For all that, the Hamlet Evaluation System of the McNamara-Johnson years was followed by new layers of technocratic fallacies in the Nixon era that followed. At about the same time that General Kinnard and the embassy official were reminding themselves that CORDS–HES statistics were irrelevant to the real-world risks they ran, Republican Secretary of Defense Melvin Laird established another Vietnam "task force" in the International Security Affairs division of the Pentagon.

> Before long the task force was living in its own statistical world. Success in Vietnamization was measured not by the body count, but by its own litany, which was the reverse of the build up period: troop-strength reduction ahead (but not too far ahead) of Presidential goals, percentage reduction of United States maneuver [combat] battalions, percentage decrease of Americans killed, increased percentage of Vietnamese Air Force sorties flown, etc. What did it all mean? Who knew? Who knows now? At least it sounded as though the Vietnamese were taking over the war, and it provided an apparently professional military basis for a political withdrawal.[77]

Political withdrawal, however, was what it was all about, a withdrawal that could not be too open or too immediate lest it worsen war-induced political tensions back home, tensions that Republican President Richard Milhous Nixon had to master before they mastered him.

## The Peace That Was No Peace[78]

Now all was a bloody denouement, the infinite fits and starts of a four-year-long withdrawal from direct involvement in a war the United States had escalated itself into during the course of the preceding four years. The two periods had more than just their duration in common. From 1965 to 1968, the U.S. leadership often consisted of proving the truth of the falsity that America was *winning* the Vietnam War; 1969 to 1973 was just as often spent creating the illusion that America was *not losing* a Vietnamese struggle it had made so largely and so completely its own.

Illusion, therefore, is a key concept to keep in mind regarding all Vietnam War–related policy after the Tet offensive—not because Richard Nixon was a uniquely criminal leader who lied and was the embodiment of all evil, but because the posturings, deceptions, self-deceptions, and political theater of post-Tet peacemaking, Vietnamization, and U.S. withdrawal were utterly bipartisan, and indeed almost universal, phenomena in official Washington. Republicans and Democrats, liberals and conservatives, members of Congress and presidential staff all shared in it for the sake of self-interest and survival.

Let us start with the mainstream Democrats, those whose Cold Warrior ideals and concrete political interests had led them to ally with Hubert Humphrey to beat off an antiwar-deescalationist insurgency that was based upon the overall idea of a negotiated settlement of the Vietnam War, one *not* predicated on proposals for unilateral withdrawal of American military forces. These Democrats' problem remained what it had always been. Vietnam was "their war" in its all-out, direct-military-involvement phase. The problem for the Democrats was how to shift most of whatever blame was sure to be apportioned for additional failure and frustration in Vietnam onto the shoulders of the Republicans before the Republicans did the exact same thing to them.

This partisan task was made easier by the fact that the many unsettling events of the year 1968 induced an I-don't-want-to-know-anymore reaction in a very large segment of public opinion in the United States. Less affluent and less schooled citizens, still tied to the Democratic Party by bonds of tradition, were particularly turned off by politics. These people were tired of hearing about black people and their problems; of "corners being turned" in a faraway war; of hearing odd-sounding names of Vietnamese leaders; of assassinations; of long-haired kooks smoking pot and acting irreverent; of a disconcerting sense that things that had seemed fixed and certain were either out of control or being looked after none too well.

These tens of millions of mostly Democratic Americans had problems of their own, and they wanted the mostly Democratic Congress and the Republican president they had elected in 1968 to do something to solve national problems quickly, especially in Vietnam. They didn't particularly care how the Vietnam mess was dealt with but they wanted it dealt with, fast. In particular, they wanted the United States to get U.S. ground troops out of Vietnam if those damned fools in Washington weren't going to go all-out and stop fighting a limited war.[79] This turning off of mass attention assisted Democratic partisans materially. It allowed many Democrats to attack their opponents for not doing things they never would have done themselves had their party happened to have won the White House. These Democrats dragged Nixon over rhetorical coals for not withdrawing American forces immediately.

The ironies were great. Throughout the Johnson presidency, mainstream Democrats had demanded that a foreign-invasion rather than a civil-war model apply to Vietnam. Using this invasion analogy, Democratic leaders affirmed and reaffirmed that no peace would ever be made by them in Vietnam until all North Vietnamese forces evacuated the country of South Vietnam, and until the Vietcong guerillas in the South ceased their insurrection against a legitimate democratic regime there. The United States would continue to supply the Saigon regime with arms, training, and money once peace broke out. After the invasion and the insurrection had stopped, then and only then would it be possible to discuss the possible creation of a coalition government in South Vietnam which might someday include representatives of the former rebels—those from the separate nation of South Vietnam. Any coalition government which might ever exist, however, would play by the rules as determined by the American-backed elite in Saigon and fully recognize its legitimacy and right to rule. Thus far—and no farther—had the Hubert Horatio Humphreys and others like him ever gone.

In a civil-war approach to what was happening in southern Vietnam, Humphrey and Co. were ridiculous. They demanded that Hanoi surrender first, and then hope to get something for its surrender later, if it could work out some sort of deal with the Saigon leaders it had been trying to kill for ten years. To demonstrate their willingness to forward what they believed to be a compromise solution, Democratic movers and shakers had agreed, by the end of the Johnson presidency: (1) to limit the number of U.S. ground troops in Vietnam to the level of just over half a million men reached just before Tet; (2) to start talking—regularly and without massive interruptions—to North Vietnamese and Vietcong representatives in Paris; and (3) to stop bombing North Vietnam (on the very eve of the 1968 elections).

Once Richard Nixon took over, his initial proposals to end the war were a variation on established Democratic precedents.

First, Nixon maintained that the Vietnamese conflict was a foreign invasion and maintained that the separate nation of North Vietnam must cease its aggression (invasion) before peace could come.

Second, Nixon substituted Vietnamization (a gradual withdrawal of American *ground troops*) for the "freeze" that the Democrats had already established.

Third, Nixon, like the Democrats, substituted high technology and air war for ground combat. Nixon accelerated this substitution approach as U.S. ground force levels started to be reduced significantly (in 1970).

Fourth, Nixon, like the Democrats, required that North Vietnam and the Vietcong recognize the legitimacy of South Vietnam and of the Saigon regime.

Fifth, Nixon, again like the Democrats, argued that the United States maintained a full and complete right to continue to supply Saigon with arms, training, and money during and after the period of gradual withdrawal and Vietnamization.

Sixth, Nixon, in a variation on a previously established Democratic theme, continued to leave the question of a possible postwar coalition government in the South securely suspended in midair. The Democrats had said zero about it, practically speaking. Nixon said the whole question should be left up to the Saigon regime's discretion.

Seventh, Nixon maintained the bombing halt of North Vietnam that the Democrats had begun on Election Eve, 1968.

Eighth, Nixon kept on talking to the North Vietnamese and the Vietcong in Paris, again as per the Democrats.[80]

From all this public activity, it is clear that Nixon wasn't doing any-thing—publicly—that the Democrats hadn't done, except to Vietnamize the war, that is, to gradually withdraw U.S. ground troops and reduce U.S. casualty levels while buying time to allow the ARVN to take over this portion of the fighting.

Privately, however:

First, Nixon continued the cross-border spying, raiding, and dirty-tricks attacks into Cambodia and Laos that had been going on throughout the Johnson presidency.

Second, Nixon promptly instituted a supersecret and very large-scale bombing of Cambodian border regions to try to destroy insurgent forces using these areas as supply, training, and rest-and-recovery bases, an initiative the Johnson White House had never undertaken.

Third, Nixon, by mid-1969, was threatening Hanoi with American use of tactical nuclear weapons in Indochina.[81]

What Nixon was trying to do (the secret bombing of neutral Cambodia and the short-lived threats of nuclear warfare excepted) was to accomplish what the Democrats had, and to do so in a fashion very similar to theirs. Nixon wanted to defeat an insurrection. His aim was, basically, to go back to the days of American Dollars and Arms rather than continue the Ameri-can Dollars and Arms *and* Blood and Guts stage of the war.

For all these basic similarities of strategy and outlook between Nixon and the mainsteam Democrats, the Democrats mercilessly harried him— rhetorically. Rhetoric was more important than reality because the main-stream Democrats who remained in control of both houses of Congress after the 1968 elections would, in all likelihood, have done nothing differ-ent had they been in the White House as well. It remained however, in the mainstream Democrats' interests to deflect as much attention as possible from their own failed, politically divisive, and potentially disastrous record on Vietnam by branding it, now, "Nixon's war."

This was drivel, and everybody with the faintest claim to be a paid-up member of the Washington cognoscenti knew it. Hanoi had never agreed with the American definition of the war as a foreign invasion, and viewed Saigon as a puppet secessionist regime created and maintained by U.S.

power. Further, Hanoi's negotiators consistently demanded (from the start of serious negotiations in March 1968 up until August 1972) that the Thieu regime be toppled and the ARVN dismantled before they'd sign any armistice or peace treaty with anybody. They also refused to withdraw their invading forces as a condition of peace. Hanoi was not about to deal on the basis of American assumptions or terms. Period and end of all but exceedingly elliptical diplomatic discussions. Given the realities of a civil-war (Hanoi) versus foreign-invasion (the United States and Saigon) approach to comprehending the war, and given that Hanoi had not been forced by Washington into accepting its terms, a negotiated settlement was a chimera. That much was, and remained, common sense.

If Hanoi wasn't going to give way, and if Nixon was not going to run the risks of escalating the war as Johnson and Kennedy had, the get-tough-or-get-out logic applied. This logic had polarized the country and the Democratic Party in 1968. To avoid the Democrats' fate and wider social and political unrest in America itself, Nixon, practiced politico that he was, tried to move in both directions at once. In secret, he escalated the hi-tech air war in neutral Cambodia. In public, he began the first stages of what was, in effect, a unilateral withdrawal of U.S. fighting forces from Vietnam.

The irony was that unilateral withdrawal was a radical more than a mainstream position, one that the left wings of the antiwar movement and of the McCarthy and Kennedy insurgencies had monopolized before and during the 1968 elections. Nixon's unilateralism, to be sure, was *not* the antiwar left's version, but it was a lot closer to unilateralism than the Democrats had ever dared to come. The left was aware of this. Its *"Out now!"* did not mean selective and gradual withdrawal with stepped-up air war, Vietnamization, Electronic Battlefields and continuing economic, political, and military support for the Saigon regime. The antiwar left, therefore, attacked Nixon as strongly as it had attacked Johnson, given that it believed Nixon was selling the same old snake oil in a slightly different bottle.

Johnson's supporters also attacked Nixon's careful unilateralism, flaying him for not quickly settling things and withdrawing our boys over there so fast as to put a weak and ill-organized Saigon regime at risk—moves they had never made, moves Johnson had never made, moves Nixon himself wanted to avoid making if at all possible. The intellectual dishonesty of these people was profound. A Democratic Congress could have tried to stop or deescalate the war any time it had wished to run the risks involved in doing so. For example, it could have denied the White House the funds to fight all or part of the war in the first place.

The Democratic House and Senate leaders, however, ran no such risks.

Instead, they sought to avoid responsibility for what was happening by giving presidents all they wanted, and then letting *them* take the heat when they exercised the War Powers they'd gotten. The justly infamous Tonkin Gulf Resolution of August 1964 is well remembered here, the "blank check" whereby the House (unanimously) and the Senate (by 88 to 2) gave Lyndon Johnson permission to take all necessary measures . . . to prevent further aggression.

What is less remembered is that the same Senate, for instance, voted down an effort by Wayne Morse to repeal the Tonkin Gulf Resolution in March 1966, by 92 to 5, as U.S. military force levels in Vietnam ascended unto the stratosphere.[82]

Of Profiles in Power there were many; of Profiles in Courage, few. Those who made it a habit to be in the know, and who had superlative opportunities to know, chose not to oppose a War President who many would later say had "misled" them—when, that is, it was safe to say so in the wake of Tet, Lyndon Johnson's withdrawal from the presidential race, and the fiasco of the Chicago convention and the Humphrey candidacy which followed it.

The Democratic Congress, it has often been said, was a "cipher" regarding Vietnam: a zero, a nothing. This was not accidental. By doing nothing, Congress hoped to avoid responsibility for the war and sanctions that could be levied against them by a Democratic president. Inactivity helped guarantee political survival. For this reason, Democratic national political leaders and would-be leaders in Congress, however frustrated and frightened they were about Vietnam events, did not even revoke the blank check they had given the president until a Republican became president. They didn't even do that until December 31st, 1970, two full years after Richard Nixon replaced LBJ.

Why didn't Nixon do unto others as they were trying to do unto him? Why didn't he put the Vietnam monkey on a Democratic Congress' back? Why didn't he bite the bullet, withdraw as fast or faster as his partisan opponents were saying he should, leave the Saigon regime to whatever fate awaited it, and watch the splintered Democrats feud, squabble, and dither about what, if anything, they wanted to do—while facing the inevitable wrath of the majority of the electorate? Why didn't Nixon take the realistically cynical counsel of "a friend in Congress" who advised that a fast exit from further direct involvement in Vietnam was the answer, and a way to dish the Democrats into the bargain?

> You didn't get us into this war [the Congressman wrote], so even if you end it with a bad peace, by doing it quickly, you can put the blame

on Kennedy and Johnson and the Democrats. Just go on TV and remind people that it was Kennedy who sent the 16,000 Americans in there, and it was Johnson who escalated it up to 540,000. Then announce that you're bringing them all home, and you'll be a hero.[83]

Nixon's answer was: Because the United States would lose face. American credibility would suffer, at home and around the world.

## The Frustrations of Saving Face

Saving face, credibility, and honor was what it was all about in Vietnam, so far as the power brokers in Washington were concerned. Johnson fought an American war in Vietnam for fear of national humiliation if he didn't. Nixon couldn't stop fighting the same war because of the same fear, a fear that LBJ's successor talked about once in terms of a dreadful possibility that America might become a "pitiful helpless giant" in world affairs.[84]

To understand what was going through Nixon's mind (and through the minds of many other politicians before and since), we need to recognize two things. First, Vietnam was fundamentally a symbolic war for the power elite in America. It was important, not so much for Vietnam or for the Vietnamese as for what it would prove to others, others who didn't live in Vietnam, but in the communist superpower states, in America itself, and throughout the rest of the world, especially the Third World. Second, this elite approach to the war was aimed at preserving the status and power of that same elite.

Vietnam, on the global abstract and symbolic level affected at the centers of U.S. foreign policy-making, assumed the necessity of a *Pax Americana* in key regions of the world (and the Third World) as the only alternative to a descent into international chaos and totalitarianism. The United States was, therefore, trapped into staying in Vietnam by a bipartisan Cold War policy elite whose habits of mind had gotten it there in the first place. Vietnam was the inch which, if given to the communist hordes, would lead those hordes to take a mile, and thereby spiral the whole world into war. If America backed down or bugged out, or if there was no Peace with Honor, the psychological edge would drift to the enemies of freedom around the world, and America, the "last, best hope" of democracy would be unable to stem the tide of disaster. Because it would, then, be critically weakened both internally and externally.

Face, then, was critical. It explained why it took America as long to get out as it had taken to get in. It explained why Nixon and his Republican followers believed—just as strongly as Kennedy, Johnson, and their Democratic followers had—that Vietnam was crucial to the American image in the world. American leaders were arriviste imperialists, parvenus whose experience of global dominion was so recent that they believed they had to be dominant everywhere and continually, and that to back down would be to give the whole world away. This mind-set was classic feast or famine, with no in-between allowed. Every communist challenge had to be beaten off, for disaster everywhere was the price of defeat anywhere. "To leave Vietnam to its fate," Lyndon Johnson said in 1965,

> would shake the confidence of all [the people in the noncommunist world around the globe from "Berlin to Thailand"] in the value of an American commitment and in the value of America's word. The result would be increased unrest and instability, and even wider war . . . Let no one think for a moment that retreat from Vietnam would bring an end to conflict. The battle would be renewed in one country and then another. The central lesson of our time is that the appetite for aggression is never satisfied. To withdraw from one battlefield means only to prepare for the next.[85]

Richard Nixon and his foreign policy aides fundamentally agreed with Johnson's assessment. And, like Johnson, they defined and rationalized what they did in Vietnam with respect to the U.S. image almost everywhere else in the world. As Jonathan Schell put it, "The aim of upholding American credibility superseded any conclusions drawn from a simple accounting of tangible gains and tangible losses, and it dictated that the war must go on, for it was American credibility, the strategists thought, on which the safety of the whole world depended." The "judgement, skill, prestige, and national honor" of America all depended on proving to Americans, allies, and foes, that American national will and determination remained strong and unsullied. "The tangible objectives of limited war had been completely eclipsed by the psychological objective. The war had become an effort directed entirely toward building up a certain image by force of arms. It had become a piece of pure theatre."[86]

The problem remained, of course, that the Vietnamese enemy wasn't playing by the rules as understood and acted upon in official Washington.

They kept on spoiling the performance. Thus the rage with which Lyndon Johnson viewed them and killed them, thus the same rage which Richard Nixon and Henry Kissinger directed toward them—rage which led Nixon to vacillate between a desire to get out of direct involvement in a limited war gone wrong as fast as possible and a desire to turn Vietnam into a charnel house. Rage and frustration were inevitable when it is considered that politicians of all sorts have an inevitable tendency to confuse their individual fates with those of their countries, in the same way they emphatically and consistently confused the fate of the United States in Vietnam with the destiny of the entire noncommunist world.

Self-preservation was also central here. Appearance became all, and reality less, because an entire generation of U.S. political leaders had *their* credibility, honor, and face to save, failing which they would probably lose their jobs, incomes, perquisites, powers, and careers. America must somehow avoid defeat in Vietnam so that *they* could avoid defeat there and thereby legitimate their own previous activity regarding the war. Peacemaking became a way to make it look as if a country had not been defeated, and to also make it look as if that country's leaders had not been defeated.

Writing a peace script like this was all very well, but getting it performed was another thing. Here, political theater fast became political bankruptcy. The continuing weakness of the Saigon regime was a key variable. Nixon and his foreign-policy eminence Henry Kissinger realized that American Peace with Honor depended upon the ability of the Thieu-Ky regime to repair the glaring deficiencies of the Republic of South Vietnam. The U.S. undertook high-technology air war and diplomatic shadowboxing with Hanoi to buy Saigon time. The weaker Saigon's movers and shakers were, however, the more time Washington would have to buy, the less willing Hanoi would be to compromise, the more Americans would die, and the greater the political risks would become.

Saigon remained weak and the fatal misstep was made. In April 1970, U.S. and ARVN forces launched a two-month long incursion (invasion) of eastern Cambodia in an effort to destroy enemy bases and disrupt enemy supply lines. Nonsecret air support (bombing) attacks accompanied the invasion.

The Cambodian escalation, whatever its military logic or results, was a political catastrophe for the Nixon administration in terms of immediate and longer-term results. Immediately, the war became "Nixon's war." Longer-term, the negative popular and political fallout of the Cambodian invasion added to a State of Siege psychology in the White House. It led to a frustrated effort to exponentially increase the level of government spying on the citizenry (via the FBI-opposed Huston Plan of July 1970) and inaugurated, a year later, the supersecret "intelligence gathering" and "dirty tricks" activities that culminated in the Watergate crisis.[87]

We will examine only the short-term effects here, reserving the others for discussion in Part Four. As Arnold R. Isaacs has said very well, the Cambodian invasion marked the point where the Nixon administration closed a political trap upon itself. "All else they had done in Indochina, Nixon and Kissinger could claim—and the American public could agree—was a matter of cleaning up someone else's mess. But Cambodia was their own."[88]

Indeed it was. Most Americans believed Vietnam was a Democratic war. They were willing to give a Republican time to do something about that war, in a way that did not involve defeat or humiliation. Nixon possessed precisely the advantage that Republican Dwight David Eisenhower had had before him in Korea, after an earlier Democratic-led limited war in Asia had gone awry. Once Nixon made the decision to Vietnamize the ground war, however, the majority wanted that initiative maintained. Withdrawal meant withdrawal; it did not mean taking troops *out of* Vietnam only to put them *into* Cambodia. That sort of thing smelled like limited-war escalation all over again. Americans had had quite enough of that.[89]

Unrest in the grass roots, then, had to do with practicality more than morality, more with galloping skepticism about *all* politicians than with ideological opposition to Richard Nixon or the G.O.P. People had had enough surprises in Vietnam. The sudden invasion of a neutral country was an additional and unwanted surprise, one that made many Americans fear that Nixon was going to get the nation mired deeper in the quagmire of limited war. All Nixon's belligerent rhetoric that Cambodia was necessary to demonstrate the strength of the national honor and will, and all his explanations that the incursion was only a temporary, rather than a permanent, phenomenon, didn't improve his standing with the electorate much. The fact was that he had widened the geographical extent of the war suddenly and without warning, and used mostly *American* troops to do it.

Cambodia, therefore, gave the political initiative to Nixon's enemies. They used it. An antiwar left which wouldn't have believed anything Nixon said about "peace in Vietnam" if he had sworn to it on his deathbed mounted hasty demonstrations at hundreds of colleges and universities, protests that resulted in the well-publicized death of students at Mississippi's Jackson State College and Ohio's Kent State University in May.

Revivifying the antiwar left was bad enough. And, although Cambodia-related college protests soon subsided for reasons to be dealt with in Part

Three, other, more important, political genies had been let out of the bottle. These were the mainstream Democrats whose fulsome support for Lyndon Johnson's war had hitherto disqualified them from scoring partisan political points against Nixon.

Cambodia, however, gave those prowar Democrats their opportunity, and they, too, seized it. Lyndon Johnson had never massively invaded Cambodia, nor had LBJ bombed it, as Nixon was now both secretly and publicly doing, nor had LBJ backed a coup that simultaneously brought Cambodian forces into the war for the first time. No, Nixon couldn't pin *this* mess on his Democratic predecessors. From now on, all the pain and frustration and destruction going on in Indochina was going to be Nixon's responsibility, and his alone. Now Tricky Dick was the bad guy springing surprises on people—*all* the people, including a Democratic Congress that had hitherto been involved in almost everything to do with the war except the post-1969 secret bombing of Cambodia and Nixon's secret threats to use tactical nuclear weapons. Once public-opinion polls showed a widespread lack of support for the Cambodian invasion, most congressional Democrats started their slow and careful Long March away from the war. Thus, for example, the sadly belated revocation of the Tonkin Gulf Resolution that occurred in December of 1970; thus, too, a congressional prohibition of funds for U.S. *ground* troops operating outside of South Vietnam that the Senate imposed on the White House during the same month: the Cooper-Church Amendment.

Richard Nixon knew how the political game was played. He knew most Democrats had been as aggressive as he was. He knew the Kennedy and Johnson people who now began to attack *him* as an Imperial President in Vietnam were practicing situation ethics of a more than usually self-serving sort. He knew that Washington, D.C., is a difficult place to keep secrets and that some of the same senators who orated against the use of ground troops in Cambodia didn't care whether he used air power (in secret or in public) to turn the geography of that country into one approximating the far side of the moon. He knew, moreover, that his Democratic opponents understood just as well as he did that Cambodia's neutrality was a selective proposition; and that Prince Norodim Sihanouk, who ruled until General Lon Nol overthrew him with U.S. support in March 1970, had regularly turned a blind eye to Vietnamese control of the eastern third of his country and to U.S.-engineered dirty-tricks raids and the 1969–70 secret bombings as well. Sihanouk had feared that to notice any subversion of sovereignty by one side would only increase the risk of Cambodia's being drawn into the maelstrom by the other combatant power.[90]

Nixon knew all these things and more about the sometimes brutal ironies of politics. But he could not tame his growing rage at what his critics were trying to do to him, for they were succeeding. Cambodia was the tool they were using to do it; and Nixon himself, by stupendous political miscalculation, had given them that tool. Nixon finally made it Nixon's war. Ironic humor, however, was never Nixon's forte.

## Finding the Fig Leaves

After Cambodia, Nixon lost the political initiative. His use of American ground troops there undermined the whole Men Out, Machines In strategy upon which much of Vietnamization was based. Once the political unrest of April and May 1970 showed him that continued withdrawal of all U.S. ground forces was the absolute minimum required for regaining status and legitimacy as a leader who was only cleaning up Democratic messes, Nixon fought to recover his pre-Cambodia momentum.

During the next two years, the Republican president won more often than not, as much because of the weaknesses and miscalculations of his enemies as of his own strengths. He weakened the antiwar left. He out-maneuvered those mainstream Democrats who were trying to define him as the only warmonger in creation. He capitalized on an ill-considered Hanoi military offensive mounted toward the end of the post-Cambodia American withdrawal period. Then, ironically, he undid all that he had done: he gave the political initiative back to his opponents via a Watergate scandal that tore his credibility, power, influence, and policy to ribbons.

The antiwar left proved to be Nixon's easiest victory. The "hard-left" minority got the cudgel; the "soft-left" majority got fragmented or bought off. Nixon's men, assisted by police forces around the country, hammered the hard antiwar left with selective prosecutions and waged war against especially vulnerable racist and violence-oriented organizations, notably the Black Panthers. Meanwhile, Nixon undermined his soft-left opponents by greatly decreasing the wartime risks faced by young college and university students who were key components of the antiwar forces. The most effective techniques here were Vietnamization itself; a "draft lottery" which, starting in 1970, exempted approximately two-thirds of all draft-eligible males from military service; and, finally, the accompanying effort to create an all-volunteer army, finally completed in 1973.

So far as mainstream Democratic politicians went, Nixon played a very different game. Most important, he played peacemaker with Moscow and Peking, and used his resultant political clout to improve his prospects of Peace with Honor in Vietnam. The curtain went up on this second component of the Nixon strategy in July 1971, a year after the Cambodian ground invasion had been concluded. Previous secret diplomacy managed by Henry Kissinger paid handsome dividends when Nixon unexpectedly announced he would visit China shortly to inaugurate a new era of U.S. recognition of and cooperation with communist power on the mainland. Thereby, Nixon put an end to twenty-five years of a pariah-among-the-nations policy of which he had hitherto been one of the most strenuous advocates.

This Nixon-Kissinger bombshell seriously discomfited Democrats in Washington, and it actively worried the Marxists in Hanoi. Hanoi's leaders, in fact, contemplated the possibility of a sellout by Peking.[91] Peking had previously supplied them with arms in a diplomatic bidding war with the Russians, but China was also coming to the end of a xenophobic Great Proletarian Cultural Revolution which had cost it heavily in political, social, and economic strength. Rapprochement with America was in the air.

Shortly thereafter, both the Democrats and Hanoi had even more surprises to ponder. Soviet leaders did not doubt what American-Chinese rapprochement could mean to them. The threat of a hostile America allied with a hostile China had at all costs to be avoided. So, shortly after Nixon consummated his state visit to Peking in February 1972, moves were well under way to insure that Moscow would be next stop on his itinerary. In May, Nixon flew off to the Soviet Union, bringing with him an agenda that included trade and technology-sharing agreements and the crucial Strategic Arms Limitation Treaty of 1972 (SALT I). The SALT treaty was based upon U.S. acceptance of the all-important principle of nuclear equality between the two major military colossi on the planet. It was diplomatic spice the Kremlin palate found very savory indeed, not least because Nixon had been the sort of American politician who had previously clamored loudest and longest for U.S. nuclear superiority, vis-à-vis the Russians, in any and all conceivable circumstances.[92]

Détente ensued. Nixon, the heretofore fervid anticommunist, relaxed his rhetoric and worked out deals based upon principles of mutual advantage. Nixon also played Moscow and Peking off against one another when he could. He sought to give Soviet and Chinese leaders more to gain from selective cooperation with America than they might gain by alienating Richard Milhous Nixon: for example, by maintaining their existent levels of diplomatic and material support for destabilizing national liberation movements in the Third World—especially, of course, the one headquartered in Hanoi.

Previous American presidents had often tried to bluster the Soviets and the Chinese into not sending arms to Vietnamese rebels and into helping to force Hanoi to bargain in a manner congenial to Washington. Now, Nixon and Kissinger added carrots to sticks. Détente, as applied to Vietnam, was aimed at weakening and isolating Hanoi by making the Indochinese struggle appear to be a messy and troublesome remnant whose continuation endangered the new cooperative arrangements that China, the U.S.S.R., and the U.S.A. were attempting to work out with each other.[93]

The détente strategy was as close to political genius as Richard Nixon ever came in foreign policy. Détente gave both international and domestic credibility to the concept of a New Nixon: a tough-minded operator who was lessening Cold War tensions and extricating America from Vietnam by bargaining with Hanoi's military and financial godfathers in Moscow and Peking. His efforts to turn Vietnam into a relic of bygone days might not have appeared in so rosy a light if Hanoi had not launched its army on a conventional cross-DMZ offensive in between the time that Nixon visited China and the time that he journeyed on to Moscow. But Hanoi did, Hanoi failed, and Nixon benefitted, at least in the short term.

Hanoi, basically, tried to knock the Saigon regime and its army quickly and completely to pieces before Soviet–American–Chinese détente took root. Starting on March 30th, 1972, its generals ordered northern-based battalions supported by artillery and armor to push south, at a time when the last divisions of U.S. ground troops in the South were also being withdrawn.

Communist military strategy backfired badly. Nixon's visits to Peking and Moscow in search of détente, together with the final pullouts of American ground troops, made it look as though Hanoi were trying to kick Nixon out of a room he was already leaving under his own power. Hanoi appeared to be the spoiler, while Nixon looked more like the peacemaker. As a result, Nixon, as the aggrieved party in the political performance, had a chance to become more of a warmaker as well. He could now demonstrate to the conservatives back home who had elected him that he was conciliatory but not soft.

Nixon responded to Hanoi's ill-timed offensive in mid-April. The ARVN's forces were supported by large-scale U.S. air attacks that savaged the now road-bound and vulnerable North Vietnamese army south of the Demilitarized Zone. Nixon also ordered the resumption of the air war against North Vietnam itself, attacks which included never-before-undertaken bombings of Hanoi and the nearby port city of Haiphong and the mining of all major northern harbors. North Vietnam was now being pummelled in ways it had not been since LBJ had stopped the bombing on Election Eve of 1968.

Escalation was possible three-and-a-half years later because Hanoi's Spring Offensive gave the political initiative to Nixon. This, in turn, wrenched the military initiative away from Hanoi. Destroyed weaponry, dead men, territory reopened to destruction, and increasingly stiff ARVN resistance all told the tale. Once Hanoi's forces retreated, however, all did not go back to square one. Instead, Nixon continued the bombing. Soviet and Chinese protests against it were pro forma, even though one Russian vessel was sunk and three more were damaged during the initial air attacks on Haiphong harbor. In America, antiwar opposition to the renewed bombing was weak, scattered, and ill-organized.

For all these reasons, then, Nixon's star was ascendant again by mid-1972. America's troop withdrawals were almost complete, and a hi-tech and relatively low-casualty conflict, just reescalated to include North Vietnam, played well—or well enough—in a mainstream America where many millions of the citizenry had turned off the war once it no longer appeared to directly affect them. By August, Nixon felt strong enough to tell Hanoi that U.S. forces would bomb North Vietnam until a peace settlement was reached and that no reduction in bombing levels would take place unless substantial progress was made toward that settlement. The best that antiwar Democrats in Congress were able to do to dispute any of this was to try, for the first time, to pass legislation demanding that the president withdraw all U.S. forces (ground and air) from all of Indochina (Vietnam, Cambodia, and Laos). They tried, in short, to put some teeth into the earlier repeal of the Gulf of Tonkin Resolution. This effort failed in the House of Representatives on August 10th by a vote of 228 to 178, but Nixon had been warned that Congress was getting restless.

Diplomacy, now, became war carried on by other means. Hanoi, pressured by Washington and fearful about future levels of support from Moscow and Peking, backed away from previously ironclad demands that the United States throw the "puppet Saigon regime" overboard as a condition of peace. The U.S. negotiators responded by moderating their inflexible requirement that Hanoi withdraw all of its "foreign" troops. An agreement on an "armistice in place" which required no withdrawal of communist forces from southern Vietnam was pieced together by October. In return for this the United States got a promise of the return of all American prisoners of war and vague agreements regarding the creation of a postwar coalition government by Hanoi and Saigon. The United States, meanwhile, promised Saigon that it would continue to supply it with money and arms and promised Hanoi that *all* U.S. forces would be withdrawn from battle in Vietnam.[94]

Saigon's head of state, Nguyen Van Thieu, hated this October 1972 agreement with a passion. All it did, after all, was put the clock back to 1965 (for the United States) while leaving him with a powerful and well-emplaced rebellion on his hands, one he would now have to fight without benefit of U.S. air power as well as without benefit of American troops. Thieu, therefore, refused to agree with the agreement, even after Henry Kissinger made an unpaid political announcement that "Peace is at hand" only twelve days before the 1972 presidential election.

Pre-election flutterings and blusterings then commenced in earnest in official Washington. Thieu's opposition made the Nixon Vietnamization program look just like the fig leaf for unilateral withdrawal of *all* U.S. military forces that it had now become. Comparatively few voters, however, were swayed by these nuances. All they knew was that Nixon was bombing the blazes out of North Vietnam and that America appeared to be almost out of direct involvement in Vietnam. If Thieu didn't like that, he himself could go to blazes, and America would stop supporting him. The Democrats, meanwhile, had been successfully branded as the party of total and unilateral withdrawal, cut-and-run, and cowardice. So people voted for Richard Nixon.

Boy, did they ever. Nixon was returned to office with a 45.7 million to 28.3 million popular majority and the Electoral College votes of all the states but one. His ability to play carrot-and-stick politics in the ongoing armistice and peace talks rose accordingly.

Nixon started off well enough. The stick was applied to Thieu via simple reminders of who was financing and supplying whom: "Get on board, or else," spoken in svelte diplomatic idiom. Carrots, meanwhile, were offered in the form of postelection secret reassurances from Nixon to Thieu that the United States would definitely reinvolve itself in the war as a direct participant if Hanoi failed to abide by any of the terms of the treaty being worked out, especially if Saigon-Hanoi "cooperation" ended up looking a lot like continued military conquest.[95]

Then Nixon made a mistake. He applied the stick to Hanoi by demanding that a previously utterly (and intentionally) vague segment of the peace treaty that Hanoi's representative was about to sign be made crystal clear. Hanoi, orated Kissinger on Nixon's orders, must provide an ironclad guarantee that Thieu would remain in power at the head of any future southern Vietnamese coalition regime. This was tantamount to requiring Hanoi to sign a binding contract not to defeat in any way a general running a regime it had been fighting for twelve years. This general had had himself reelected Saigon's president in 1971 by 99 percent of the vote in an unopposed race characterized by wholesale fraud; and only after an earlier experience of electoral politics in a balkanized eleven-way presidential race, where fraud was more retail than wholesale, had ended up giving him only 35 percent of the total votes cast. Hanoi's Marxist-Leninist leadership, of course, didn't care about Thieu's being a dictator, but he wasn't *their* dictator. He was their enemy-in-chief in what they saw as a civil war. To agree that they wouldn't overthrow Thieu by ballot or bullet was to lose that war in the flourish of a pen. Hanoi, accordingly, refused to do so.[96]

Nixon, however, kept on trying to stop a civil war by fiat, after American military might had failed to accomplish that over the preceding eight years. He further demanded that this civil war be ended by joining the sides which had been fighting that war into a peaceful coalition government, one in which the rules were going to be made by the man (Thieu) who embodied the most anticommunist and most pro-American Vietnamese political forces available. Even Henry Kissinger later argued that logic like this was an "absurdity." Nixon could not win diplomatically what he had not won militarily.[97]

During November and December 1972, however, ambitious political operators like Kissinger argued nothing of the sort, not if they wanted to go on being employed by a president who had just won one of the biggest election victories in U.S. history. These same people also rarely told themselves the civil-war facts of life, because the war was all about a foreign invasion, wasn't it? So almost nobody said anything, and a frustrated and angry Nixon began to bomb on a scale never before seen. Twelve days of round-the-clock B-52 raids pounded Hanoi back to the bargaining tables between December 18th and 30th, at the cost of enraging Democrats who did not like it when spurious Election Eve peace breakthroughs became a political technique the Republicans also tried on them.

Once the artful evasions of diplomacy were renewed in January 1973, smaller artifices were contrived to cover the gaps in the larger artifice of the armistice process between Washington and Hanoi. Hanoi promised not to send any *more* northern troops to the South; America, in return, promised not to significantly increase its arms shipments to Saigon beyond their present levels. Both sides agreed that a "balance" of military resupply should be maintained for forces already in the field while some form of "national reconciliation" that might lead to elections for a coalition government was attempted by procommunist, anticommunist, and neutralist "South Vietnamese" political-interest groups without any "North Vietnamese" involvement. The people of South Vietnam, President Nixon claimed, had now been guaranteed the right to determine their own future without outside interference. Peace had come to all of Vietnam and Southeast Asia.[98]

In fact, nothing of the sort had been guaranteed. Hanoi had no intention of compromising anything with Saigon, unless it was forced to by pressure exerted by the Soviets and the Chinese. Hanoi wanted the United States as far out of direct involvement in the Vietnam portion of the Indochina war as possible. This it got. Washington, for its part, wanted its prisoners of war back, and desired only vague limits on its right to continue to supply and train the ARVN after the Hanoi-Washington ceasefire. These things it got. Saigon, which didn't want the Americans out at all so long as Hanoi's troops still occupied parts of the territory over which it claimed sovereignty, got nothing except continued aid and Nixon's promises that the U.S. military would directly re-involve itself in the conflict if Saigon's military could not do the job. The Vietnam War that had produced so many graves would produce many, many more.

For all that, Nixon's primary aim was to get America out of direct involvement in Vietnam without appearing to lose an American war there. Further, he fully intended to assist Saigon and harry communist forces by continuing the high-technology air war in *Cambodia* and *Laos,* where the White House had signed no armistice of any sort with anybody. If *Saigon* later lost the war in Vietnam, that would be too bad, but it would not be an *American* problem that could undermine America's ability to lead elsewhere around the globe. The symbolic, as so often in Vietnam, was more important than the real. So, on January 23rd, 1973, almost eight years after Lyndon Johnson had finally Americanized the war in Vietnam, Richard Milhous Nixon announced that it would finally be de-Americanized by a peace treaty signed four days later.

Here, for most Americans, was the end of the country's Longest War. An end, even, for Lyndon Baines Johnson, who had died in Texas, aged only 64, on January 22nd, one day before the treaty announcement was made by his presidential successor.

## The Last Gasps

It was not the end. Not for the Vietnamese, and not for the Americans. War raged on in Cambodia and Laos, as Americans bought more time for Saigon by destroying communist supply lines and reinforcements while trying to shore up an even weaker Cambodian regime—one which, by the spring of 1973, had lost control of almost the entire countryside to Hanoi-backed Khmer Rouge rebels and left General Lon Nol and his government penned up in the Cambodian capital, Phnom Penh. Bombing, as so often before in Indochina, became the substitute for men, a way to kill a lot of communists without killing enough Americans in the process to set the grass roots of public opinion alight back home.

The trouble was that Saigon and Phnom Penh stayed weak, and the Nixon regime also began politically hemorrhaging so fast that it was unable to make up, in terms of firepower, what its allies and itself increasingly lacked in strength and believability. The first problem was the scale of the bombing, the next was popular and congressional reaction to it. Between February and July 1973, U.S. warplanes dropped more high explosive on ever-widening "target areas" in Cambodia than America had dropped on Japan during all of the Second World War. This bombing killed more and more Cambodians, produced more waves of refugees swelling into the few major cities still held by the Lon Nol regime, and did nowhere near enough to stop defeats of the Cambodian army on the ground, defeats to which the indiscriminate destruction Americans meted out from the air only contributed.

Mega-destruction in Cambodia—and Laos—produced bad political results at home. Most Americans were profound about Southeast Asia in only one way: they were profoundly tired about hearing about it. Peace meant peace, tens of millions of Americans assumed, in Vietnam and everywhere else in a messy, obscure, and psychologically distant part of the world. When these same people discovered that an American peace in Vietnam did not mean that American pilots had ceased fighting in Cambodia or Laos, grumbling became widespread and continual—especially as more and more bombs produced fewer and fewer results. Weren't American boys still fighting wars for Asian boys? Hadn't this been the way the whole mess had started? And wasn't it about time to get everybody out of a conflict that still, after almost a decade, looked unwinnable, because we were trying to protect people who couldn't protect themselves?

This practical, as opposed to either ideological or moral, impatience with continued direct U.S. involvement in the wider war beyond Vietnam's borders was an item of no little import to politicians who had been fighting unsuccessfully to decrease presidential War Powers ever since the escalations following the Tonkin Gulf Resolution. Up until the January 1973 peace treaty between Hanoi and Washington, those most anxious to reassert congressional primacy had had only one major success, the Cooper-Church Amendment passed six months after the Cambodian invasion of April–July 1970—legislation which, recall, only prohibited Nixon from using U.S. *ground* troops outside of South Vietnam. As the bad news from Indochina continued, however, Nixon's opponents had a chance to attack again on the War Powers front. And, as luck would have it, they were able to do so successfully because of a festering wound the Nixon White House had given to itself.

The fight began on January 2nd, 1973, when House Democrats caucused and voted 154 to 75 to vote to cut off *all* funds for *all* types of U.S. military activity in *all* of Indochina when future appropriation bills came before them. The Democratic House had been much more hesitant to criticize the war than the Democratic Senate had been up to this point. The straw vote now made it plain, however, that House Democrats, by a two-to-one majority, were going to cut themselves loose from further support for direct U.S. involvement in the war once peace accords were signed and the last American troops and prisoners of war returned home. Nixon recognized the dangers this posed to his continued freedom of action in Laos and Cambodia and to his ability to send U.S. air forces into action in Vietnam again if the ARVN needed them.[99] Nor did he underestimate the significance of growing congressional urges to reduce levels of U.S. military and economic assistance to Saigon, and even to set a three-year limit on such aid.

Nixon, however, could do less and less to try and convince hitherto sympathetic Democrats or frighten hitherto timorous ones, for he had, by now, "brought the war home" in a notably self-destructive fashion by utilizing spying and political sabotage previously reserved for radicals against the largest political party in the United States. This, more than any other single action, destroyed his presidency and his ability to continue leading in Southeast Asia or anywhere else.[100]

Watergate will be analyzed in Part Four. What we need to keep in mind here is that by March 1973, the Watergate cover-up had started to unravel and that, by mid-April, Nixon was fighting for his political life. On April 30th, 1973, Nixon fired his personal counsel, John Dean, his two chief White House aides, John Ehrlichman and H. R. Haldeman, and his attorney general, Richard Kleindienst, meanwhile protesting his own utter innocence of anything and everything. By May 17th, the Senate's special

Watergate Committee began nationally televised hearings which soon showed John Dean accusing the president of fully participating in the cover-up of a crime. One day after the Senate Watergate Committee began its hearings, a special prosecutor, operating independently of the White House, the attorney general, and the Justice Department, was named to conduct an investigation to complement a judicial one by the Federal District Court for the District of Columbia, Judge John J. Sirica, presiding.

Early in 1973, then, Nixon was reeling from repeated blows. Many Democratic politicians who had not previously dared cross him on issues of war or patriotism decided to start running such political risks, if only because they thought that this president had to be gotten before he got them. As a result, ideology fused with interest and the Vietnam War came home at last. And it affected the crucial power relationships within the American government itself, relationships which had allowed the war to be waged as it was in the first place.

Congress counterattacked to take back what it had lost. Not for the Vietnamese or the Cambodians, but for itself. There was no heroic charge against the bastions of executive and "expert" power. Instead, a careful advance occurred, one that expanded upon opportunity and weakness. In late June, as John Dean was presenting his sensational testimony to the Senate Watergate Committee, the full Senate passed a bill ordering Nixon to end all U.S. military action in Cambodia and Laos immediately. The House joined in, and Nixon promptly vetoed the legislation. Two-thirds of the Senate then passed the bill again, but the required two-thirds majority was not obtained in the House.

Nixon's veto stood, but only just. The president had utterly lost control of the Senate, and was within an ace of losing the one-third-plus-one support that he needed to sustain his war policy in the House. Nixon had no choice but to deal, and deal he did. To protect his ability to keep on sending arms and money to Saigon and Phnom Penh, he offered to surrender his power to order American airmen into combat as of August 15th, 1973. Congress, anxious to avoid a head-to-head confrontation, agreed to the compromise and Nixon signed a bill to that effect on July 1st.[101]

For fifteen days, all went well enough. Then Richard Nixon's political world exploded. On July 16th, former White House aide Alexander Butterfield publicly testified to the Senate Watergate Committee that Nixon had been secretly tape-recording all his White House conversations for three years. When Capitol Hill got over reeling about this bit of political lèse-majesté, it reeled some more when Secretary of Defense James Schlesinger first publicly admitted the same day that then-neutral Cambodia had been secretly bombed in 1969 and 1970 without any official notification of Congress.[102]

The combined effect of these two revelations was disastrous for Nixon's continued political survival and for his remaining war policy. Lying is not rare in politics, but a leader had better not get caught lying to his friends—about bombing a neutral country for two years, for example. Recording sensitive conversations in some manner to insure that you know what you said—and what they said—is, likewise, far from rare: but, again, a leader had better not do that often to his political friends or allies, and *never* do it unless they *know* he is doing it.

Nixon made both mistakes, and ended up losing a lot of political friends, because these people came to believe that they couldn't even trust Nixon to play straight with them when they were on the same side. Once any politician loses such calculated trust, he is in deep trouble. So it was with Richard Nixon. By August 3rd, he'd been backed so far into a corner by Congress that he had to "reaffirm" that all U.S. bombing of Cambodia would end on the day (August 15th) that he had agreed it would only a month before.

From here, all went downhill at an even faster pace. Once the American portion of the Cambodian and Laotian wars ended on schedule on August 15th, it was back to the pre-1965 game of only indirect U.S. support. But the United States had not Vietnamized a peace; it had only Vietnamized a war. It had also "Cambodianized" another bloodbath it and Hanoi shared responsibility for. The United States had spent almost $150 billion, chalked up fifty-eight thousand dead and perhaps five times that many disabled in American loss accounts, and left behind a peace that was no peace for anybody. Not, especially, for the several million who had already died in Indochina or for the several million more who would.

American leaders, however, did not spend much time pondering such matters in late 1973. Washington focused on its own internal power struggle, especially after the Saturday Night Massacre of October 20th began the impeachment stage of the Watergate battle. Crises elsewhere (most particularly the Arab-Israeli War of October 1973 and the subsequent Arab OPEC producers' oil embargo on the United States) also distracted attention from the remaining messy realities of a failed war. Henry Kissinger, who assumed the post of secretary of state in August, ran around trying to make an unworkable peace work so far as Hanoi and Saigon were concerned. In November, a War Powers Act aimed at making another Tonkin Gulf impossible was passed over Nixon's veto. American aid, meanwhile, continued to flow to Saigon, $1.5 billion in 1973 (78 percent of the total spending that the Thieu regime devoted to the war that year).

The American figure was halved to $700 million (65 percent of Saigon's spending) in 1974. Saigon wanted more, lots more.[103] But few in official Washington now had the faintest hope that any agreement on anything would be worked out between Hanoi and Saigon. Russian and Chinese military-aid levels to Hanoi were also falling at approximately the U.S. rate. Détente and U.S. withdrawal had put Indochina off the communist superpowers' list of number-one priorities as well. 1974 was a quiet military year in Vietnam, but a year of a wrenching political passion play in America, one climaxed by Nixon's resignation in August and Ford's pardon in September.

The quiet, however, did not last. Husbanding its now scarcer military resources, Hanoi's leadership began another all-out offensive in March 1975. This time, unlike 1968 and 1972, it succeeded. Economics played a major role in the result. Inflation and unemployment became endemic in South Vietnam after the final U.S. withdrawals and, by 1974, the average ARVN trooper's pay bought only one-fourth as much as it had ten years earlier. Ninety percent of the soldiers weren't earning enough to even support their families.[104]

The Saigon regime, unable to turn back a tide of economic disaster, and with many another frailty besides, was a disaster waiting to happen. Once the communist forces pushed for a third time, and no U.S. military re-involvements such as those secretly promised by Nixon occurred, panic set in at the top and quickly communicated itself to the dissatisfied bottom. The ARVN and the regime it maintained fell so fast that Hanoi's military commanders were initially hesitant to believe the extent of their good fortune. As Hanoi's army marched toward Saigon and the rot spread to Cambodia as well, a Gallup Poll published in mid-April 1975 showed that no fewer than 79 percent opposed any additional military aid for South Vietnam or Cambodia.[105] Congress did not ignore figures like this, and it did what the voters told it to, which was to do nothing more than it was already doing. Its final wartime act was to allocate $400 million toward emergency refugee relief as hundreds of thousands of Vietnamese and Cambodians began to stream out of countries that had ceased to be theirs.

It was all a loss of nerve, the believers in the war said. America had failed in a crusade for liberty and forfeited its national honor. The war could have been won, and it would have been. Lily-livered liberals and unpatriotic radicals had sold out freedom somewhere else so that they could feel mindlessly progressive about themselves. Here were idiots useful to Moscow, Peking, and Hanoi; punks who mouthed pinko slogans they would never have to fight for; hairy young people who listened to barbarous sounding music, who honored morality more in the breach than in the observance, and who were so hopelessly innocent and mindlessly self-centered that they would, one day, present the Marxist hangman with all the rope necessary to execute the world. The radicals of the New Left, the strongest prowar advocates argued, were the only real winners of the Vietnam War in America. They kept the vast majority of their countrymen from fulfilling their duties and responsibilities to preserve liberty around the world.

The New Left, however, was not as powerful, organized, or monolithic as its conservative opponents supposed. Most New Leftists were, in fact, neither particularly "left" nor particularly "new" about translating what radical beliefs they had into the sphere of action. The irony, in fact, was that the same realities which left their most thoroughly committed right-wing adversaries behind (for the moment) left them behind more thoroughly and more completely. The New Left is discussed at length in Part Three, which follows.

# PART THREE

# THE NEW LEFT
# AND AFTERWARD

*Dreams and Realities*

Claiming to be a socialist of any type in the United States is like arguing that elephants nest in trees. People look at you funny and wonder whether you suffer from some mental malady. There are fewer members of the American affiliate of the Socialist International, a United Nations of ballots-not-bullets Democratic Socialist parties, than there are in its sister organization in the Republic of Ireland, even though the Irish Republic has one-eightieth the population of the United States and is the most conservative country in Western Europe. If all the Marxists, Leninists, Maoists, Trotskyists, Democratic Socialists, and others within the wildly varied socialist spectrum were gathered together in one place in the United States, they might compose a town of one hundred thousand. Almost none of these people are elected officials in local, state, or national government.

The Revolution, should you happen to be waiting for it, is a very long way away in the United States. Should you prefer the votes-not-guns route, you also have a long march to make. Americans of all sorts rarely comprehend the ideological or other differences between, say, a socialist

and a communist. Thus the elephants nesting in trees problem, or, ideologically, a Socialism = Communism = Bad Thing equation which stops
thought before it starts. To be even a Democratic Socialist in the United
States is to be classified as a radical in a manner that is unknown in Europe
or among its other democratic diaspora.

And yet, for all these disadvantages and weaknesses and for all their
experience of being but humble servants to political events, there have
been times when American radicals have been prey to a belief that they
could direct the future.

The late 1960s was one of those rare periods. As Vietnam divided the
nation and challenged its leaders' assumptions about America's power and
place in the world, socialists thought they had perspectives which explained both what was wrong and how it could be made right.

## To Hell with the Liberal Establishment

In the radical view, what was happening to Vietnam and to America was
the result of conceits that had hardened into imperialism abroad and a
go-as-slow-as-possible approach to redistributing political and economic
power at home. Leftists had been making such critiques for sixty years.
Late in the 1960s, however, they gained currency because of the activities
of the mostly under twenty-five-year-old radicals of the New Left.

The New Left began with an attack on what sympathetic sociologist C.
Wright Mills characterized in 1962 as the "bipartisan banality" of "smug
conservatives, tired liberals, and disillusioned radicals." What had happened was that the Cold War era had induced more reactionary paranoia
than usual on the right, and intellectual cowardice among liberal and
radical forces. The two decades after the Second World War had been a
great barbecue of Church Militant anticommunism abroad and New Deal
era fragmentary welfare statism at home. This, together with heresy hunting, great waves of postwar prosperity, and a loss of faith in the imperialist
and purge-prone Soviet Union as the model for the shining socialist tomor-
row, had combined to create a society fit only for conformist ideological
invertebrates.[1]

Liberals were the special villains of the piece. The right was slack-jawed,
Social Darwinian, and predictably hopeless; while the old left were a
bunch of political fossils arguing who-really-did-what-to-whom in Russia

in 1917 or Spain in 1937, meanwhile living out their lives in the sectarian wombs of the Socialist Party or the Communist Party, U.S.A.

The liberals, however, embodied what political tradition there was in America during the Vietnam era; and they had most of the power into the bargain. They had succeeded in defining themselves as the vital center of American politics. They had had primary responsibility for creating and implementing national policies ever since Franklin Delano Roosevelt had become president in March 1933.

But these vital-center liberals, the New Leftists went on, were neither vital nor centrist. They were closet right-wingers. Their misplaced sense of mission had led them, like the conservatives, to see everything as forces-of-light versus forces-of-darkness. Liberals were caught in the same grim escalatory duet as the right was. More and more ambitious policies aimed at exerting American power abroad excused the creation of ever more armaments; then the possession of ever more armaments provided steadily expanding opportunities for interventionist policies. The liberals couldn't stop the resulting imperialist cycle, because they wanted to do the same things the right did, in smaller ways. And what started out small almost always got larger because the liberals were usually terrified that the right-wingers would red-bait them mercilessly if ever they failed to be as tough as the rightists wanted them to be.

It was all self-defeating stupidity, the young radicals argued. It was so stupid it had to be planned that way. The liberals reassured the troglodytes of the far right who equated communism with whatever it was that they happened to dislike the most at the moment. John F. Kennedy started to Americanize the killing in Vietnam and then said that McCarthyite heresy hunts would develop if the Democrats didn't follow through. The result was that Kennedy and Johnson vastly expanded the war. Nonleftist Gary Wills summarized the logic:

> Over and over again in recent history Presidents have claimed that they had to act tough in order to *disarm* those demanding that they act tough. The only way to become a peacemaker is first to disarm the warmakers by making a little successful war. And if the little war becomes a big one, it must be pursued energetically or the "hawks" will capitalize on the failure. War wins, either way. If you are for it, you wage it. And if you are against it, you wage it.[2]

President John F. Kennedy tried a little war to overthrow Castro, which failed, and then almost fought a third world war after Castro offered Cuba as a military base to the Soviets in return for protection in the event that the Americans came back again. Kennedy also told critics that conservatives would have done worse and that the right would surely get *him* if he didn't tough it out with the communists.

Thus, the New Left argued, an almost-Armageddon in Cuba in 1962 and a full-scale Americanization of the Vietnam War in 1965 demonstrated there was no real difference between Cold War liberals and Cold War conservatives. They were two peas in the same pod. The right-wingers were wolves; the vital-center liberals claimed to be lambs, cried wolf about the conservatives, and then proceeded to act like wolves themselves. Only the rationalizations differed, not the actions the rationalizations were devised to explain. Ignoring the fact that there was a very hard, hard right (led by George Wallace or Ronald Reagan, for example) and underestimating the aggressive elements of public opinion in regard to foreign policy (because they believed that political leaders *made* that opinion rather than being in any substantial way *made by* it), the New Left accused liberalism of being just another name for status-quo-oriented imperialism trying to freeze the globe in America's chosen image.

Given this logic, the young radicals repeatedly used the term "the Establishment": a British import designed to describe an unchanging Old Boy Network (another British import) or a "Power Elite" (to use an Americanism, courtesy of C. Wright Mills) which existed independent of party politics, election results, or explanations of what the United States government was doing in the world at any particular moment. What it was doing, the New Left charged, was what the Establishment told it to do.

There was enough truth in the radical claim to give it credibility far beyond the left- and right-wing realms where democratic politics are equated with ruling class conspiracy. The War Managers of Washington had operated as a mostly unelected foreign-policy elite which assumed itself to be superior Platonic Guardians of freedom around the world. Their expertise had signally failed, but very few modified their thoughts and actions accordingly. To let anything new into their system of beliefs was to undermine their status and their self-image as disinterested and supremely necessary persons.

Large and growing numbers of people in whose best interests these elite foreign-policy Guardians were supposedly acting, however, were hardly so shy about disbelieving. It was not *their* status and power that was at risk, after all. Tet and what came afterward made fine-tuned "limited war" look like so much lunacy, and bred wholesale and retail cynicism regarding the political, military, academic, and other elite groups that had been looking after America's burgeoning foreign-policy interests for twenty years. People became bluntly skeptical that the gentlemen of the foreign-policy

Establishment knew whereof they spoke. Activists of many ideological persuasions demanded that the system be opened up to a new clientèle— chiefly, of course, themselves.

This withdrawal of belief and demands for the inclusion of the hitherto excluded, ignored, or just plain disinterested left the Old Boy Network open to immediate and thoroughgoing attack. Most of its members promptly fought back, arguing that nobody else could do any better, given unexpected circumstances.

Equally clearly, it gave the nascent New Left a chance to make a lunge for the liberals' throats, an opportunity its members did not hesitate one second about taking. The radical attack, initially, went well. New Left fledgling organizations, including the Students for a Democratic Society (SDS), joined their protests to those coming from a wide variety of other groups, most of which were not leftist at all. The terrible year of 1968 gave the New Left a hearing and vaulted radicalism into an uncustomary position of national visibility. Perceived crisis gave radicals particular entrée to a clientèle, especially young collegians, who did not have direct electoral or political responsibility for the war but who feared that their lives were hostage to the quick solution of its dilemmas.

Then came the much harder part. Relatively large audiences were paying attention to what the left had to say. Now it was up to the young radicals to demonstrate that they could replace liberal ideology with one of their own. In this, the New Left fared none too well. Here, in fact, it essentially self-destructed.


## The Ideology of the New Left


A key attribute of the New Left throughout its history was vagueness: a blurry approach toward clarifying ideological basics like who the central agents of political and economic change would, could, or should be; or about whether to confront established authorities via peaceful, nonviolent, and democratic means or by a violent revolutionary vanguard unrelated to popular decision making or consent.

The New Left was easier to define in terms of what it usually was not, rather than in terms of what it normally was. New Left was a generic term, and contained important differences of derivation and emphasis. Analysts of its five-year history as a significant national movement have often perceived it to be about as organized as a cross between a revolutionary cell meeting and an orgy, a mixture of Power to the People, Gee Whiz, and Far Out, Man.

This oddity stemmed, in large part, from the fact that the New Left was a child of affluence much more than of poverty. Sons and daughters of toil were rare in New Left ranks at any time during its brief prominence; sons and daughters of the upper-middle class studying in the better-known universities and colleges were the norm. Here was a peculiarity for old-left socialists and communists to contend with. Whereas they saw the working class or a revolutionary proletariat as the necessary agent of change in a hostile capitalist world, the New Left most emphatically did not.

Who would serve as the inevitable and irresistible gravedigger of capitalism was a matter that started out inexact and remained that way. Most committed New Left activists were initially clear, however, that the working class was a hopelessly inadequate force for historical progress. The worker's paradise (socialism) might come one day, but most of the workers wouldn't have anything to do with producing it, especially if they were enrolled in trade unions.

The problem with these latter sorts of workers, New Leftists believed, was that they'd been co-opted and bought off by the System. Wily capitalists, their political henchmen, and union leaders who were traitors to their class had muzzled the revolutionary awareness spawned during the debacle of the Great Depression by a combination of "corporate liberalism" (big-business sponsorship of social welfare and labor legislation such as the Social Security Act of 1935 and the Wagner National Labor Relations Act of 1935) and a return to affluence dependent largely upon foreign economic imperialism and the vastly expanded military spending that accompanied the Second World War and the Cold War which followed hard upon it.[3]

War, Cold War, and a bit of prophylactic reform was great for business, the New Left's argument went, because it drowned rebellion in prosperity. On average, for example, U.S. paychecks rose 13 percent in "real" (after inflation) terms during the politically supine 1950s. The rise doubled (to 25 percent) during the seven years from 1965 to 1972, i.e., the average wage or salary earner's income increased by a quarter between 1965 to 1970, when the New Left was in flower.[4]

These gains were averages, of course. Some did better, others not so well. But those among the blue-collar workforce who did the best were those with the greatest collective organization and clout: the largely unionized industrial workers of long-established socialist hopes. The very people who were supposed to be leading the radical charge from the factory gates to the citadels of capitalist power, then, had been beguiled to sell out shining socialist tomorrows for messes of materialist pottage.

Plainly a "new proletariat" (a new revolutionary working class) was required. And, as long-time Democratic Socialist Michael Harrington noted in 1966, that is precisely what the New Left spent a lot of its ideological energies trying to define. It searched for "a social class that would be driven by the very conditions of its [exploited] existence into [serving as the inevitable historical agent of change behind] a total transformation of the society; a group whose plight was so extreme that its definition of reform would be revolution."[5]

This search proved elusive. Blacks were a near-universal candidate for most thoroughly oppressed revolutionary substitute. So, at a more distant remove, were American Indians and Mexican Americans. Women got added to the list after the coalescence of feminism as a national force by 1969; and gays, later still.

It was "youth," however, that was the New Left's major discovery in terms of hoped-for revolutionary potential, youth being that one-quarter of the population aged eighteen to twenty-five attending a college or university from which they would graduate, or the just under one-half of that age group who had any college experience at all. Committed collegians were the key element in the radicals' organizing strategy, especially after Black Power briefly spurred separatist tendencies among many younger blacks. This selection was natural enough, SDS pioneer Todd Gitlin recalled, because the New Left "had started, after all, from the isolation of an elite university social base."[6]

It certainly had. And the New Left, for all its insurgent efforts, never strayed far beyond that base. Several score community organizing campaigns modelled on the work of veteran Chicago activist Saul Alinsky were undertaken during the five years preceding 1968. But these nonacademic efforts were brief, withered among minority populations after the long hot summer of 1967 and the assassination of Martin Luther King in 1968, or became subsidiary to the wider efforts to mount a national campaign to stop a war that had swelled the numbers of Americans in Vietnam from fifteen thousand to 37 times that figure in the three-and-a-half years between the Gulf of Tonkin Resolution and the Tet offensive.[7]

In frenetic limited-war circumstances and a period of heightened racial tensions, short-term organizing displaced longer-term, and ending the war became the prime New Left consideration. War-related anxieties also impelled most New Leftists to build from collegiate locales they already knew and to base most of their off-campus effort in university towns and a few cities clustered with higher educational establishments.

There, appeals to oppose the war could be made with the least risk, Let Ideas Contend being a folkway of academic life—so long as academe itself did not have to contend with any actions that flowed from acceptance of any of the ideas.[8]

Clustered as small groups of self-defined prophets in the Cold War wilderness, radicals such as those in the Students for a Democratic Society sought to build a mélange of unsettled youth into a movement to stop a hot war in Vietnam. It was just as well, frankly, that the New Left had an academic base. Bolsheviks they were not. The radical activists' burgeoning concerns quickly led them into confrontational politics. But confrontation, New Left style, was too often media theatrics and catharsis and too rarely a base from which to build bridges to a wider political clientèle.

Here, again, the problem went back to the composition of the movement, which was at once favored by present circumstances and relatively unencumbered with knowledge about past events which had been formative in the historical experiences of other generations.

First to the favored circumstances, and then to the history. In the here-and-now of the late 1960s, campus radicals were often what sociologist Kenneth Keniston termed "post-adolescents." They were an insurgent minority of a much wider group of young people involved in expanded periods of training customary in technical, scientific, and other upper reaches of a progressively specialized society. The postadolescents were adults, chronologically speaking, yet they were not settled into practical affairs of occupation, marriage, and family. Such people were still in training to get their preferred tickets into the professional reaches of the labor force. Like the adolescents whose new status was defined during the Industrial Revolution of the late nineteenth and early twentieth centuries, they were betwixt and between.[9]

Postadolescents were relatively unhindered by long-term social, emotional, and economic investments and responsibilities. A graduate student, for example, could take time off from reading densely footnoted monographs and try to do something about the war: go to a March on Washington, for example, or perhaps sit in at a draft board or military induction center and spend some time in jail afterward waiting for bail money and a good lawyer. Student protest of this sort usually could be undertaken without risking immediate expulsion, loss of scholarship assistance, or other punishment, since colleges or universities were crammed with people who knew what the First Amendment specified. These people tended to observe the legal niceties of social discourse—even if they disagreed with the interpretation of free speech or peaceful assembly for redress of grievances being made—either because they believed in the majesty of the law or because they wanted to avoid fights within the ivory towers.

Such protection, logic, and niceties seldom applied to an autoworker or a secretary: they were not part of a system that could be challenged only when they chose to challenge it. Autoworkers could be faced with direct, immediate, and compelling threats to their livelihood and status in a community that was considerably more stable than the temporary college environment that only someone who wanted to become a professor could be part of permanently. A nonacademic locale might well be run by people who didn't care to be instructed about First Amendment anything if our autoworkers decided to take a week off to march on Washington or got arrested at a sit-in.

It was far easier for postadolescent youth to protest. Postadolescents, like youth generally, hadn't firmly put down roots of their own. Few postadolescents ever availed themselves of their comparative advantages in the rebellion department, but those who did still enjoyed an oft-repeated witticism of the period: "A liberal is a radical with a wife and two kids."

A mot like this got a laugh among New Leftists, as among eighteen-to-mid-twenties collegians generally, because very few had families and because they were children of scientific and technological revolution in another respect, too. They avoided many of the traditional trade-offs between procreative instinct and higher-level careerist training. Erudition simply didn't cost them nearly so much in terms of sexual opportunities missed or not taken along the way. By 1965, the birth-control pill was widely available on college and university campuses, and avoiding pregnancy became very much easier for the female, she doing the job for herself via the wonders of chemistry. The pill sparked the Sexual Revolution on campuses all over the country, and it made postadolescence more attractive than ever before. Increasing numbers of men and women didn't have to postpone, severely limit, or purchase sexual favors. Shotgun weddings and abortions were less of a threat. Male and female alike could throw many traditional upwardly mobile cautions to the winds.

Short-term romance, then, made long-term education a lot easier for postadolescents to bear. And it only further differentiated them, the campuses that trained them, and the New Left that sought to recruit them from the remainder of America, where birth-control data and devices were rare at best and where opposition to premarital sex as subversive of discipline, family stability, and long-established moral and ethical precepts was as widespread, heat-inducing, and subcortical as lechery often was on campus.

If postadolescence had been only a matter of favored educational—or even sexual—opportunity, the New Left's effort to use campus-based protest as a lever to move a society would have been difficult enough. But college kids were special in two other very important ways. They were a lot more affluent, and they weren't fighting the war. The several hundred (of three thousand) American colleges and universities notable for their level of antiwar protest during the Vietnam era were a score of state universities (including the University of California campuses at Berkeley, San Diego, and Santa Cruz; the University of Michigan, Ann Arbor; and the University of Wisconsin, Madison); larger private universities (such as Columbia, Brandeis, Harvard, Northwestern, and M.I.T.); and a collection of unconventional small private colleges including Antioch, Goddard, Oberlin, Swarthmore, Bard, Smith, Reed, Carleton, and Grinnell. None of these schools claimed to be anything but selective in its admissions policies, and superior in its student bodies, characteristics for which students (or, far more often, students' families) paid handsomely—because they had the money to pay.

Once a student was admitted to such select precincts, a further bonus was conferred: the famed 2-S deferment which exempted all draft-age (eighteen- to twenty-six-year-old) males from military service during their educational careers, provided they maintained full-time student status and passing grades. Until February 1968, midway through the Tet offensive, the 2-S deferment covered all graduate study as well, so that undergraduate study followed by immediate admission to graduate school was an almost certain way to avoid any military service during one's entire period of draft eligibility. This deferment alone was a marvellous protection as military requirements cut wider and wider swaths through noncollegiate males.

What all of this meant was that the New Left, in trying to erect an economically, socially, and educationally favored youth as the centerpiece of a new proletariat, stood socialist theory on its head. Instead of a revolution set off by a class forced by grim imperatives of survival to change the world, the New Left hoped that an elite, protected, and comfortable group would deny itself economic and other benefits and then go on to impel a revolution. Radical change, therefore, was a trickle-down, rather than bubble-up, proposition.

Trickle-down, however, led to the cathartic element of the New Left radicals' organizational problems. The radical minority of an elite favored by circumstance, opportunity, and noninvolvement sought to stop a war and change a society in an immediate purifying fashion, one which did not remind them that they were favored and did not threaten their advantages substantially. In this ambivalent effort, appearance often replaced reality.[10]

## The Revolution as Theater

The New Left saw itself as the conscience of a generation. It and the 1960s Generation of which it was a small part, were formed, like all generations and protest movements, by its habits of mind. These habits of mind were conditioned largely by the history that the young radical activists had experienced in their politically aware lifetimes and by the short-term contexts in which they placed those formative historical events. This generational memory—particularly, memory formed by *televised* national events—was central to understanding both what New Leftists believed and how they translated those radical beliefs into action.

The New Left was young. Its mostly eighteen- through twenty-five-year-old activists had been born between 1943 and 1950. In 1968, a twenty-five-year-old leftist had been conscious of political events since only about 1958; while eighteen-year-old radicals hadn't seen themselves as a part of wider political environments before 1965—in other words, since each had reached approximately fifteen years of age. The historical memory such young people embodied, in terms of direct experience, was and remained, therefore, *very* different from that of the Second World War politicians who led the nation into the Vietnam War. The historical experience of that generation had usually begun in the 1930s, with worldwide depression, the debate about the New Deal, and increasing fascist aggression abroad. Its generational memory had matured within the context of global war and Cold War.

To a John Fitzgerald Kennedy or a Richard Milhous Nixon, events between the failed effort to appease Hitler at Munich in 1938 and the U.S. nuclear bombing of Japan in August 1945 demonstrated obvious truths. Totalitarian aggression must be stopped sooner, rather than later, or global disaster ensued. America was the strongest democratic nation in the world and, therefore, essential to the postwar peacekeeping process. Postwar Soviet imperialism led such leaders to substitute communism for fascism as the chief threat to global peace and accelerated their efforts to vastly expand America's military and political role in world affairs to stop renewed aggression. Peace through Strength was a logic which appealed with special force to young veterans like JFK (twenty-eight in 1945), Nixon (thirty-two), George Corley Wallace (twenty-six), and Ronald Wilson Reagan (thirty-four). It also appealed to twenty-one-year-old U.S. Naval Academy Cadet James Earl Carter and thirty-six-year-old U.S. Representative Lyndon Baines Johnson.

Most New Left activists on the scene by 1968, however, had different formative experiences. Young radicals of the post-1945 baby boom had no direct experience of Cold War events much before 1960. They remembered Kennedy's assassination, of course. They might, if they were historically minded, even recall the Soviet suppression of the Hungarian uprising of 1956 or the Suez imbroglio of the same year. Depression, fascism, communism, Korea, and the Cold War, however, were all ancient history.

What wasn't ancient, and what had involved them, were more recent events like the Bay of Pigs invasion of April 1961 and the Cuban Missile Crisis of October 1962. Neither had struck the young radicals as good guys (us) versus bad guys (them). Hadn't Kennedy taken the world to the brink of holocaust trying to recoup status lost during his earlier botched effort to overthrow Cuba's Fidel Castro?

The Vietnam oddities which followed the Missile Crisis—Diem's assassination in November 1963 and the subsequent coup-after-coup in Saigon for two years—increased radical skepticism regarding U.S. activity in the Third World. So did Gunboat Diplomacy like the marine-assisted overthrow of Juan Bosch's regime in the Dominican Republic in April 1965, just as the all-out Americanization of the Vietnam War was under way.

An additional and simultaneous concern was the decade-long surge in the nuclear arms race sparked by Kennedy's claims of a "missile gap" during and after the 1960 election. Domestically, too, Cold War anticommunist rhetoric looked especially threadbare, particularly because "communist" epithets were being thrown at the Reverend Martin Luther King and his nonviolent followers by diehard segregationists trying to equate the civil-rights movement with a Moscow-orchestrated conspiracy to destroy freedom.[11]

Given such events and contexts, it is understandable that *Time* magazine, in a November 1963 article on U.S. colleges, cited a poll conducted immediately before JFK's assassination which indicated that "campus discontent with Kennedy stretches far and wide."[12] It is also understandable—if not agreeable—that Jack Newfield, the author of the first book on the New Left, observed that the archetypal young radical of 1966 "has seen Communists only as victims, never as executioners." New Left spokesmen Tom Hayden and Staughton Lynd early stated that "we refuse to be anticommunist. We insist that the term has lost all the specific content it once had [and is now merely a rhetorical fig leaf aimed to justify a foreign policy] that often is no more sophisticated than rape."[13]

Radicals like Hayden and Lynd were guilty of more than a bit of rhetoric of their own, but the difference between their historical experience and memory compared with that of their generational predecessors remained.

To the Second World War political generation, America was savior; to the alienated segments of the 60s generation, America had become a bully.

Formative experiences, then, were important and remained so. The ways in which these experiences were most often recorded, disseminated, and remembered were also crucial. For this was the *how,* as opposed to the *what,* of the generational "habits of mind" equation. Of fundamental importance was television. New Left radicals, like their peers, were the *first television generation,* the first generation to whom breaking news, in striking visual form, was relayed from around the nation and around the world. This, as we shall see, was crucial to understanding them and the wider antiwar movement of which they were a part.

Few twenty-one-year-olds in 1968 could even remember when television did not serve as the major information and entertainment medium for a majority of the populace. Kennedy's assassination in 1963, for instance, (when our twenty-one-year-old was sixteen) led national networks to cancel regular programming for three days and give incessant coverage to the murder, the police investigation, the national mourning, and the funeral of the slain president. A more riveting example of TV's ability to involve the nation in a process of grief, hope, and renewed determination could hardly be imagined. The like of it had never been seen anywhere in the world up to that time. No one with the slightest claim to expertise in the black arts of politics would ever ignore television again.

Involvement was the key. Television was the picture worth the thousands of words read in newspapers or heard on the radio. Television could pick people up from the privacy of their living rooms, pull them into the action, and give them the feeling of participation in political processes and events. It was also almost instantaneous, unlike, for example, the weekly movie newsreels that many of the Second World War generation had been weaned on.

Almost-instantaneous involvement opened up politics, and especially political wars, in ways that had never been seen before. It allowed people— particularly, young people—to "see for themselves" (or to believe that they had) what abstractions like the Cold War, containment, national defense, and so forth meant in far-off lands that most had never even heard of before.[14]

This opening up of foreign policy spelled disaster for Lyndon Baines Johnson and his two presidential successors, because he and they simply were not adept at using the new tool of television to maintain their authority in the face of growing attacks upon it. Johnson and Nixon, in particular, failed because they couldn't sufficiently control the images being relayed home from Indochina. Second, neither (especially Johnson) could mount

a televised counterattack to the domestic unrest spawned by the first
Television War. Both failures, in turn, initially helped the New Left before
helping to instill it with delusions of grandeur, addiction to overly theatrical tactics, and assumptions of crises everywhere that led it into self-
destruction.

All politics—whether televised or not—is largely theater, in the sense
that what any leader does cannot be divorced from the way that he or she
does it. Issues are debated, policies arrived at, and actions taken—and the
rhythm and timing and appearance of events are all important. Anyone
who has ever engaged in "sexual politics" knows precisely the point being
made here. What you say or do is often far less important than the way
you say or do it. If you get the theatrics wrong, you may well end up
accomplishing nothing or less than you might have preferred to.

TV enabled radicals to play to large audiences quickly. The New Left
and the wider antiwar movement of which it was a part promptly, therefore, emphasized television-based political theater as its major device for
mobilization, opinion changing, and recruitment. The New Left, however,
played appearances more than realities.

The reasons were due to two of the New Left's basic characteristics. It
was operating from a narrow class base within a couple of hundred elite
schools; second, it was anxious—and, by 1968, desperate—to end the war
as fast as possible. These two characteristics spelled disaster for New Left
hopes—unless an almost instantaneous mobilizing device could be found,
to do in months what radicals had repeatedly failed to do since the Cold
War began.

Television resolved a large part of the conundrum, or seemed to. A
media-based rebellion could be mounted to stop a media war on the home
front. Prowar forces were using television to tell their side of the story
wholesale and continually. Their performance, however, was not very
good, and thus the New Left had its opportunity.

It would have been different, perhaps, but Vietnam was a new kind of
war for Americans. A war without front lines and secure rear areas and,
most important, without the military censorship of pre-TV-era wars. Vietnam was a war where enemies were rarely even identifiable, and images
of this type of struggle proved difficult to equate with visions of a grand
bipolar struggle between the U.S.S.R. and the U.S.A., a struggle of nuclear
weapons and big battalions. The images from Vietnam were often different—of a supremely undramatic war fought by small units moving
through villages, looking for an enemy they seldom found. Vietnam had
a lot of gray in it, a lot less black-and-white certainty, and much more

frustration, particularly after the Tet offensive demonstrated the American failure to achieve a widely assumed and widely promised quick solution.

After Tet, official public relations and political theater about the war took a nosedive from which they never recovered. The key components of the Cold War rationale that had created the war looked artificial; besides, Johnson and Nixon no longer acted upon them come hell or high water. The crucial principles were national security and national credibility, and they were based upon the idea that to lose anywhere was to lose everywhere. If southern Vietnam was a domino whose collapse would cause many other dominoes to fall subsequently, then the United States had no choice but to win there. To do anything else was to face disaster—a communist "world offensive," as JFK once called it. Vietnam, as its supporters often proved extraordinarily adept at forgetting later, had been sold precisely in all-or-nothing terms. That's why there were five-hundred-and-fifty-thousand Americans in Vietnam in 1968, and that is why a majority of Americans wanted further escalation, not limited war as usual, in the immediate aftermath of Tet.

The motifs of crisis and all-or-nothing in Vietnam, however, had been overdone. The part had been overplayed. Therefore, LBJ's unwillingness to go all-out to win immediately after Tet destroyed him: it angered the prowar "hawks," gave the antiwar "doves" greater opportunity to try to deescalate a war that had run away with itself and the United States at one and the same time, and confused the middle-of-the-road majority who didn't know what they wanted done—except that they wanted it done very fast and at the least possible cost in American lives. Here was the New Left's opportunity and the antiwar movement's as well. Both took it and began what Schell has well called a "public relations insurrection" against a "public relations war."[15]

The New Left's countertheater worked from late 1967 to mid-1970. These were the years of well-publicized and televised mass marches, demonstrations, and civil disobedience. But then the radicals' efforts to use TV as their chief organizing tool ran straight off a cliff. Image displaced reality because New Leftists forgot that theater was only part of the equation and because the rest of that equation was *power*—power which the New Left's opponents still possessed but which the radicals never had.

The New Left tried a bluff which failed, and paid the price accordingly. Anxious to create some revolutionary replacement for the working class and suspect of all established institutions, including working-class ones, the New Left fell back primarily upon television as a way to grab attention and take power. The attention it got aplenty, but the power it never got.

Its only clear and certain "substitute proletariat" was postadolescent college and university youth, a privileged social sector it devoted its attention to with diminishing results as the radical alternatives it espoused were swallowed up in a much larger antiwar movement with which it had little in common.

## The Antiwar Movement versus the New Left

The New Left and the antiwar movement were never one and the same thing. The first was a small subset of the latter, a radical vanguard-in-waiting that never led the much broader and more diffuse antiwar alliance of which it was a part.

This simple truth has been obscured for three major reasons. First, relatively few young Americans ever participated in any form of public political protest during the wartime years; thus, most tended to dimly equate New Left and antiwar. This equation, second, was made a lot easier by prowar activists' tendency to brand all antiwar and deescalationist forces of whatever sort as "radical," partly out of genuine anger and partly as a strategy to undermine their opponents by lumping them all together as proponents of extremism and violence. The New Left, too, was usually only too anxious to gloss over very real differences between itself and the antiwar mainstream for purposes of its own, chiefly that it wished to use the antiwar movement as a recruitment base for itself. The result was that an inaccurate picture of a coherent and well-organized something called "the movement" was common then, and is still common now.

The movement, however, was a loose coalition, somewhat united on the goal of ending *direct* American involvement in the war as fast as possible but very divided on the means to achieve this end. To be antiwar could mean that you were a pacifist opposed to all wars. It could mean that you were an old-left communist or a member of the antiwar section of the Socialist Party of the United States. You might be a New Leftist. You could be a liberal deescalationist like those who supported senators William Fulbright, Eugene McCarthy, or Robert F. Kennedy. You could be a postadolescent anxious not to get yourself drafted. You could be somebody who thought, as recorded by Myra MacPherson, that protesting was a great way to "get laid, get high, and listen to some great rock [music]."[16] You could even be a grim street-corner realist who wanted out of the war for no grand intellectual reason at all, other than the compelling one that you no longer thought Vietnam worth the effort.

A stewpot full of differing motivations and viewpoints like this demonstrates the futility of relying on public opinion polls for very much, so far as antiwar opinion is concerned. It is true, for example, that the Tet offensive changed public views and that 60 percent of the citizenry polled shortly afterward agreed that it was a "mistake" for the United States to get directly involved in Vietnam in the first place. But almost the same percentage of people wanted America to take a "stronger stand" in Vietnam, even if it meant invading the North. Millions who were against the war were against it because they opposed the way the limited war was being fought. As Godfrey Hodgson put it with refreshing brevity, "Almost as many who thought it had been a mistake to get [directly] involved wanted to get out by escalating the war as wanted to get out by simply withdrawing." "Most of those," Hodgson continued, "who disliked the war disliked the peace movement even more." In 1968, more than half of those who thought that the United States should *immediately* and *totally* withdraw from Vietnam (a standard New Left demand) had *negative* opinions about the Vietnam war protesters among whom the New Left was numbered.[17]

Now we can see why it was that most of the antiwar vote that Senator Eugene McCarthy got in the New Hampshire primary was directed against LBJ for not doing enough rather than for doing too much. This "get serious or get out" opinion was supremely unradical. The majority of Americans who turned against Vietnam after Tet were never against the war on moral or ideological grounds. Their opposition to long-continued direct American military involvement in Vietnam was thoroughly pragmatic. They were against a war that looked less and less winnable the way it was being fought. "The swing of public opinion against the war," Hodgson concluded, "did not mean that the peace movement had succeeded in achieving its dream of mass conversion. It reflected the cannily realistic judgement that winning the war didn't seem worth the price." The accompanying view that the war was a "mess" or a "mistake," but not a "crime" or an exercise in failed imperialism flowed from this.[18]

Hard-eyed analysis like Hodgson's—published in 1976—was rare, because frenetic gush substituted for fact on all sides of the political equation. Besides, umbrella movements in America are often set afoot, organizationally speaking, by pragmatic characters who realize that it is a great deal easier to create a political movement based upon a loose agreement about an *end* (stopping direct U.S. involvement in the war as fast as possible) than one based on agreement about a particular *program* to achieve that end.

Curtis Gans, an antiwar activist who had helped found the SDS in 1961 and 1962, and who worked for Eugene McCarthy in 1968, argued succinctly and logically, in March 1967, against an effort to try to dump LBJ by forming an antiwar third party under the leadership of the Reverend Martin Luther King: "while it might be possible to get a broad consensus against the war," Gans said, "the snag was that you couldn't get such a consensus [for] any particular remedial program." In other words, getting too specific too soon would get you nowhere politically.[19]

Gans was absolutely right. That was why he ended up working for McCarthy. It was also why the antiwar movement was often studiously vague about exactly how to bring peace about, as vague as befits *any* movement seeking to recruit as much support in as short a period as possible. The National Moratorium Committee to End the War in Vietnam, established in 1969 to help organize marches on Washington that symbolized the antiwar movement in most participants' minds, exemplified the studiously vague strategy. "Moratorium" was a bit of legalese meaning "postponement" or "delay"—a postponement or delay, for example, of further military offensives (like bombing North Vietnam) while ways to end the war were decided upon. In other words, "Let's stop attacking, and think about what to do then": hardly a blazingly radical prescription.

Such calculated inexactness privately infuriated the immediate, total, and unilateral-withdrawal New Left even as it sought to recruit from the mass base that such a broader and blurrier mobilization strategy created. The all-inclusive National Moratorium Committee, for example, was counterpointed by the "Mobe" and the "New Mobe," National Mobilization Committees—organized by alliances-of-convenience of old-left communists and Trotskyists, New Left SDSers, and some socialists—to steer mass protest into more ideological, radical, and exclusivist directions. The Moratorium and the Mobilizations sponsored and even cosponsored marches, but they were rarely differentiated in the minds of even the hundreds of thousands of Americans who repeatedly marched upon Washington throughout 1968, 1969, and 1970 to protest the war. Inclusivity triumphed. A broad consensus to end the war existed within antiwar ranks, while no consensus for any particular remedial program was ever achieved.

New Leftists, for all of this, kept on trying to transform "antiwar" into "radical." They realized that the antiwar movement was chock-full of the college and university students they hoped to weld into a substitute proletariat. The young radicals even had a name for their strategy—not the "popular front" or "united front" of the old left of the 1930s, but "participatory democracy." Participatory democracy was both an organizing principle for New Left activity and an expression of its anti-institutionalist and anti-organizational bias. Here, again, embodied history is important. For if the Cold War was the New Left's longer-term formative experience, the civil-rights movement was its shorter-term one, especially for the TV-oriented mobilization of a television generation.

The civil-rights movement, during its heyday from 1961 until 1965, was the essence of participatory democracy, an all-inclusive alliance which ostracized none while seeking to convert all. Southern states and localities had denied blacks their basic constitutional rights to vote or to hold office, thereby excluding them from the political system, and had done this with federal connivance. Therefore, working within the system was impossible. Those systematically excluded took their protests to the streets in peaceful demonstrations aimed at proving their right to full and complete participation in the American Dream. Gandhian nonviolence was the rule. It was risky, especially when segregationist violence entered the picture. But Martin Luther King and others succeeded in turning worldly weakness into spiritual strength because civil rights meant only equality of political and social opportunity then (as it no longer did after 1965), because the means to achieve that equality were already spelled out in long-unenforced constitutional mandates, and because TV and print reporters were usually there to see just how unsubtly the powers-that-were in the South reacted to any effort to end American apartheid.

The media-oriented aspect of civil rights, before 1965, was immensely important. Civil-rights marches—masses of diverse people getting together to peacefully petition elected officials for a redress of grievances—was theater and practical politicking combined. It was the mobilization of power and recruitment of wider support via television. Southern black civil-rights leaders could not operate through government; a century of bitter history had shown that. Nor could they operate through established institutions of almost any sort. Apartheid was all-pervasive, to the point where the many members of the black bourgeoisie who were dependent upon white-controlled power structures were often notable for their absence from civil-rights activity. The black elite who did lead were those best protected from white institutional wrath: black ministers whose salaries were paid by their all-black congregations.

The nonviolent but direct confrontations that resulted from the efforts of hundreds of such courageous and capable preachers, and from the hundreds of thousands who followed them, was media-oriented from the start. Civil-rights demonstrations like the March on Washington of 1963 appealed over the heads of all the elite political, economic, educational, and other groups of the South—and most of those within the nation gener-

ally—straight to the people of the United States. The whole process occurred very largely on television.

If the civil-rights movement wasn't successful mass mobilization via TV,
nothing was. The most systematically excluded minority in American
society won in only a few years the enforcement of civil and political rights
first tendered a hundred years before. By 1965, the white economic and
political power structure in the southern third of the nation had been
outflanked, outmaneuvered, and outfought. It had been made irrelevant by
images of the reality of its exploitation relayed quickly around the nation
and around the world.

A better moral lesson for young radicals weaned on TV would have been
hard to imagine. They had grown up with civil rights. Well-known New
Left leaders had participated in early demonstrations and voter registration
drives in the South. The radicals, too, felt excluded from "the system," and
they realized, before some later succumbed to revolutionary visions, that
they too were a weak and isolated group within American society. It was
even easy—too easy—for young radicals to believe that they *were* blacks,
menaced by men with uniforms and guns, exploited by uncaring and
distant bureaucracies. The only way to replace weakness with strength,
most believed, was to take a page out of the civil-rights movement's book.
This meant working with other forces that had gotten people, and TV
cameras along with them, into the streets. Only as part of such a mass
participatory movement could the masses be appealed to over the heads
of all the warmongering leaders without working through any of those
leaders' institutions. Only as a vanguard within a larger antiwar coalition
that New Leftists often criticized did they have the faintest chance of
winning without having to cut organizational deals with the devil. Or so
they thought. So participatory democracy, and the antiwar movement
which exemplified it, it was.

The student radicals = blacks analogy paid psychic dividends, legitimized the use of television as a mobilization tool, and rationalized cooperative alliances of convenience within a diverse and diffuse antiwar movement. But the analogy also gave a hysterical ring to much of what the
radicals were saying about themselves and the society of which they were
a part, firmed up anti-institutional and anti-organizational attitudes within
the New Left itself, made radicalism too dependent upon televised demonstrations and too little dependent upon everything else, and led, very often,
to desperation, burnout, and ennui, both individual and collective. The
combined effect was to keep radicals relatively weak within antiwar organizations and make them notably unpopular outside of them. The same

New Left which burst on the national scene after Tet was in tatters just over two years later.

The hysterical element of the civil-rights model and the blacks = student radicals analogy was a result of sheer self-indulgence. Fellowship in suffering was all very well, but to argue, as New Leftists very often did, that antiwar youth were as "exploited by the system" as a southern black long accustomed to living at the bottom of the political and economic pyramid was to broaden the concept of suffering until it meant nothing— until it became mental masturbation, or the "radical chic" so mercilessly delineated in Tom Wolfe's essay of that name.[20] Radicals making such analogies forgot that blacks were usually fighting to *get into* a System that the radicals considered exploitive and unjust, including an educational system that most blacks deemed to be the surest path to upward mobility in an affluent society. The spiritual misery of a sophomore at Harvard or a graduate student at Berkeley simply was not on a par with the problems of a black farmer or laundry worker. To argue that it was was smug, silly, and infuriating to many.

Rash efforts at self-legitimization like this might have been avoidable if the New Left had not had such an anti-organizational bias. Radical youth too often forgot that the civil-rights marches they had seen on television were only a small part of the story. Supremely undramatic, untelevised, and constant politicking, joined to a thoroughgoing use of the judicial system (by, for example, the N.A.A.C.P.), were associated elements in black success. Without such a combination of forces, the civil-rights bills of 1964 and 1965 would have been impossible. Radicals also forgot that civil-rights activists like Martin Luther King had utilized a national *religious* network, mostly of black churches, to build and maintain their movement. The young radicals also forgot that the black congregations whose commitments had made victory possible had many local and undramatic things to do to keep themselves occupied and aware during the many interims between the occasional demonstrations that became national news.

Radicals generally forgot all this because most never particularly wanted to remember it most of the time. The New Left was new, after all, precisely because it was a reaction against what it perceived as a too-organized, hierarchical, disciplined, dogmatic, and intellectually constipated old left. The New Left sought to replace the incestuousness of such organizations with a wide open and wild blue yonder political style, A "hang loose" approach which often looked like a cross between a communitarian movement, a New England town meeting, and a university seminar. A major precept of participatory democracy, New Left style, was that organizations should be kept as decentralized and minimalistic as possible so that radicalism would be part of a human-scale, grass-roots, built-from-below movement which would not smother creativity under layers of bureaucracy, conformity, and dictation by leaders to led.

Organization, in short, was a trap, of which the true radical had to be careful. To structure, arrange, or systematize was to be part of the problem rather than part of the solution. *"Fidelismo,"* Jack Newfield called it, referring both to the New Left's anti-organizational bias and to the type of leader (Fidel Castro of Cuba) who appeared to be making new revolutions instead of getting hung up in debates about old ones. Learning by doing was the New Left style; and the best way to do it, radicals presumed, was to get together in informal networks to change the world, just as they thought the black civil-rights marchers had done. Or as the supposedly simple guerillas in Cuba's Sierra Maestre mountains had before they overthrew Fulgencio Batista, or the socialists in Israel, who had apparently fulfilled near-utopian goals by creating kibbutzim that made the deserts bloom. Social change, even revolution, was a matter of unconcentrated energy applied to problems in a decentralized fashion.[21]

The radicals of the New Left, therefore, often looked as much like Daniel Boone or Henry David Thoreau with hefty dollops of Robert Owen and the Utopian Socialists thrown in as they did like Karl Marx or V. I. Lenin. Their idea usually was that freedom had been made moribund by obedience and conformity to ever-larger private and public bureaucracies and that groups had to be determinedly antibureaucratic to survive as more than empty husks of departed dreams. Personal liberation was, therefore, supposed to go hand in hand with fundamental shifts in who had power and who didn't—so long, of course, as the "we" of the New Left didn't turn into the "they" who ruled the world through big organizations that spindled, folded, and mutilated people and stifled their freedoms.

This anti-organizational habit of mind was suicidal, especially for a political movement trying to operate in a large, federal, and diverse immigrant society. Fearful of being captured by the system, New Left activists never created a system of their own and didn't organize bureaucratically in a bureaucratic world. They tended to assume, instead, that change—radical or otherwise—was equivalent to marching across a television screen, especially if you could see yourself doing it later on a news program. Rebuilding the world began to look an awful lot like turning it into a sort of mega-university without required courses, grades, or teachers involved in the heavy joys of listening to their own voices booming out platitudes, and with lots and lots and lots of media. All, in this roseate vision, would be uncoerced energy devoted to determining who would get what and who would pay the bills for the getting.

When it came down to the details of giving and getting, however, the anti-institutional assumptions that were commonplace in young radical circles normally produced platitudes all too similar to those of a merely academic variety. So far as New Left economic thinking went, what ought to replace capitalism was a collection of small producer and consumer cooperatives held together by nothing: a decentralized economy of self-sufficient and egalitarian worlds-in-miniature, where communities of workers made and carried out decisions, microeconomic worlds without a macroeconomic capitalist marketplace to set priorities, prices, and incentives, allocate resources, or distribute income and wealth—*and* which did not require large state planning structures that replaced the market. The New Left preferred planning to marketplace capitalism, of course. Socialists of any sort almost always do. But New Left socialists wanted national planning without a bureaucracy, planning that would be undertaken on the grass roots and magically coordinated and synthesized without large-scale administrative agencies, and that would mediate fights about who got what and who didn't and enforce agreements.

As Swedish economist Assar Lindbeck argued after a visit to collegiate America in 1968–69, the New Left's decentralized economic arrangements looked more like Robinson Crusoe's island writ exceedingly large than like any modern industrial society of any description. Their socialism was of a utopian and communitarian variety, a socialism of the heart that aimed to restore justice to European industrial society and which had often moved to the American frontiers to attempt it. When the New Left believed that they, too, were going to build society anew and so avoid the private hierarchies of the marketplace or the public hierarchies of a planned economy, they were badly mistaken. For if, Lindbeck wrote, "economic decisions are not coordinated by markets, they have to be coordinated by central administrative bodies. New Left writers avoid the real problems of the economic system by not realizing that they have, in reality, to choose between markets and centralized administrative procedures, or various combinations of these two methods."[22]

Lindbeck, however, was preaching to the winds. He represented a society where Social Democrats had administered a modern economy for fifty years, consciously planning and just as consciously keeping the market intact. He was speaking, however, to Americans who very often didn't recognize where marketplace criteria had been fully or partially replaced in their own economy; and to a mostly student New Left unencumbered with responsibility for administering anything. Warnings that the world's largest economy couldn't be run like a collection of kibbutzim, without large-scale planning bureaucracies, without markets, or without any substantive ideas about how to mix planning and markets got nowhere fast. Most New Leftists continued to assume, when they thought about it at all, that the economy should be like an idealized college faculty, a firmly pre-industrial enclave within an industrial society, a medieval guild with lifetime tenure and with castes of workers able to control the pace, duration, and extent of their labor because their "tools" were still theirs, and located between their ears. The New Left too often wanted a well-protected world whose members mostly didn't know and mostly didn't care how somebody else paid the bills and minded the store for them. Here, indeed, was its way to avoid the organizational trap, to ignore the vexing questions of scarcity and private ownership versus allocations of public resources. Assume the world could be a university. Assume neomedieval guilds. Assume that income and wealth redistribution would only rarely be downward, rarely enough so that the rich didn't include one's self. Then economic questions would not involve hierarchies or rules but, instead, would consist only of egalitarian voluntarism. Participatory democracy was what the New Left and the antiwar coalition were mostly all about.

Burnout, however, was also what the two movements were all about. Participatory intensities, which arose and peaked quickly within the ranks of postadolescent collegians, receded equally quickly—so quickly that mass antiwar protest of *any* kind became rare after the middle of 1970.

## Mass Protest Ebbs Away

The New Left was never more than a small proportion of antiwar ranks, and most antiwar protest was not equatable with revolution of a political or economic nature. "The movement" remained a disparate alliance whose members were never united by any particular program to achieve the goal all desired: the ending of the American war in Vietnam.[23]

Reality, however, was obscured by the rhetoric and imagery of events. The enemies of the antiwar effort made too much of it because of their fears, while its friends made too much of it because of their hopes. A television-based mobilization strategy and the visual drama of mass antiwar marches that aped civil-rights marches of preceding years made excellent political theater. Marches called attention to the existence of a mass movement in concrete, dramatic, and visual terms—television terms. Media attention, in turn, inflated the perceived size and importance of the antiwar coalition as a whole and of the New Left within that coalition. The biggest posters in antiwar marches were often those carried by radicals. The minority-within-a-minority in New Left ranks whose True Believer Marxist-Leninism assumed a Chinese Maoist direction (e.g., the Progressive Labor Party faction within the SDS) or a Trotskyist one (e.g., the Socialist Workers Party–Young Socialist Alliance) passed out leaflets to all explaining what any demonstration was really, *really* all about. Marxist, Leninist, and Maoist sectaries tended to crowd next to speakers' podiums at protests—especially national ones held in Washington—and fill the air with Vietcong flags and staccato shouts of "Ho, Ho, Ho Chi Minh, N.L.F. [National Liberation Front, the official title of the Vietcong] is gonna win!" and the flags and shouts were choreographed to obtain maximum attention from TV cameras and voice recorders. No matter that they almost never attracted the crowds located behind them.

These masses of the antiwar ranks were—N.L.F. flags and Ho Chi Minh chants to the contrary—about as cataclysm-and-convulsion-oriented as senators Fulbright, McCarthy, and Robert Kennedy were, and about as Marxist as mashed potatoes. The large majority of those who marched and demonstrated throughout the three-year heyday of antiwar protest wanted the United States out of direct military involvement in Indochina, but they were often prepared to support good-faith efforts to accomplish that end by gradual progress toward a negotiated settlement of the war. Time (but not too much) and continued support for Saigon (but not if it involved American men) were generally acceptable to them.

"End the war," then, mostly meant ending the American portion of a war in Vietnam. Richard Nixon came into office saying he intended to accomplish this. Antiwar moderates, however, had no more faith in Nixon than they had in Hubert Humphrey or Lyndon Johnson. All were perceived as unreconstructed Cold Warriors with naught but rhetorical commitment to U.S. military withdrawal or peace. Nixon, in fact, struck antiwar protesters of all types as just another old used-up man who would blow up anyone who got in his way, including themselves.

Nixon, once he assumed the presidency in January 1969, did little to seek to split moderates from radicals within the antiwar alliance during the crucial early months of his administration. Recent and wrenching events had pushed hefty numbers of liberals into moderate antiwar ranks and antiwar moderates toward occasional cooperation with their radical opposite numbers. Nixon did nothing to undermine this "hang together, or we will most assuredly hang separately" cooperation based on fear. In fact, he started off by adding to his antiwar problems by equating moderates who saw Vietnam as a mistake or a mess with radicals who viewed it as a premeditated imperialist crime. Vice President Agnew did the dirty work early in 1969, by expounding about "radical liberals," radicals in moderate's clothing who intended to rend and tear at America with bloodthirsty and unpatriotic vengeance.[24]

Conservative equations of antiwar moderates with Leninist revolutionaries had some basis. Nixon believed that hypocritical liberals had ineptly waged war and then started to blame him for their failure—and for not immediately withdrawing—once he became president. So he smeared them as they sometimes smeared him, using guilt-by-association techniques that conservatives had found congenial in the past. Not all was artifice. Nixon genuinely believed that radicals, operating through front organizations such as the New Mobe, would beguile naïve liberals into extremism. Hyperthyroid speculations, courtesy of the FBI and the military intelligence services, and COINTELPRO, a spying and political sabotage program launched against New Left organizations in 1968, fueled the White House's grimmer assumptions. They also resolutely ignored realities like the inability of the communists and Trotskyists (who used "front" tactics repeatedly) to either attract or retain large numbers of new members at any time during the Vietnam era. Also underestimated was the organizational harm being done by the infantile ultraleftist fantasies and the internal sectarian splits burgeoning within the SDS.[25]

But even antiwar moderates who didn't marry lunacy to Lenin or debate the capitalist world to death on college campuses were, on practical political levels, dangerous to Nixon's policy. Richard Nixon came into office a deeply divided man. He wanted to get the United States out of a limited war gone wrong (if only to protect more important American interests elsewhere), on the one hand. And he wanted to blast stubborn Hanoi communists into atoms, on the other hand (because Hanoi would not, until very late in the game, make the compromises that he wanted them to make to buy Washington out—rather than force it out—of Vietnam). Nixon never resolved this ambivalence in his mind or that of his administration. Instead, he squared the circle by escalating and deescalating the U.S. war in Southeast Asia simultaneously, using the "Men Out, Machines In" strategy discussed in Part Two. Nixon hoped that a carrot-and-stick combination could allow a withdrawal that nobody—least of all the Kremlin— would perceive as a surrender.

The problem with Nixon's dualistic Vietnam strategy was summarized in a phrase often heard in Vietnam and America after 1969: "Who wants to be the last man to die for a mistake?" Once deescalation of the highest-profile ground war with the highest U.S. casualties began, the desire to withdraw all American forces quickly gathered force; and the riskier a two-pronged escalate-deescalate strategy became. And here was precisely where the moderate antiwar opposition *was* most dangerous and discomfiting to Nixon. The moderates, goodly numbers of whom had been sturdy Cold War liberals before Tet, were not radical. They were talking about moratorium, bombing halt, withdrawal, and negotiated settlement, but they also wanted all U.S. military forces out fast. They demanded this of a president who had begun a supersecret bombing of Cambodia just after entering office and who was secretly threatening Hanoi with a thermonuclear holocaust by the summer of 1969. His secret acts indicated just how tough Nixon intended to be in the air while the first detachments of U.S. ground troops were being withdrawn that same year. Nixon didn't want to be crowded by the moderates, and so he sought to limit their popular influence by branding them as closet extremists. They were people, said Spiro Agnew, who burned the American flag before breakfast and went on to spit on returning Vietnam veterans in the afternoon.[26]

Then Nixon got smarter, or some of his people did, because the lump-them-all-together red-baiting strategy angered many of the moderates. It also produced, in October and November 1969, the two largest demonstrations in U.S. history in Washington. During one, a small fracas vainly organized by a Maoist SDS faction outside of the massive locked doors of the Justice Department building to heighten the contradictions in the capitalist system (i.e., produce violent scenes that looked bad on television) reminded then U.S. Attorney General John Mitchell of a scene straight out of the Russian Revolution.

The scene, however, had more to do with Laurel and Hardy than it did with Lenin. Intelligent observers recognized this when, following a few theatrical shouts and poundings, detachments of Washington, D.C., police arrived on motor scooters, and the radical vanguard speedily decamped. The rest of the crowd followed shortly afterward, when tear gas clouded the atmosphere. So far as the revolution was concerned, it was just another day's work for the Washington cops and the crowd ended up running in the wrong direction.[27]

Following its initial right-wing frenzy and lots colder and more germane political calculation besides, therefore, the Nixon administration changed direction. It began to split moderate from radical within the antiwar coalition and it throttled relatively vulnerable radical groups. The splitting began in December 1969 with the "draft lottery." Convinced—now—that most antiwar demonstrators were young people anxious, above all, not to get themselves put at risk in war, Nixon acted on the basis of that theory, which worked wonders. Two-thirds of the eligible draft-age males were exempted from the threat of future Vietnam (or other) military service by the lottery and also decisively separated, in personal interests, from the remaining third, as any collegian who remembers that December evening draw on television can recall. Those who got lottery numbers about 1 to 60 (and, thus, almost-sure-to-go-after-graduation status) tended to walk off alone for a bit of very serious thinking, but the majority tended to remain clustered around the TV to whoop it up about their good fortune.

Simultaneously, bureaucratic and legislative moves got under way to replace the draft with the All Volunteer Army, a process Congress completed in 1973 to the hosannas of antiwar liberals, most collegians of all political persuasions, and even most of the military brass (whose increasingly high-technology approach to waging war seemed to require a smaller professional army, rather than a larger and largely nonprofessional one).

Meanwhile, as more exemptions from military service to collegians were distributed wholesale, repression became fierce. COINTELPRO moved beyond spying to concentrate upon agent provocateur activity. Operatives were planted to advocate or initiate violent activity and sway others to join in or follow along. Radicals thus crossed the legal dividing line between advocating something when no "clear and present danger" of riot existed and advocating or doing something when it did. Thus, more and more of them ended up in jail.

Legal distinctions were not so important in dealing with the Black Panthers. Their mixture of racism, violence, radical posturing, and oddball ideological mix of Mao Tse-tung, Marx, and black separatism (ghettos in the United States were deemed to be minority outposts of a nonwhite world that would one day rise up and overthrow its Caucasian oppressors) made them unpopular with blacks and absolutely hated by all others. Moves against the Panthers started well before Nixon reached the White House—in 1967, in fact. But in 1969 and 1970, the FBI and urban police forces went after the Panthers with a vengeance: imprisoning leaders, shooting others in suspicious circumstances, and fracturing the tiny membership of the organization into pussycat quiescence. The Panthers helped by killing each other as fast or faster than the police were killing them.[28]

Quiescence was also exacted from the three major commercial television networks. Each was discreetly informed that it did not pay to anger a president who could launch antitrust investigations against commercial broadcasters, hold up station license renewals, and otherwise complicate corporate existence in expensive ways. Tremors in the boardrooms followed. Thus, no network provided live coverage of the largest-ever antiwar marches of October and November 1969. TV coverage of continuing military activity by U.S. forces in Vietnam, Cambodia, and Laos diminished greatly after late 1969. That the United States was on its way out of Vietnam became the Good News story henceforth. In 1970, Walter Cronkite, the avuncular and respected anchor of the CBS Evening News, allowed that "the industry as a whole has been intimidated." He was absolutely right.[29]

As the television coverage upon which the New Left and the broader antiwar movement had pinned so much of its mobilization efforts dried up, moderates and radicals alike added to their troubles by revolutionary posturing, sectarian vendettas, and whining responses to violence directed against them. The Kent State University shootings of May 1970 were symbolic of the trend, and they went a long way toward explaining why the protest against Nixon's decision to invade eastern Cambodia with American ground troops was also the last large national upsurge of collegiate antiwar unrest.

Had Cambodia been a Saigon, rather than a Washington, operation, the final wave of moderate antiwar protest might not have risen and crested at all. Vietnamization, the draft lottery, and the "Men Out, Machines In" strategy had all removed much of the personal threat faced by most collegians. The TV network intimidation had decreased the usefulness of mass demonstrations as a recruitment and organizing device. The National Moratorium Committee closed its national office in Washington, D.C., just before the Cambodian "incursion" occurred.

But Cambodia was a largely *American* operation, and so posed the threat that U.S. ground forces were being withdrawn from Vietnam only to begin fighting another war right next door. Even self-interested collegians (and there were many of those) had reasons for protest, and protest they did, until Kent State reminded them that colleges and universities were special safe places for special people only so long as the larger society accepted (or chose not to dispute) that traditional view of matters academic. The four dead, one crippled for life, and twenty wounded from several quick volleys of bullets from the national guard at Kent State became an almost instantaneous national trauma, in collegiate circles, precisely because it demonstrated that conservative state governors, including James Rhodes of Ohio and Ronald Reagan of California, intended to use force to repress disturbances at state university campuses and that private schools might well be next on the list.

Levels of college and university dissent sagged accordingly. Elite collegians were special and they knew it. So did the administrators who ran their schools. They were special on political, military, sexual, and drug-related grounds, grounds that would cause wholesale anxiety if the laws, statutes, and draft regulations of the Real World were ever invoked. Kent State stripped away the ivory tower's assumptions that its special status would likely be continued.

Kent State's small-scale human tragedy was also traumatic because it demonstrated the hot-shot, self-righteous, and smug elements of all-too-much college-based moderate and radical antiwar protest. These attributes existed because collegians rarely built bridges to local groups (such as churches or unions) whose membership they often gratuitously assumed to be reactionary. Nor were student antiwar moderates or radicals ever willing to renounce their 2-S deferments in more than tiny numbers. Pacifists, not SDSers, were the collegians most willing to assume such real-world risks and to go to prison for draft resistance if necessary.

Here, some data, courtesy of Lawrence Baskir, William A. Straus, and Myra MacPherson, demonstrate just how prone the collegiate antiwar movement was to *avoid* the war rather than *resist* it. Throughout the war, male collegians tended to oppose the war by: (1) seeking medical or psychiatric exemptions from military service; (2) seeking "conscientious objector" (pacifist) status; (3) committing indictable offenses like burning their draft cards or failing to show up for draft physicals or military inductions; and (4) choosing exile in foreign nations—especially Canada—in preference to military service. Noncollegians, for their part, usually registered their discontent by never registering for the draft, by receiving less-than-honorable discharges from the military, or by deserting. The collegians' techniques were different because they knew the arcana of draft regulations better than their noncollegiate peers. The students were also almost always denied the opportunity to refuse to register for the draft in the first place because the law required all colleges and universities to regularly report all draft-eligible students' academic status to their local draft boards.

Avoiders were by far the largest antiwar group among collegians. Numbers are a guesstimate at best, but a minimum of several million young men, mostly upper-middle class, probably made use of the system to avoid military service by flooding into physicians', psychiatrists', and psychologists' offices with tales of woe. A far smaller number, 172,000 (of whom not all were collegians) received conscientious objector status. A still smaller number, 60,000, chose exile. And a yet more modest 3,500 (of 25,000 indicted for draft offenses) went to prison rather than go into the military. One-third of this last group were Quakers, Black Muslims, or Jehovah's Witnesses. The noncollegians, meanwhile, accounted for most of the 250,000 who never registered for the draft in the first place, the

93,500 deserters, and the 790,000 with other-than-honorable military discharges.

If, now, we add up all of the pacifists, exiles, indicted draft offenders, prisoners, deserters, nonregistrants, and less-than-honorably discharged, and assume that *all* paid a personal price (or, as in the case of the nonregistrants, faced reduced employment opportunities for evading the law), we come up with some humbling figures. First, only about 5 percent (1.4 of 27 million) draft-eligible men in America during the American war in Vietnam resisted the war in *any* major way at *any* time. Second, a larger group of several million, mostly upper-class and collegian Americans, confined their opposition to the war to occasional marches and avoiding military service in some fashion (e.g., medical and psychiatric deferments) that did not require them to fight authority but only to slip past it, using the draft's own rules and exceptions to do so.[30]

Such is not the stuff of which revolutions or resilient social reform movements are made. Avoiders often saw themselves as resistors, but people have to put themselves and their interests on the line. They have to take big risks for moral politics; as black civil-rights marchers in the American South usually did and as collegiate antiwar demonstrators usually didn't. Avoiding the draft because you knew a cooperative physician, going to an antiwar rally for reasons that were often miscellaneous, talking about what a wonderful world it would be if there were no wars and everybody was as good and true as yourself, or simply not wanting to get shot at was not often equatable with courage, with taking a stand and accepting real risks when you did so.

That was, however, what Kent State was all about, real-world risks that couldn't be eased around. That was what made Kent State so scary for many collegians who had never seen violence except on television, kids who had always "talked out difficulties" and who had never felt, and rarely even feared, the force of paternal fists or maternal broomsticks, young people who found it too hard to conceive that very large numbers of other Americans assumed that every generation had "its war" and that willingness to go to war was a badge of manhood.

Putting oneself on the line in demonstrations that looked too dangerous for comfort, then, was not what college and university life was all about, and most especially not after Kent State. "The masses like guts," Charles Macomb Flandrau wrote of his long-ago Harvard days, "while the upper classes prefer expression."[31] After Kent State, political guts decreased markedly and expression assumed a higher and higher profile—the "counterculture" or "a search for new life styles," its supporters called it. "Sex 'n Drugs 'n Rock 'n Roll," said the cynics of a humorous bent. "Solipsism run amok," snarled those appalled by how easily many acted on the "Do Your Own Thing" assumption that whatever they wanted was, therefore, right. "Chaos," screamed innumerable conservatives.

What the counterculture mostly was was a habit of mind which was upper-class self-expression personified—a habit of mind which sought to *be* rather than to *do*, one which assumed affluence, and one which ignored institutions entirely. The counterculture was "cultural revolution" of a sort. It had been ever since it had assumed a high national profile by the middle of 1967. But it was *also* one that was basically private and between-the-ears. Private dissent did nothing to change power relations (except in the male-female realm) in the wider society. It also did nothing to stop the American—or other—wars in Vietnam, because the salvation it sought was personal, not social.[32]

A personalized path to salvation it was, however, especially after Kent State. Youthful narcissism flowered. Self-involvement was even increased by the comparative technological advantages of the Sixties Generation which made them the peculiar bearers of the Sexual Revolution. Narcissism, self-expression, and avoidance, however, were not nearly enough when discussion turned into violence, as it had at Kent State and as it did several days later when a large crowd gathered at the mayor's mansion in New York City to demand that the American flag flying there be lowered to half-staff to mourn the slain students of Kent State. Shortly after the demand was acceded to and the flag lowered, several hundred construction workers at a nearby building project heard about what was going on and got mad. Some picked up clubs, and all pushed through the crowd to demand—equally successfully—that the flag be restored to the top of the flagpole. Kent State was no tragedy to them; punks had just got some of what they deserved.

Now another traumatic event was assumed to have occurred, and an opprobrious phrase entered the language: "hard hat," from the protective helmets worn by all construction workers on site. The term was redolent with fear of an aggressive, working-class backlash that many collegians, intellectuals, Jews, and blacks found particularly threatening. "Hard hat fascism," histrionic academics worried at one another, was only a matter of time, especially after Nixon, scenting a symbolic event, promptly invited New York City construction-union representatives to the White House, where the president was presented with his own hard hat in front of a bevy of photographers.

Here, then, was put up or shut up expressed in symbolic terms. Black civil-rights activists had always had far more violence to contend with. Avoidance, however, meant continued exclusion, subservience, discrimination, and poverty for many southern blacks. Avoidance, for the much more comfortable and protected collegians, produced utterly different results: safety, continued affluence, career opportunity, and the restoration of the university as a special and protected postadolescent world, a world where miracles of modern chemistry—and modern birth control—could be savored.

Not surprisingly, then, most of the collegiate antiwar left lapsed into quiescence after Kent State. The young radicals who sought to bond such favored people into a substitute proletariat, meanwhile, self-destructed, a fact which only further accelerated the decline of antiwar protest.

## The New Left Commits Suicide

The New Left faced difficult tasks after Richard Nixon assumed the presidency and would have had trouble fighting off COINTELPRO's dirty tricks and simultaneous efforts to isolate the radicals from the moderates within a loose antiwar coalition. The difficult was turned into the impossible when the New Left promptly, figuratively, and sometimes literally blew itself to bits. By late 1969, the ideological and organizational coherence of the New Left approximated that of a cauldron into which somebody had thrown an assortment of boa constrictors, rabbits, mice, wolverines, and camels by way of experiment. In other words, it was a howling, thumping, heaving, sad, silly mess.

How such slapstick came to be is a tale of children of affluence succumbing to apocalyptic visions and roaring off into the political outback in search of some infallible lever of change, meanwhile becoming more and more dogmatic, hypertensive, sect-ridden, and full to the brim with rhetoric and abstractions. All these never-never oddities were precisely those that C. Wright Mills had wisely warned New Leftists against at the very beginning of their radical effort in 1962. "Infantile ultra-leftism," these New Left vaults into the revolutionary-millennium were called in Leninist lingo, or "putschism," in another abstruse socialist phrase.[33]

The internal characteristics of the New Left which made such behavior possible were very many. To call the New Left a "movement," in fact, was accurate more as an impulse or thrust of energy than as a description of a structure of thought or action. Too much organization was a trap, after all, and working through the institutional channels of the system was even more of a trap, so far as most young radicals were concerned. The anti-organizational bias that limited the New Left's ability to reach out to a wider clientèle rebounded to destroy its own political base. It started with a utopianism that led young radicals to ignore the differences between *revolutionary* and *evolutionary* approaches, between socialism of the ballot and socialism of the bullet.

The New Left believed it could avoid a hundred years of suspicion and fifty years of ideological conflict by ignoring the differences between evolutionary and revolutionary, between democratic and democratic central-ist, and between advocates of the ballot and advocates of the bullet. The SDS let everybody in, thereby internalizing a conflict that could have been kept external, and it ended up an organization like unto a cross between a rhinoceros and a kangaroo.

So long as youthful attention was directed overseas, the difference be-tween ballots and bullets advocates didn't seem to matter much. There was a war on, and most younger radicals saw Vietnam as equivalent to the Second World War, in terms of forming united fronts against common enemies. Their immediate goal was to stop the American war in Vietnam and further military or economic support for the Saigon regime. Vietnam, where that war was, had never been democratic before and wasn't demo-cratic then. A conflict had begun, against French imperialism, and con-tinued against American imperialism. The distinction between ballots and bullets in Vietnam didn't mean a lot to most young radicals. The simple fact was that ballots don't stop civil wars, and bullets do.

Then, however, the war "came home" for the New Left following the 1968 election. As it did, the distinctions between ballots and bullets, and violent confrontation and nonviolent protest increasingly mattered, and tore the fragile unity of radical organizations apart. The disintegration was well under way by June 1968. The SDS's national convention at Michigan State University resembled a Hollywood set for a mini-epic on Marxist–Leninist–Stalinist–Maoist–Ho Chi Minh–Castroite Old Time Religion. The young fogeys of the old left past were back in force, by virtue of the influence of the Maoist Progressive Labor faction, a sect which had entered SDS en bloc in 1966 after being expelled from the Communist Party, U.S.A. for being pro-Chinese rather than pro-Soviet.

Between June 1968 and December 1969, the SDS's Old Time Religion became religious war.[34] Democratic Socialist fought revolutionary; revolu-tionary Maoist fought Trotskyite "wrecker"; Stalinist struggled with Leni-nist; and the Weatherman faction of the by now faction-happy SDS vaulted off into the utopian empyrean by heightening the contradictions in the imperialist system with explosives. What the Weathermen and

Weatherwomen of the Weather Underground mostly wafted into the heavens was themselves, for instance, in a premature detonation of a bomb factory in an exclusive New York City townhouse in March 1970. This, together with the destruction of a toilet in the Capitol Building in Washington, D.C., about a year later, was the finest hour of the would-be revolutionary vanguards.

Most Americans, antiwar, prowar, or turned off, no longer gave a damn. Rhetoric about Revolutionary Suicide and Destroying Monster Amerika seemed nonsensical. Not least in 1970, the year of the first large-scale Vietnamization of the ground war, the first wholesale draft-lottery exemptions, the invasion of Cambodia, the Kent State aftermath, and the beginning of an economic recession which brought an end to the decade of affluence upon which much of the upwardly mobile worldview of post-adolescent collegians was based. A New Left that had started out as an all-inclusive search for a substitute proletariat had, during the four short years from 1965 to 1969, recruited few, retained fewer, and had pulled the plug on itself at precisely the time that it began to face the fact that it was irrelevant to most of the political currents roiling through the country during and after the 1968 election.

The New Left's banzai charge into nowhere provided a wonderful instance of a truth coined by Isaac Asimov: "The falsely dramatic drives out the truly dull."[35] Outer-space revolutionary posturing provided instantaneous celebrity for that small minority of collegians who liked to think of themselves as hardened Leninist revolutionary operators in a violent world, especially if they did not have to learn how to operate a rifle to do so. Here, again, was a television generation's belief that image was reality, that no one needed to worry about the grubby realities of organization or the power that organization can bring.

False dramatics was also a reason for the decline of the antiwar protest as a whole. After 1970, the Movement never went anywhere—into, for example, a *mass civil disobedience* stage à la Mohandas Karamchand Gandhi, Martin Luther King, and civil rights in the American South. Nonviolent sit-ins there were, but they were rare phenomena carried on by far too few to make them effective. Washington, in April and May 1971, saw the two largest and best-organized of these events. The first was the unauthorized protest of several thousand members of the Vietnam Veterans against the War (V.V.A.W.). The vets testified and lobbied against U.S. war policy in Congress and staged demonstrations at the White House during which some ex-soldiers renounced their Vietnam decorations by the stark procedure of heaving them over well-locked gates. Nobody interfered with the V.V.A.W. Their marches were headed by cripples in wheelchairs such as

Ron Kovic, author of a searing personal memoir of the war. Jonathan Schell summarized it: "They, virtually alone among Americans, had to resolve within themselves the full dilemma posed by the Indo-China war . . ." to travel the "entire measureless distance" between guilt and redemption, in a society full of others who were far-too-short on direct experience and all-too-long on abstract moralistic posturings.[36]

The embodied personal tragedies of the V.V.A.W. were followed, a month later, by the May Day Tribe, about forty thousand demonstrators who arrived in Washington determined to "shut D.C. down" by lying in the streets and engaging in other forms of passive resistance. Ten thousand of these people were arrested, warehoused in an empty football stadium, and shortly thereafter released by the courts. Richard Nixon received half-hourly reports during a fear-ridden period that he advertised to the nation as a "normal business day." We Shall Return! vowed May Day spokesmen. In a month, in fact.

But June came with no renewed demonstrations. And the V.V.A.W., having seized the attention of the nation once, also faded away following an occupation of the Statue of Liberty a few months later. A young man from Maine who had returned from a year's voluntary exile in Canada in June 1971 to participate in the promised second wave of mass civil disobedience was looking for what no longer existed. Ennui and enervation reigned everywhere—even at Antioch, the young man's alma mater, the only college or university in the nation selected for "universal coverage" by the FBI-run COINTELPRO program. In mid-1971, the antiwar movement, like the New Left before it, was a burnt out case.

## Illusions and Realities in Retrospect

Few cared, in 1971 or even 1968, about what was happening in Vietnam. Americans cared, instead, about what was happening to *America* and, more particularly, to *them.* They cared about what they wanted other people to do for them: by waging war, waging peace, negotiating chimerical settlements, or assuring the nation (as President Gerald R. Ford eventually did) that national amnesia was the best way to put Vietnam behind us. The Vietnam War, ironically, was never about the Vietnamese, not so far as most Americans of *all* political persuasions were ever concerned. It was about Americans, about America's image of itself, and about the ideological universalisms on which those images are based. Thus the view, currently renascent, that the United States failed to win in Vietnam only because of political timidity or wrongheadedness at home. "We" could have won, and almost as easily as the War Managers thought we were going to before the Tet offensive—if only U.S. forces had the shackles taken off and there had been a lot less shilly-shallying and effete, impudent intellectual snobbery on television.

The view is comforting. It is another version of a logic that Thucydides the Athenian put in the mouth of one of his dramatis personae arguing for draconian punishment of a rebellious Athenian ally in 427 B.C. "[T]he three failings most fatal to empire," Thucydides had it then, were "pity, sentiment, and indulgence."[37]

But there is another mistake, the name for which also comes down to us from Classical Greece. It is hubris. The Vietnam War was a Vietnamese war, first and last and all the time. Americans waltzed into the middle of a civil war, insisted that a foreign invasion was also going on, and assumed that they were so powerful that they didn't need to know anything about those Vietnamese allied or opposed to them. A quick limited war against the foreign invaders would destroy the opposition and teach the friendlies to get their act together on the American plan. That would be that.

That was nonsense. They are a peculiar sort of fool who believe their own lies, yet that is precisely what most Americans did. They are also an odd kind of fool who think they have all the answers, when they aren't usually even asking the right questions. This, too, was America's Vietnam experience.

The New Left, meanwhile, had different prescriptions, most of which were equally irrelevant to what was actually happening in Vietnam. *Fidelismo* was thrown against megalomaniacal Cold Warrior assumptions, and the Good Guys and Bad Guys roles were reversed. The assumption was still that politics was a simple bipolar contest between right and wrong, a kind of grand ideological football game rather than a many-sided struggle whose contestants were using Western ideas to try to solve some of the most pressing problems of ancient—and non-Western—societies.

By the time Marxist-Leninism à la Hanoi triumphed and the inevitable postwar terror, flight, and expulsion began, there were precious few winners left in Vietnam, or in America, either. The grand ideological assumptions of New Leftist and Cold Warrior alike had been humbled by events and by their own ineptitude and hauteur.

What was left was a heritage of distrust, distrust both of glowing and universalistic claims to virtue made by a government that had failed in another limited war in Asia and pronouncements made by a New Left or a much larger antiwar movement which had done relatively little to stop that war. Vietnam, increasing numbers of people assumed, had been a mistake, as opposed to either a crime or a failed crusade: a mistake because it had never been worth the lives of Americans in the first place.[38]

The list of American casualties in Vietnam, however, was not complete, not yet. The war had already driven one overwhelmingly elected U.S. president out of office and out of power in 1968. And as Richard Milhous Nixon geared himself up for the 1972 reelection campaign he was to win overwhelmingly against the hapless George McGovern, and put the final touches upon the phony peace which accompanied the later stages of the withdrawal of U.S. ground forces from Vietnam, he made a series of fatal missteps which doomed him as well—a "third-rate burglary," a cover-up, and much, much more. We discuss Watergate in the next part of this book.

# PART FOUR

# WATERGATE

## History as Kaleidoscope

It is easy to enunciate brittle profundities about Watergate. Americans who lived through over two years worth of break-ins, cover-ups, hearings, resignations, and on- and off-camera debates know that this political trial of a president and his closest associates mattered. We know it proved something about Richard Nixon, presidential power, government in general, and the laws upon which this nation is dependent. When it comes to being precise, however, eloquence often evaporates into knee-jerk phrases: "Nixon is a crook"; "No one is above the law"; "Nixon got railroaded"; "All politicians are only out for themselves"; and so forth.

This imprecision is hardly surprising. Watergate was a many-sided skirmish that roiled into a full-scale war. As combat proliferated, utterly ambitious people found their careers in danger and fought to protect them. Loyalties were strained or broken by fear; alliances were formed and re-formed; associates were destroyed and replaced; and layers of rhetoric, lies, evasions, ad hominem abuse, guesstimation, press leaks, and instantaneous analysis obscured the landscape.

It was, to millions of concerned Americans, just one damned thing after another—surprises galore, a wildly burgeoning cast of characters, crisis rhetoric, and a review of basic principles about as easy to keep straight as a catalog of volcanoes on Mars or gaseous layers of Neptune. Watergate certainly wasn't the intellectualized government of political-science text-books. It was a soap opera come to life, with a plot that was like the layers of an onion.

Watergate produced a result which Vietnam never had. The war made the United States look ineffective and divided, but Watergate made America look ridiculous in the eyes of its own people. The leaders often appeared to be buffoons, and the led hedged their political loyalties accordingly. The view that "government is the problem" grew. Washington looked as illegitimate and pathetic as it did misguided or criminal. The process—full of fits, starts, alarms, and diversions—took place in five major stages, which are summarized here and will be discussed in detail later.

An initial judicial and journalistic stage of the Watergate investigation lasted for eleven months, from June 1972 to May 1973. Then, during May, June, and July, the first stage of the political trial commenced before the Senate Watergate Committee. Once John Dean and Alexander Butterfield did so much to legitimize the Watergate investigation and to put the criminal spotlight on Richard Nixon himself, a second judicial and journalistic struggle took place from July to October 1973. At issue was whether the courts could gain custody of the Watergate tapes. After the first special prosecutor was fired for his legal troubles in October, and continuing on until April 1974, political, judicial, and journalistic opposition gradually, and sometimes hesitantly, converged on the White House. Finally, from April to August 1974, this process of convergence had gone far enough so that the second and last stage of the political trial of Watergate drove Nixon from the presidency.

By the end, almost nobody felt triumphant and almost everybody was emotionally drained. Watergate, in this important sense, marked a watershed in American innocence. It symbolized the end of three decades when Americans could assume, in bland arrogance, that they were a special, powerful, and uniquely favored nation existing outside of history. If there was one thing that everybody, from Richard Milhous Nixon himself to the most thorough Nixon-hater, agreed with after two-and-one-third years of repeatedly failed cover-up, it was this maxim from La Rochefoucauld: "Almost all our failings are more pardonable than the means we use to hide them."[1] The adage captured the mood of unflattering self-awareness that characterized the period.

Watergate was a twenty-seven-month struggle during which all the unsettling factors of the Anxious Years previously and separately discussed in this book flowed together, and during which America's constitutional system of checks and balances was faced with its most divisive and overt challenges since the Depression decade of the 1930s. In the process of attempting to resolve the conflict about the proper scope of presidential, congressional, and judicial power in the United States, the judges, legislators, and executive branch officials—with assists from investigative journalists—were faced with the fact that presidential power had vastly increased during the Cold War which had characterized United States foreign policy since the end of the Second World War. Watergate had flowed from Vietnam and from the polarized domestic politics the failed American war in Indochina had induced.

It was now up to the Congress and the courts to determine how far to scale back executive privileges and the assumptions about national security that rationalized so many of those privileges. The process was daunting and threatening. Courts and Congress alike proceeded carefully and often hesitantly. Had Richard Nixon not made the incredible error of tape-recording his own conversations, and then of needlessly alienating many of his own congressional allies—as, for example, by claiming a right to impound funds—it is more than likely that he would have survived Watergate and that only a relatively small number of deniable intermediaries would have been punished for activities in which he was fully implicated.

The system worked, in the end, but only just. The process was prolonged, often calculatedly complicated, and full of fits and starts, any one of which, given different circumstances, could have marked an end to the ongoing criminal and political investigations. Even so, the investigations did not coalesce until almost two years after the break-in and the cover-up.

To comprehend what happened and why, and to discuss the realities as opposed to the images of present-day political power in America, we will depart somewhat from the organizational scheme of the preceding two parts of the book and return to the approach used in Part One. Matters will be discussed topically, but along a clear chronological line. This is so the reader will better understand that a great deal of the complexity of Watergate resulted from the fact that the Congress and courts evaded their constitutional responsibilities as often as they performed them during the first four stages of the power contest. Then, once Nixon had left office, neither contested the legal surrealism of a president pardoning his predecessor before any criminal charges or penalties had been assessed against him. From such evasions have come the constitutional lunacies of the Iran-Contra affair and the continuing need to clarify the still proliferating boundaries of presidential War Powers in a sometimes unfriendly world. Other Vietnams—and more Watergates—will surely be the price if we don't meet this need.

## How It All Began

Personal factors were important.[2] They helped determine why Nixon did not survive Watergate, as Kennedy survived the Bay of Pigs and Reagan the Iran-Contra affair. Richard Nixon was a leader who felt himself in opposition, who viewed politics as war carried on by other means. His rise was quick and hard. He went from being an unknown to vice president in six years, then lost a heartbreakingly close presidential contest eight years after that. For the next eight years, he struggled back from the status of also-ran. He lost an election for California's governorship in 1962, briefly gave up politics, then agonizingly rebuilt support. He backed Barry Goldwater after he was nominated in 1964, delivered endless speeches, raised endless money, and accumulated endless political IOUs from endless power brokers. Yet he almost failed to get nominated for the presidency in 1968, and then almost snatched defeat from the jaws of victory in the election. Afterward, he faced a Congress where both houses were controlled by Democrats (the first president in one hundred years to do so). He faced the same situation again in November 1972, even though he had won a resounding victory against a fractured Democratic Party and a lackluster antiwar moderate, George McGovern.

None of it was easy. Loser Nixon had fought back; all his life he had fought back. He was, as a former speech writer wrote in 1972, "the born second-stringer who captains the varsity by hard-plugging, self-discipline and perseverance."[3]

Perseverance like this was possible partly because Nixon hated well. He, the outsider, was surrounded, in his own mind, by supercilious insiders— people of wealth and privilege and connections, Midwest aristocrat Adlai Stevenson, haughty Harvard Boy JFK, Good Old Boys on Capitol Hill who bought votes with federal handouts, collegians who thought communism was stuff you read about in books and who didn't want to know how wealth was created or how national power and credibility were maintained in a dangerous world, people who laughed at him and pilloried him as an unctuous hypocrite with sweaty palms and a ski-jump nose and a never quite fully shaven face and who orated over cocktails that Richard Nixon was a fellow whose sense of honor and virtue approximated the reptilian. Nixon saw himself, David Halberstam has argued, as a victim of the insiders with the prestige, the connections, and the power. Therefore, he "permitted himself to victimize others" by getting them before they got him.[4]

A key element here was symbolic, symbolically taking charge and demonstrating status and power. Two events illustrated the pattern. The first occurred immediately after Nixon became president; the second during his second inaugural in January 1973.

In early 1969, what was lampooned as The Palace Guard appeared: White House police decked out in redesigned white uniforms, epaulettes, and special headgear—comic-opera dandification, rumors had it, created by Nixon himself. Who, humorists wondered, did Nixon think he was, some emperor or king? Why weren't standard blue police outfits good enough for him? Was he somebody special? Of course, Nixon was somebody special. He was *President* Nixon, symbol of national unity and politician-in-chief all rolled up into one. Yet, it still did not do to demonstrate such status with fancy security guards during an unpopular war, and after squeaking into office in a three-way race which pitted him against the Democrats and the Democrats against themselves. So off went the new White House police uniforms, to be warehoused for eleven years before some were sold to a high-school marching band in Iowa, and others were loaned to musicians at Southern Utah State College.[5]

The second symbolic misstep was of a piece with the first. In January 1973, an Anti-Inaugural demonstration brought perhaps thirty thousand people to Washington. This rear guard of the by now dissipated antiwar coalition was protesting, one last time, against the war. Washington and Hanoi had just brought a sham peace to Vietnam, but, simultaneously, had expanded their conflict in Cambodia and Laos. The demonstrators, accordingly, had no love whatsoever for Nixon—and Nixon reciprocated. He lined both sides of his inaugural parade route down Pennsylvania Avenue with armed detachments from all the military services, including paratroops from the elite 101st Airborne Division.

The thousands of soldiers and police deployed in force were as disciplined as befitted the occasion. They more than overawed the vanguard party revolutionaries who passed out leaflets, talked loudly about disrupting the inauguration, and then did nothing except chant behind police barricades once the antiwar masses decided not to fight their battles for them in a revolution that was no longer being televised. The presence of so many armed men, however, was overkill. The crowds along Pennsylvania Avenue were overwhelmingly friendly. The far less numerous antiwar demonstrators were forlornly standing witness against a war very few Americans still cared about. Bringing in the 101st Airborne and other units was using the military to make law-and-order points that the Washington cops could have made by themselves, as they had done in preceding years. Something in the president and the president's staff, however, impelled them to overassert their control, to deploy elephants to control mice when a cat or two would have done. A young man from Maine, in town to stand witness as forlornly as others, wondered about this, as he watched well-officered units of the 101st alight from two-and-a-half-ton trucks, form-up, and march off to their destinations as Richard Nixon's second term officially commenced. What was Nixon doing, the young man wondered? Hadn't he just won big? Why did he seem so fearful of those who had lost?

Just so little did the young man know, as little as almost everyone else temporarily in Washington that day. He and they saw only exterior trappings, soldiers guarding a president-elect who reaffirmed in his second inaugural address the points he had made in his first presidential speech four years earlier. The day of the nay-sayers "taught to be ashamed of their country, ashamed of their parents, ashamed of America's record at home and around the world" was, mercifully, over. The time had come to "renew our faith in ourselves and America" and "make these next four years the best four years in America's history." Americans would "answer to God, to history, and to our conscience for the way in which we make use of these years." Americans should help make these "best four years" possible, so that the United States of America, two hundred years old by 1976, "will be as young and as vital as when it began, and as bright a beacon of hope for all the world."[6]

And yet, and yet, the very president who enunciated glowing visions on the symbolically rich political occasion of January 20th, 1973, had already set in motion a return to "a long night of the American spirit" that he took credit for ending during his first term.

Hatred for his enemies was at the base of it all, a hatred which obscured the difference between enemies and opponents, between those who despised him and those who disagreed with him. Richard Nixon, the victim, victimized and allowed others to victimize for him so ineptly that he was caught, even on his second inaugural day, in a web of crime and cover-up that only increased his obsessive concerns about enemies lunging for his throat. Nixon was not paranoid. There *were* people who *did* want to get him. But he was driven to equate all opposition to him with aggression, and then to equate his fate with that of the presidency and the nation. The web that bound him, he believed, bound all America as well. So Nixon hated, and his hatred destroyed him. To cite another maxim from La Rochefoucauld, "Excessive hatred brings us down below the level of those we hate."[7]

Nixon hated too well because he trusted too little. The wounds he inflicted upon himself throughout Watergate stemmed from that basic fact. Trust is rare and valuable in politics, for power is a lonely profession.

Power attracts legions of people who want you to accomplish their purposes, and causes aides to swell your repute (and your head) as a means
of swelling theirs. Presidents, therefore, learn to ration themselves, and to
keep frankness and honesty to a minimum. Yet all politicians also have to
talk with those they trust. They have to possess friendships personal
enough so that others will risk that friendship for friendship's sake by
telling them that what they are doing is wrong or is less right than they
suppose. In the web of suspicion that politics can too easily become, the
powerful must be reminded that they can be as silly, self-defeating, or
stupid as anyone else; that self-delusion is the worst delusion of all; and
that without mutual trust, power cannot be effectively delegated by any
leader.

Friendship like this, for any politician, is hard to obtain, and harder to
maintain. It was especially hard for a loner like Dick Nixon, whose alone-
ness largely stemmed from having been a winner who had become a loser
and who had then fought back to become a winner once again. Nixon
lacked friends who "knew him when," longtime comrades who could help
cushion both the rises and the falls. Nixon's friends were political friends
who shared the good times but not the bad, people whose loyalties were
conditional upon success or the prospect of success and which evaporated
with failure. Nixon had suffered through a "long night of the spirit"
himself. He had emerged from it as one who could reach out to very, very
few, and who kept control more and more in his hands alone.

Such personal qualities might not have been self-destructive, but they
gathered virulence from their environment, the political circumstances of
Richard Nixon's presidency. What resulted from the interaction of the
White House and its environment was Guerilla Government, one where
the president and his aides functioned as a cabal fighting to liberate America from the bondage of what Nixon termed an "iron triangle."[8]

This iron triangle had nothing to do with the checks and balances beloved of constitutional scholars. It was legislative parochialism run amok.
The political spectre that haunted Nixon and other conservatives was
made up of a mostly liberal Congress, well-organized interest groups seeking favors, and federal bureaucrats administering public programs. Together, Nixon believed, these unscrupulous legislators, interest groups, and
wily bureaucrats were perverting the Republic, throwing billions down rat
holes, and turning government into a bedlam. This unholy trinity had
created a mutually reinforcing alliance whereby Congress doled out
money, regulatory authority, and social welfare programs to baronial
bureaucrats for distribution to modern-day guilds and syndicates masquerading as "the people." The members of Congress got votes and cam-

paign contributions in return, the bureaucrats got ever-larger organizational domains and appropriations, and the interest groups got largesse. "Interest-group liberalism," Professor Theodore Lowi of Cornell called it in a respected analysis published at the time.[9]

Conservatives proved especially receptive to Lowi's arguments. They were a balm to those who had been powerless to stop the wave of social-welfare legislation and spending that occurred after the political slaughter of Barry M. Goldwater and many Republican members of Congress in the 1964 elections. A right wing which had long believed that welfare state liberalism was mostly a giveaway now argued that giveaways had degenerated into organized pillage of the public purse and the public interest, with parochial claims assuaged by booty paid out by a Congress that equated patriotism with reelection. Spoils like this used other people's money to buy votes and keep them bought in a welfare state where manna was offered to those with the loudest voices, as opposed to those with the best, or better, claims.

Nixon could do little about a problem he perceived as profound. Republicans controlled neither house of Congress during either of his terms. Their failure to halt the continued growth of the American welfare state only accentuated Nixon's frustration, suspicion, urge to control, and preferences for Guerilla Government. Both of Nixon's major domestic policy initiatives of his first term, for example, suffered the death of a thousand cuts on Capitol Hill: the Family Assistance Plan (guaranteed minimum income) welfare reform package and an unprecedented peacetime wage-and-price-control program. This happened when federal spending for social welfare had doubled in ten years and when stagflation increased both unemployment and inflation in grim tandem. Defensive Democratic demagoguery was frequent during both domestic policy debates, which occurred simultaneously with other demagogic attempts by liberals and conservatives to foist the responsibility for failure in Vietnam on each other. Richard Nixon, however, was far better at giving abuse than he was at taking it, especially about Vietnam. He did not lack excuses for starting secret wars, at home as well as abroad.

Wage wars he did. Mid-1971 was the watershed, the point at which Nixon's frustrations over domestic affairs and his ongoing efforts to conduct a partly secret Men Out, Machines In escalation-deescalation campaign in Indochina congealed into Guerilla Government at home.

The seminal event in translating frustration into self-destruction was the leaking to the press of a supersecret study of policymaking during the pre-Nixon phases of America's involvement in Vietnam, known as the Pentagon Papers. This exhaustive and exhausting analysis, put together by defense intellectuals at the order of JFK's and LBJ's Secretary of Defense Robert S. McNamara, covered the years from 1945 to 1968, and sought to learn confidential lessons from confidential history.[10] Alas for secrecy. Most of McNamara's staff gained access to the innermost sanctums, kept their mouths shut, and profited accordingly: leaving office for posts at think tanks and with up-and-coming Democratic politicos. But two, Daniel Ellsberg and Anthony Russo, broke faith, photocopied the closely guarded report, and threw away their government careers by contacting the *New York Times.*

It didn't take the *Times* editors long to figure out that they had one of the better headlines of the century: warts, bloodletting, nonsense, and all. The Pentagon Papers proved the existence of deceptions that critics of the war had long suspected. The Johnson administration, for example, had played a dual game of affirming that it intended no massive American involvement in Vietnam as it was privately planning just such a war. On June 13th, 1971, the first installments of the Pentagon Papers were published. The Nixon White House, fearing more leaks which might blow the cover on deceptions of its own, such as the secret bombing of Cambodia in 1969 and 1970, was not amused. It persisted in equating Ellsberg's and Russo's action—against repeated CIA advice—with a radical conspiracy programmed by foreign communists.[11] Mistaken fear that the mass civil disobedience undertaken by the Vietnam Veterans against the War and the May Day Tribe in Washington in April and May 1971 were curtain raisers to new rounds of antiwar militance added to White House anxieties.

Nixon came out swinging. A court injunction was slapped on the *Times* forbidding further publication. A legal merry-go-round ensued as the *Washington Post, Los Angeles Times, St. Louis Post-Dispatch, Boston Globe,* and *Chicago Sun-Times* all subsequently picked up the story and ran further installments of the Papers. A blizzard of injunctions followed, and the newspapers appealed. Finally, on June 30th, the Supreme Court stopped the carnival by ruling against the president's effort to choke off further publication on "national security" and other grounds.

The publication of the Pentagon Papers seemed like the last straw. Nixon the outsider had lost to the insiders again; to an establishment that was conspiring against him and nibbling the United States to death from within. America was becoming a pitiful, helpless, impotent giant in world affairs, and ungovernable at home. The liberal establishment that was making Nixon powerless was an evil alliance of media idiots, longhairs, subversives, do-your-own-thing lawyers, spineless jurists, Georgetown high society, bureaucratic barons, and members of Congress without any awareness of foreign affairs. Nixon had hated such people all his life or had come to hate them during his hard path to supreme political power in America. Nixon would get them and show them who was boss. But he'd do it carefully and indirectly, using only especially trusted subordinates, people who were entirely dependent upon him for all the political authority they possessed.

The creation of a super-secret Plumbers unit within the White House early in July 1971 was the first step. Presidential adviser Charles Colson, of the "When you've got them by the balls, their Hearts and Minds will follow" school of political discourse,[12] recruited former CIA agent E. Howard Hunt and former FBI agent G. Gordon Liddy to execute a leak-plugging and covert-action operation. Liddy and Hunt, in turn, were overseen by the White House inner circle and by representatives of three of the four most powerful Cabinet-level departments: State, Defense, and Justice, all acting through intermediaries. Emil Krogh, for example, carried the ball for White House Chief of Staff H. R. (Bob) Haldeman at the supervisory meetings concerned with the Plumbers unit; and one David Young did likewise for chief White House domestic policy adviser John Ehrlichman.

Oversight notwithstanding, the Plumbers started off badly. Colson assigned Hunt and Liddy to an Ellsberg Project. The effort to discredit Ellsberg as a subversive by breaking into his psychiatrist's office in September 1971 in search of incriminating self-revelations got nowhere, even after the *right* office was burgled on the second attempt.[13] As Hunt and Liddy's failures in the psychiatric department became known, a subsequent half-baked Liddy proposal—to firebomb the Brookings Institution, a liberal Washington, D.C. think tank, in order to ransack its files and prove that Ellsberg or Russo had used it as a base of operations when photocopying the Pentagon Papers—was quashed.[14]

Presidential politics soon proved a more fruitful arena for transgression. There, character assassination could be carried on with comparative ease because the Plumbers didn't have to pick any locks to accomplish results, at least initially. But once the Plumbers shifted from covert action against Ellsberg to covert action against the president's political opponents, a crucial line was crossed. Nixon's people ceased to concern themselves primarily with plugging leaks and began to engage in spying, sabotage, and dirty tricks. They started to do unto others what they supposed those others had done unto them. Defensive efforts were replaced by offensive ones.

Offence was easy, given the circumstances. There were a lot of inviting political targets in mid-1971, all launching campaigns aimed at the presidency in 1972. Democrats had a herd of opponents in the field against Nixon, notably senators Birch Bayh, Fred Harris, Hubert H. Humphrey,

Henry M. Jackson, Ted Kennedy, George McGovern, and Edmund Sixtus Muskie. There was also, as in 1968, Governor George Wallace's powerful populist insurgency to contend with. With so many opponents around, Nixon's covert actors found it impossible to resist playing them off against one another so that a Democratic Party which had divided against itself in 1968 might engage in even worse internecine bloodletting in 1972.

Racial, ethnic, and sexual slurs were favorites in the Plumbers' arsenal. Spies in all the major opponents' campaign staffs stole stationery on which middle-level saboteurs like one Donald Segretti composed fake official communications redolent with slime. Candidate A was a homosexual, Candidate B hated French Canadians, Candidate C wanted blacks to enjoy too much open housing for most white folk's comfort, and so forth. The purpose wasn't to create any one lie that would be widely believed for long; it was, instead, to engage in verbal thuggery to keep all the Democratic campaigners off balance, on edge, and at each other's throats, bleeding each other to death during the crucial *candidate selection* stage of the election. Nixon would then run against a weak survivor unable to compromise the claims of embittered factions. Nixon's men centered their attentions on moderate contenders, especially Edmund S. Muskie, in hopes that "radical" candidates, particularly George McGovern, would benefit. Nixon could thus occupy the sacred middle ground between Wallace on the right and an "extreme" Democrat on the left; and walk off with the presidency.

The secret war the Plumbers waged to polarize the Democrats was on par with the government-by-surprise strategy that came to characterize the Nixon presidency as a whole when the Plumbers operation began. In the summer of 1971, two veiled strokes badly discomfited a Democratic Congress that Nixon had been feuding with ever since he'd become president.

First, in mid-July, Nixon, in a surprise TV address, announced that months of secret negotiations had paid off. Relations between China and the United States would be "normalized."[15] To begin this new era in Sino-American diplomacy, he would soon visit China's capital, there to eat Peking duck with Mao Tse-tung, Chou En-lai, and others whom Nixon had been equating with the political anti-Christ for decades, leaders whose revolutionary machinations Nixon still said Americans were struggling to foil in Vietnam. It was as if the Pope suddenly announced he was getting engaged to a Lutheran.

As a Nixon-the-peacemaker media offensive followed the White House's surprise announcement, many liberal Democrats who had been too cautious to support diplomatic recognition of China, for fear of being branded closet Bolsheviks, privately fumed. Publicly, however, they had no room to maneuver, and so added their applause to that of others. Many liberals, after all, had wanted the United States to get less livid about the Chinese for years, so as to be able to play Peking against Moscow. Conservatives of what Nixon liked to call Middle America, for their part, didn't know exactly what the president intended, but they also remained sure that Dick Nixon could not be gulled into giving away American interests by sweet words from Marxists.

Then, only a month after the China surprise, Nixon further confounded the Democrats by taking charge of a policy arena that they had assumed as their peculiar property since the era of Herbert Hoover. That arena was the nation's economy: which by mid-1971, was in bad enough shape so that many liberals conceived it to be their political passport to regaining the presidency in 1972. Stagflation, the problem was called: simultaneous increases in inflation and unemployment. This, together with other factors such as the unwillingness of many foreigners to keep on holding vast amounts of overpriced U.S. dollars, made for gloomy economic prognostications.

In mid-August 1971, however, the secretive dramatics of the Nixon economic controls program were revealed. A conservative president suddenly took the unprecedented step of announcing a peacetime wage and price freeze and quickly followed that up with an equally unprecedented series of peacetime anti-inflationary regulations. In the process, Nixon ran off with most of the Democrats' clothing so far as economic recovery policy was concerned.[16] Nixon's business-oriented controls subsequently withered on the vine, especially after the political hemorrhage of Watergate began. But, for the first year of the controls, all that most Americans realized was that a president in whom few had much economic faith before August 1971 had suddenly done unprecedented and dramatic things that liberals had berated him for not doing for more than a year. Nixon's success was deliciously ironic. He used blank check emergency powers that Congress granted in August 1970 to begin the controls program, end the intergovernmental gold standard, and end a system of fixed international monetary exchange rates that had existed since the end of the Second World War. It was a blank check that the Democrats had assumed Nixon was too conservative to ever cash, but he cashed it and the ensuing partisan protests rang hollow.

The Democrats thus lost their economic policy advantage, and Nixon, the decisive and more secretive leader, dominated the chief domestic issue of the 1972 presidential campaign. Once the freeze and the controls began, moreover, political attention often shifted back toward foreign policy. Here, Democrats of all sorts were hindered by their previous support for the war. Nixon might be a not-so-nice guy, but he was getting things done at home and abroad. The Democrats often appeared to be a collection of nay-sayers and ideologues by comparison.[17]

Government by surprise paid off handsomely for Richard Nixon during the summer of 1971, so handsomely that secrecy became a habit, and Guerilla Government began to flourish. C. P. Snow argues that there is a euphoria about secrecy, and that this "euphoria of secrecy goes to the head . . . normally prudent men become drunk with it. It induces an unbalancing sense of power."[18]

Thus it was in Nixon's White House. Little people swelled with the belief that only they knew what was going on, that only they understood how things really worked, that they were tough while others were weak. Stupidity and miscalculation were concealed by a secrecy which preserved arrogant assumptions. That was what the insider technocracy and war management of Vietnam was all about. That was what produced Watergate as well—little people presuming to behind-the-scenes control over a political society they barely knew. Politics became layers of secrets to which only they possessed the answers because they had created the mysteries, or thought they had. The Iran-Contra affair was only a later example of the phenomenon.

Plumbers and War Managers, however, knew little enough. Secretiveness exacerbates suspicions and breeds situations where others keep secrets, too. A politics of the lowest common denominator results. Politics shifts away from public bargaining and toward conspiracy; wheels revolve within wheels and mystery is piled upon mystery; nothing is as it seems or even as others say it is; trust evaporates and politics becomes war.

Richard Nixon wanted it that way. He revelled in the euphoria of surprises and secrecy, so much so that he forgot that one essential thing keeping insiders from running amok is the existence of "no-men," people who can short-circuit the extremisms of those drunk with secrecy. Nixon, however, hated no-men. There were few of those close to him whom Nixon had not made or who could operate from independent bases of status, influence, and power—only a couple of Cabinet-level officers like Nixon's second Secretary of the Treasury John Connally or Bryce N. Harlow, his chief congressional liaison.

Bob Haldeman and John Ehrlichman and Howard Hunt and Colson and Liddy, however, were not self-made anything. They were yes-men incarnate, creatures of Richard Nixon, planets to his sun. Senior aides Haldeman and Ehrlichman were advertising executives who had joined Nixon in the dark years after 1960, never been elected to public office, never worked for any other power broker. They were Nixon's men, men without independent standing who owed everything to their maker. From such men, Richard Nixon could expect indiscriminate loyalty and get it.

Nixon, then, was in control. Since the delegation of authority is difficult when trust doesn't exist, and Nixon was not a trusting man, he surrounded himself with people whose knowledge of electoral politics was marginal and who did his bidding. The Plumbers unit *was* a secret White House spying and dirty-tricks operation because Nixon didn't trust the FBI and the CIA to break the law in the ways he wanted it broken. In late 1971, Nixon created yet another personal political organization, the Committee to Re-Elect the President (CREEP), which raised money and otherwise operated entirely independently of the Republican Party and of the Republican National Committee. It, too, would do his bidding.

Shortly after CREEP was formed, Plumber G. Gordon Liddy had new outlandish ideas. He proposed ways to disrupt the forthcoming Democratic presidential convention in Miami. Pungent political information, Liddy argued, could be gathered by establishing mugging and kidnapping squads and by hiring prostitutes to service delegates. Sweet nothings whispered in the hookers' ears would be recorded and opportunities for blackmail ensue.

Liddy's proposals, put forward on January 27th, 1972, struck other Nixon loyalists in attendance at the political sabotage planning meeting as too weird for comfort. White House Counsel John Dean, CREEP director and former Attorney General John Mitchell, and Mitchell's CREEP deputy Jeb Stuart Magruder told Liddy to devise a less expensive and risky program. Liddy complied, but Mitchell apparently remained unimpressed. Following pressure by Colson and Haldeman in the White House, however, Mitchell underling Magruder OK'd a scaled-down and refocused $250,000 covert operation at a meeting on March 30th. A break-in and bugging at the Democratic National Committee headquarters in the Watergate apartment and hotel complex in Washington was the centerpiece of Liddy's new scheme.[19]

Now the little people who saw themselves as hard-eyed loyalists had their chance to prove how tough they were and how well they could serve Richard Nixon's will. Conspiracy to commit a crime, when followed up by the crime itself, however, soon became comic opera.

## The Break-in and the Beginnings of the Cover-up

Political intrigue, Watergate style, began with a conspiracy which turned into farce. The slapstick of the break-in illustrated the process.

The Plumbers, as we've seen, weren't brilliant at burglary. When Howard Hunt and G. Gordon Liddy began their felonious escapades in September 1971, they botched the job. Instead of burgling Daniel Ellsberg's psychiatrist's office, they tried to pick a lock, failed, smashed through a door with a crowbar, and then discovered they'd broken into the wrong place. Only on the second effort did they get it right. Even then, the incriminating evidence they were sure existed utterly eluded them.

Eight months later, their criminal expertise hadn't much improved. Their effort to break into the Democratic National Committee (DNC) offices resembled an airplane without a propeller. On the first attempt, Hunt and Liddy, together with four Cuban Americans, posed as salesmen, entered the Watergate Hotel, loitered while two hid in a closet in a banquet hall until the hotel closed, and then tried to sneak from the hall into the adjoining apartment complex to do their dirty work. No such luck. Hunt and a Cuban were locked into the banquet hall by departing staff and then couldn't pick the lock. They cooled their heels until the next morning and aborted their mission.

Round two was more successful. Waiting until May 28th, a Memorial Day weekend when downtown Washington was about as populated as the Sahara Desert, Hunt, Liddy, and the Cubans broke into the Democrats' lair, bugged the telephones of the DNC director's secretary and his deputy, and left undetected. Later that same night, they also made the first of several unsuccessful efforts to bug the campaign headquarters of by then Democratic presidential frontrunner George McGovern. New problems soon surfaced, however. The signals from the DNC bugs, beamed to a former FBI man in a nearby hotel, contained nothing of value to CREEP and White House functionaries. Liddy and Company were wasting a quarter-of-a-million bucks, so far as those paying for the job were concerned. The pressure was on Nixon's political saboteurs. On June 17th, Liddy and Hunt ordered the Cubans back to the Watergate to bug the DNC director's personal phone and otherwise tidy up their act.

What ensued was asinine. The four Cuban Americans were accompanied, on their return engagement, by former CIA agent James McCord. An entrance door lock was picked and then taped open, but the tape was placed over the lock so that it lay across the inside and outside faces of the door instead of along the vertical edge of the door—where it would have been invisible to passersby. And glaringly visible it was. When security guard Frank Wills arrived, he saw the tape, removed it, and relocked the door. McCord and Company returned and retaped the lock in the same conspicuous way. Back came Mr. Wills, put two and two together, and called the police. Washington, D.C. detectives quickly arrived in an unmarked car.

Now another element of McCord's expert operation misfired. McCord had given walkie-talkies to his Cuban counterparts, and issued another one to a lookout stationed in a hotel room across the street from the Watergate complex. The lookout, once he belatedly determined that police had actually arrived, tried to warn the break-in team. Alas, the Cubans had decided to conserve the batteries of the walkie-talkies by turning them off during the re-bugging operation. The police and Watergate security personnel apprehended the unknowing burglars red-handed in the Democratic National Committee offices.

Now things got even stranger. New recruit James McCord was also none other than the security director for Nixon's Committee to Re-Elect the President. McCord's personal participation in the botched burglary— which former FBI man Gordon Liddy had allowed—was ridiculous. It also violated an elementary rule of spying—never use anyone who can be easily and directly traced back to you. If you try to burgle the Kremlin, you don't send a Pentagon general or the White House chief of staff to do it. You hire a Latvian cleaning lady instead. You work through deniable intermediaries.

This point the Plumbers partially understood, enough to hire the four Cuban Americans in the first place. They were anti-Castro emigrés who could be perceived to be acting against the Democrats on private grudges of their own. Liddy queered the whole deal by letting McCord go along with the Cubans. McCord connected the crime and the conspiracy to commit it directly to CREEP; and, through CREEP, to Nixon, whose personal political property CREEP was.

Deniability didn't even work with the Cubans. All happened to be carrying several-score crisp new $100 bills whose sequential serial numbers were eventually traced to a secret CREEP account. Two of the Cubans, moreover, had brought address books with them, in which Howard Hunt's name was listed, together with the suggestive abbreviations "W.H." and "W. House." One also had a check in his wallet signed by Hunt.

Two junior *Washington Post* reporters assigned to the break-in on the assumption that it was just another local burglary story now began capitalizing on such mistakes. "W.H." and "W. House," Bob Woodward and Carl

Bernstein discovered, meant White House, and Howard Hunt turned out to be a protégé of Charles Colson. Colson, in turn, was one of only four men (Haldeman, Ehrlichman, and Henry Kissinger being the others) possessing the bureaucratic right to report directly to President Richard Nixon in the Oval Office.

Now Watergate was connected back to Nixon in two ways. First, through CREEP (via James McCord); and, second, through the Cubans-Hunt-Colson link. Three months more of journalistic detective work uncovered even more linkages between CREEP, the White House, and the burglary. Gordon Liddy's name was discovered in a Cuban's address book, and then Liddy's White House connections were uncovered. Liddy, it also became clear, had moved over from the White House Plumbers to CREEP at the end of 1971 to take up the post of "general counsel" there. One of his earliest official duties had been to hire fellow Plumber Howard Hunt on the recommendation of Chuck Colson. Liddy, finally, had bankrolled the burglary from a secret "intelligence gathering" fund at CREEP, one overseen by CREEP director and former Nixon Attorney General John Mitchell.

Now the break-in ceased looking like an isolated event, and started looking like Guerilla Government. The fact that McCord and Hunt were former CIA men, that the Cubans all had CIA connections, and that Liddy was a former FBI agent did nothing to reassure those who believed that the Democratic Party was being equated with the New Left or the Vietcong. The additional discovery that McCord was an officer in an air force reserve unit assigned to draw up lists of radicals to be arrested and news media to be censored in time of war or "national emergency" didn't either.[20]

Evidence like this, to be sure, was only circumstantial. But "some circumstantial evidence is very strong," observed Henry David Thoreau, "as when you find a trout in the milk."[21] It did not take a genius to suspect that the burglars were an extension of CREEP or that CREEP was an extension of the White House. The challenge was to prove it with legal rigor—and, in so doing, to challenge the authority of the most powerful politician in the United States.

Richard Nixon consequently faced new problems. He had to protect himself, but how? Should he cut his losses by admitting crimes by CREEP subordinates only four months before the election? Or should he erect a stone wall, deny everything, and hope investigations of burglary and conspiracy would blow over quickly and leave him in office and in power?

Nixon toughed it out; he lied. And, in order to limit his own personal involvement as much as possible, he had others lie for him. Lies, however, were not enough. Action was necessary. Felonies designed to cover up a crime were necessary. Public officials also had to fail to do things they should have done so that crimes whose existence they should have recognized would not be punished, but official looking-the-other-way like this was also felonious.[22]

Further crimes were necessary because five men had, after all, been apprehended at the Watergate. These five, the four Cuban Americans and James McCord of CREEP, had to be offered money to take the fall and not implicate their immediate superiors, Hunt and Liddy. At this point, it was not obvious that a luckless Hunt and an inept Liddy had been implicated by traceable $100 bills and names written in address books. The burglary, remember, was only part of a wider picture, and the two ex-Plumbers knew too much about other political sabotage such as the Ellsberg Project and the Segretti sleaze. If Liddy ever talked, for example, he could implicate CREEP director Mitchell, Mitchell's deputy Magruder, and White House Counsel John Dean in the planning of Watergate-style operations. This would take the criminal trail right up to the president's re-election campaign manager and his personal lawyer at 1600 Pennsylvania Avenue. Nixon pondered such possibilities with all the joy of a man playing tag with a shark.

Hunt and Liddy, therefore, were not quickly offered up as masterminds of a botched burglary. Nor were they ordered to take the rap in absentia by disappearing abroad. Nothing immediate was done, except to have Liddy approach Attorney General Richard W. Kleindienst to ask him to order all five burglars freed immediately, to shred lots of papers, and to otherwise organize the effort to bury the Watergate criminal investigation.

Kleindienst, however, had no interest in risking his neck, so the White House looked elsewhere. John Dean received more and more operational responsibility as the cover-up progressed. The belief apparently was that McCord and the four Cubans would keep quiet in return for hush money, legal support, or promises of postelection presidential pardons. Nixon did not seem to think beyond November, and delay was the key. Thus the burglars initially pled *innocent* to the charges against them, though they'd have ended the criminal investigation a lot sooner if they had pled guilty. Their initial arrogant pleas demonstrated that the White House believed the situation was manageable.

Liddy and Hunt's connections, however, threw a monkey wrench into everything. The burglars couldn't connect the crime back to the White House, but Liddy and Hunt could. Howard Hunt had the *Washington Post* reporters, Woodward and Bernstein, after him only two days after the burglary. The FBI was right on their heels; nine days later, FBI agents, using investigatory powers newspaper reporters didn't possess, interviewed an uncooperative Gordon Liddy at his CREEP office. Liddy's obstructionism accomplished nothing, for the FBI agents were also following the trail of $100 bills that stretched from the burglars' pockets to Liddy's dirty-tricks fund at CREEP.

This simply wouldn't do. If Hunt and Liddy were bagged by the FBI, the courts could have a field day. Watergate would no longer be perceived as a simple burglary undertaken by individuals because of personal grudges, and proof would exist that Watergate was part of a wider pattern of illegality. The FBI data would be turned over to federal prosecutors investigating a burglary committed in a federal enclave, the District of Columbia, and federal prosecutors would then present that same evidence to a grand jury impanelled to determine whether "probable cause" existed to try the burglars and their associates for crimes against the state—in this case, for political conspiracy as well as for violation of criminal law.

Hunt and Liddy, therefore, had to be protected. Long before either was ordered to answer prosecutors' questions before a grand jury in July, three illegal steps were taken to insure that the two would not be involved or that, if they were, the Watergate investigation would end with them. Four of the five apprehended burglars were already being paid to keep silent. Now money was also given to Hunt and Liddy, and more vague assurances were now given to all seven men that they would be pardoned in the event they were indicted and convicted. Finally, the ongoing investigation of the crime by the FBI was short-circuited. All these activities were "obstructions of justice," a cover-up.

The seven failed political saboteurs, McCord alone excepted, got hush money—at least $400,000 during the first eight months after the break-in. It was never enough, but it bought temporary silence. Subtler efforts were required at the Federal Bureau of Investigation, efforts aimed to convince the Bureau that the Guerilla Government that had led to Watergate had noble and patriotic purposes, because the Democrats had compromised the national security of the United States.

It was a new version of standard red-baiting, but with a more secretive twist. On June 23rd, a plot was hatched by White House Chief of Staff Haldeman and by Nixon to make it appear that the Watergate burglary was part of a wider CIA operation.[23] By bringing the CIA into the picture, the widest possible national-security blanket could be thrown over do-it-yourself political spying and sabotage. The Democratic Party had been infiltrated by subversives, so two former CIA men, four participants in previous CIA operations, and a one-time FBI agent had gone into action to save the Republic. Any effort by the FBI to blow the CIA's cover would only give aid and comfort to the nation's enemies.

It was a clever idea, but it had a flaw. It could require the CIA to walk the plank for Nixon to stop the FBI from probing further. The CIA, recall, *had* previously investigated possible treason networks for Nixon: overseas networks that Nixon mistakenly believed tied together antiwar liberals and New Leftists with Moscow, Peking, or Hanoi. The FBI had done the same about domestically based subversions. Neither had found proof that Nixon's political opponents were traitors to the country, as White House toughs like Chuck Colson enthusiastically believed. The CIA, moreover, was a *foreign* spying and dirty-tricks agency, one specifically prohibited by its charter from performing such activities within the United States itself. For the CIA to take responsibility for Watergate, then, was very dangerous, especially if Nixon and his men claimed—as they probably would—that they had never ordered the CIA to break the law.

Protection, however, was what Nixon and his staff also wanted. Having mired themselves in Watergate, they wanted the CIA first to pull them out and then to jump into the quicksand in their place. The CIA could do this, the White House argued, precisely because the agency *was* so secretive. Nothing it did had to be done publicly, nor would it ever become public. Nixon's people wouldn't leak anything to the *Washington Post* for angry Democrats to read. All that was necessary was for CIA staff to go over and have a quiet chat with FBI staff and tell them to lay off further investigation of Watergate. To get the point across, Nixon ordered Haldeman to threaten the CIA with exposure of embarrassing details of the Bay of Pigs fiasco, its best-known failure to that date, unless it complied.

Once CIA Director Richard Helms and Vernon Walters, Nixon's recent appointee as deputy CIA director, heard all this from H. R. Haldeman on the afternoon of June 23rd, they knew they were in trouble. They realized that Nixon's chief of staff was ordering them to cover up a crime for the president so that Nixon would be spared the risk of doing it himself. They also knew that if they did what Haldeman was telling them to do, and it blew up in their faces, they would be saddled with the responsibility for Watergate and all it represented. Some cold political calculation was in order. Both men realized it simply wouldn't do to refuse Haldeman. Nixon might attempt to pin Watergate on the CIA anyway, given McCord's, Hunt's, and the Cubans' CIA connections.

Helms and Walters also knew that acting FBI Director L. Patrick Gray, a Nixon loyalist, was caught in the same bind as they were. The FBI was investigating a political crime in which its number one boss, the president of the United States, had a distinctly personal interest. They realized that if Gray persisted in an all-out probe of Watergate, he would be risking *his* career. Helms also knew that Gray understood this very well. On June 22nd, the day before the CIA men met Haldeman, and only five days after the break-in, Gray, according to Helms's biographer, Thomas Powers, called Helms to say that some of his FBI investigators "were wondering whether it might have been a CIA operation of some kind."[24] Helms knew that Watergate wasn't a CIA operation; he also knew that Gray realized the CIA couldn't spy domestically without presidential authorization be-cause that violated the law and trespassed on the FBI's domestic turf into the bargain. Helms understood, therefore, that Gray was beginning to feel the heat and was looking for a way out of Watergate. So when FBI inves-tigators, in the process of tracking the source of the money found in the burglars' pockets, discovered that it had been laundered through a *Mexican* bank account, Gray seized the opportunity to assume that the CIA's inter-national spy network was somehow involved. If Helms would so certify, Gray would be off the hook. He could try to smother the investigation—before it became clear, as it soon did, that the Mexican laundering opera-tion had nothing to do with the CIA and everything to do with Gordon Liddy at CREEP.

Simultaneously, Gray tried to protect himself on the presidential front by carefully informing the White House of everything his agency was doing. White House counsel John Dean, the man with primary day-to-day responsibility for the cover-up, was provided, on Gray's order, with all details of the FBI's investigation of that same cover-up—to the point of being allowed to sit in on FBI interviews or read full transcripts of them. Dean was also informed in advance of leads the FBI planned to pursue and could plan his obstruction accordingly. Gray was so anxious to be of assistance that, when a nervous John Dean actually handed him evidence of Hunt's dirty trickery from Hunt's personal files in the White House on June 28th and told him to commit a felony by destroying it, Gray destroyed the evidence on July 3rd. Using the CIA as a foil to end the Watergate investigation for Nixon was Gray's way out from between a rock and a hard place.

The question for Helms and Walters became how to let Pat Gray and the FBI take the risks involved in muzzling Watergate while putting the CIA and themselves in the least possible danger. The CIA's Helms could have performed these ticklish negotiations himself, but number one men rarely do. They operate, especially in the spying and dirty-tricks business, through intermediaries, deniable intermediaries.

Vernon Walters, the CIA's deputy director, was the obvious choice.

Walters was Nixon's man at the CIA, one who had performed secret missions for Nixon on many occasions in the past, and who had been his personal translator in foreign diplomatic negotiations off and on for fifteen years. Walters knew how to keep his mouth shut and had—Helms suspected—been sent over to the CIA early in 1972 specifically for the purpose of gathering intelligence for Nixon about *him.* Walters was, therefore, the best man for a very quiet and dangerous job. And so, just hours after the Haldeman–CIA meeting on June 23rd, CIA's Walters and FBI's Gray sat down for a little chat.

Walters did *not* tell Gray that Watergate was really a CIA operation, nor did he tell him to quash the FBI's investigation. This is not the way political survivors operate. Especially if they think, as Walters and Helms probably both did, that Nixon was putting them and the CIA at risk only to cover up partisan political sabotage and the third-rate saboteurs who had done it, all the national-security oratory to the contrary.

Vernon Walters proceeded very carefully. The FBI's efforts to trace the burglars' money through a Mexican bank account, he told Gray, *might* imperil the CIA's operations *in Mexico.* Nothing definite was provided, nor was it requested. Pat Gray, after all, also knew how survival games are played. The FBI's Gray didn't expect direct statements. The CIA didn't have to say that Watergate was their own. "Maybes" were good enough, possibilities that could put Gray's investigators on hold and constrain them from going any further for fear of ruining something the CIA had going south of the border.

Thus matters were arranged. The CIA did not take responsibility for Watergate, but it gave Gray all the excuse he needed. The FBI's investigation suddenly stopped one crucial step short of connecting the Watergate burglars' money with Liddy and the coffers of the Committee to Re-Elect the President. This careful acquiescence with Nixon, Haldeman, and Company's effort to fob off the cover-up on the CIA might well have worked. But then Nixon's people got greedy. Haldeman, Ehrlichman, and Dean "decided to press their advantage."[25] Helms had given them something, but they needed more because their do-it-yourself dirty trickery had been so inept.

And so, as Thomas Powers relates, John Ehrlichman, whose arrogance was often profound, told John Dean to demand more of the CIA's Walters. On June 26th, 27th, and 28th, Dean told Walters, and through him, Helms, that the CIA's careful going along wasn't enough. The CIA was going to do more than just warn off the FBI in an oblique fashion. It was going to take over *entire operational responsibility for all ongoing aspects of the cover-up,* payoffs to the burglars and the whole program. Putting the CIA in the least possible danger was not acceptable. The CIA was going to do everything the White House told it to do, and in precisely the way it told the CIA to do it.[26]

The mistake was profound. Helms had already had himself and his agency dragged in to clean up somebody else's mess. Walters was even more at risk. This is why both men had played it so conditionally and cautiously with Gray. Now here was young hot-shot Dean ordering Helms and Walters around. Didn't Nixon know that old-timers like Vernon Walters and Richard Helms had seen many presidential acolytes come and go, that they weren't going to risk gutting the CIA just because the fools who had planned the Watergate operation didn't have a hope of getting clear of the mess without at least a few of them having to take some lumps? What was Nixon doing putting *their* heads on the block for such people? Didn't he know that Washington was full of leaks, particularly when peoples' careers were at stake? Didn't the White House appreciate the bureaucratic subtleties of the Walters-Gray deal? Why didn't Nixon just fire some people over at CREEP and have done with the whole thing? Who or what was he protecting? What wider threats faced Nixon so directly that Haldeman, Dean, and Ehrlichman were telling the CIA to get involved so dangerously and completely?

Vernon Walters and Richard Helms would have been fools if they had really wanted answers to questions like these. To have wanted or found answers would have risked making themselves and the nation's premier foreign spying force fair game for every Nixon hater who existed or who might soon come along. All Helms and Walters knew was that Nixon was in deep trouble, and they didn't mortgage any more of their fate to his. Then, instead of taking over complete responsibility for the cover-up as ordered, the CIA apparently retreated from further involvement. Helm's agency was not going to be mousetrapped between an arrogant White House and the FBI's tremulous Patrick Gray. Nor was the CIA going to be crucified to save Nixon.

The strategy Walters and Helms used to accomplish their retreat was simple: they demanded that Nixon first put *his* head on the chopping block before asking anything further of them. No, replied Vernon Walters to John Dean, the CIA would not manage the cover-up for Nixon, not without an explicit presidential order to do so. It was hardball and, of course, no presidential order was forthcoming. To have provided one, Nixon would have had to act directly and without benefit of deniable intermediaries. He would have had to put himself on record as being a part of the cover-up and risk having his orders made known if the CIA were ever caught out and shredded by the press or by politicians.

The FBI also knew how to play the CIA's game. By July 5th, Gray, having just burned Hunt's dirty-tricks files for John Dean, faced an in-house insurrection by FBI agents who were angry at delays in the Water-gate investigation. The CIA-operation excuse hadn't worked for long, and Gray telephoned Vernon Walters to say that he couldn't keep his own people on the leash any longer without a formal request from the CIA that he do so. Gray now needed a direct statement to cover *himself*. The CIA, of course, gave the FBI's Gray no such written hostage to fortune; Helms would as soon have sat on a time bomb.

None of this bureaucratic jungle fighting, however, meant that either the FBI's or the CIA's leaders would *oppose* Nixon actively; it just meant that they weren't going to help the White House as much as he wanted them to. The FBI's Gray continued to funnel up-to-the-minute information about the progress of his agents' investigations to Dean at the White House, and he continued to tell Dean about leads that were being uncov-ered—all of which allowed the White House to alter its cover-up plans accordingly.

The CIA, meanwhile, sat passively on the sidelines. It did nothing, for example, to inform anybody that former agent Howard Hunt had made use of CIA hardware to perform the dirty trick at Ellsberg's psychiatrist's office, ten months before Watergate. Not getting involved, Helms hoped, would keep the CIA's hands clean enough of prohibited domestic spying and covert action to avoid being drawn any further into Watergate. It was Nixon's play from now on. Helms may well have stayed mute so that Nixon, who was then headed for one of the greatest electoral victories in U.S. history, would not punish Helms or the CIA for disloyalty after November.

The CIA and FBI also made no move to broaden Watergate beyond Hunt's and Liddy's level, even after Liddy's secret CREEP fund, which had financed the burglars, *was* uncovered by reporters in July and August. Any FBI men who suspected that Hunt and Liddy were only small fry were sabotaged by the acting director of their agency. The CIA's directors, meanwhile, kept mum about the little chats they'd had with Haldeman and Dean, and about those they'd later had with John Ehrlichman and others. They did nothing to disturb the cover-up.

The CIA had no wish to court disaster. Nixon's men probably had Watergate covered. Who, aside from the court trying the Watergate bur-glars and a few *Washington Post* reporters, had any chance of proving that a burglary had been complemented by a criminal conspiracy to cover up the political sabotage of which Watergate was only one part? Were federal prosecutors working for recently appointed Attorney General Kleindienst ever going to unravel the cover-up? Probably not, especially because the Justice Department chiefs were letting Nixon know what they knew just like FBI's Patrick Gray. Then, too, CREEP had also become a focus of investigation after CREEP's Liddy joined CREEP's security director James McCord in the Watergate net. And CREEP was John Mitchell's turf—the same John Mitchell who had preceded Kleindienst as attorney general of the United States.

For the moment, then, the political and bureaucratic elite held back. Leaks there were, but they were carefully handled. Few, even within Washington, yet grasped Watergate whole. Their chances of doing so now depended upon the federal judiciary and on the ability of journalists to keep gnawing away at the edges of the cover-up in hopes that it would unravel.

## Here Come De Judge

Once the secret infighting with the FBI and the CIA in late June and early July 1972 was over, the Nixonians who had raged at iron triangles and sabotaged the candidate selection and election prospects of their opponents were left a lot more on their own than they wanted to be. The CIA wasn't going to ride to the rescue, take over the cover-up chores, and pull a mantle of national security over everything. The odds, however, still looked good. The CIA's Helms paid for his careful neutrality by being fired as director two weeks after Nixon was overwhelmingly reelected in November, and then sent off to become U.S. ambassador to Iran. Others who had opposed Richard Nixon were put on a special "enemies list" to be singled out for tax audits, delays or refusals of TV station license renewals, and other punishments.[27] Revenge was going to be sweet, once a third-rate burglary became third-rate news and once the efforts to investigate Watergate in court were stymied.

It should have been easy, but it wasn't, not after the CIA refused to legitimize the national security excuse the White House needed to choke off further investigation of the wider patterns of political sabotage. When the Nixonites failed to transform Watergate into patriotism early in the cover-up, just enough people, including Bob Woodward's highly placed source, Deep Throat, talked to reporters. This kept the *Post* reporters on the trail for the crucial five months between July 1972 (when the CIA refused to risk destroying itself for Nixon) and January 1973 (when the trial of the Watergate burglars began). What the reporters discovered gave the court just enough evidence to work with to elicit damaging new facts and allegations, especially from James McCord. This, in turn, undermined the White House's stone wall, led Nixon to throw more of his people to the wolves, scared CREEP's Jeb Stuart Magruder and White House Counsel John Dean into turning state's evidence, and kept Watergate high-profile enough to give Congress the courage to begin a political investigation of the *cover-up*, as opposed to the *burglary* that preceded it by almost a full year. The White House's failure during the first stage of the Watergate struggle, then, led to a gradual and obscure process that left Nixon open to cautious political attack from Congress.

The first major public step toward political disaster occurred on September 15th, 1972, when, at the end of a long effort to tie Hunt and Liddy into Watergate, the grand jury returned indictments against them and the five failed burglars. The judge before whom all stood at the subsequent court hearing was John J. Sirica, a Republican nicknamed Maximum John for a tendency to give stiff sentences to convicted criminals, including white-collar varieties. Why, Sirica asked himself, were some of the accused acting so innocent of charges of burglary, wiretapping, and conspiracy, especially the five who had been caught in the act by the police?

Then, however, the at best skeptical Judge Sirica made a decision that allayed White House anxieties. He issued a judicial gag order to help guarantee the defendants a fair trial and an impartial verdict by the trial jury. This meant that all witnesses and *potential* witnesses in the upcoming trial were not supposed to talk about the case to anybody, especially reporters.[28] On the eve of a presidential election, this was pure gold for the White House.

Sirica's gag order, however, came too late to stop further damaging illuminations in the *Washington Post*. By the end of September, former CREEP director John Mitchell, who had resigned in July to protect Nixon, was linked to the secret fund from which Liddy had paid the Watergate burglars. This was manageable. Whatever happened to Mitchell, he was from CREEP, not the White House. Mitchell could also be guaranteed to keep quiet about CREEP–White House connections.

What came next, however, wasn't so manageable. First, Donald Segretti and his bag of sleaze surfaced, and lights went off in Woodward and Bernstein's brains. "By itself," they later recalled:

the Watergate bugging made little sense, particularly since it occurred when the Nixon campaign was at its strongest [in the polls during the course of the year 1972]. But if it had been a part of something much broader, it might make some sense . . . And there was evidence [once the existence of the Segretti dirty-tricks campaign was definitely known] of a broader scheme. . . . Perhaps the White House had been involved in a much bigger way and for much longer than most people figured.[29]

It had indeed. Then, during the second week of October, Woodward and Bernstein discovered that Dwight Chapin, a student who had been associated in campus politics with Segretti at the University of Southern California (U.S.C.) had drafted the "Canuck letter," a phony ethnic slur with which Segretti had helped sabotage Senator Edmund S. Muskie's presidential campaign. Dwight Chapin, moreover, was Richard Milhous Nixon's presidential appointments secretary. *Now* the dirty trickery of which Watergate was a part had reached into the White House *directly.* Now the CREEP–White House interlock was clearer. The argument that Nixon was not involved became less tenable.

Once the Segretti-Chapin link was made, White House staff reacted ferally. Press Secretary Ron Zeigler, who had also politicked at U.S.C. with Messrs. Segretti and Chapin, took the lead. "Hearsay, innuendo, and guilt by association," Zeigler charged, were being used by unscrupulous reporters. Still, these reporters knew, for instance, that Zeigler, Chapin, and Segretti had all engaged in collegiate election frauds they'd titled "ratfucking."[30]

Election frauds at U.S.C. could be bragged about and leered over by Big Men on Campus. But political fraud in the real world was different, especially when you got caught at it. Segretti and Chapin, therefore, began to sweat. Woodward and Bernstein also began to think, by early October, that the "head ratfucker" might be Nixon himself, as Deep Throat told Woodward that a sense of reality finally had dawned on the young "switchblade mentality" boys Nixon had surrounded himself with. They weren't brilliant, Deep Throat reported, and they were afraid it had all gotten out of hand.[31] It had indeed. Only a month after Nixon's men thought they had finally stonewalled the Watergate investigation—and after Hunt, Liddy, and the five burglars *and no others* were indicted in mid-September—loose ends like Segretti and Chapin began to unravel.

Sirica's gag order, however, helped keep the fabric of the cover-up intact. So did the momentum of the fast-approaching November election. The *Washington Post* was a Democratic paper, and its occasional Watergate stories were pilloried as part of a smear campaign by discredited liberals to turn the electoral tide in their favor. Many believed such charges. More

didn't pay any sustained attention to Watergate at all because the fragmentary reporting of the story confused them, because they were unfamil-
iar with the legal issues and proceedings involved, or because they figured
that there was no way that Nixon could lose the upcoming election, however guilty he might be. Still more citizens figured it was "all politics," just
pots calling kettles black. Democrats didn't help their own case, in this
regard, by using rhetorical smear that rivalled Spiro Agnew's during the
final weeks of the campaign.

Partisanship, lack of coherent information, cynicism, and the fact that
the Democrats were heading for almost certain defeat in the presidential
contest all combined to mute the impact of journalistic investigation. It
also persuaded newspapers other than the *Washington Post* that Watergate
was not a very big story. Editors certainly thought so: 753 of the nation's
daily papers endorsed Richard Nixon that November, as against 56 that
endorsed McGovern. Popular perceptions were only slightly less supportive. Voters *under* twenty-nine believed Nixon was a more sincere and
believable politician than McGovern by a 57-to-28 percent majority in a
poll taken just before the election. And, on election day, Nixon beat
McGovern by almost two-to-one, winning 61 percent of the ballots.[32]

Although the Democrats hung on to control of Congress, with 243 of 435
seats in the House, and 58 of 100 seats in the Senate, the drubbing McGovern had received, and the already parlous state of Democratic party unity,
restrained postelection vengeance. To keep yelling foul after losing betok-
ened a sore loser. So long as the break-in and *not the cover-up* remained the
focus of the Watergate story, political retribution had to be restrained.
Only when the cover-up that the *Post* reporters had started to unravel
replaced the burglary itself as the major component of Watergate would
Nixon, the sore winner, become vulnerable to renewed Democratic attack.

Transforming the Watergate story from break-in to cover-up, however,
was not something the politicians accomplished, nor was it something a
handful of reporters accomplished independently. It was a process that
really began with the court trial of the seven Watergate defendants.

This judicial contest was not joined until January 8th, 1973, six months
after the burglary and a convenient two months after the election. Then,
Liddy, Hunt, and their five fellows faced Judge John J. Sirica. It did not take
Judge Sirica long to feel disappointment about what was happening in his
court. All the defendants were still pleading innocent, like unto angels.
Worse, the federal prosecutors seemed, to former boxer Sirica, to be pulling
their punches. "Liddy was the boss," coprosecutor Earl Silbert argued. A
single Nixon loyalist had gone off half-cocked and planned and orchestrated the crime. Liddy had acted politically; maybe Hunt had, too. Every-

body else probably had financial motives, including McCord, CREEP's security director.

Sirica, however, refused to buy the Liddy-as-kingpin argument. He was distinctly unimpressed by Liddy. "No political campaign committee," Sirica later wrote, would have turned over almost $200,000 to "a man like Gordon Liddy without someone higher up in the organization approving the transaction. How could I not see that?"[33] How, indeed? Especially with an arrogant Gordon Liddy facing him in his own court. Liddy refused to testify or to cooperate in any way, silently daring Sirica to do something about it.

As if Liddy's insolent claims to rectitude weren't enough, there were also the five burglars. Yes, their lawyers said, their clients *had* all been caught breaking in and wiretapping. That was indisputable. But their motive had *not* been personal gain, as the prosecution alleged. They had acted on patriotic motives. Somebody had convinced all five to do what they had done for the greater good of the nation. They were innocent of intent to commit a crime. Misguided they might be, but not criminal.

None of the defendants named names. None told whom they had acted for. Had Liddy alone sounded the clarion call to save the Republic? Unlikely. Then who had? A resounding silence followed this crucial question. They'd only followed somebody's orders, the burglars replied. Maximum John was distinctly unimpressed. The burglars were simply doing with words what Liddy was doing with silence. All intimated they were backed by powerful political forces, and then dared the court to proceed. This was not a smart move against a stubborn jurist who viewed political power and the people who held it as a lot less majestic than most Americans of the period.

Then the fix really went in, and Sirica's sometimes not too courtly temper worsened. First Howard Hunt, upset by the recent death of his wife in an airplane crash while on a trip to pay hush money, tried to plead guilty to some of the indictments against him. No way, replied Sirica. Hunt had to plead all or nothing. Hunt caved in and pleaded guilty to all the charges against him on January 11th. Sirica now had one guilty party, and six innocents, but not for long. The day after Hunt's mea culpa, Sirica heard that the four Cuban Americans were on the verge of pleading guilty to everything as well. They did so on January 15th.

A stone wall was rising fast, and there didn't seem to be anything Sirica could do about it. A judge cannot fail to accept a full guilty plea by defendants but, in so doing, the court forfeits its chance to prosecute further and find out more than it already knows. Somebody was trifling with Sirica. The defendants couldn't intimidate him, so now they were trying to protect the higher-ups in another way. Five innocents suddenly admitted guilt after trial had begun, and Sirica smelled a payoff. These men were all going to plead guilty and march out the door, mocking him and the legal system he represented. It was too much.[34]

But it didn't happen the way Sirica feared it would. The door didn't fully close. Gordon Liddy and James McCord kept the courtroom investigation alive. Instead of pleading guilty like their fellows, the two maintained their innocence, thereby allowing the trial to continue.

Sirica had his opportunity and took it. Once Hunt and the four Cuban Americans had all pled guilty, the judge told the jury to leave the courtroom temporarily, called the five men before him, and asked if anyone had ordered them to change their pleas. No. Was a payoff going on? No. Had any of the five ever worked for the CIA? No. Nonsense, replied Sirica, you should all expect heavy sentences, and so should anybody else who impedes the progress of this investigation. Gordon Liddy laughed and leered, and Sirica fumed some more. Why Liddy leered, rather than plead guilty and end the trial, is an oddity of history and of Liddy's mind. The behavior of the remaining defendant, McCord, was less odd.

McCord had been a Company (i.e., CIA) man, just like Howard Hunt and the Cuban Americans who had occasionally been on CIA retainers were. But, unlike those others, McCord *admitted* his CIA connection. McCord also hated what Nixon was still occasionally trying to do to America's foreign spying agency. Saddling the CIA with the rap for Watergate and the by-now-associated dirty tricks of Segretti and others would, McCord believed, destroy its effectiveness. McCord was not about to allow that, and had so informed the White House. He'd written a friend of his there in December 1972, for instance, that "every tree in the forest will fall," Watergate would be a "scorched desert," the "whole matter is on a precipice right now," and that an explosion would result if Richard Helms was fired or if "the Watergate operation is laid at the CIA's feet."[35] McCord was angry, very angry, but the war of whispers against the CIA did not cease. McCord, accordingly, threatened the White House with partial exposure and hoped that this would be enough to save the CIA— and himself—from further harm.

Gordon Liddy's was a stranger case. A self-described strong man who remained utterly loyal to the bitter end, Liddy was more histrionic than realistic. He had recruited James McCord and thus allowed Watergate to be directly connected to Nixon's Committee to Re-Elect the President. Liddy had much to answer for, and he knew it. He had even told a bemused John Dean that he would stand out on a street corner and allow someone to come along and shoot him, only two days after the Watergate burglary exploded in his face. Dean never took Liddy up on his offer, nor did Liddy prove his devotion to his superiors by shooting himself.[36] Instead, Liddy apparently sought to prove himself another way. He demonstrated that he was a Real Man by pleading innocent and then not defending himself. Tough Guy Liddy would take his medicine, and no one would ever be able to say that he was a wimp who had botched everything in the first place. Liddy would thus achieve heroic stature, not least in his own eyes. During the trial, the federal prosecutors were arguing that Liddy was the kingpin of Watergate: attention, therefore, was focused on him, even by those who believed that small-fish Liddy had got his orders from somebody else. Such attention only further legitimized Liddy's courtroom posturing in his own eyes. By ostentatiously not talking, Liddy would show he was loaded with *will;* and cock a snook at those who hated or pitied him. Liddy was probably determined to achieve heroic repute, and achieve some he did. Yet, ironically, by allowing the trial to go on, he also helped to destroy the administration and the president he was supposed to be trying to protect.

Judge Sirica despised Liddy's theatrics and didn't believe he was the kingpin of anything. So, once Liddy and McCord were the only innocents left, Sirica began to take an unusually active role in examining witnesses. Some successfully pulled off perjury, temporarily, Magruder of CREEP among them. Former CREEP treasurer Hugh Sloan was another matter. He confirmed the earlier *Washington Post* story that both Magruder and John Mitchell of CREEP had knowledge of monies Sloan had paid out to Liddy to finance sabotage. Sloan also testified that Secretary of Commerce Maurice Stans, CREEP's finance chairman, had known about the expenditures. And Magruder had ordered Sloan to make all dirty-tricks payments in cash.

Sloan, innocent of involvement in conspiracy or cover-up, gave the courtroom and journalistic investigations more impetus. Liddy had not, as the prosecutors were arguing, gone off on a wild escapade of his own after stealing funds out of campaign cookie jars. It now looked as though the Watergate conspiracy went higher, at least as high as CREEP's Magruder and Mitchell. Magruder, who had just testified that everything felonious was Liddy's doing, had OK'd payments of almost $200,000 in supposedly untraceable cash. He was now very suspect. Where did the cover-up end?

Where, indeed? By the time that the Watergate burglary trial concluded, on January 30th, 1973, three weeks after it began, all seven burglars were convicted on all charges. Sirica had made sure that the Watergate grand jury which had brought in these charges stayed in existence to investigate new information and levy new charges in a case that was getting more complicated by the day. Journalists investigating the case were now joined by a righteously indignant judge. The trial jury's verdict alerted increasing numbers of people that something important *had* happened at Watergate, even though Nixon had triumphantly won reelection.

Popular assumptions about the nonpartisan way that judges and juries behave legitimized the desire to know more about crimes, especially about the crime of conspiracy to obstruct justice. So, only eight days after a jury convicted the burglars, the very often partisan U.S. Senate edged into the investigative fray for the first time, voting 70-to-0 on February 7th, 1973, to create a special committee to delve further into the increasingly murky waters of what was no longer simply a third-rate burglary.

## *The Cover-up Unravels*

Before the first stage of the political trial of Watergate began, however, the court and the journalists still had very important parts to play. Their combined efforts blew the case wide open and further encouraged elected politicians to risk entering the Watergate arena.

Sirica set the stage for what was to follow when he read the riot act to the Justice Department's prosecuting team in open court on January 30th for arguing throughout the trial that Liddy, Hunt, McCord, and their four confederates were running the only criminal game in town. "I have not been satisfied," Sirica declaimed, "and I am still not satisfied that all the pertinent facts that might be available have been produced before an American jury." A cover-up was going on, and the prosecutors hadn't gotten nearly to the bottom of it yet. "Everyone knows," Sirica continued, "that there is going to be a Congressional investigation in this case." This implied that the Justice Department's prosecutors had better get busier if they didn't want to end up looking like fools or worse. The prosecutors assured Sirica they'd bring the burglars back before the grand jury, after their sentencing, for additional grilling.[37]

Sirica's airing of the cover-up provided important assistance to the few reporters who had been unravelling the cover-up from almost the instant it began. Until Sirica expanded the scope of Watergate from break-in to cover-up during the trial, spirits at the *Washington Post* were sagging badly. The *Post* did not even mention Watergate in a retrospective on Nixon published when he began his second term. Nor did senior staff at the paper yet feature the story in their columns. Watergate remained the almost unique property of Woodward, Bernstein, and the *local* news division of the *Post.* Woodward and Bernstein, moreover, were stalled. Efforts to involve cover-up principals were being frustrated. H. R. Haldeman, in particular, proved a hard nut to crack. Evidence accumulated that he was implicated, but it remained circumstantial and Haldeman remained— Haldeman, Nixon's right-hand man in the White House. To take on Haldeman was very risky, and sources clammed up, especially after Haldeman's boss, Nixon, smashed McGovern. No, Haldeman was too big. Deep Throat told Woodward on January 24th that *everybody* in the upper reaches of the White House staff and the FBI was in on the cover-up, including Haldeman, but Deep Throat added nothing to what he'd earlier intimated about Haldeman's involvements more than a month earlier. "Insulation" was the order of the day. Evidence had been stifled, shredded, and burned. The stakes were simply too risky, now, for most of the inhabitants of the political jungle.

That thought, apparently, also occurred to an important U.S. senator, Sam Ervin of North Carolina. Ervin, shortly to be selected as chair of the Senate Watergate Committee, called Woodward into his office for a confabulation in January as the burglary trial was in progress. Woodward allowed that big fish like Haldeman were bathed in Watergate rascality and argued they should be caught in the upcoming Senate investigation's net. To try to convince Ervin to do this, Woodward told Ervin about leads he and Bernstein had developed. He summarized what they definitely knew and much of what they still only guessed. He and Bernstein, Woodward continued, had only scratched surfaces. What they had pointed toward was a massive political sabotage operation against the Democrats. Would Ervin's committee stop the White House's cover-up effort from succeeding?

Yes, said Ervin, he would try. So far, at least, as calling upon people to testify before the Senate Watergate Committee, up to and including Haldeman. Ervin, however, was not optimistic. "I'd be content if we discover Mr. Magruder's role," he told Woodward.[38] Almost as Ervin spoke, however, the cover-up began to disintegrate. The decay involved Nixon loyalists losing faith in their superiors, becoming fearful of being made sacrificial lambs, and then deciding to try to save themselves by getting their superiors first. Five men were central: Watergate burglars Frank Sturgis and James McCord, the FBI's L. Patrick Gray, CREEP's Jeb Magruder, and White House Counsel John Dean. Between mid-January and mid-April 1973, their combined trepidation destroyed the cover-up that all had helped create and focused the investigation on President Nixon.

Frank Sturgis, a one-time guerilla commander for Fidel Castro who later worked for the CIA to overthrow his former boss, was first. Sturgis was being paid to keep his mouth shut, but he became the first of the Watergate crew to sing like a bird, and his song served as an overture to the symphony that followed. As early as November 1972, Sturgis was talking to a reporter. Later, a *New York Times* reporter got hold of Sturgis and informed his editors that Sturgis was charging that a White House silence-buying operation, utilizing fellow burglar Howard Hunt, was under way. The *Times,* however, hesitated. Skeptical editors demanded exhaustive confirmation which delayed publication until January 14th, 1973. The story, however, was important, for it reached Judge Sirica just before January 15th, when the four Cuban Americans (including Sturgis) joined Howard Hunt in suddenly changing their pleas from innocent to guilty. Sirica, already testy, became furious when his cover-up suspicions were confirmed by the story about Sturgis in the *Times.* The *New York Times* had not previously devoted much attention to Watergate, even though it was a national newspaper of great repute. Its publication of Sturgis's charges demonstrated that the *cover-up* aspects of Watergate were now important national news and that Sirica might look silly if he didn't stop the fraud occurring in his court.

Sirica didn't want to look like a patsy. He was too combative a jurist for that. He pushed the defendants and the prosecutors hard, and said he intended to be Maximum John when sentencing occurred.[39] His threats gave all the pled-guilty or convicted burglars pause for reflection after January 30th. James McCord, for one, had over seven weeks to ponder his prospects between his conviction and the scheduled sentencing date of March 23rd, 1973.

McCord, however, didn't make it to the 23rd. On March 20th, he blew the Watergate case wide open. The former CIA man did this by confessing the cover-up in a fashion that did maximum damage to the White House. Fellow burglar Sturgis had talked only to reporters. McCord, who, unlike Sturgis, had never received hush money, addressed a letter to Judge John Sirica.

In his letter, delivered three days before the sentencing, McCord did not name names and confined himself to generalities. But what generalities they were! The Watergate burglars were being pressured not to talk. Perjury had been committed at the trial. Others involved in the break-in and conspiracy could have been identified by witnesses, but were not. Watergate was not a CIA operation, even though his Cuban confederates had apparently been persuaded that it was. McCord's motives for committing crimes were different from those of all the others. McCord handed Sirica legal dynamite. The judge now had a weapon to keep the criminal investigation of Watergate very much alive. For the first time, Sirica had a legally admissible confession that a cover-up was going on. "This is the best damned birthday present I've ever gotten," Sirica enthused to an aide.[40]

The question was how to get the biggest bang out of the legal weapon McCord had placed in Sirica's hands. Sirica and his advisers decided to make it public just before he levied stiff sentences on all of the political saboteurs, except McCord, on the morning of March 23rd. When he did, shock waves went out all over official Washington. Watergate was *big news* now, national news. And it was the cover-up, not the burglary, that was crucial.

Adding to the shock was another charge of cover-up and perjury, a charge that *did* name a name—a very big name: John Dean.

The charge against Dean was levied by a man who had been between a hammer and an anvil for over eight months, L. Patrick Gray of the FBI.[41] On March 22nd, the day before Sirica read the text of McCord's confession in court, Gray testified, before a congressional committee, that Dean had "probably lied" to the FBI early in its Watergate investigation. His was a specific accusation that a high-ranking official in Nixon's White House was involved in a cover-up. Nobody had legitimized Woodward and Bernstein like this before.

John Wesley Dean III began to sweat. Gray was jumping ship, even though he was more a part of the cover-up than he wanted to admit. It began to look to John Dean as if Gray was trying to protect himself and the FBI by incriminating John Dean. Gray's statement requires some explanation. In a stupendous miscalculation, the White House sought to get Gray appointed "permanent," rather than "acting" FBI director in February 1973, in order to protect itself from the threat of further investigations. By February 28th, Gray began testifying before the Senate Judiciary Committee as the first step in the Senate confirmation process.

The timing was awful. Gray tried to evade Watergate entirely, but courtly Senator Sam Ervin wouldn't let him. Ervin finally had a chance to administer some political punishment to Nixon, and he grabbed the opportunity. Gray was induced to discuss some of the more odoriferous details and, in the process, revealed just how cooperative an accomplice he had been in that whole process. The senators were very anxious to know more, particularly about key White House aides like Haldeman, Ehrlichman, and John Dean. The Judiciary Committee, accordingly, requested that such key cover-up principals start coming up to Capitol Hill to testify at Gray's hearing.

This, Richard Nixon had no interest whatsoever in allowing. Gray's fitness for office had become synonymous with his lack of involvement in

Watergate in many senators' eyes, and Watergate was something Nixon wanted to make past-tense as fast as possible. So, on March 2nd, he issued a presidential order prohibiting all present *and former* White House aides from obeying the Judiciary Committee's summonses. The blanket of obstruction of justice was being rolled over Watergate again.

Senator Ervin and others were furious. The president, they argued, was claiming executive privilege he didn't possess. They tried to get Dean and others to come anyway, but they steadfastly refused. As the discussion began to turn into a nasty legal argument, Senate subpoenas were threatened, and Patrick Gray began taking more and more senatorial punishment all by himself. Take it he did. By March 13th, his nomination was in deep trouble. Gray regularly checked in with cover-up operations officer Dean about his ongoing testimony, and he also did the same with John Ehrlichman. But Dean's optimism about Gray and Ehrlichman's loyalty—not least to himself—began to sag.

For all the consultations and mutual assurances, Gray had become a lightning rod for congressional opposition to the cover-up. Dean, anxious about his own growing visibility, made the point clear to the president. He and Nixon met on March 13th and agreed that Gray, then before the Senate for two weeks, was having his ability to serve them shredded. Nixon concluded that, "After going through the hell of the hearing, he will not be a good [FBI] Director, as far as we're concerned." The problem, Nixon and Dean went on, was as much internal as external. Gray's own bureaucracy might stab him in the back even if he did manage to be confirmed. "Not that Pat wouldn't want to still play ball, but he may not be able to," opined Dean. "I agree," spake Nixon.[42]

The stage was set for abandoning Gray, and Gray probably realized it. The longer the confirmation hearings stretched on, the more his neck was in a noose. Senate Democrats wanted to brand him as a stooge who had purposely bobbled the Watergate investigation. If that gambit succeeded, Nixon would behead Gray himself or, worse, leave him hanging in a political limbo as Watergate was fought out around him. Dean, Nixon, and John Ehrlichman believed that limbo was good enough for one who could no longer do their bidding. Gray faced ruin—all because he had played along with cover-up artists like Dean.

What to do? Get out from between a legislative rock and an executive hard place by nailing Dean. Shift the burden of the cover-up to somebody else, somebody who could not implicate Gray in illegalities like destruction of evidence without also incriminating himself. So Dean it was. The president's counsel, hitherto a shadow on the edges of Watergate, got vaulted to stage center. Gray compromised other people at CREEP and Justice during his Senate testimony, and he scared Mitchell, Magruder, Attorney General Kleindienst, and others in the process. But John Dean was the one on whom the spotlight really focused.

Dean began getting an education in the ways in which people became part of the political food chain. So, just as Gray helped turn eyes in his direction, Dean returned to the Oval Office to have some weighty conversations with the president. One took place on March 21st, 1973, on the eve of Gray's and McCord's revelations.

Dean had been an enthusiastic rabbit previously, but now he was at risk, and Nixon had to listen to news he didn't want to hear. Pat Gray's testimony was disastrous. Nixon's blanket prohibitions against testimony by present or former White House employees were infuriating Capitol Hill. The Segretti aspect of Watergate was likely to crack wider open. Demands for hush money from the about-to-be-sentenced burglars, especially Howard Hunt, were escalating. And, finally and most important, little hope any longer existed of isolating the White House from widely perceived involvement in a cover-up already nine months old.

Dean used a punchy metaphor to make the point. "We have a cancer—within—close to the Presidency, that's growing. It's growing daily. It's compounding, it grows geometrically now, because it compounds itself," Dean began. There were simply too many people involved; too many weak reeds; too many demands for payola or pardons or whatever. Too many people were going to have to start perjuring themselves—or perjuring themselves more—to keep the Watergate cover-up a secret. It was getting out of hand, like a metastasizing and spreading cancer. It was time, said Dean, that Nixon knew all that Dean knew about how far the Watergate mess extended. Dean was apprehensive about continuing as point man in the cover-up. He was too visible now, and too much at risk. The cover-up, not the burglary, was the primary political problem. This was the cancer within. What was, wasn't working. It was time for a change of tactics, strategy, or both.

In rambling conversations with Nixon, Haldeman, and Ehrlichman that took more than two-and-a-half hours, Dean presented four major alternatives to more-of-the-same. One was to simply stop paying off whiners like Howard Hunt, let them talk, and face the criticism that would cause some heads to roll within CREEP and White House ranks. Two other alternatives concerned making prophylactic arrangements: to try to find a new (and, thus, relatively ill-informed) judge and grand jury for the Watergate case, or to appoint a special prosecutor from within the Department of Justice to carry on a carefully limited investigation of political sabotage and obstruction of justice. Both of these proposals were attempts to substitute watered-down judicial proceedings for the more threatening and more public political investigations already going on in the Judiciary Committee and soon to be start in the Senate Watergate Committee, established the month before. Dean's final and most important proposal was that a sort of collective political suicide pact be worked out among himself, John Mitchell, Bob Haldeman, and John Ehrlichman to allow these aides to remove the cancer from the presidency by walking the plank for Nixon. "[E]verybody is now starting to watch out for their own behind," Dean declared. This had to be stopped before it drew Nixon himself into the mess. "Sometimes it's well to give them something," Nixon restated Dean's logic, "and then they don't want the bigger fish."[43]

The president, however, didn't bite at any of the proposals made by his counsel, nor did he throw anybody to the sharks. Instead, he ordered Dean to do more-of-the-same by continuing to pay hush money to Hunt and other burglars. As much as a million dollars over the course of the next two years was budgeted, and a first installment was shortly delivered to Hunt. Dean had been "turned around" during the discussion.

It didn't take Dean long to understand the mistake he'd made. More-of-the-same and tough-it-out made him no worse off than he was already. But then Nixon, with an assist from Ehrlichman, put something else on the plate later in the March 21st meeting. A proposal Dean had not made, and one he wanted at all costs to avoid—a proposal that Dean be set up to take the fall for the Watergate cover-up all by himself. Paranoia now began to make good sense to John Dean: somebody *was* out to get him. That some-body appeared to be John Ehrlichman, and he was nothing if not thorough. For months, he had pressed Nixon and Haldeman to order Dean to prepare a thoroughly deodorized "Dean Report" about White House and CREEP involvement in the cover-up. From November to March, Dean stalled and evaded Ehrlichman. On March 20th, however, according to Dean, Nixon called Dean at home and vaguely enthused how nice a Dean Report would be. Dean, then, had his "cancer on the presidency" meeting with Nixon the very next day as a means of protecting himself from Ehrlichman, as well as from Gray.

But Dean failed. He muffed his opportunity to get Nixon to support any alternative to more-of-the-same cover-up, and gave Ehrlichman another opening. Ehrlichman proposed a Dean Report *seven* times during the final forty minutes of discussions on March 21st.

Ehrlichman's strategy was brutally simple. The cover-up was messy and likely to get messier. The idea was to get Dean to write a report protecting everybody from everything, and then say that that report had been pre-pared months previously—in August 1972, for example. Dean could be advertised as a super-sleuth who had been assigned to ferret out evil within the administration. Then, if anybody in the White House got thoroughly enmeshed in Watergate during the ongoing criminal investigation or the forthcoming Senate investigation, blame it on John Dean. The president and his topmost aides like John Ehrlichman and H. R. Haldeman, the argument could go, would have known all about the nasty cover-up all along—except that Dean's nefarious report had misled them all.

It was a nice idea, except that it would ruin John Wesley Dean III. The question was posed: Would Dean write a report to give Nixon and his topmost advisers instantaneous alibis if anything more went awry with the cover-up? No order was given to Dean by Nixon during the course of the March 21st meeting, but the axe was poised and Dean knew it. Dean also knew what he should do: be loyal at all costs. He should write a report, mount the guillotine, and hope the axe didn't fall. If it did, he was to sacrifice himself to protect his superiors. But Dean bridled, for what appear to have been six major reasons.

First, the Dean Report proposal had been initiated, in Dean's mind, by precisely the wrong person, the one man in the White House John Dean most feared and hated, and whom he had the least desire to protect: John Ehrlichman. Second, Dean believed he would receive no reciprocal loyalty from the White House for the sacrifice he was being asked to make. Ehrlichman had steadily expanded his power over many domestic matters that interested Nixon a lot less than foreign affairs. Dean might well, then, be dependent upon a saurian Ehrlichman for the legal and other assistance he would need after the axe fell. Third, Dean wanted to throw somebody else to the wolves—anybody else, but particularly John Mitchell and Jeb Stuart Magruder of CREEP, men whose political incineration could keep the cover-up separated from the White House and John Wesley Dean.

Fourth, Dean had reluctantly come to believe that no one sacrificial lamb would suffice. Lambs simply wouldn't line up for the slaughter alone. Each, including Dean, felt increasingly isolated, angry, and cynical about the behavior and motives of their fellows. The only solution was a mass slaughter. That way, no one of Nixon's aides would feel that *he* was acting to protect the president while the others were acting only to protect themselves. Fifth, collective suicide was also the answer because the cover-up simply had too many loose ends. The way to keep this house of cards from falling was to knock down all the cards at once. Otherwise, the trail of conspiracy and cover-up could lead to Nixon himself. If everybody walked the plank, none of them would incriminate Nixon—not if they remembered their all-important pledges of loyalty to *him* as their bonds of trust with each other strained or broke in whatever ordeals were in store.

Sixth and finally, John Dean wouldn't sacrifice himself alone because the timing was dreadful. Gray, as we have seen, told the Senate that Dean had "probably lied" to FBI investigators the day after Dean failed to talk Nixon out of a Dean Report on the 21st. A public charge by the FBI's acting director that he'd "probably lied" meant John Dean was going to get it right in the neck in court and in the upcoming Senate Watergate Committee investigation as well. Who, Dean must have wondered, could benefit from such a mess? Who, perhaps, but Ehrlichman?

Then things got even worse. The day after Gray dropped his verbal bombshell, Judge John J. Sirica dropped his. On the morning of March 23rd, Sirica read McCord's letter charging the existence of a widespread and thoroughgoing cover-up during the Watergate trial.

DEAN PROBABLY LIED read the headline in the *Washington Post* of March 23rd. Dean and his new wife Maureen awoke that day to find their home surrounded by reporters and television cameras. There was blood on the floor in the Watergate case now, and mobs of journalists were now out to demonstrate that there was a lot more where that came from. As Dean furiously tried to figure out what to do, the phone rang. It was the private line from the White House relaying the news about McCord's letter to Sirica. "The dam was cracking," Dean later recalled. Dean, too, was cracking. But the final crack was yet to come.

Later that day, Nixon invited a still hidden-at-home Dean and his wife Maureen to go to the presidential retreat at Camp David in Maryland for some well-deserved relaxation. Dean didn't need to be asked twice, but the vacation had lasted about five minutes when the phone rang in their well-appointed cabin. It was Haldeman on the line from the White House. After verbal preliminaries, Dean reported Haldeman saying that "While you're up there, the President would like you to take a shot at writing up the report we talked about on Watergate."[44]

Dean was finally being ordered to exonerate Nixon, Haldeman, Ehrlichman, and whoever else Nixon might choose to protect, by writing a report which would inevitably ruin himself. He was to become the mastermind of the cover-up whenever Nixon chose to release that report. . . . and in whatever final form he chose to release it. It was all up to John Dean now.

## What John Dean Did During (and After) His Spring Vacation

Dean was no hero. He took no forthright stands and issued no immediate challenges. He tried, instead, to play both sides of the street and save as much as he could. Only gradually and reluctantly did he move into open opposition to Nixon, and so destroy his presidency.

John Dean had cause for reluctance. He was a committed conservative whose first political idol was Barry Goldwater of Arizona, and he had even roomed with Goldwater's son Barry, Jr., at private school. Dean saw himself as part of an elite that would bring order and stability back to a nation which had lost its soul during strife-filled years like 1968. John Dean was also a good soldier—the "White House platoon sergeant," as lawyers Richard Ben-Veniste and George Frampton, Jr., later put it, of the Watergate campaign. For nine long months, Dean had plugged holes and kept his superiors informed about what was going on down in the dust of the White House cover-up. "Like any good non-com Dean did not have to consult the White House brass at every step," Ben-Veniste and Frampton concluded; "he knew what was required." The White House, in the persons of Haldeman, Ehrlichman, and Nixon, made major decisions, planned strategy, and gave the orders. Dean carried those orders out; now he was being set up as the commanding general of the cover-up.[45]

It seemed that Dean had company. To further protect themselves, the men at the apex of the administration were planning to throw two CREEP eminences to the wolves: former director John Mitchell and Mitchell's deputy, Magruder. The break-in and other political sabotage could thus be advertised as CREEP-only operation, at the same time that Dean was to be saddled with the blame for the White House end of the cover-up. By March 25th, for example, the *Los Angeles Times* and the *Washington Post* were reporting that Dean and Magruder both had advance notice of the Watergate break-in. These were leaks aimed at putting Dean, Mitchell, and Magruder on the menu.

But it did not take John Dean long to stop writing the report he'd been ordered to prepare. One day was enough. Political suicide was not in Dean's nature, not if he had to do it alone, so he stonewalled. Playing the good soldier, he tried to stall long enough to convince Nixon to include Haldeman and Ehrlichman—especially Ehrlichman—in the political sacrifice that now included Dean, Mitchell, and Magruder. He did this out of hate, revenge, envy, and desperation. He also believed, as he told Nixon on March 21st, that only major surgery would work, that only by firing the general staff of the cover-up could Nixon be saved.

Meanwhile, other people kept on cracking. McCord had already talked to Sirica, and by March 28th, he was talking to the Senate Watergate Committee as well. This testimony, supposedly secret, was leaked all over Washington. Other convicted burglars might tell what they knew. None of this could get Nixon, but parts of it might nail Haldeman, Ehrlichman, and Dean. It could also get Mitchell and Magruder, and, while Mitchell didn't panic, Magruder did. It was a mess and getting messier, and a rush to the lifeboats was in order. The point was not to be the last person to enter the lifeboat, especially as the Calvary of the Senate Watergate Committee investigation loomed. These hearings were to be held in front of television cameras and were finally—in the wake of Gray's and McCord's statements—going to focus more on the cover-up aspects of Watergate than on the burglary itself. Thus, some lower- and middle-level participants in Watergate started thinking about self-preservation and began arranging to surrender on the best possible terms. By the end of the first week of April, the process was well under way and people were talking to lawyers.

John Dean got his lawyer during the final days of March, and used him to feel out to the opposition. If Nixon didn't sacrifice Haldeman and Ehrlichman, Dean was going to do it for him, before they threw him overboard and tried to sail away scot-free. Magruder, meanwhile, was also trying to find out about others, including John Dean and John Mitchell. The legal poker involved was complex.[46] Dean, Magruder, and the others all remained cognizant of one thing: Richard Nixon was still president, and a man to be respected and feared. The fear was especially relevant because Dean, Magruder, et al. were all playing most of their poker with men who worked for Nixon's Justice Department—the federal district attorneys who were the original prosecutors of the Watergate case.

When last we met these prosecutors (Earl Silbert, Seymour Glanzer, and Donald E. Campbell), they were arguing that "Liddy was the boss" of the Watergate break-in before Judge Sirica back in January. Sirica, remember, was distinctly unimpressed by their performance, because they were ignoring the *cover-up* aspects of the case and only going after small fry. But, only two months later, much had happened. Silbert and his compatriots were starting to get real earfuls as Dean, Magruder, and their lawyers began cutting deals. The information hinted at a thoroughgoing conspiracy to obstruct justice and implicated the president's closest aides in political sabotage of which the Watergate break-in was only a small part.

The prosecutors, however, were between a political hammer and an anvil themselves. They worked for Nixon's Attorney General Richard Kleindienst and Kleindienst's deputy, Henry Peterson. If they told their superiors all that Dean and Magruder were telling them about Haldeman, Ehrlichman, and Mitchell, Nixon would know, because Richard Nixon was their president. Still, neither Dean nor Magruder was trying to implicate Nixon in a blessed thing. Nevertheless, Dean knew full well that Nixon *was* involved in a conspiracy to obstruct justice. He also knew, from previous experience, that anything the prosecutors reported to their superiors at Justice got back to Nixon almost immediately, and to Haldeman and Ehrlichman immediately after that.

Dean, therefore, through his lawyer, demanded that the prosecutors keep his statements to them confidential. He still had one foot planted in the White House, and had no desire to make more enemies there any sooner than necessary.

So Dean wanted a pledge of silence. Equally important, Dean wanted as much judicial immunity as possible. He knew Nixon was throwing him to the wolves and that it was also only a matter of time before he ended up in Sirica's court on criminal charges. If Dean didn't make some sort of deal with the prosecutors, Maximum John might very well send him away for forty years. Immunity was the way out. Dean could incriminate higher-ups in the cover-up, *but not Nixon;* in return, the prosecutors would buy his testimony.

The purchase could be made in one of two ways. Dean could get total immunity or limited immunity. Total immunity meant that any crime Dean testified to in court could not be charged against him later in any way. This was the type of immunity that Dean wanted. Limited, or use, immunity was another possibility. Under this type of immunity, Dean could testify about his involvement in various crimes, and that specific testimony could not be used against him. But if *others also testified* that Dean had committed the crimes, and used different evidence to prove it, Dean could be convicted on the basis of their testimony. This type of immunity Dean didn't like at all. First, Dean didn't initially intend to testify to everything he knew (especially about Nixon); second, if Dean forgot one thing about any crime he had committed, somebody else could come along and hang him with it later. Dean had committed a lot of perjury and obstruction of justice in the last nine months, and it wouldn't take many lapses of memory to risk growing old behind stone walls.

Dean's lawyer, Charles Shaffer, knew all about this. So Shaffer told Dean they must do two things: hold out for total immunity if they could get it, and make sure the federal prosecutors stayed mum about the meetings he and Dean were having with them. Shaffer also advised Dean to get in the lifeboat fast to maximize his chances for full immunity and prosecutorial silence.

The prosecutors listened. They had to. Their case against cover-up principals was not very strong. They didn't, however, give Dean and Shaffer what they wanted. They refused full immunity; worse, they blabbed about the Dean-Shaffer meetings to their superiors at Justice a week after Dean had started to talk with them.

Now Dean was in *big* trouble. No immunity deal had been worked out, yet Nixon knew that Dean was trying to make a deal with the prosecutors precisely when he was still officially supposed to be beavering away on the Dean Report. On April 15th, 1973, John Dean received his last summons from Nixon. In a frosty meeting, Nixon posed leading questions to Dean, questions designed to elicit admissions that Dean had done this and that during the Watergate cover-up. Dean, now older and wiser, began to suspect he was being secretly tape-recorded by Nixon so Nixon could use what Dean was saying to inform newspaper reporters or courts at some later date. Dean's suspicions were exactly right.

Worse, however, was what Nixon did on April 17th, when he read an announcement to reporters who were by then rabid for news about the White House's supposed investigation of itself in connection with the cover-up. "Major developments," Nixon allowed, had just come to his attention. Watergate was now a presidential responsibility, by God, and he would get to the bottom of it. White House aides whom Nixon had prohibited from testifying to Congress on grounds of executive privilege during Gray's disastrous confirmation hearings would now obey legislative summonses, including those from the Senate Watergate Committee. Anybody indicted by the courts would cease their active association with the White House. There was one final thing, added Nixon: "No individual holding, in the past or present, a position of major importance in the Administration should be given immunity from prosecution." That meant John Dean. Dean, or anybody else, who talked should be punished for every crime they admitted to.[47]

It was, as even Dean admitted, a clever stroke. Nixon—on the Machiavellian advice of John Ehrlichman, Dean thought—was posing as a law-and-order president, while, at the same time, trying to scare federal prosecutors away from giving immunity to Dean *and* thus scaring Dean into silence.

What to do now? If Dean continued to go the judicial route, he might get nowhere. Immunity deals with federal prosecutors were now iffy at best. The most they'd ever offered was exemption from all *but* one charge of conspiracy. Dean had refused, and then the prosecutors had tried to force him to testify before the Watergate grand jury. Dean had refused again, citing his Fifth Amendment right to avoid self-incrimination. The prosecutors, meanwhile, were also getting evidence from others, chiefly Jeb Stuart Magruder of CREEP, that implicated Dean and undercut his bargaining power. By April 19th, the *Washington Post* reported that Magruder had charged Dean and Mitchell with helping plan the break-in and with organizing payoffs to the burglars.

It looked—again—as if Dean, Mitchell, and Magruder were being set up to take the fall to save Haldeman, Ehrlichman, and whomever they chose to protect. It also looked as if Nixon would continue to find out everything Dean told prosecutors, thus allowing Haldeman and Ehrlichman to plan their defense against Dean's charges. The White House was already making use of press leaks and countercharges from the likes of Chuck Colson, who were buying themselves protection from prison by saying whatever Ehrlichman, Nixon, or Haldeman told them to say. Colson's leaks to nationally syndicated columnist Jack Anderson resulted in an April 26th story that Colson and Ehrlichman were sterling fellows who had uncovered Dean's skullduggeries only twelve days before.[48]

What to do now? Answer rough with rough. Say to hell with *judicial* trials, and try to make a deal with the *politicians* of the Senate Watergate Committee. After all, it was the Democrats who controlled the Senate and chaired its committees.

John Dean proceeded carefully. Nixon finally fired him on April 30th, but he continued to meet with federal prosecutors until early May while he and his lawyer began sounding out Samuel Dash, chief counsel of the Senate Watergate Committee. Although Dean didn't finally meet Dash until May 12th, his decision about what to say to Dash was very largely made for him by Nixon.

Had Dean been purely idealistic, the way he got fired should have insured his silence. He was sacrificed the way he'd offered to be a little more than five weeks earlier. He had company, lots of it. Joining him on the plank out of the White House were Haldeman, Ehrlichman, and Attorney General Kleindienst: the collective suicide pact he'd proposed on March 21st. The Ship of State sailed grandly on without them as Nixon rooted out the cancer by firing the aides he had labored so particularly and so long to protect.

Nixon arranged the Dean-Haldeman-Ehrlichman-Kleindienst departures, however, in a fashion that alienated Dean, and which didn't appease the growing appetites of his opponents. Only six months after winning one of the greatest presidential election victories in U.S. history, Nixon tried to recover fading political initiative and failed.

But it was too late. There were, by now, too many loose ends for Nixon to explain without appearing to be either foolish or criminal. He had also made too many enemies and lost the affection of too many political friends, often in connection with events not related to Watergate. Third, Vietnam had provided what national-security rationale existed for the Watergate crimes. But Watergate began to peak—in terms of mass public awareness—just as the Vietnam War began to disappear into limbo.

## The Recipe for Disaster

April 30th, 1973, was a good day for political theater, or so Richard Nixon hoped. In an address broadcast on national radio and TV, Nixon spoke to the people "from [his] heart" on a subject "of deep concern to every American."

The subject was Watergate. Political sabotage and a cover-up of that sabotage had occurred, Nixon admitted. The burglary was not the only— nor even the major—problem. He, however, had had nothing to do with such grisly matters. He'd been too busy solving international and national problems. He had ordered immediate investigations, been repeatedly lied to, and so had remained convinced that no major administration or CREEP official was involved in skullduggery until over ten months after the break-in.

This was standard apologia. Ruthless advisers had deceived the Good King for impure purposes. So spare the king and punish the powers near the throne. The Good King, moreover, had now "personally assumed responsibility for coordinating intensive new inquiries into the matter." Had since March 21st, in fact, when John Dean and the unnamed others responsible for obscuring the truth about Watergate had been grilled by Nixon at the White House. These men had all failed a president who intended full cooperation with the congressional and judicial investigations of the case. Now, "two of the finest public servants it has been my privilege to know," Bob Haldeman and John Ehrlichman, had to leave— not because they had done anything wrong, but to maintain and restore confidence in legal and ethical standards of government. Attorney General

Kleindienst, a distinguished friend "with no personal involvement what-ever in this matter," had also resigned for the public good and because he was a personal friend of some of those now involved in the case. "The Counsel to the President, John Dean, has also resigned," Nixon appended with the dullest of rhetorical thuds. Nixon thus pointed his finger squarely at John Dean as the wrongdoer. All had resigned; but Dean alone was uncomplimented—and, therefore, guilty.

Having tried to dispose of Dean, Nixon went on to say that a new Attorney General had been named with "absolute authority" to "make all decisions bearing on the Watergate case and related matters." These pow-ers included the "authority to name a special supervising prosecutor for matters arising out of the case" if the attorney general–designate, Elliot L. Richardson, chose to do so. (Or if, as Nixon did not say, Senate Democrats forced him to—as they soon did—as a precondition of his confirmation.)

In what he added about a new *judicial* investigation, Nixon tried to accomplish two goals: first, to decrease the threat of the forthcoming political investigation of the Senate Watergate Committee; second, to un-dermine the ongoing criminal investigation by adding a new wrinkle to the White House's investigation of itself via the good offices of the Justice Department. Self-investigations, as we've seen, had allowed Nixon and his men to know where problems were developing in the Watergate cover-up well in advance. Nixon had evaded accordingly, and wanted to go right on doing so, using a special prosecutor who was officially part of the Justice Department.

Then Nixon, in a classic rhetorical device, performed an "I will not place the blame for Watergate crimes on subordinates—on people whose zeal exceeded their judgment and who may have done wrong in a cause they deeply believed to be right" routine. Thus he blamed others while denying he was doing so, and reiterated the Good King–Bad Advisers argument earlier made.

Finally, Nixon explained that he respected the majesty of the law, char-acterized Watergate as "a series of illegal acts and bad judgements by a number of individuals," and talked about the many vital things his ad-ministration had yet to accomplish. "Campaign excesses" had occurred in both parties in recent years, but these bad old days were behind us now. Americans had a job of moral and institutional renewal to complete. "This is my goal," he concluded, "I ask you to join in making it America's goal."[49]

It was one of Richard Nixon's best performances, but it failed to mobi-lize public opinion on his behalf. It did the opposite, in fact. And in so doing, it gave John Dean, identified as Public Enemy Number One in the president's version of Watergate, a chance to destroy Nixon in order to save himself. Dean benefitted because of the timing of the April 30th speech, just as Nixon was hurt by it. Nixon's popularity sagged badly after Dean, Haldeman, Ehrlichman, and Kleindienst were sacrificed to reassert the president's stature.

As we said earlier, Watergate was becoming a matter of mass public (and mass media) awareness just as the Vietnam War ceased being an object of primary national attention and concern.[50] The point is crucial. The sink-hole known as Watergate was national security run amok. The president and his men had violated the Constitution and the law ostensibly to save the nation from imminent subversion. They'd fought fire with fire, and their politics was not for the squeamish. Before *direct* American participa-tion in the Vietnam War finally ended in January 1973, most Americans bought such hard-line logic or weren't apt to oppose it. Most citizens believed that national unity *was* threatened by some dimly understood radicalism. Most also believed that presidents had the right to tell trou-blemakers to put up or shut up, so they accepted Kent State, COINTEL-PRO, the Black Panther raids, and a national atmosphere that allowed for sabotage and cover-up alike.[51]

A fragile left had shut up. What remained by early 1973 was scattered and impotent. *Direct* American involvement in Vietnam, after all, was what most of a diverse antiwar coalition was mostly against. After January 1973, that problem was gone. The country was back to fighting its wars with money and materiel, but not its own men. And the radical threat, therefore, was gone, real gone. George McGovern, whom Nixon and millions of voters in the 1972 election viewed as a New Left dupe, had been slaughtered at the polls. The Vietcong and the North Vietnamese Army were a very long way away. Some sort of peace agreement had been worked out with them; the average American didn't much know, or care, what sort it was. If the reds cheated, U.S. arms in South Vietnamese hands would be there to kill them. The limited war that had gone wrong ten thousand psychological and actual miles away was over for America and America's boys. The pressure was off, including the pressure to rally around the flag and the presidency in circum-stances of external danger. The crisis that served as a rationale for Watergate had begun to evaporate as people developed sudden amnesia about a war they had never known much about to start with.

This helps to explain why the attack on Nixon's credibility started to gain ground during and after the events of March and April 1973. The national atmosphere that made Watergate possible began to lift. The grow-ing controversy in Washington even filled the emotional and political void left by America's blunder in Vietnam. Government had failed. Leadership had failed. Something was rotten in Washington.[52] Watergate, therefore, was a lightning rod for frustration. It started to become big news precisely when Nixon needed it to fade into the deep background of American politics.

Here reference to the press is instructive. Until the Gray-McCord-Sirica-Magruder-Dean-Nixon dramatics of March and April 1973, very few papers gave Watergate any sustained attention. The *New York Times* didn't jump on the Watergate bandwagon to stay until January 1973. The *Washington Post* was unique in its continuing coverage of unfolding events.

In a complex case that had to be read about to be understood, this lack of printed attention helped insure that most people outside of Washington rarely knew what was going on. Network television news, when it covered anything, usually presented a cast of characters that very few viewers had ever heard of before. TV, as a visual medium, communicated a sense of a worsening mood, but it could not, and did not, clarify the legal and consti-tutional aspects of Watergate. Not until TV cameras were let into the hearings of the Senate Watergate Committee did this aspect of affairs begin to change.

While television remained on hold, however, the press surged forward. After March and April 1973, major newspapers in the Midwest, West, and South picked up the Watergate story and stuck with it. Notable, here, were bellwethers including the *Los Angeles Times, Chicago Tribune,* and the *New Orleans Times-Picayune.* Meanwhile, Watergate coverage in the *Washington Post* and the *New York Times* had become daily and unrelenting.[53] Reporters were clamoring for the big story. Bad news about the Nixon administration was good news for its opponents and enemies. Watergate was no longer peripheral, precisely because the Vietnam and the domestic radicalism it had spawned *were* peripheral. With peace returned, Nixon's opponents in a Democratic Congress could attack him without appearing to support Commie hordes or the "sell-out brigades." Members of Congress didn't wait long to avail themselves of the opportunity, one for which some had been waiting a long time.

## The Senate Watergate Committee Whets the Knife

To begin their attack on Nixon's administration, Senate Democrats needed the best weapon available. They found that weapon in John Dean. Dean and the Senate Watergate Committee used each other, pure and simple. Dean wanted as much immunity as he could get, and he needed protection from the wrath of Richard Nixon. A relatively low-profile judicial approach to Watergate gave him very little of either. Legal complexities, TV cameras banned from the courtroom, and reams of testimony were fine for John Sirica, but his court had still not gotten very far with its criminal investigation of the cover-up. Sirica could take his time and think long and hard on the majesty of the law; John Dean, meanwhile, had to think about saving himself.

Salvation was unlikely to occur judicially. On April 30th, Nixon sandbagged the three federal prosecutors with whom Dean had been unsuccessfully bargaining for total immunity and who now knew more about Watergate-related crimes than anyone else in Washington. Nixon did this by saying that his new attorney general–designate could appoint a special prosecutor and give that special prosecutor "absolute authority" to prosecute the Watergate case from here on out.

This was at once a play for time and a surrender on a key judicial and political point. No longer was Nixon going to be trusted by Congress to use his own Department of Justice to investigate a cover-up which had expanded to include his closest White House aides and two of his former attorney generals. The special prosecutor will be discussed later. For now, it is sufficient to say that the Senate Judiciary Committee demanded that Attorney General–designate Richardson agree to appoint a fully independent special prosecutor before recommending that Richardson be confirmed by the Senate. Richardson agreed to these terms and selected Archibald Cox, a professor from the Harvard Law School, on May 18th.

Archibald Cox, however, was not Earl Silbert, Seymour Glanzer, or Donald Campbell, the three federal prosecutors who had been probing Watergate for almost a year. Their involvement was finished. Cox, their successor, had to familiarize himself with a new case with as many tangles, loose ends, and political considerations as any he had ever handled. Cox's case wasn't going to reach the courts for many months more, and these were months John Dean did not have.

Dean had been in an emotional pressure cooker for too long. He was still playing two games. He wanted to get back at John Ehrlichman and Bob Haldeman, but he still did not want to do this in a way that would harm Nixon. They were still Nixon's men, however, and Nixon still intended to protect them at John Dean's expense. Dean was between the devil and the deep blue sea. If he didn't get Haldeman and Ehrlichman, they'd brand him as the mastermind of the cover-up; if he fought them, he had also to take on the president. Dean didn't want to ruin Nixon, and he was deeply afraid of Nixon's power, but it didn't look as if he had any real choice in the matter. Nixon's April 30th rhetoric showed that.

It didn't pay to be stupid in such a situation, and Dean was not stupid. He was as manipulative as anybody else. He began doling out leaks and apparently tried to persuade some journalists to support his campaign for maximum immunity in return for further information. These back-door efforts, however, were minor compared with the resolution Dean made about two weeks after he was ushered out of government. This mid-May decision was to talk during a nationally televised political trial before the Senate Watergate Committee, rather than to put primary emphasis on a much slower and lower-profile judicial trial by the new special prosecutor and Judge Sirica.

Dean knew he was going to face Sirica and Cox in court eventually, but he decided to take on Ehrlichman, Haldeman, and even Nixon first in the political arena. He did it, moreover, without the grant of total immunity that he had sought for so long. Dean still *wanted* total immunity, but he couldn't *get* it. Nobody trusted him enough to sign away all the incriminating evidence they already had against him, courtesy of songbirds like CREEP's Jeb Stuart Magruder. Nor did they want to give him, on faith, any kind of blanket immunity about crimes he might tell them about later. Dean's reputation was hardly good. Nixon was blaming the entire cover-up on him. To trust a guy like Dean to be truthful wasn't easy, and it proved impossible.

Dean, however, had dealt directly with cover-up principals including the president, and he said he was willing to talk. Would he really tell *everything* he knew if he was immunized in advance? And if he didn't, what might Richard Nixon's revenge very likely be on those politicians who had tried to use Dean as a weapon against him and failed? The result was that Dean got no total immunity from anybody, even though he tried to play off the Senate Watergate Committee against Silbert et al. and, later, Special Prosecutor Cox, to accomplish precisely this result. Dean, however, had been in the upper echelons of the White House, so he got something from the skeptical senators: limited immunity and national television time to state his case.[54]

Limited immunity meant, to reiterate, that Dean could still be prosecuted for crimes he testified to, if the prosecutors could show that the evidence they had against him was obtained independently of his testimony. Dean, then, got protection only at the price of being a completely forthright and unbreakable witness. For if he weren't, he'd end up with very little immunity at all.

Legal conditions like these are a marvellous spur to candor. And so it was with John Dean. But Dean made a virtue of necessity. The idea of going before the Senate Watergate Committee, he wrote in his best-known memoirs, "grew increasingly attractive."

> I mulled it over with [my two lawyers] and listed the advantages. For one thing, I was not as uncomfortable with a Senate forum as with grand juries and courtrooms. Capitol Hill was familiar ground from my [several years as chief counsel to the Republican minority on the House Judiciary Committee in 1967–68: a period during which—ironically—limited immunity statutes began to be incorporated within federal law]. I had testified [before Congress] many times, and I knew how hearings worked. Also, the televised proceedings [that the Senate Watergate Committee had scheduled] would give me a chance to lay out my whole testimony before millions of viewers. I was not faring well with the written press. I could use a piece of the President's own philosophy against him and "go over the heads" of the written press straight to the public. [As Nixon had done in his April 30th speech explaining what nice guys Haldeman, Ehrlichman, and Kleindienst were . . . and what a nice guy John Dean was not.] Finally, I was drawn to the technical ramifications of the Senate's immunity powers. [The Senate Watergate Committee was only offering Dean limited, instead of total, immunity. But there were advantages to this.] The squealer image would be limited somewhat if I were granted [limited and conditional] immunity by the Senate. There would still be a strong possibility I would go to jail; I would not be guaranteed a free ride. It might make me a more credible witness.[55]

Yes, indeed it might. And so, by mid-May, Dean agreed to testify against the president of the United States. Dean might be a "squealer," "Judas," "rat," "turncoat," or "bottom-dwelling slug," but he could present himself to the nation on television as a contrite man who was reluctantly "breaking faith" with Nixon for the greater good of the political order.[56]

None of this would have happened if John Dean did not have allies, *political* allies who realized that Watergate was an essentially political struggle. But Dean had those allies of convenience, people willing to run the risk of using Dean to get Nixon's highest White House aides and perhaps even Richard Nixon himself.

## Nixon Isolates Himself

How all this happened was not a saga of innate republican virtue. Political people made political decisions based on political calculations. Growing numbers of, above all, pragmatic political survivors began to equate their best interest with a struggle with the White House. Many Democrats, for instance, were angered by political defeat due to fissures that had opened within their party during the Vietnam War and to Nixon's ability to exploit—indeed, heighten—those divisions. They also still needed somebody to blame Vietnam upon, somebody who wasn't a Democrat. Watergate gave many of Nixon's partisan opponents the chance they needed to attempt to finally and completely blame Nixon for Vietnam.

How? Simple. *Nixon had lied.* Only his lies and secret bombings and sub rosa sins, it was argued, had kept the United States in the war. The growing miasma of Watergate, coming precisely when the final withdrawal of U.S. ground and air forces had been accomplished, allowed the idea of blaming Nixon, the Universal Liar and Mad Bomber, for Vietnam to take root and flourish. The Democrats were attempting, to quote Charles R. Morris, to "exonerate themselves from complicity in the war." "It was easier," Morris continues, "to claim deception by a renegade President or Presidents than to concede collective responsibility."[57] It sure was, especially as Nixon's moral stature was starting to seem a whole lot grayer to growing numbers of Americans, even those who had reelected him to presidential office only a few months before.

Nixon knew what the Democrats were doing. He had done the same to them often enough. Now, however, their liberal hypocrisy and self-exoneration started really getting to him. But with growing anger came more mistakes which added to Nixon's troubles. We have seen how Nixon stonewalled everything after the break-in and continually frustrated the criminal investigations of the case. But that was not all Nixon did. He also counterattacked in other ways that cost him dearly in political Washington. As one result, Democrats found it easier to exonerate themselves at Nixon's expense. This was not because they got stronger, but because Nixon's political support became weaker.

To understand this point, we have to go back to November 8th, the day after the 1972 presidential election. The scene was the Roosevelt Ballroom of the White House, and the entire senior staff of that White House was gathered together to hear Nixon congratulate himself—and them—on beating the competition by 45.7 million to 28.3 million votes.

President-elect Nixon did so, briefly. Then the meeting was turned over to White House Chief of Staff Haldeman. Let John Dean paint the verbal picture:

> Bob moved to the head of the table and, never long for words, went straight to the point. "As the President indicated [in his speech to you,] some things are going to change around here. I want you all to send me a written description of the responsibilities your office now has, plus a description of the responsibilities you would like to have in the second administration, and the reasons you think you should have them. Now, don't get carried away on the reasons you think you are qualified to handle everything. Make it simple. We can get your flowery reasons later, if we need them." Bob laughed nervously at his joke, coughed when it didn't go over, and composed himself for his important lines. "Now, the President and I are meeting with the Cabinet shortly. We are going to direct them to obtain written letters of resignation from all [two thousand or so] appointed sub-Cabinet officers in the government and [have the Cabinet officers] submit them along with their own resignations. And the President has directed that everyone in this room also hand in a letter of resignation. This doesn't mean that you won't be asked to stay on, of course. We will review each situation individually. We just want to show that we mean business." And he departed for the Cabinet meeting.
>
> All the President's men and long-time servants had been fired at the post-landslide thank-you meeting. The news hit with a thud, leaving a few seconds of silence before the Roosevelt Room buzzed with shock, complaints, and outrage. I slipped out. I was unaffected, secure on the inside.[58]

The problem was that the "inside" of the Nixon administration was becoming a very cramped set of quarters indeed. Guerilla Government was now being waged against the president's own men. A state of siege powered by Watergate flowered in the White House. Cabinet officers who were not "loyal" were being pushed out of government, including most of the men whom Nixon had *not* made, men like Secretary of Defense Melvin Laird, Secretary of Commerce Peter Peterson, Secretary of Housing and Urban Development George Romney, and Solicitor General Erwin Griswold. Other Cabinet-level independents including John Connally and Bryce N. Harlow had already left. Nixon's palace guard was increasingly left in charge.

The second Nixon administration was, accordingly, far more centralized than the first one. Decisions were taken away from Cabinet officers and removed to the White House. There, super-Cabinet officers like Henry Kissinger coordinated policy, prevented bureaucratic sabotage, and handled more and more executive branch operations. None of this received congressional approval, nor were the new super-Cabinet officers or their superiors Haldeman and Ehrlichman deemed accountable to Congress. The White House not only made policy, it sought to insure that policy was always carried out by White House staff whose total loyalty was to Richard Nixon.

Members of Congress of many descriptions had no love for a power grab that equated the entire executive branch with the White House and decreased congressional influence over Cabinet agencies. Such executive branch reorganizations, invisible to most voters, were key items of discussion in Washington as Nixon's second term began. The debate got even more intense by the second week of March 1973. For then, on the eve of the Gray-McCord-Sirica shocks, Nixon announced that he intended to "impound" congressionally approved funds.[59]

Impoundment was a constitutional challenge which hit Congress right in the pocketbook. Nixon argued that if the legislators funded programs he disapproved of, or voted more funds for something than he thought sufficient, he would veto the bills. *Then,* if Congress passed the bills over his veto, he would *still refuse to spend the money.* Impoundment was a red flag to most members of Congress, for it took away their power over the purse strings, and gave it to the president. Political temperatures on Capitol Hill rose. Some members were most concerned about pork barrels, others about social-welfare programs, and still others about funding for everything from subsidies to agriculture to regulatory agencies. Nearly all, however, were united in opposition to impoundment. Congress was being told to give Nixon what he wanted—or else, and at precisely the wrong time.

Then, during the second week of April, and as a result of the Gray hearing fiasco, Attorney General Kleindienst had gone before Congress to argue that presidential "executive privileges" were nearly absolute. *Any* employee of the executive branch could be ordered not to testify before Congress if Nixon decided it might harm "national security." Congress could damned well try to impeach the president if they disputed Nixon's claims, Kleindienst added. It was another constitutional challenge. Nixon backed away from Kleindienst's constitutional interpretation several weeks later, but he and his administration had won no laurels. In the argument over executive privilege and national security, impeachment had been mentioned openly for the first time.[60]

Late April was a period of White House retreat, but Nixon and his staff had threats still in store. Kleindienst's Justice Department, for example, had a bill pending in Congress which would have made it a crime for any government employee to give "classified information" to a reporter or for any reporter to receive such information. This was leak plugging par excellence, particularly since no one, according to the White House version of national security, could challenge the reasonableness of any "classified" designation put on any document by anybody at the summit of the executive branch.[61]

Many congressional moderates and some conservatives were concerned as the Watergate situation intensified from March to May 1973. New presidential claims threatened interests far broader than those directly involved in Watergate heretofore. Powerful liberal Democrats—notably, senators Muskie, McGovern, and Fulbright—exploited the wider opportunities by warning of the dangers of dictatorship. McGovern had made such charges during his unsuccessful presidential bid; now he and others were listened to, and not by Democrats alone. One important result of such bipartisan disaffection occurred on May 23rd, when John Dean paid a private visit to Senator Barry Goldwater.[62]

Goldwater, as we've seen, was important to Dean, both as a politician and a man. Dean went to him with some serious questions about the possible effect of his forthcoming testimony before the Senate Watergate Committee: What might happen if his testimony against Nixon gave communists the wrong ideas? Might nuclear arms limitation talks fail? Would the Soviets likely become aggressive while the United States was distracted by Watergate? No, replied Goldwater, he didn't know what verbal bombshells Dean might drop, but it was unlikely that real bombs would explode because of it. Then Dean showed his hand: What would happen if he weakened Nixon by testifying that he was lying about complete lack of involvement in the Watergate cover-up?

Goldwater, according to Dean, said such news didn't surprise him at all. Nixon had been lying all his life. Dean should tell what he knew and not worry about sanctimonious people who'd criticize him for saying shocking things. Hypocrites like these didn't matter. Dean's charges weren't going to surprise most senators, so he should make them and not worry about the consequences.[63]

Advice like this was very important to John Dean. Dean knew that liberals wanted Nixon's scalp, but he was no liberal. When thoroughly conservative Barry Goldwater advised him to take on Richard Nixon, it was precious reassurance that the upcoming political trial of Watergate was *not* a struggle between the president and the Congress which might destroy the Republic.

What Goldwater told Dean also helps explain why Nixon was increasingly beleaguered. With congressional moderates, and some conservatives, alienated from him and his administration, Nixon's unilateralist instincts flowered, and so he threatened impoundment and such like, threats that only created more opposition to his policies. Nixon was shooting himself in his own foot.

He sensed this, but did nothing to stop it. Instead, as early as February 1973, the president began to isolate himself. Press conferences ceased for four months. He spent progressively less time in Washington. There were rumors that the president was acting depressed, drinking heavily, and taking sedatives. By April, he'd become "a more desperate and less coherent President." "Over and over," Ben-Veniste and Frampton wrote, Nixon "questioned his aides about details and vulnerabilities in the cover-up, never seeming to get the story straight. He would announce a decision about strategy to his assistants, and then abruptly back away from it when one or the other suggested that that might not be the best way to go."[64]

Nixon wavered as he isolated himself, and this only worsened his problems, including problems with his own people. John Dean refused to fall on his sword for a vacillating president whom he thought was being maneuvered by unscrupulous palace guardian John Ehrlichman. Nixon's problems were all of a piece: the actions he initiated—or allowed others to initiate—alienated his congressional allies just as his opponents were opening the all-important first act of the Senate Watergate Committee investigation.

## The Political Trial Begins

Now began the second, and crucial, stage of Watergate. Within four months, Nixon's opponents staged a nationally televised investigation which decreased support for the president, faced him with a charge of obstruction of justice from John Dean, showcased his former aides Haldeman and Ehrlichman to their disadvantage, and, finally, uncovered the existence of secret White House tape-recordings which could resolve the question of whether John Dean or Richard Nixon himself was the chief architect of the cover-up. Once Nixon refused to release these tapes to either the Senate Watergate Committee or to the courts—including the Special Prosecutor's Office—the political trial and the judicial trial of Watergate began to converge. Even worse for the president, Watergate began to be perceived, by the public, as less a struggle between political partisans than as a constitutional issue of whether a president was "above the law."

The political preliminaries began slowly. The Senate Watergate Committee was composed of practical politicians, people who knew—or could be advised—how to go about carefully building a case in a highly charged atmosphere where the penalties for carelessness were apt to be high. These members, chaired by conservative Democrat Sam J. Ervin of North Carolina, started low and worked up. First they dealt with underlings in the cover-up; then they went on to middlemen like Jeb Magruder of CREEP; and finally they graduated to key witness John Dean, who moved the cover-up into the Oval Office itself. None of it was easy. The committee was full of leaks and there were frequent efforts to sabotage the effectiveness and credibility of the public hearings which lasted from May 17th to August 11th, 1973.

Republican Senate Minority Leader Howard Baker of Tennessee was a villain in many eyes. The pressure on him to protect the president was intense; Baker was also ranking minority member and co-chair of the Senate Watergate Committee. If Baker could tie the investigation into knots or make it look like a partisan vendetta by mudslinging Democrats, the bipartisan credibility of the investigation would be destroyed.[65] Baker tried for a time, using procedural techniques. He attempted to deny Dean *any* immunity at all. He tried to prepare schedules of testimony that were confusing, and left key witnesses like James McCord off these lists. He proposed that administration witnesses like Haldeman, Ehrlichman, and Mitchell testify before the committee *before* any evidence had been presented against them and before they had any *specific* allegations of wrongdoing to explain. In the process, Baker enraged Dean and angered Samuel Dash, the chief counsel hired by Ervin for the Democratic majority on the committee.

Baker's backroom machinations, however, failed. Dean even used Baker's obstructionism as a bargaining chip in secret immunity negotiations with Dash, about which only Ervin knew. Then Dean, with the assistance of Dash, his lawyers, and others, put himself through a crash course on Watergate in preparation for his televised testimony. He was tired of behind-the-scenes infighting, and he organized an assault on the credibility of the White House.

Dean succeeded for three reasons. First, he kept his testimony against

Nixon, Haldeman, Ehrlichman, and others specific. He related distinct instances of wrongdoing, rather than making—or being led into making— general accusations for which he lacked proof, or of which he knew only by hearsay (i.e., not from personal experience but only because someone else had told him about them). Dean's narrow and legalistic presentation paid dividends because it made it far more difficult for pro-Nixon members of the committee to pick holes in his case; to distract the proceedings with rodomontades about how Dean was just a mealymouthed begrudger out to pillory the president and destroy America; or to blacken the committee hearing by treating it like a circus rather than a political investigation.

Dean's lawyerly presentation benefitted from an exceedingly good memory. Since it was Dean's word against Nixon's and the others, it behooved Nixon to deny Dean access to as much information as possible. This he did. When Nixon announced the Dean, Haldeman, Ehrlichman, and Kleindienst resignations on April 30th, he also ordered FBI agents to seal off Dean's office and impound all his files. This meant that Dean's memory *had* to be good about important events like his March 21st "cancer on the presidency" meeting with Nixon.

Dean also benefitted from the fact that, legally, he could not afford to lie to himself. He couldn't selectively forget things that made him look like something less than a servant of the True and the Beautiful. Dean had to remember things that led him to title his later memoirs of Watergate *Blind Ambition* and *Lost Honor;* he could not portray himself as a passive *Witness to Power,* as John Ehrlichman did later. Nor could he dress up Watergate as a CIA plot, as H. R. Haldeman subsequently attempted. Dean couldn't make excuses, or ease around things he found it inconvenient to recall. Success in such unvarnished remembering required that Dean successfully present himself as a guilty man who was levelling with himself and the American people. This was more than honesty for the sake of self-preservation. It was "media smarts."

Media smarts Dean had, and this was the third and final reason Nixon's effort to brand him as the failed "mastermind" of the entire Watergate cover-up failed. Dean knew that he would be the televised centerpiece of the Senate hearings, and he knew that his performance had to be good. He worked hard at scripting his testimony. He spent two months writing a 245-page opening statement to tighten his charges. He also watched a TV interview which aired on May 17th and which introduced Dean to most Americans for the first time.

Dean knew, after watching that interview, that he had an image problem. He changed his hair and his speaking styles, replaced his contact lenses with sober glasses so he wouldn't blink a lot before high-intensity

TV lights, stopped laughing nervously and larding his speech with "you knows," and determined to present himself as if he were a corporate accountant who knew precisely which numbers didn't really add up. Calm, cool, understated, and alone in front of the TV cameras, Dean presented himself as David in a business suit versus a White House Goliath.

The cameras loved it, and so did the Democrats on the Senate Watergate Committee. Dean was good, and the high point of their case against the Nixon White House. His five days of testimony from June 24th to 29th dramatized Watergate, allowed millions to get a handle on the cover-up aspects of it for the first time, and helped shift the public's perception of Watergate from "just politics" to a "serious matter." By the time Dean finished testifying, a majority of the population believed either that Nixon planned the break-in (8 percent); that he didn't plan it, but knew about the crime before it was committed and did nothing to stop it (28 percent); or that he found out about the crime afterward and then tried to cover up some aspects of it (31 percent).[66] As any and all of these actions were criminal, it was the president of the United States who now had an image problem. Matters became even worse, for John Dean wasn't through with Richard Nixon.

The crunch came as Mitchell, Ehrlichman, and Haldeman began to testify during the second week of July. John Dean, remember, had kept his testimony narrow and specific. He talked about what he knew, not about what he suspected or about what others had told him. He made, however, one crucial exception. Dean strongly suspected that he had been taped by Richard Nixon during their final meeting on April 15th, 1973. Word reached Dean by April 18th that Nixon did, in fact, have him on tape and would discredit Dean with his own words if Dean told tales about presidential involvement in the cover-up. Dean claims he replied—through his lawyers—to go right ahead and threaten and, further, that he had his lawyers tell Justice Department officials to tell Nixon to put up or shut up.[67]

Nixon did nothing, and the tape threat apparently faded away. In mid-June, however, while preparing his long opening statement, Dean included a brief paragraph in which he said that he suspected he had been taped by Nixon on one occasion, and that the committee should seek to get hold of an unadulterated version of that recording if they believed one existed. This careful allusion was ignored. Dean was not even questioned about it by the senators. The committee's *lawyers*, however, acted differently. Majority Counsel Dash knew of Dean's suspicions in mid-June. During Dean's testimony two weeks later, others began to share his suspicions.

Included among them were Donald G. Sanders, a deputy counsel for the Republican minority, and Scott Armstrong, a Democratic committee investigator.

Sanders and Armstrong became suspicious because Nixon apparently gave his new White House counsel, J. Fred Buzhardt, sanitized summaries of some of what he had said to Dean and allowed Buzhardt to send written versions of those summaries over to the Senate Committee to be used in cross-examining Dean. Buzhardt's various efforts to derail Dean were harmless enough. A new kid on the block, Buzhardt was in no position to trip up a predecessor who had been poring over the cover-up's entrails for months. Buzhardt's real failure, however, was that the questions the Senate Watergate Committee allowed him to pose for the president were too detailed, and the White House summaries of the Nixon-Dean conversations were more detailed still. Either Nixon had a photographic memory or a way to refresh his memory a very great deal. Thus it was that, on July 13th, while interviewing a former White House aide, Armstrong and Sanders hit the Mother Lode of Watergate.

The former aide, Alexander Butterfield, was shown the Buzhardt-supplied summaries of the Nixon-Dean conversations. Then Armstrong and Sanders told Butterfield of Dean's supposition that he was taped. Finally, Sanders popped the question: "Do you know of any basis for the implications in Dean's testimony that conversations in the President's office are recorded?" "I was hoping you fellows wouldn't ask me that," Butterfield replied. Nixon had taped *all* such conversations for several years.[68] Butterfield was one of the tiny handful who knew that the president had secretly bugged the Oval Office and another, more private retreat next door to the White House since the unsettled spring of 1971. Butterfield also knew, as the aide once responsible for the operation of the tape-recording system, that Nixon had also had his office telephones and the Cabinet room wired at the same time—all with voice-activated recorders that registered everything automatically.

Nixon had taped himself! When Butterfield reluctantly told that to the committee's investigators—for fear, perhaps, of a later perjury conviction if he didn't—another fault line opened in the cover-up case. Now there was proof-positive of whether Dean was lying or everybody else in the White House inner circle was lying. "Why Sam, this is nothing less than providential," Senator Ervin enthused to Dash when he got the news.[69]

After July 13th, the Committee finally had its case against Nixon, courtesy of Richard Nixon. Senator Ervin proceeded with dispatch. Butterfield was called as a surprise witness on July 16th, after Ervin threatened to have him arrested by writ of Congress and jailed in an almost-never-used cell in the basement of the Capitol if he refused. Butterfield had to choose between shredding his career or talking.

He talked. Nixon had secretly taped *everybody* for over two years: friend, enemy, and foreign dignitary alike. To imagine that many power barons would fail to seek revenge on Nixon for preserving their private conversations for posterity or whatever other uses Nixon might choose to make of them was to be sublimely innocent. And Butterfield, like Dean, had lost his innocence, sublime or otherwise. The news about the secret tapes reached Congress on the very day that news of Nixon's secret bombing of neutral Cambodia finally surfaced on Capitol Hill.

Congress began buzzing like a hornet's nest. Secret tapes and secret bombing and secret political sabotage—too much was going on as if Congress didn't exist. It was time, now that the crisis atmosphere of wartime had moderated, to call Nixon on the carpet. The Senate Watergate Committee did just that. It proceeded in two ways at once. First, it interrogated Nixon's former aides, Haldeman and Ehrlichman, to their disadvantage. Second, the committee tried to subpoena the most relevant portions of Nixon's tapes for use in the Watergate investigation: thus drawing the president directly, immediately, and, above all, *legally* into the case for the first time.

Haldeman and Ehrlichman's testimony proved to be disastrous for them and for the president. When the two began their eight days of testimony on July 24th, Dean—and Dean alone—had implicated Nixon in the cover-up. Then Butterfield had testified that presidential tapes existed which could resolve the matter of who was lying and who was not. The committee promptly and unanimously asked for the tapes (July 17th), was refused by Nixon (July 23rd), and responded by trying to serve Nixon with a judicial writ commanding that he produce the requested evidence later the same day.

This was hardball, real hardball—one of the few times in U.S. history that a congressional body had ever demanded that a sitting president produce evidence in a criminal investigation. The committee's action put Nixon on the Watergate firing line without benefit of intermediaries for the first time.

Nixon loyalists now had to get the president and his tapes back out of the public picture. One way to do that was for someone to fall on as many swords as possible, and thus take the spotlight off Nixon and his face-off with Dean. Dean, remember, was an admitted criminal testifying under a grant of limited immunity. Dean knew he had a "squealer" image, and so did Haldeman and Ehrlichman. Most people still doubted Dean's legally induced veracity. Dean was not an insurmountable problem. Somebody immediately below Nixon could have taken all of the discredit for Watergate and relegated Dean and his charges to the deep background. But nobody did, especially not H. R. Haldeman or John Ehrlichman. Ehrlichman engaged in mincing legalisms and obfuscations, arrogantly allowed that he was guilty of nothing in the conspiracy, cover-up, or political sabotage departments, and said Dean was a liar incarnate. That took five days of hearings to accomplish.

Then Haldeman, much better behaved, came along, and announced he was innocent of everything too. Dean was still the bad guy who'd deceived everybody. Haldeman knew this positively, he added at one point, because he had recently taken Nixon's secret tape of the crucial Dean-Nixon meeting of March 21st, 1973, home with him one night and listened to it.

What? Taken a tape home with him? Yes. The same tape Nixon wouldn't let Congress see? Yes. And the Senate committee was supposed to take Haldeman's word about exactly what was on that tape, and to believe that it exonerated Nixon and convicted Dean? Yes. Statements better calculated to offend senatorial sensibilities and to keep Dean's testimony in the limelight were impossible to imagine. The tapes' importance had been underlined further, and in a fashion distinctly uncomplimentary to the president. Nixon had let an aide no longer in his employ—because he was a suspect in a criminal cover-up proceeding—take the tapes home with him for inspection, but wouldn't let others see them, especially not the senators investigating the cover-up.

It was absurd. But Haldeman's and Ehrlichman's performances had cause, other than their unwillingness to sacrifice themselves for Nixon. Both men viewed their interlocutors as hypocrites, as "a shabby collection of posturers and politicians, winding themselves up in swaddles of self-righteousness," John Ehrlichman later wrote in his memoirs.[70] No bunch of drunks, lechers, and parochial power brokers was going to lecture *them* on the true and the beautiful before television cameras. Not when Ehrlichman knew that Congress was full of undisciplined and evasive types.

What Ehrlichman and men like him ignored, however, was that their public images were no better than those of the politicians they derided. Thinking of themselves as hard-eyed realists, they often came across, on television, as brittle and evasive men who did not understand give-and-take. When faced with some successful verbal artists, Nixon's men came off looking bad. Haldeman, Ehrlichman, and others prided themselves upon understanding public relations. Once their testimony brought the hearings to a dramatic end, however, "simple country lawyer" Sam Ervin, Senator Howard Baker, and John Dean ended up looking a lot better than

they and their president did. This was not good. Worse still was that the
tapes *shifted the burden of proof to Nixon,* and made Watergate more understandable to millions of people. Obstruction of justice was an abstraction; Dean
versus Nixon was not. The president's former lawyer had accused him of
doing something wrong, the president responded that his ex-lawyer was
a liar, and Nixon's tape recordings could resolve the issue one way or the
other.

Watergate, then, was *personalized* by this first stage of the political trial.
The misdeeds became less confusing, less peripheral, and more personally
threatening to millions of interested Americans. Burglaries, dirty tricks,
hush money, slanders, and other offenses were translated into the idiom
of individuals. Most people still found most of the lawyerly issues opaque,
executive privilege, for example, but Dean versus Nixon was easy to understand. So were the Enemies Lists which had sensationally surfaced
during John Dean's interrogation. The White House's desire to go after
opponents with the bludgeons of the tax code and the IRS were not at all
difficult to get queasy about. John Ehrlichman's out-thrust Sawdust Caesar
jaw and vulpine disposition radiated abuse of power. The idea occurred to
many that a president might be lying *to* the country instead of lying *for* the
country. All this meant trouble, lots of it. The Senate committee's hearings
alienated many an American who had, until then, wished Richard Nixon
well.[71]

These shifts in popular perception were important, and helped provide
the political momentum that allowed investigations to go forward. Momentum, however, was suddenly snatched away from Congress and returned to the judiciary by the courts. This shift back to a judicial trial from
a political trial was abrupt, but the judiciary had had enough of the Senate
Watergate Committee's trial by television and public opinion. It was time,
the judges thought, to return to disinterested justice. By mid-August, the
transition to the second judicial (and journalistic) stage of Watergate was
complete.

## The Judiciary Tries Again

The tool the judiciary used to take back control of the cover-up investigation from the politicians who had broken it wide open for them was a
subpoena. Specifically, the subpoena the Senate Watergate Committee had

requested—in the name of Congress—for the portions of Richard Nixon's White House tapes relevant to Watergate.

What judges John J. Sirica and Gerhard Gesell of the Federal District Court for the District of Columbia did with the committee's demand for evidence was simple: they refused it. They said that a committee of Congress had no right to issue a writ to require a sitting president to produce records of key importance to a merely political investigation. Simultaneously, however, these same judges allowed a *judicial* subpoena for the same tapes to be delivered to Richard Nixon. This writ was requested of them by the Special Prosecutor's Office, created back in mid-May to conduct a criminal investigation of the Watergate case. Special Prosecutor Archibald Cox wanted the tapes to prepare his case to the grand jury that would determine who should or shouldn't be indicted for the cover-up.

The legal relations between the special prosecutor, the judge, and the grand jury were demonstrated nicely on July 26th, 1973, when Nixon refused to obey the special prosecutor's demand for the tapes. Prosecutor Cox promptly informed both the grand jury and Judge Sirica, who had issued the writ. The grand jury responded that it wanted the subpoena enforced. Sirica met with jury members, polled them as to whether they wanted a "show cause" order issued, got a unanimous vote for just that, and then *ordered* the president either to provide a convincing explanation of why he couldn't provide the court with the best available evidence in a criminal investigation or face possible criminal charges himself—contempt of court proceedings. The judicial struggle to obtain the Watergate tapes had begun.

There were ironies aplenty in this sudden switchover from a political trial to a judicial trial. As we have seen, Judge Sirica's initial effort to use the court system to get to the bottom of Watergate had been stymied. It was only through the well-televised intervention of the politicians in the Senate hearings that the logjam was broken. But for Judge Sirica, in fact, there might never have been any Senate Watergate Committee hearings at all.

This was because of a protest from—of all people—Archibald Cox. The special prosecutor, newly installed one day after the Senate Watergate Committee's public hearings began on May 17th, made it almost his first official act to try to stop those hearings dead and to keep the television cameras from recording them. Cox attempted to turn a power struggle between Congress and the executive into a neat exercise in the gymnastics of jurisprudence. He argued that an investigation by politicians would interfere with the rights of the accused, and those who might later be accused, to a fair and impartial judgement because of negative "pre-trial publicity."[72] Had Cox's logic persuaded Sirica, Watergate might not have destroyed Nixon's presidency. But it didn't. The majesty of the law, on the eve of the Senate Watergate Committee's sensational hearing, was a tattered has-been in rags facing a still-daunting stone wall.

A little over two months later, however, much had changed. After Dean's and Butterfield's revelations, the lawyers and the judges apparently thought they were back in business. Now that Nixon had been directly involved and the existence of the White House tapes had been determined, Watergate was taken back out of the political arena, and placed safely in the hands of elite jurists.

The lawyers and judges wanted the case back for two major reasons: one political, and the other procedural. Politically, Watergate was now strewn with possibilities of constitutional crisis. A legislative effort to embarrass and weaken Nixon had, suddenly and unexpectedly, turned into a struggle that could very well destroy him. The tapes transformed the Watergate case into an intimidating matter of striking at the head of a sitting president of these United States.

This meant, in turn, that any strike had better not miss. The lawyers and the judges elected themselves to wield the axe, if it had to be wielded. Any hint of partisanship could have catastrophic effects upon constitutional checks and balances, so the judicial elite took back the action from the politicians, to many politicians' discontent. The process was made easier because, once the tapes' existence was known, the Watergate case could be—and was—perceived in narrow procedural terms, as a case where the courts, at the request of the special prosecutor, were requiring the White House to produce the best evidence in a criminal proceeding without judging guilt or innocence in advance.

This narrow view of what Watergate was about was neat, antiseptic, procedural, and very, very wrong, as we shall see.


## The Special Prosecutor versus Nixon

The Special Prosecutor's Office that seized the investigative initiative after the Senate Watergate Committee's failure to execute its subpoena of the White House tapes was an odd bureaucratic creation. It was *in* the executive branch, but not *of* it. This oddity resulted because few in Congress expected Nixon to investigate or prosecute himself after almost a year of Watergate had demonstrated otherwise. The Democratic majority in the Senate, therefore, had enforced conditions upon Nixon and the man he nominated as attorney general following the resignations of Dean, Haldeman, Ehrlichman, and Kleindienst.

The deal was simple. Either Nixon stop the farce of having officials within his own Department of Justice investigate the involvement of top members of his own administration (including himself) in possible crimes or the Congress might just decide to deny him any new attorney general at all.

This threat was credible because highly placed Republicans on the Hill had joined Democrats in proposing a bipartisan quid pro quo. The proposition was that a new and unusual special prosecutor be appointed as an *independent* investigator of transgressions, including Nixon's. Congress sent Nixon a message in late April and early May 1973, a message that the day had passed when Nixon could continue, in his own interest, to set the rules of a criminal investigation.[73]

Thus neither Nixon nor his Justice Department nominee, Elliot Richardson, opposed the creation of the Special Prosecutor's Office. Nor did Richardson play bureaucratic hardball when a Kennedy Democrat, Archibald Cox, was recruited to head that office in mid-May. Cox, in fact, got guarantees that Richardson would have no veto power over what he reported about the case, or when he reported it. Nor did Cox have to inform or consult with Richardson regarding whom he intended to prosecute or why, except at his own discretion.

This blank check for an independent special prosecutor served many interests, including those of Nixon himself, congressional Republicans, and conservative Democrats. The special prosecutor, therefore, became a sort of Golden Mean. Liberals wanted him because they didn't trust Nixon. Conservatives desired him (especially after Dean's and Butterfield's revelations in July) because they wanted to get the Senate's investigation of Watergate off the nation's television screens as fast as possible. Nixon accepted him because he hoped to decrease the political hemorrhaging afflicting him and his administration. Lawyers and judges preferred him because a judicious process of levying specific criminal charges against specific individuals would thereby replace the Senate's hunting expedition.

The Special Prosecutor's Office also served another, less obvious, purpose. It allowed the White House to play opponents off against one another, and attempt to separate *power* and *information* in the Watergate investigation. By August 1973, it was obvious that the Senate Committee had lots more information about the cover-up, and lots more power. If Congress got any more, Nixon was in even deeper trouble. The special prosecutor, on the other hand, had information and wanted more, but he had no power, independent of the politicians the judges distrusted, to destroy Nixon's presidency. The central element of this phase of Watergate is made clearer when we examine White House strategy from August to mid-October 1973.

The White House strategy was both legal and political, and had three components. First, Nixon and his men sought to deny evidence to anybody, and most especially to Congress. Second, they tried to frighten off both their judicial and political pursuers by arguing that the courts had no right to prosecute or convict a sitting president no matter what proof they had against him unless Congress first impeached that president. This was a classic Catch-22: The courts which had, or might get, the information didn't have the power, while the Congress that had the power didn't yet have enough information to risk impeaching Nixon. Third, Nixon and his supporters attacked all efforts to investigate Nixon further as a *vendetta against the institution of the presidency* and, thus, disruptive of good order and all warm, safe, and constitutional things. By definition, therefore, Watergate couldn't be an investigation of a *man* who had misused his presidential *office* or allowed others to misuse it for him.

This White House strategy initially paid dividends. Watergate was not a struggle of political heroes and antiheroes. It was a long and drawn-out contest between political technicians and their legal counterparts, people concerned that one misstep would betray them into the hands of their enemies or cause them to be crucified in the court of public opinion. Because of such thoroughly unromantic considerations, Nixon's opponents moved slowly and hesitated often, particularly after TV coverage of Watergate slumped badly following the Senate Watergate Committee hearings.

For two months, all was abstruse debates about executive privilege. Maybe one American in a hundred had a definite idea about what they were about. But the power question was clear: could a president refuse to provide evidence to a court in a criminal trial because of his position as a national leader and his involvement in weighty matters of state? Or was Nixon like any other citizen in this regard? Like everything else in American law, the answer depended upon the circumstances.[74] When it came to military or diplomatic secrets, arguments for executive privilege were hardest to attack. There, national security had almost always allowed presidents to withhold information.

National security as a rationale for executive privilege regarding the Watergate tapes, however, was a nonstarter in the political atmosphere of mid-to-late 1973. Red-baiting failed to convince people that presidential opponents were KGB dupes, fellow travellers, or unwitting antipatriots. Watergate looked much more like a *domestic* political issue, and much less like one involving foreign policy.

A second approach to executive privilege was to defend it on the basis of confidential reporting. If, say, the FBI completed a confidential background check on an applicant for federal office and discovered some failing in that person's past which did not negatively affect suitability for present trust and employment, presidents or their representatives could refuse to release such a report on the grounds that unscrupulous politicians might use it to defame someone. The problem with this second argument against turning over the tapes was that courtly Harvard Law School honors graduate Sam Ervin was the furthest thing from a bomb thrower, Judge Sirica was hardly Senator Joseph McCarthy, and Archibald Cox of Harvard was the complete Boston brahmin. They didn't act like avenging angels, vendetta artists, or Inquisition brokers. In terms of public relations, Nixon and his men had a problem. They also had the logical difficulty that what the special prosecutor wanted were tapes bearing on a judicial proceeding. The prosecutor and the courts were not prejudging guilt or innocence and were bound by legal confidentiality and the rules of evidence in all proceedings. These rules prohibited things like hearsay testimony, abusive ad hominem, and many another item that Congress rarely prohibited itself.

Nixon, therefore, had to ground most of his legal argument against turning over the subpoenaed tapes on a third argument. This concerned the politicians' right to keep confidential private deliberations with their aides, so that aides wouldn't be inhibited from offering the frankest advice on important policy questions. The problem with this last type of explanation for privilege and noncompliance with a court order was that Dean had testified that Nixon was part of a cover-up whose only relation to public policy was his own continued political survival.

Nixon's lawyers, therefore, were not in spectacularly good shape to argue executive privilege on any grounds. Nixon claimed he was above the law only in order to keep secrets of state for the greater good of the nation. So his lawyers dutifully argued that any subpoena, of any tapes for any reason, would destroy the entire principle of the confidentiality of high-level political conversations. A key part of this argument was that Cox was on a glorified fishing expedition involving demands for all sorts of secret material unrelated to Watergate. The claim was false, but the irony was that Nixon's own people had already provided the Special Prosecutor's Office with exactly what it needed to determine which of the four thousand hours of taped conversation were most relevant to Dean's charges against the president and his topmost aides.

How did the special prosecutor know which tapes of which meetings to demand as evidence? Dean's memory helped; and the prosecutor also quickly realized the March 21st "cancer on the presidency" encounter was crucial. March 21st was only the beginning, however. For most of the rest of what it wanted, Cox's office made enthusiastic use of White House logbooks detailing Nixon's daily schedule and the personal desk diaries of Haldeman and Ehrlichman which noted the times of their meetings with the president. Such records, obtained by Cox *before* Butterfield's revelations about the tapes, allowed the prosecutors to make very specific demands for additional information.[75] The Nixon White House had again unintentionally given its opponents the tools with which to destroy it. For, had Cox been forced to guess or make vague requests for evidence, Nixon's supporters might have made their fishing expedition argument stick. As things were, however, the special prosecutor made his request for evidence specific enough to be believable.

As if all this weren't enough, career federal bureaucrats now began attacking the Nixonites on their own account. In the month after Alexander Butterfield's testimony, hitherto cautious political animals reared up and bit the president on the by now all-important personal honesty front. On August 2nd, for example, Vice President Spiro Agnew was privately informed that the Justice Department had had him under investigation for bribery, extortion, and tax fraud since early 1973. These probes were not directly related to Watergate, but Agnew refused to resign, and defended himself against Justice's charges—when they became public a week later—on one of same grounds as Nixon was basing his own claim to privilege. Justice, declared Agnew, had no right to try and force him to turn over personal financial records for purposes of a criminal proceeding. He'd have to be impeached first.

Agnew's logic was pure "come and get me," a.k.a. a Catch-22 version of executive privilege. Deny the courts the information and then hope Congress couldn't throw him out of office without that information. The vice president's argument for privilege achieved headline status, however, the week before Judge Sirica was due to hear arguments from the special prosecutor and the White House counsel on why the grand jury's "show cause" order should not be honored. The timing couldn't have been worse, so far as Maximum John, jury members, and the special prosecutor were concerned.

Simultaneously, another story hit town. This one emanated from the General Services Administration (GSA), a federal agency responsible for maintaining U.S. government property. Since Nixon had arrived in office, the GSA said, the very tidy sum of ten million dollars in federal money had been spent to renovate two of Nixon's personal homes in California and Florida, and on the homes of his two daughters. This news, released on August 6th, simply disgusted millions of Americans. Padding the expense account was something lots of red-blooded Americans could understand, because they knew precisely what it would mean if *they* got caught playing that game. Taken together, therefore, the Justice Department's and the GSA's revelations blasted the White House claims to personal honesty precisely when Nixon most needed to be believed.

On August 15th, Nixon leaped over his pursuers and went directly to the people in another nationally televised address. The day before, Agnew had dropped his executive privilege claims and agreed to turn over his records to prosecutors after Nixon had ordered him to. The day after, Nixon hoped to make his version of Agnew's privilege argument stick. It didn't, not quite. Nixon reasoned on TV that it was time to put Watergate behind us. It was only Dean's word against his, and Dean was the bad guy of the whole cover-up, anyway.[76] Sirica, however, had more than a few doubts. Two weeks later, he ordered the president of the United States to *partially* obey Cox's subpoena for the tapes.

What Sirica suggested was yet another compromise. On August 29th, he ordered the White House to turn over the subpoenaed tapes *to him alone* for inspection. "The point was to walk a sort of middle ground," he later wrote. Sirica would examine the evidence in private without enunciating any legal principle about executive privilege. If Nixon's arguments for privilege were convincing, the tapes would go no further; if they were not, the judge would forward them to the special prosecutor.[77]

Now commenced another period of backing and hauling. Nixon, who by now probably had listened to just enough tapes to know that he was in deep trouble if Sirica or Cox also heard them, refused Sirica's offer. The Sirica-Nixon face-off was then kicked upstairs to Federal Appeals Court, and Nixon began to have the intimate records of his presidency transcribed, secretly editing a private face that might later become public. During September, Watergate receded. Congress was on vacation, and so were lots of other people. There was a widespread popular assumption that the courts would somehow handle the problem.[78]

## The Saturday Night Massacre

Little did the citizenry know, and just as little did its hopes become realities. In October 1973, Watergate exploded into all-out guerilla warfare. Nixon sought to scare off the lawyers and the judges, but succeeded only in leading them to make their belated alliance with the politicians.

This convergence of the judicial trial and the political trial of Watergate took place gradually. During the month that it took the Court of Appeals reviewing Sirica's decision to make up its mind, Nixon and the people around him were increasingly aware that they were behind the power curve on Watergate and a lot else besides. Their legislative agenda was stalled, rumors of presidential ill-humor and depression were rife, and Spiro Agnew was on the verge of being indicted for taking bribes before and during his vice presidency. When Agnew went, one of Nixon's major protections against indictment or impeachment was also going to disappear. Politicos who hesitated about replacing Nixon when Spiro Agnew was the required alternative could easily change their minds if there was another option.

Nixon, therefore, had to do something to replace his "No" with "Yes, but . . .". A negative position had to be packaged in a positive way. The president and his staff tried to recover the initiative by *appearing* to compromise in the not unlikely event that Sirica's compromise offer was upheld on appeal. One way to accomplish this was by excising incriminating or politically suicidal material from the tapes before Sirica even saw them. This partial and fragmentary process began no later than September.[79]

Another, and much preferred, approach was to try to use Sirica's offer to frustrate any judicial review at all. Sirica, remember, had said he would examine the tapes to decide whether or not they should be given to the special prosecutor and the grand jury. Sirica was casting himself as a solitary Platonic Guardian of the Republic. So Nixon's men scouted the possibilities of replacing Sirica with a Guardian of their own, someone who would see only what Nixon wanted him to see, and then insure that even that never got seen by anybody else. By October 12th, the appear-to-compromise strategy was given impetus when, after over a month of silence, the Appeals Court finally ruled that Nixon must accept Sirica's compromise.

Wheels started moving in earnest. Nixon's White House executed a classic "Yes, but . . ." aimed at flouting the court's decision without appearing to do so. *Yes,* it would turn over information, *but* not to Judge Sirica. Nor would it turn over the tapes themselves, only transcripts of the tapes. Senator John C. Stennis of Mississippi would do any private reviewing that was to be done. Senator Stennis? What did he know about such a complex case? Either nothing, or practically nothing. These may have been Stennis' major qualifications, along with being an utterly conservative Democrat who had publicly advised Nixon to tough it out about Watergate: some thought Stennis wasn't going to look hard, and that he didn't really know what to look for, anyway. He was a legal eunuch.

Once Nixon ordered the "Stennis compromise" announced on October 15th, 1973, selling and intimidating began in earnest, all dressed up in grave and polite phrases. Senators Baker (supportive) and Ervin (befuddled) were asked for input, Ervin in a fashion designed to maximize his confusion. Attorney General Richardson, meanwhile, had a brahmin-to-brahmin chat with Special Prosecutor Cox, telling him that serious consequences would ensue if he opposed the Stennis compromise.[80] Go along with this, or else—was the name of the game. Nixon sought to extricate himself from an ongoing criminal investigation on his own terms while pretending to obey the Majesty of the Law.

The second and third weeks of October 1973 were a good time to make such an effort. For crisis loomed again in the form of a foreign war Nixon hoped to exploit to repair his sagging presidential fortunes. Fears of a holocaust were, for the moment, daily fare. The occasion was a sudden and unexpected war between Egypt, Syria, and Israel that began on October 6th, the Hebrew festival of Yom Kippur. The Day of Atonement has been an occasion for fasting, prayer, dust, and ashes for Jews for millennia, and in 1973 reparations were assessed against Israeli Jews in dead earnest. Two Egyptian armies attacked across the Suez Canal, surprised Israeli defenders, and won unprecedented military and political victories.

The shock of the Yom Kippur War was profound, and not only to Israelis. Israel, in order to counterattack successfully, required lots of American arms, intelligence, and diplomatic muscle. Using such assistance, Israeli troops mounted a counterattack across the Suez Canal. Victory hung in the balance and Egyptian leaders increased their demands for Soviet assistance. The danger of a U.S.–Soviet military confrontation rose fast, particularly after Egypt upped the ante by calling upon the U.S.S.R. to send paratroop units to its aid. But United States and Soviet leaders decided on deescalation and pushed for an armistice and mutual withdrawals which allowed both Egypt and Israel to argue it was the real victor in the war. Washington and Moscow reined in their mercurial allies in order to avoid

war with each other. This was the wild and woolly atmosphere of official
Washington in early to mid-October 1973. The White House was involved
in brinksmanship of the most compelling kind.

In such a crisis, any president's political stature rises. Nixon hoped that
the storm swirling up out of Middle Eastern sands would give him the
opportunity to ram through a compromise on Watergate that would gut
the investigation of his personal involvements. He almost succeeded. But
a week of coldblooded political bargaining left Nixon and his staff with
one insoluble problem: the special prosecutor.

Archibald Cox simply refused to play ball. Nixon's whole "Yes, but"
strategy to foil the judicial probe required Cox to look the other way.
Without Cox to prepare a strong criminal case against him, Nixon would
be home free. The special prosecutor's suit for the original tapes had to be
stopped; once it was, further judicial or political efforts to involve Nixon
in the Watergate cover-up would be doomed.

So Nixon moved to isolate Cox during the crisis atmosphere of early to
mid-October. The move was so powerful and well orchestrated that it
made most of the special prosecutor personnel feel like pariahs. The White
House was better organized this time. And when new White House Chief
of Staff General Alexander Haig insistently advertised that the president's
diplomatic and military authority was being weakened too much by Watergate and that the debate about the tapes had to be ended, many Washington insiders agreed. The Stennis Compromise now looked good enough.
Nixon's counterattack was even benefitting from the fact that Spiro Agnew
had resigned on October 10th. Within two days, Nixon had nominated
Agnew's successor—House Minority Leader Gerald R. Ford—with considerable stage-managed drama. It looked like Nixon's star was on the rise and
that Cox or Sirica were going to lose if either kept insisting upon the
enforcement of the Appeals Court's ruling.[81]

Cox bent with the wind and tried some "Yes, but . . ." of his own. *Yes,*
it would be OK for somebody other than Sirica to decide whether or not
he and the grand jury ever got to see any of the tapes. *But* that should not
be a task for Senator Stennis; instead, "special masters" should be appointed by the court. These masters, moreover, should *not* be provided just
with transcripts; they should receive copies of the original recordings, plus
technical assistants to make sure the recordings hadn't been tampered
with.

What Archibald Cox proposed on October 18th was pure theater. Neither he nor Nixon wished to compromise, but both wanted to appear to
be doing just that. The White House had to make Cox look like a pettifog-
ging lawyer who was aggressively uncompromising. Cox had to bend to

avoid being broken, in hopes that Nixon would overreach himself before the Special Prosecutor's Office was emasculated.[82] It was a waiting game, a game to see who would make the first mistake—and, like all such contests, it was emotionally and physically exhausting. Power was what was being played out here, not the majesty of the law.

Enter John Dean again, stage center, with a guilty plea that shocked and discomfited the White House and which helped impel Nixon into the decisive misstep known as the Saturday Night Massacre. When last we saw John Dean, he had directly involved Nixon in Watergate by both his Senate testimony and by his fruitful speculation about Nixon's secret taping system. Dean had done all of this under a grant of limited immunity from the Senate Watergate Committee. The Special Prosecutor's Office, however, hadn't liked the committee's immunizing of Dean one little bit. It still suspected Dean was a self-serving liar and wanted to get as much criminal leverage on him as possible.

Dean knew this, too. And he knew that Cox had been careful to deposit all the proofs the special prosecutor had against him in the judicial equivalent of a safe-deposit box *before* the committee's immunity grant was finalized, in order to try to bring a case of his own against Dean later. So, following his Senate testimony, Dean and his lawyers spent months plea-bargaining with the special prosecutor. Dean's strength in these negotiations was that he was still the only witness there was against Richard Nixon, and still the strongest witness against Haldeman and Ehrlichman.

The special prosecutor had to deal. After his Senate Watergate Committee testimony, Dean was pure gold; in the absence of the tapes, Dean was also the centerpiece of Cox's case. Cox moved slowly, however, and let Dean sweat. Meanwhile, he prepared stronger cases against Dean on specific counts. Chief Watergate trial prosecutor Jim Neal carried on these negotiations for Cox, but Neal also knew when to stop the legal foreplay and consummate a marriage, of convenience if necessary, with John Dean. The week of October 14th to 20th was a watershed for Neal. By then, the tide was turning against Cox and the Special Prosecutor's Office. Something had to be done to regain the political initiative. Neal therefore made an unusual deal with Dean and his lawyer Charles Shaffer. Neal would conclude a plea bargain allowing Dean to plead guilty to only *one count* of conspiracy, *if* Dean came to court no later than Friday, October 19th, to enter his guilty plea *in open court.* Here was the touch of a master, the touch of a courtly U.S. attorney from Nashville who knew how to knock opponents off balance in public.

Timing was everything in such an exercise, and Neal got the timing very right. The Neal-Dean deal was completed at 3 A.M. on October 18th. At

10 in the morning of the 19th, Dean appeared before Judge Sirica to enter a guilty plea. The news flashed through Washington: Neal had got John Dean lined up and ready to go as a witness in the criminal trial! What other surprises did the special prosecutor have in store?

What surprises, indeed? many in the White House may have wondered. For they were about to spring a surprise of their own, one Jim Neal strongly suspected was coming. Nixon was about to forswear appearances and fire Cox outright, thus removing the chief impediment to the Stennis compromise on the tapes. When Neal whispered his suspicions about Cox's imminent firing to lawyer Shaffer as Shaffer and Dean were on the verge of entering their plea before Sirica on October 19th, the action was all in John Dean's corner again. Neal was honorably informing Dean that he still had a chance to back out of the plea bargain if he wanted to. Dean's deal with the Special Prosecutor's Office might very well be meaningless before the weekend was out. Dean could well plead guilty, go to prison, and then watch all other major Watergate players go free after Nixon abolished the special prosecutor's criminal investigation of the cover-up. John Dean could have run for legal cover, but he bit the bullet. He went ahead and entered his guilty plea anyway. Dean's courageous willingness to honor his agreement with the special prosecutor at Cox's worst moment helped keep pressure on the White House and pushed it further toward self-destruction.[83]

The day Dean pled guilty was one of frenzied press speculation and verbal warfare between Nixon's staff and Cox and his band of lawyers. On Friday, October 19th, the drama culminated in renewed White House attempts to make it appear as though Cox were at fault for refusing to accept Nixon's effort to violate court orders without seeming to.[84] Many and various were the legal liberties taken by all sides this day. Nixon's power play was obvious. Less obvious, though equally relevant to the fact that power, not law, was now what Watergate was mostly all about, was the fact that many people at the Special Prosecutor's Office busily photocopied documents from their files and hid them so that proofs already gathered wouldn't be destroyed by the White House, and so that they might be available for future use.[85]

As lawyers on all sides turned into guerilla warriors, the axe fell. Friday evening, White House Chief of Staff Haig ordered Attorney General Richardson to fire Cox, hinting at all manner of political rewards if he did as he was told. Richardson had been playing along with the White House for months, but playing behind the scenes was one thing and acting openly was another. If Richardson fired Cox, he would be risking his career. He wouldn't do it. The special prosecutor hadn't been boxed into the aggressive and uncompromising role the White House had tried to script for him. The attorney general refused to solve Nixon's remaining problems for him by playing the role of political executioner while Nixon sought refuge in the atmospherics of international crisis. Archibald Cox helped to sustain fellow-Bostonian Richardson's fortitude. On the morning of Saturday, October 20th, as pressure mounted on Richardson to remove Cox, the special prosecutor held a press conference at which he took a page out of simple country lawyer Sam Ervin's book. "I read in one of the newspapers this morning," Cox began, "the headline Cox DEFIANT. I don't *feel* defiant."

No, indeed. Cox, as his able press secretary James Doyle put it, presented himself in a determinedly modest light as the honest and forthright Jeffersonian yeoman in a land of political slickers. "It is sort of embarrassing," Cox allowed, "to be put in the position to say, 'Well, I don't want the President of the United States to tell me what to do.'"[86] Cox cast the negative spotlight on the president, not on his attorney general. Nixon was a power grabber, but Richardson was too honorable to be mixed up in such unseemly goings-on. "Admiration, respect, and affection" were what he felt for Richardson. Archibald Cox simply stood still, to give Richardson a way out and to force the White House to fire him without benefit of intermediaries. He didn't resign in a huff; he didn't do what Nixon told him to do; and he didn't go to court with another demand that Nixon turn over his tapes. Instead, Cox drew a line in the sand and dared Nixon and Haig to cross it. The next move was theirs.

This was not what the White House had expected. Alexander Haig, a devotee of the Pentagon approach to problem solving, had "war gamed" Cox's moves for him. Cox simply slipped out of Haig's net; instead of surrendering or attacking, he threw matters back at the White House and waited for *it* to act.[87]

When it did, all hell broke loose. Following Cox's folksy press conference on the morning of Saturday, October 20th, Richardson received the full crisis-of-national-security treatment from Haig: If Cox didn't go, Nixon would be weakened. If Nixon was weakened, international emergencies could easily get out of hand. Did the attorney general want to weaken America and risk blowing up the world? No, Richardson didn't, but neither was he going to commit Nixon's crimes for him. Richardson resigned his Cabinet post rather than fire Cox and so behead the Watergate criminal investigation. Then Richardson's number two man, William Ruckelshaus, also refused to wield the axe. "Your commander-in-chief is giving you an order, Bill," Haig angrily observed. But orders-are-orders and national-security logic failed again. Finally Robert Bork, number three at the Justice Department, decided to be a good soldier and fired Cox. Haig and Nixon thus maintained the fiction of noninvolvement.[88]

The fiction did not survive for long. Within hours, Nixon's staff made a stupendously maladroit move. Haig ordered FBI agents to go to the offices occupied by the special prosecutor's legal staff, seal all the rooms, and impound all the criminal evidence Cox and his predecessors had put together during the preceding fifteen months. This sort of obstruction of justice was preeminently visual. The legal to-ings and fro-ings described above were arcane, abstract, and impenetrable to most Americans. But FBI agents seizing offices and cordoning off their contents were a lot less abstract, a lot more personally threatening, and very much easier to see. And the seeing was made possible by television cameras, which were there because of people like Cox's press officer James Doyle, who knew a fantastic TV story when they saw one. Network news cameras, they fervently hoped, would illuminate the mailed fist descending on the special prosecutor's head.

Doyle et al. hoped correctly. "You would turn this country into a banana republic if you allowed defiance of the President," White House Chief of Staff Haig railed at reporters in defense of the seizure orders he'd just issued. But Haig had created a supremely public confrontation between FBI agents, the special prosecutor's lawyers, and the policemen responsible for guarding Cox's offices which made the scene look awfully like a banana republic undergoing a late-night coup.[89]

Reactions were instant. What Haig later termed a "firestorm" followed what was almost immediately dubbed the Saturday Night Massacre. One angry citizen had a stroke of grass-roots genius and arrived in front of the White House on Sunday morning dressed in a Nixon mask and a convict's uniform and carrying a sign reading "Honk for Impeachment." Many motorists driving by were happy to oblige, and the resulting cacophony did nothing to calm worried spirits within the Nixon administration.

Auto horns were only the beginning. Congress was deluged with waves of wrath. Although Cox was fired on a weekend, in an effort to minimize media coverage, an estimated 250,000–300,000 telegrams cascaded into Congress and the White House during the ten days following. The phone calls and letters to congressional offices on and after Monday, October 22nd, grabbed more attention. Such an outpouring of overwhelmingly negative opinion had never been seen before, even during the worst days of America's war in Vietnam. Western Union alone was carrying ten times its previous daily record of messages to government officials.

It didn't take long for Congress to recognize that the Saturday Night

Massacre was not a Washington story or an overnight sensation short on staying power. Public opinion like this was pure dynamite—just as it was late in 1986 for the Reagan administration in the Iran-Contra scandal and had been for the Carter administration after the failure of the Iranian hostage rescue mission in 1980. Political antennae started vibrating with a vengeance.[90] Former Representative Edward Mezvinsky of Iowa described part of the resulting congressional scene:

> When the House [of Representatives] convened at noon [on Tuesday, October 23rd, three days following the Saturday Night Massacre], the mood inside the chamber was wild. The talk was of the avalanche of mail and telegrams and telephone calls descending on Capitol Hill and demanding impeachment. Senior members assured me that the outpouring of public rage was unprecedented . . .

> I heard someone inside the cloakroom repeat the latest instant cliché: "Nixon is a Cox sacker."[91]

Nor was the House the only arena for gallows humor or fright. Iowa's Senator Harold Hughes, shortly after the Massacre, told Mezvinsky, "Ed, you just can't tell about this guy [Nixon] . . . you could have tanks in your front yard."[92]

Thus far had Richard Nixon fallen. He had sought to destroy his chief criminal pursuer, and the blows had rebounded against himself. "[T]hings unnoticed are forgotten," Tacitus once observed, "resentment confers status upon them."[93] Now the Special Prosecutor's Office had more status and visibility than it had had since its creation.

Moreover, it still had staff. Several-score lawyers and others had not resigned, any more than Archibald Cox had. These men and women of the Special Prosecutor's Office ruined Al Haig's game plan; they, too, stayed put and forced Nixon to fire them.

Once the firestorm set in following the Saturday Night Massacre, however, Haig and Nixon couldn't afford to fire anybody. The White House had gotten the politics of firing Cox very wrong, and had branded itself as the aggressor. Worse, the televised theatrics of FBI agents at the special prosecutor's offices further personalized millions of peoples' concerns about what was going on in Washington. What had started out cool, judicial, and abstract was now increasingly being perceived in direct, immediate, and compelling terms—like "tanks in your front yard."

The press reflected the climate of wholesale disenchantment. *Time* magazine, which supported Nixon during the 1960, 1968, and 1972 presidential elections, now stated that he had "irredeemably lost his moral authority, the confidence of most of the country, and therefore his ability to govern effectively." Important regional papers like the *Detroit News, Denver Post,* and *Atlanta Journal* joined the carefully liberal *New York Times* in editorializing that Nixon should resign. The *Washington Post* called for impeachment.[94] Commercial TV networks made unusual noises. CBS, scared away from Watergate late in 1972 by White House threats of economic sanctions, belatedly began almost nightly coverage of the case. Watergate still bemused most citizens, but the Saturday Night Massacre, like no other single event, riveted attention on the face-off between Nixon and his judicial opponents over the Watergate tapes. "Watergate" now became equivalent, to most, to the struggle for those tapes.[95]

This struggle was one Nixon wasn't winning. In November 1973, the first anniversary of his 61 percent victory over McGovern, Nixon's support ratings were 27 percent. Only eleven months earlier, 68 percent had sustained his leadership.[96] Worse, far worse, was that the Saturday Night Massacre pushed Congress back into the Watergate action and showed the judiciary that its efforts to prosecute the case without Congress's political muscle were exercises in futility. After October 20th, therefore, the political trial and the judicial trial started to coalesce and, with a journalistic assist, began the fourth stage of Watergate. From now on, it was political and judicial hardball all the way.

## Congress Moves to Renew the Political Trial

Congress was again a central focus of the Watergate drama. But, within Congress, the scene shifted from the Senate to the other house of the national legislature. This was ironic. The House of Representatives, up to then, had been an almost invisible player in Watergate. After the Saturday Night Massacre, however, a fault line now ran straight through Nixon's moral authority and eroded that fragile divinity which doth hedge presidents. Nixon had failed to set the terms for his prosecution. Impeachment, a political trial of a sitting president, was the topic of the hour.

That meant that the House had to enter the picture at last. Its Judiciary Committee had to draw up a bill of charges against Nixon, vote that bill out, and get it passed by the full House. Then, and only then, could the Senate determine whether or not to impeach by a two-thirds vote. It sounded august, but it wasn't. The House was quick off the mark, that is, eighty-four Democratic representatives were, either by introducing bills for Nixon's immediate impeachment (which meant nothing, but made nice headlines back home) or by supporting legislation to allow an impeachment process to begin. *That* meant everything, especially after Peter W. Rodino, the chairman of the House Judiciary Committee, told reporters on October 24th that his panel was going to proceed "full steam ahead" with an impeachment investigation.[97]

"Full steam ahead" was mostly rhetoric, but House members who had done nothing about Watergate for fifteen months and let the more electorally protected Senate take the lead now had their own political interests to consider. For when Nixon overreached himself, and produced a never-before-seen wave of grass-roots rage that hit Capitol Hill, the logic of political survival in Washington changed. Congress had at least to begin to begin an impeachment investigation to protect itself from the electorate.

Nixon, a power player in his own right, knew what had happened and tried to repair the damage. On October 23rd, only four days after he'd fired Cox, Nixon's lawyers went before Judge Sirica to say, "This President does not defy the law."[98] Of course, this was nonsense. Nixon had defied two federal courts and fired a special prosecutor to avoid providing evidence in a criminal investigation—contempt of court, and a whole lot more. Nixon had stymied the judiciary. But once the political trial resurfaced and impeachment threatened, Nixon had to change his tactics. He did so in two ways. First, he played appearances with the judiciary (again) in order to forestall his political opponents (again). Second, he sought to restrain the House from probing very far.

Political theater was made easier by the hesitancy of House leaders. The full House, for example, did not *formally* vote Rodino's Judiciary Committee the power to organize an impeachment investigation until three-and-a-half months after Rodino had announced "full steam ahead." That meant that the House Judiciary Committee was engaged in an informal fishing expedition, rather than a formalized constitutional process, until February 9th, 1974.

For those same three-and-a-half months, Nixon and his men kept stonewalling the judiciary. It was "Yes, but . . ." all over again. Court hearings to get the subpoenaed tapes turned over to Sirica for review and for possible later release to the Special Prosecutor's Office turned into a carnival. First, several of the subpoenaed tapes were claimed never to have existed. Then it was discovered that Nixon had spent at least twelve hours listening to important tapes as early as July. Cover-up suspect Haldeman, meanwhile, had taken no fewer than twenty-two tapes home with him "for review" shortly after his departure from the White House. Finally and most damningly, Nixon's personal secretary, Rose Mary Woods, claimed to have accidentally erased eighteen minutes of an important tape while transcribing its contents. All this and more had been known by the White House *before* it had offered to provide its versions of *all* tapes to Senator Stennis as a "compromise" in early October, and before it had fired Cox for opposing this phony "compromise."[99]

Week after week the "Yes, buts" obstructed the courts. Sirica and the Special Prosecutor's Office were being gulled, and they knew it. Every day the White House delayed in turning over the originals of the Watergate tapes—instead of transcripts or copies—made it less likely that anybody was ever going to get anything other than perfumed garbage. Nixon couldn't destroy all the tapes, for fear of impeachment if he did, but he could nickel-and-dime the courts to death by losing or erasing tapes and finally turning over nothing of any substance.

The question was: What was the judiciary going to do about it? The answer was: Nothing heroic. They kept the pressure on the White House by making sure that every one of its excuses had to be made in open court before hordes of reporters. But they did not force the White House to stop its delaying tactics.

Until November 21st, that is. On that day, when the electrifying news of the eighteen-minute gap broke, Sirica had had enough. Evidence was disappearing too fast for the judge's comfort, and he finally acted. Not by holding Richard Nixon in contempt of court—that was still too risky—but by demanding that Nixon at last begin turning over the tapes for review.

Starting on November 26th, Nixon complied. By December 8th, Sirica had what remained of the Watergate tapes originally subpoenaed by Cox. "Yes, but" no longer worked. Missing tapes and especially the eighteen-minute gap had worsened presidential public relations problems to the point where Nixon could no longer afford wholesale destruction of taped evidence. The logs in the possession of the special prosecutor prevented that. Other White House records were thoroughly sanitized. But the tapes—and the logs—remained. "I am not a crook," Nixon explained to an audience of editors early in November just after the news of the eighteen-minute gap broke, but most Americans had become skeptical. A poll commissioned by Congress found that the populace had "more confidence in garbage collectors than in (in declining order) the police, the press, church, business, Congress, or the White House."[100]

Sirica and others capitalized on Nixon's growing weakness. Sirica secretly vetted the original tapes between December 8th and 12th. After listening to the March 21st Dean-Nixon conversations, he decided that the president had probably obstructed justice, and he therefore did what justice required. He let executive privilege apply to some unrelated materials after specific appeals from White House lawyers and vetoed efforts to apply it to others. The main body of the recordings was finally shipped over to the Special Prosecutor's Office after almost five months of legal surrealism, delay, and failed *diktat.*

What the special prosecutor would do with the tapes was anybody's guess. His lawyers listened to the same material Sirica had, and also concluded Nixon had convicted himself in his own words. They remained uncertain, however, of their ability to build a case against the president and other higher-ups in the cover-up—even though a new special prosecutor had recently been appointed for precisely that purpose.[101]

Leon Jaworski of Houston, Texas, was a large part of the political and judicial conundrum. Immediately after the Saturday Night Massacre, energized members of Congress had sought ways to replace Archibald Cox and keep the Watergate prosecution alive. Three alternatives presented themselves. The first was to begin an impeachment process. Congress moved very cautiously here, as we have seen. It still didn't know whether any "smoking guns" actually existed on the subpoenaed tapes. Until early December, nobody except Nixon and his inner circle did. Even afterward, only Sirica and the special prosecutor's lawyers were added to that select list, but judicial custom forbade them from talking before indictments were handed down. The House wanted proof before it moved, but the courts had already prohibited the Senate from subpoenaing evidence from Nixon. The judicial process remained the easiest way to proceed.

Alternative two was for Congress, in order to put its muscle behind the criminal investigation, to appoint a new special prosecutor *responsible to itself alone.* Congress could get Cox's successor out of the executive branch and make him an investigative arm of the legislature. Precisely this had been done during the odoriferous Teapot Dome scandals of the Harding and Coolidge administrations in the 1920s. But many members who were hesitant about impeachment also hesitated to get out in front of the judiciary and take over the primary burden of Watergate. To do so was to risk assaults on their "political partisanship," the possibility of further court rulings that Congress had exceeded its legitimate constitutional authority, and the possible disenchantment of the electorate. This approach got nowhere.[102]

Judge Sirica and John Stacks have explained the political hesitation nicely. At the end of 1973, and during the early months of 1974, Nixon was very unpopular, but public opinion was still opposed to having Congress or the courts remove him from office forcibly.

In late January the Gallup poll found that only 27 percent of those polled approved of Nixon's performance as president; 63 percent disapproved. Despite this low rating, there was no consensus on whether he should leave office. The country was split 46 percent to 46 percent over whether he should resign. And opinion was two to one against impeaching President Nixon, in spite of the fact that, according to the Lou Harris poll, three out of four believed Nixon knew about the Watergate cover-up attempt [and thus was legally guilty of obstructing justice in a criminal investigation]. It was this contradiction that I found most troubling: we seemed to have a president who was trusted or believed by very few, yet could not be removed from office [because public opinion was too ambivalent and potentially volatile for Congress to act decisively].[103]

Sirica and Stacks put it in a nutshell. Half the country wanted Nixon out, but only a third wanted to force the issue. And so, the same Congress which did not formally begin an impeachment investigation until February also avoided the political risk of appointing a special prosecutor of its own. Congress played it safer, did only what it had done before, and chose the most careful alternative. They forced Nixon to appoint another prosecutor who was, once again, *in* the executive branch but not *of* it: Leon Jaworski.

When Jaworski was appointed on November 1st, when he received Senate approval on November 8th, and for several months afterwards, his power, status, and purposes were vagueness incarnate. Nixon had already fired one special prosecutor, and few Watergate veterans doubted that he'd fire another one if the opportunity ever presented itself. The special prosecutor's staff knew this better than anybody. Many of them also feared that their southern Democrat boss Jaworski was a conservative who would go light on Nixon and other cover-up heavyweights. Jaworski looked like a Good Old Boy without principles to many young lawyers who had just received the lesson that law is what the powerful say it is unless competing powers are saying different and fighting hard for their views.[104]

Cox's men and women needn't have worried. Jaworski was a Good Old Boy in Senator Sam Ervin's mold. He revelled in manipulation, greased, and glad-handed. But Jaworski also knew how to fight for the principles of law and order in which he believed. Jaworski fought, moreover, with Cox's experienced legal team, not new staff of his own. That meant big trouble for Nixon. Judicially, Jaworski speedily renewed Cox's suit for the originally-demanded tapes. This reassured his frazzled staff that he wasn't going to sell out the criminal investigation for a mess of political pottage.

That was only the beginning. Once Jaworski and his newly adopted staff got the tapes in mid-December and realized smoking guns did tie Nixon, Haldeman, Ehrlichman, and others directly into the cover-up, they peppered the White House with requests for *more* tapes. Beginning on January 9th, they requested twenty-five additional recordings of presidential conversations. This number eventually increased to forty-four (in mid-March), and then sixty-four (in mid-April). Nixon provided nothing, and travelled the country arguing that Jaworski, like Cox, was engaged in a fishing expedition which could require the White House to supply boxcars full of national secrets that might fall into unfriendly hands. The fact that Jaworski wanted specific records of specific conversations among Watergate principals was, once again, thoroughly obfuscated.

The White House's smokescreens, however, had a diminishing effect, for Jaworski began by *asking* for more evidence instead of *demanding* it. Cox had subpoenaed, and been fired for it. That had made Nixon look over-reactive. Exploiting this, Jaworski maneuvered Nixon into a negative light again by demanding nothing and continuing to ask, anyway. Later, he demanded—just as Cox had—but he realized that only congressional threats of impeachment had gotten any tapes released at all and that only more political muscle would get more released. He first waited to see what the House would do about an impeachment investigation. Meanwhile, there were prosecutions to prepare on the basis of proof already in hand, and media games to play.

On the prosecutorial front, Jaworski prepared transcripts of the first seven tapes and started playing those tapes to the Watergate grand jury on January 16th, 1974. This jury, at work on Watergate for a year and a half, finally had enough evidence to consider indictments against higher-ups. While the grand jury pondered, Jaworski spent time with the press. Jaworski's media activity was a matter of broad hints and strong nudges. Sometime in February 1974, for example, he had dinner in Washington with the top editors and writers of *Time,* the nation's largest news magazine. *Time's* editors, recall, had already said that Nixon should resign. Impeachment, however, was a question on which *Time* (lacking the evidence before Sirica, Jaworski, and the grand jury) had not yet taken any position.

Jaworski intended to change that. So, saying nothing about what the evidence definitely was, the special prosecutor used a lawyerly and hypothetical approach. What if X had obstructed justice, and X happened to be the president of the United States: Would that be an impeachable offense? By using such rhetorical devices, Jaworski told *Time* that the tapes showed Nixon was guilty of criminal offenses.[105]

Richard Nixon also knew how such games were played. Operation Candor was his media and public-opinion offensive. Explanations were com-

plemented with veiled threats and by crises (notably a worldwide alert of
U.S. military forces on October 25th). "One year of Watergate is enough,"
he told Congress in his State of the Union Address on January 30th, 1974.
Congress should either impeach him *immediately* or drop the issue for
good.[106]

Congress, meanwhile, still hadn't seen any Watergate tapes and remained afraid to go after Nixon without them. Those who *had* the evidence
(under pretrial legal wraps), on the other hand, couldn't proceed against
a sitting president without strong congressional support. So Nixon again
told Congress to put up or shut up; trying, as often before, to keep power
and evidence separate in the Watergate case.

It didn't work—largely because, after Nixon fired Cox, too many journalists began devoting too much time to presidential involvement. When,
for example, court-appointed experts investigating the eighteen-minute
gap on a key Watergate tape reported on January 15th, their conclusions
were another public-relations disaster for the White House. Five separate
erasures had almost certainly occurred, instead of one secretarial "accident."[107] Eighteen months of obstruction were producing one major result.
The president's continuing efforts to choke off the criminal proceedings
were only legitimizing the attack upon him. Nixon's transgressions had
unsettled a nation established and maintained by agreements on means—
on legal procedures by which disputes should be resolved. The longer
Nixon offended these procedural canons of America's civil religion, the
worse off he was. Buggings and break-ins could be downplayed on the
grounds that politics was a dirty business. Sabotaging the courts repeatedly
was another matter; *that* was refusing to play by the rules. Millions of
concerned citizens were becoming a sort of massive jury listening to Richard Nixon and his judicial opponents argue in the court of public opinion.[108]

This gets us back to the special prosecutor, who was now a very busy
man indeed. Between January and March 1974, Jaworski and his office
slowly backed Nixon farther into a corner on the tapes. Nixon couldn't risk
intensifying Congress's nascent political trial, so he had to appear to cooperate. So long as the judiciary's information and Congress's power remained separate, Nixon could play both ends against the middle.

But time was running out. Evidence presented to a grand jury is kept
secret before indictments are brought down, but an indictment is not
supposed to be made in secret. Nothing, however, was usual about Watergate. The walls of judicial secrecy finally and thoroughly eroded, and in
a fashion most damaging to Richard Milhous Nixon.

The process had far more to do with power than it did with law. Special Prosecutor Jaworski made unprecedented legal moves which gave Congress, in the form of the House Judiciary Committee, the full benefit of all the evidence, particularly the seven tapes that had so far been pried loose from the White House's grip. What happened resulted from the careful manipulation of judicial and political technicians. The twenty-three women and men of the Watergate grand jury, however, rose to the occasion. These grand jurors, after listening to the tapes Jaworski provided on January 16th, finally started to hand down indictments for cover-up and political sabotage against White House and CREEP principals.

The grand jury had had enough of delay, and so decided to indict *all* the still unindicted or unpunished principals: Haldeman, Ehrlichman, Mitchell, Colson, Haldeman aide Gordon Strachan, Mitchell aide Robert Mardian, CREEP lawyer Kenneth W. Parkinson, *and President Richard Milhous Nixon* for crimes including obstruction of justice, perjury, and conspiracy. But when the special prosecutor's lawyers got wind of this, they blanched. The others OK, but not Nixon.

There were legal reasons for their concern. No president had ever been indicted while in office. Nixon—presuming the courts would try him—would have to be convicted on *criminal* grounds, that is, on narrow grounds and on the basis of proof which Nixon was refusing to provide. But considerations of power were primary. Jaworski simply didn't think the courts had the will or muscle to indict or convict Nixon. So he compromised with angry grand jury members who were threatening to act on their own unless *something* was done about Nixon, and then cut a deal with House Judiciary Committee staff lawyers, in order to insure Congress would do that something.

The procedure unfolded in stages. First, Jaworski persuaded all the grand jury members not to indict the President, but, instead, to list him as an "unindicted co-conspirator." This information was not included with the indictments the jury sent to Judge Sirica. It was a secret decision, known only to the jury members themselves and to Jaworski's staff. The legalese involved was wondrous and unprecedented. The president was not being charged with any crime, even though all the jurors and the prosecutors thought him as guilty as some or all of the others who were indicted. Instead, he was secretly classified in a fashion reserved for criminals who had pled guilty or those who had agreed to testify against their fellows after receiving immunity. This legal gambit allowed the special prosecutor to restrain the grand jury from pushing him into a confrontation with Nixon which Jaworski feared he would lose. At the same time, it also allowed the jury to avoid *not* indicting Nixon. They could and did put him in a temporary legal limbo, one which allowed them to say that they had done *their* part of the job.

Now Jaworski had to do his. Keeping the grand jury's almost-indictment of Nixon on March 1st in reserve for the moment, he moved to insure that Congress realized that more than enough evidence existed for them to politically indict Nixon, just as more than enough evidence existed for the grand jury to criminally indict Nixon's cronies. This meant more wondrous legalese by Jaworski. He filled a suitcase with the best evidence he had against Nixon and the other Watergate conspirators—tape transcripts, for example. Then, he added a 55-page road map to that evidence, one that his lawyers had put together during the long year that they'd been on the case. This map pointed straight at Richard Nixon by tying him directly into the cover-up and associated misdeeds.

The grand jury was very happy to include the raw evidence and the Nixon-is-guilty-too road map with the indictments of Haldeman, Ehrlichman, Mitchell, and others which it sent to Judge Sirica on March 1st. The jury, moreover, also followed Jaworski's lead in asking Sirica to send all these materials over to the House Judiciary Committee immediately so that it could be used to impeach the president of the United States.[109]

Now it was up to the judge. If Sirica sat on the evidence and the road map, it was all over. But Sirica didn't. He knew what Jaworski was telling him: the courts simply didn't have the power to indict or convict Nixon while he was in office and in power. He knew, too, what the road map meant: both the grand jury and the special prosecutor wanted Nixon punished, but believed that Congress had to do that.

By March 18th, therefore, Sirica ruled that he would comply with the request of the special prosecutor and the grand jury, and send the tapes and other documents over to the House Judiciary Committee. Three days later, a federal appeals court upheld his ruling, and the coalescence of the hitherto-separate judicial and political offensives against Richard Nixon was complete. Finally, Congress would know as much as Jaworski did about what Nixon had done. In terms of the majesty of the law, the procedure had all the grace and clarity of a bogged-down hippopotamus bellowing in a swamp on a moonless night. Grace and clarity, however, meant little at this point. Sirica, the grand jury, and the special prosecutor all wanted Congress to get serious about formulating indictments to serve as the cornerstone of the political trial of the president. A court system which had hitherto stymied a political trial of cover-up principals by denying Congress the right to subpoena Watergate tapes was now providing the tapes and pushing the politicos to go ahead. The courts would try all the Nixon men who had fallen from power during the preceding twenty months, but they were going to move aside when it came to the single remaining defendant still in power.

To accomplish this, Jaworski and Sirica engaged in legal legerdemain. They proceeded cautiously because they didn't yet know whether the politicans would proceed on their own account. The House Judiciary Committee had to take the first step toward impeachment. Even when it finally got the tapes and the road map in late March, it was unclear whether the committee would move. Remember that Peter Rodino's brave words of October 24th were followed by extreme caution. The Judiciary Committee didn't hire its chief counsel, John Doar, until December 20th, significant numbers of staff weren't on hand to assist Doar until early February, and the hiring of all forty-five lawyers and fifty-five support personnel wasn't completed until mid-March—two weeks *after* the grand jury had issued its indictments. And it wasn't until February 6th that the full House voted to reassert the principle of Congress's right to subpoena White House tapes for its investigation; not until February 21st that the Judiciary Committee's staff issued a preliminary report on what the constitutional grounds for impeachment might be; and not until mid-April that the first Judiciary Committee subpoena of tapes was issued. Given such sluggishness, it took until February 19th for the Senate's Special Watergate Committee to finally stand aside to give Rodino's committee total responsibility for future investigations by voting to hold no further public meetings of its own. It required approximately four months for the House Democratic leaders to get their impeachment inquiry going. Discretion, legal and otherwise, was far more characteristic than valor. Cynics still had cause to question whether the dynamite on the tapes would ever go off.

Many of Jaworski's lawyers and most Watergate grand jury members were frankly skeptical. They hoped that Congress would try Nixon, but they didn't expect it. To get their point across, jury members warned Jaworski that they had deferred to the House Judiciary Committee in regard to unindicted co-conspirator Nixon "at this time." Jaworski reiterated the point privately during the second week in March: the grand jury members were reserving the right to charge Nixon and throw the issue into a court's lap if Congress did not act.[110]

The pathway to impeachment was finally open. Almost two years after the Watergate burglary and five months after the Saturday Night Massacre, the criminal trial and the political trial of the case had been joined. From March 1974 onward, the Special Prosecutor's Office cooperated with the Congress. The politicians controlled the action now, but it remained to see what they'd do with their opportunity.

## Congress Bites the Bullet

Most Watergate actors were cautious people, But there were reasons for caution. Such logic applied especially to the House of Representatives.

By March 1974, much more was happening in America than the legal and political gymnastics of Watergate. The economy, in particular, was suffering spasms that hit most Americans right in their pocketbooks.[111] The problem had a name: stagflation. "Economic law," as Nixon's Federal Reserve Board chairman Arthur F. Burns ruefully summarized, wasn't "working quite the way it used to." Inflation and unemployment, instead of being "inversely related," as economists had supposed for twenty-five years, rose in a grim duet. By January 1974, inflation rates, spurred by the Arab OPEC oil embargo of 1973–74, were at double-digit levels, the worst in twenty-seven years. Unemployment rates also edged—and then galloped—higher. An estimated 4.4 million were jobless in 1973; 5.2 million in 1974; and just under 8 million the year after that. By the autumn of 1974, the United States had entered what was its worst economic downturn since the Great Depression of the 1930s.

Lots more people, then, were worrying about dollars and cents than were insomniac about Watergate during 1973–74. Freshman Representative Edward Mezvinsky of Iowa recalled that he and other young liberal Democrats had surprises in store for them when they went back home to visit their constituents in August 1973. "Whether it was Barbara Jordan of Texas, Gary Studds of Massachusetts, Pat Schroeder of Colorado, Andy Young of Georgia, or Pete Stark of California, the assessment of the general mood on Watergate was the same I brought back from Iowa. The scandal was coming in a poor second to the cost of living.[112] Meat and potatoes politics, therefore, was a priority for most members of Congress desiring reelection, and many hesitated to get vehement about the constitutional debates increasingly central to Watergate.

Slander, however, helped push Mezvinsky and many others into action. Abuse had become a mainstay of the Nixon administration. Throughout Watergate, undertones of defamation were ever-present. The mostly black Watergate grand jury members, for instance, were libelled as racists in-reverse out to crucify the president. The *Washington Post* was part of a Jewish plot. Chairman Peter Rodino of the House Judiciary Committee had Mafia connections. And so forth. Innuendo like this was not unique to the Nixon years. Politically, it is as perennial as the grass. What was different, in early 1974, was the scale of the abuse. The air resounded with slander, and more members of Congress became willing to try and get Nixon before he got them.[113] The desire for unperilous courses of action delayed direct contests of power, opinion, and will, but between October 1973 and March 1974, the little kingdom of political Washington suffered "the nature of an insurrection."[114]

The insurrection, however, was a quiet one. Congress hoped to proceed "boldly, but not wrathfully." Nixon must be toppled, but the job had to be begun by a committee and this committee was a cautious and many-headed beast. Bipartisanship was all important to its Democratic leadership, in order that "This shall make/Our purpose necessary, and not envious;/Which so appearing to the common eyes,/We shall be called purgers, and not murderers."[115]

The purging began in earnest on May 9th, when House Judiciary Committee members, all thirty-eight of whom were lawyers, were at last presented with the outstanding evidence in the Watergate case. Two years after the break-in, twenty-one Democrats and seventeen Republicans had to determine whether to indict a sitting president for high crimes and misdeeds for only the second time in U.S. history.

The members of this political grand jury bent over backward to appear as impartial and unmurderous as possible by doing things no judicial grand jury ever would have done. They allowed Nixon's lawyers to hear the evidence against the president as it was presented to the House Judiciary Committee by the committee's legal staff, and they also allowed his lawyers to cross-examine witnesses testifying before the committee. Congress had never previously allowed such privileged access to any closed accusatory proceeding against a government official.

But times were not normal. When the House Judiciary Committee finally had the evidence before it, Richard Nixon had ridden even farther down the road to self-destruction. Just before the committee opened its investigation into Nixon's personal involvement in Watergate, impeachment suddenly appeared more necessary and a lot less envious. For April 1974 was the month of taxes and tapes. What interested Americans finally learned about both involved them emotionally in Watergate to an extent beyond anything except the firestorm following the Saturday Night Massacre.

First to taxes. Taxes were matters of special concern to Americans in the depressed economic climate of 1974. Taxes also destroyed Richard Nixon's credibility with a large portion of the electorate in a way that more abstract elements of Watergate never did. Taxes became front page news by April 3rd, when the Internal Revenue Service announced that Richard Nixon owed them a very great deal of money—$467,000.[116] Via creative and illegal accounting, he had contrived to pay almost no income tax after becoming president. The scandal of the preceding summer regarding monies spent on Nixon's family homes had been bad enough, but tax cheating induced visceral bitterness. Representative Mezvinsky wrote that his constituents understood what paying taxes involved and that they expected any president to set standards of honesty in that regard. "The people of the first district [of Iowa] were far more interested in the tax issue than in the more abstract, constitutional questions to be studied during the impeachment inquiry. The President's nominal tax payments struck a raw nerve."[117]

They did indeed. Nixon owed (and quickly agreed to pay) to the Internal Revenue Service more money than most Americans could conceive of earning in their lifetimes. Tax cheating, coming only a month after the grand jury indicted seven of Nixon's former top aides, pushed millions of Americans over a conceptual line and allowed them to view their president as a crook who *had* to be investigated—and *maybe* even tried—by Congress for the good of the country.

Then there were the tapes—or, rather, sanitized versions of tapes—that Nixon released in a forlorn effort to appeal to an electorate which still hadn't seen any of the taped evidence which had been the focal point of contention for nine months. On April 29th, 1974, Nixon attempted this, his final bold stroke to escape the judicial and political pincers closing around him. He tried to continue to refuse to provide the courts with any more evidence than he already had and also tried to provide Congress only with evidence that least hurt his case.

As so often before, appearances were deceiving-by-design. On April 29th, Nixon went on prime-time TV to announce he was freely making available information about his knowledge and actions relating to the Watergate break-in and cover-up which would demonstrate that both were "just as I have described them to you from the very beginning." Framing the president as he spoke were several score bound volumes of transcript, or so it appeared.[118] The volumes were stage props. Four-fifths of their pages were empty. The 1,200 pages remaining were heavily edited. Even with the White House's editing, however, the transcripts demonstrated no such "from the very beginning" honesty as Nixon claimed before an audience of over half the nation's adult population.[119]

Honesty, however, was the last thing on the president's mind. Nixon was using his office as an "electronic pulpit" to make it appear that he was doing what he was not, in fact, doing—that is, providing evidence long desired by the courts and two special prosecutors and which had been demanded of him only two weeks earlier by a Congressional Judiciary

Committee subpoena. All presidents engage in this sort of prevarication, but Nixon's lies were more brazen than most. For not quite ten months, the tapes had been a slowly tightening noose around his neck. So Nixon finally tried to slip the noose by "letting the people know" what was on the growing numbers of tapes the special prosecutor and Congress wanted to see, in hopes that his judicial and political opponents would then be forced to keep pressing for genuine evidence.

The strategy almost worked. Nixon gave one of his better Watergate performances, one good enough to elicit kudos from the *Washington Post* and the *New York Times.* He did this because he was initially able to make it appear as though he was finally obeying the law, and the appearance briefly cast Nixon's opponents as partisan villains. Here was the president giving everyone all anybody could ask for, so who was Congress to refuse it? Who was the special prosecutor to keep insisting on more? Congress now had all it needed to determine whether an impeachment trial was necessary.

Nixon's was a bold and unexpected stroke which only just failed. Had the House Judiciary Committee accepted the edited transcripts that Nixon advertised as genuine, Nixon could have eviscerated the political trial, continued to stymie criminal justice as it applied to himself, and kept his presidency alive. But the committee's staff, of course, knew that appearances were not realities. They knew that Nixon had released only sanitized versions of the tapes—including those which Sirica, grand jury members, the special prosecutor's lawyers, and the committee had seen entire—to avoid a clear refusal to obey a special congressional subpoena for many Watergate tapes which the Judiciary Committee had finally made on April 11th. Nixon submitted his *sanitized* transcripts the day before the deadline which the House Judiciary Committee had set for their receipt of the *unsanitized* evidence. It was all another "Yes, but" effort of a sort Cox, Sirica, and Jaworski had repeatedly refused.

They knew all of that. Still, they almost played Nixon's game. The reasons were various, and the details are engagingly presented in Elizabeth Drew's memoir of the final year of Watergate. On the evening of May 1st, the House Judiciary Committee's members were called upon to decide. Would they accept the transcripts Nixon had made public several days before as sufficient, or would they not?[120] They wouldn't, but only just. By a vote of 20 to 18, the committee refused to allow Nixon to set the terms of his own investigation any longer. Lone Republican William Cohen of Maine joined the Democratic members to vote that Nixon had failed to comply with the subpoena. Had Cohen voted the other way, the president's last robust effort to remake law in his own image might have succeeded. But Cohen didn't, and the Democrats didn't. They guessed what the public's reaction to Nixon's edited tapes might be, and they guessed right. Within two weeks after Nixon released his version of Watergate, his presidency was on the road toward dissolution.

Nixon's staff had deleted a lot from the transcripts—pithy instructions, for example, which the president gave John Mitchell on March 22, 1973, one day after his "cancer on the presidency" meeting with John Dean: "I want you all to stonewall it, let them plead the Fifth Amendment, cover up or anything else" to "save the plan."[121] But the transcripts were peppered with "(expletives deleted)" and the expletives mattered. Off-color expressions, present and absent, shocked the majority of Americans who did not then believe that their presidents swore.

The idea seems quaint now, yet it existed then. The United States of 1974 was steeped in an era of American Greatness, weaned during decades when presidents loomed ever larger in the nation's political imagination. America had become the greatest country in the world, a land with missions to match its greatness. Majesty was accordingly expected of the men who led that nation and who symbolized it to hundreds of millions at home and abroad—and majesty meant moral grandeur and spotless behavior. "Give 'em Hell" Harry Truman had used salty language, but Richard Nixon and many another rising politician had pilloried such verbal pyrotechnics as unacceptable. Truman was common, and the day of the common president who used common language was over. Nixon and others cast their words and actions in heroic styles pioneered by successful presidents like Franklin Delano Roosevelt and John F. Kennedy. Heroic strategies paid off for presidents. It gave them a divinity which doth hedge kings and leaders of nations with thermonuclear arsenals. It allowed their power and repute to survive shocks which other leaders, like "fixer" Lyndon Johnson, did not survive.

But it also exacted a price. Richard Nixon paid that price after April 30th, 1974. Politicians who knew what presidential image making was all about guessed what was coming, as House Judiciary Committee member James Mann of South Carolina did when he talked with journalist Elizabeth Drew on the eve of the committee's crucial vote of May 1st. Mann referred, Drew wrote:

> . . . as people have been doing all day, to the "(expletive deleted)"s. They all seem curious to know what those parentheses are hiding. "The more that people know about him, it seems, the more trouble he's in," he says. "It's not that they think he's guilty of an impeach-

able offense, necessarily, but that he's not the man they thought he was."[122]

No, Nixon wasn't the man they thought he was, any more than Jack Kennedy had been, but Kennedy hadn't been exposed while still in office. And it cost Nixon heavily with those who had come to expect their president to be a democratic monarch. Nixon's image problem then was a major reason that the Judiciary Committee risked moving ahead—though only just—on May 1st. Enough members believed that Nixon's edited words would explode in his face.[123] Congress fought to replace Nixon's evidentiary agenda with its own and, during the next several weeks, the truth of perceptions like Representative Mann's was borne out. Mann's constituents didn't like what they read or heard about the tapes, and they heard and read lots more than the White House reckoned they would.

The reading began when the *New York Times,* in a repeat of its Pentagon Papers revelations, serialized the White House's transcripts verbatim. On May 1st, CBS News broadcast a prime-time special in which reporters read segments of the tape transcripts. Three days later, NBC News used professional actors to do the same thing. Meanwhile, both the *Washington Post* and the *New York Times* rushed the transcripts into paperback, with commentaries to help readers make sense of seven hundred pages of text. Both books, available on newsstands by May 14th, quickly became best-sellers.

The more exposure Nixon's edited transcripts got, the less willing congressional Republicans and conservative Democrats were to defend their content. Republican House Minority Leader John Rhodes of Arizona and his Senate counterpart, Hugh Scott of Pennsylvania, somersaulted from complimenting the president for supplying bowdlerized evidence to damning what Nixon had made public. Rhodes branded the transcripts a "deplorable, shabby, disgusting, and immoral performance by all," and later added that he'd be willing to accept Nixon's resignation if Nixon chose to offer it.[124] Such strategic withdrawals by Congress's Republican leadership sent strong messages to fence sitters on the House Judiciary Committee. These political reactions were also beneficial to staff lawyers preparing evidence for House Judiciary Committee members to consider. House Judiciary Committee's Chief Counsel John Doar, a Republican, and his boss, Democrat Peter J. Rodino, wanted all the conservative support they could muster: bipartisan deliberations would hurt Richard Nixon more. The more Republicans who were willing to go after Nixon, the better for the Democrats. The Judiciary Committee would become a Chinese army, and Nixon simply couldn't shoot them *all.* The benefit of bipartisanship was obvious, but so was the cost.[125] The Democrats had barely enough votes to demand more unsanitized evidence from the White House. But there was a lot of difference between doing that and deciding to indict Richard Nixon for high crimes and misdemeanors against the Constitution and laws of the United States and thus begin the nitty-gritty of an impeachment struggle. There was no guarantee the Democrats had the votes to indict yet, nor were the Republicans going to push them into an impeachment struggle likely to weaken the G.O.P. electorally.

The cost of bipartisanship thus made itself felt. The House Judiciary Committee wanted to scare nobody, including itself. Its staff took four months, from early January to early May, to arrange evidence for presenta-tion—even though the most important evidence—with accompanying guidebook—had been supplied by Sirica and Jaworski early in March. The House Judiciary Committee moved like a pregnant turtle. And it continued to do so once it began to hear evidence in May. The Judiciary Committee didn't want to look as if it was prosecuting anybody. *Investigating,* yes; *prosecuting,* no.

The irony was stellar. Whatever Watergate required, it was not more investigation. That had been going on for almost two years. But further delays served an important political purpose: they maintained just enough of a united front on the House Judiciary Committee. Investigation (via a lengthy presentation of raw evidence) was all right. This would allow the committee's members to see for themselves. But organized arguments re-garding what Doar called a "pattern of misconduct" could be equated—just as it had been all along—with persecution, by the president and the president's staff. Prosecution, therefore, was not what Congress was about. Not yet.

The House Judiciary Committee, instead, bought time, more time to see which way political winds blew, more time to see whether Nixon would get Congress off the hook by resigning, more time to dot factual *i's* and cross evidentiary *t's,* more time to make it appear that Congress was doing everything possible to give its prime suspect the benefit of every doubt. Least-common-denominator politics resulted.

This investigatorial rather than prosecutorial strategy also explained, as reported here earlier, why the House Judiciary Committee had earlier made a unique allowance for Nixon's latest and last White House counsel, James D. St. Clair (who replaced an ailing Fred Buzhardt in January), to attend the closed sessions of the committee. But lousy law made good politics. St. Clair's special privileges made it harder for Nixon to present himself as the victim of a kangaroo court or a star-chamber proceeding. The White House argued this anyway, but such arguments had been rendered less than persuasive to conservative Democratic and moderate Republican members of the Judiciary Committee.

For six months, the House Judiciary Committee moved glacially. Evidence which required four months to organize took another month-and-a-half to present. By mid-July, however, the House Judiciary Committee's staff lawyers (with back-door assists from their opposite numbers at the Special Prosecutor's Office) at last began to prepare a bill of charges. It finally specified five types of presidential misconduct: (1) obstruction of justice; (2) abuse of power; (3) contempt of Congress; (4) unconstitutionally waging war by secretly bombing Cambodia from 1969 to 1971; and (5) tax evasion and selling of political favors. The House Judiciary Committee's staff lawyers had been careful not to get too far ahead of their congressional superiors, who had themselves been careful not to get very far ahead of public opinion, in the matter of impeachment.[126]

Through all of this, Washington's power brokers watched public-opinion polls like hawks, especially after Nixon's tape transcripts gambit failed. During May, June, and early July 1974, polls, more than anything else, gave Congress the reassurance it required to edge toward impeachment.

May began badly for Nixon in several respects. A majority of people came to believe that enough evidence now existed to warrant a Senate impeachment trial. A plurality had concluded that Nixon's actions were serious enough that he should be forced from office if he refused to resign.

Never before had the grass roots wanted Nixon out so badly. "Expletive deleted"s and a lot else besides had undermined Nixon to a point that a political indictment and a political trial were now acceptable. Three identically worded Gallup polls conducted between May 2nd and June 3rd and published between May 5th and June 17th illustrated the trend. In the poll reported May 5th, less than a week after "(expletives deleted)" hit the headlines, 44 percent wanted Nixon tried, 41 percent did not, and 15 percent weren't sure. On May 23rd, Gallup reported that 51 percent wanted Nixon tried, 31 percent didn't, and 18 percent were not sure. The June 17th numbers were almost identical: 50 percent wanted a trial, 32 percent didn't, 18 percent still sat in silence.

Opinion about Nixon's guilt or innocence was no more reassuring to the White House. Thirty-eight percent believed Nixon should be impeached at the beginning of May, while 49 percent did not and 13 percent had no opinion. By mid-May, 48 percent wanted Nixon tossed out, 37 percent didn't, and 15 percent weren't sure. At the end of May, 44 percent wanted Nixon removed, 41 percent didn't, and the remainder stayed bemused. Six percent more of the adult population wanted Nixon tried at the end of May than at its start. Six percent more also believed that Nixon was guilty of crimes unbecoming a president, 9 percent ceased their opposition to trying Nixon, and 8 percent ceased opposing his impeachment. The release of the tapes had backfired. Millions of Americans had believed the president when he'd stated repeatedly that he hadn't been involved in Watergate at *all*. Nixon might be a dupe, but they didn't think of him as a liar or crook. Even with excisions, however, the White House tapes showed that Nixon *had* been involved. Sloughing everything off on bad advisers like John Dean no longer worked: the question was no longer whether Nixon was involved, but how involved he was.[127]

The answer to this "how involved?" question, too, provided no reassurance. A Lou Harris poll taken May 4th to 7th and published almost a month later disclosed that two-thirds of those questioned had negative feelings about the accuracy of Nixon's edited tapes and believed he was withholding important information. Seventy percent had a negative opinion regarding Nixon's cooperation with the House Judiciary Committee; 82 percent were negative about Nixon's overall handling of the Watergate case; and no less than 56 percent thought Nixon *should* be indicted by the committee if he continued to refuse to hand over the unadulterated evidence it was demanding. Such shifts of opinion quantified the growing alienation which allowed Nixon's opponents to continue their judicial and political attacks.[128]

Attack they did. Gallup reported on May 23rd that a majority believed Nixon must be tried for possible political crimes. For the first time since Watergate had surfaced twenty-three months earlier, 51 percent of the voters wanted their president to have his day in court whether he wanted to or not. Figures like this were manna to Special Prosecutor Leon Jaworski. He made his final push to put judicial muscle behind Congress's impeachment effort on May 24th. Bypassing all time-consuming appeals procedures, Jaworski asked the Supreme Court to rule whether the president had the right (which he had been claiming for ten months) to refuse to obey judicial subpoenas demanding that he turn over Watergate tapes to prosecutors preparing criminal cases against his former aides. When the Supreme Court justices agreed to take the case on May 31st, 1974, the courts finally and completely coalesced with Congress. No one in official Washington doubted, now, that Leon Jaworski was out after Richard Nixon's scalp. Given what he'd already done in March by sending over raw evidence and a road map to the House Judiciary Committee with the cooperation of the Watergate grand jury and Judge Sirica, it was certain that whatever Nixon was ever forced to give to Jaworski would be in the hands of the political grand jury shortly thereafter, and Nixon's fate would be sealed.

The circle had not closed on Nixon yet, however. The Supreme Court appeal bought Nixon more time, but not the usual amount. The Court decided to accelerate normal procedures and allow Jaworski to argue before them on July 8th. They further agreed to hand down their decision as fast as possible. The Court, like Leon Jaworski, could also apparently read the public opinion polls.

So, too, could the House Judiciary Committee's Republicans and Democrats. On May 30th, one day before the Supreme Court agreed to rule on the tapes instead of allowing the political deadlock to continue by avoiding the case, the committee made its strongest statement yet about what continued refusals to provide evidence to *them* would mean. By a vote of 28 to 10, they warned Nixon that it would be grounds for impeachment.[129]

This vote—which mirrored the popular majority's opinion that Nixon should be indicted if he refused to cooperate with the House Judiciary Committee—was important, for eight Republicans joined twenty Democrats against the president. On May 1st, only lone-wolf Republican Cohen had allowed the HJC a bare 20-to-18 majority, saying that deodorized transcripts were not enough. By the end of that month, however, eight of eighteen Republicans on the committee felt confident enough to take the same position. A month later, fourteen of eighteen did. Bipartisanship was becoming a reality.

The tide turned in earnest after June 6th, during a second month that began badly and speedily got worse. This time, the agent of Nixon's ill tidings was the *Los Angeles Times,* which finally broke the single element of the Watergate prosecutions that was not already public. The *Los Angeles Times* reported that the Watergate grand jury had secretly and unanimously named Nixon as an "unindicted co-conspirator" three months earlier. This information, unknown to Congress, was confirmation that Nixon had already been deemed to be as guilty as any of his underlings already sentenced or being tried by the courts. Plainly, someone leaked the news that had been kept secret for three months at a time when it might do maximum political damage to Richard M. Nixon.

It was lousy legal procedure, but great power politics. The strategy worked marvellously. The *Los Angeles Times'* June 6th headlines about the secret charge against Nixon, coming after the release of the Gallup poll and Jaworski's Supreme Court appeal, firmed up congressional backbones and mousetrapped Nixon more firmly between his political and juridical opponents.

Nixon had no choice but to counterattack with whatever he had left, but June was not a propitious time. Too many chickens were coming home to roost. A second expert report reiterated that the infamous eighteen-minute gap had almost certainly been engineered by the White House. On June 3rd, Chuck Colson, after undergoing a religious conversion and endless plea bargaining, pled guilty to a charge of obstructing justice, thus becoming the highest Nixon aide to admit fault about anything. And John Ehrlichman, facing trials of his own, was threatening a court suit against Nixon to gain access to his personal White House files to better prepare his defense.[130]

Nixon made a last-minute deal with Ehrlichman by June 14th, but another White House aide was getting distinctly nervous about suffering the fate of Dean, Ehrlichman, Colson, and others. That aide, Stephen Bull, privately told the special prosecutor's lawyers that Nixon had been listening to some of the most important tapes that the special prosecutor and the House Judiciary Committee had subpoenaed at various times in May. Thus, if Nixon destroyed any more tapes, the prosecutors now had the proof they needed to charge him *personally* for it.[131]

Everything still hinged on the tapes, tapes that Nixon couldn't afford to release and couldn't afford to destroy. To stave off the growing judicial and political challenge of the tapes, Nixon had to try and intimidate Congress and somehow reassert his fading presidential status.

The status game was the simplest to play, so Nixon began there. From June 10th to 19th, he flew overseas for visits with Middle Eastern leaders. The trip was risky, for Nixon had developed phlebitis: a blood clot which, if it passed into a major organ, could kill him. Presidential physicians and Secret Service agents were traumatized when Nixon ignored warnings and engaged in strenuous politicking for nine days. They were similarly appalled by Nixon's subsequent decision to make a diplomatic visit to the Soviet Union from June 25th to July 3rd. Nixon, however, was more worried about his political than his physical health, so he made use of foreign travel as a strategy for obtaining headlines utterly unrelated to Watergate.

The other blade of the scissors began to cut shortly before Nixon returned from the Middle East. During the week of June 15th to 22nd, a series of leaks and White House pronouncements charged that the House Judiciary Committee, not the president, was the truly deceitful party regarding the Watergate tapes. The House Judiciary Committee's members were examining the first tapes they'd received from Jaworski and the Watergate grand jury, but they were doing so in a dishonest and deceitful manner. Partisan committee members were leaking transcripts to the press which were far less accurate than the transcripts Nixon had released on April 30th.

The White House was accurate in one respect. The House Judiciary

Committee was leaking like a sieve. But the charges of deceit, instead of intimidating the committee, angered it. One result was that, on June 25th, the committee voted, by 22 to 16 (the majority included six Republicans), to release the unexpurgated contents of the few Watergate tapes they'd been examining. Push had led to shove—at a period when 54 percent of the public expressed approval of a globe-trotting Nixon's foreign policy but only 18 percent approved of the way he was handling domestic policy and only 26 percent liked his overall performance as president.

Once the House Judiciary Committee's Watergate transcripts were made public on July 9th, life got nasty. Expletives and a lot else were *un*deleted. Reporters could finally read all of what Nixon had told Dean and Mitchell on March 22nd, 1973, during a discussion of the possible further payment of hush money to the convicted Watergate burglars: "I don't give a shit what happens. I want you all to stonewall it, let them plead the Fifth Amendment, coverup or anything else, if it'll save it—save the plan. That's the whole point."[132]

It sure was, and Nixon's repute suffered more. Watergate, though still a complex "conglomerate of various illegal and unethical activities" to most Americans, was also a conglomerate increasingly headed by one man: Richard Nixon.[133]

Nixon faced new drumbeats of bad news. On July 8th, the Supreme Court heard oral arguments on the tapes. The next day, the House Judiciary Committee issued its transcripts. On July 12th, John Ehrlichman was convicted of perjury in a lower court in connection with the Plumbers' break-ins during the 1971 campaign to discredit the Pentagon Papers' principal, Daniel Ellsberg. The same day that Ehrlichman was branded a liar, the long-silent Senate Watergate Committee released a 2,200-page report which its staff had worked on for a year. The Senate committee's bipartisan statement tried to tie all the many strands of the Watergate case together for the first time. On July 18th and 19th, the staff lawyers of the House Judiciary Committee—still quietly assisted by the Special Prosecutor's Office—stopped their brick-by-brick laying of evidentiary foundations and began tying evidence together. The House was finally specifying patterns of misconduct.

There was a practical political reason for all of this specificity. Unless the House Judiciary Committee drew up a list of charges against Nixon before the congressional elections in early November, Nixon's political trial could be put right back to square one. Committee members who were retiring and others who might fail to be reelected would have to be replaced by January 1975. The more substitutions, the harder Nixon's lawyers would argue that the political grand jury which had heard the evidence was not the same jury voting whether or not to indict, and the more legal gymnastics would ensue.

So the House Judiciary Committee moved fast. Seven months of preparation and two months of secret hearings were followed by a final frenzied week during which a bill of charges was presented to committee members by staff lawyers, and then amended largely as a result of last-minute negotiations between the Democratic leaders and those conservative southern Democrats and moderate Republicans whose support was crucial to the bipartisan strategy the committee was following—a strategy aimed at presenting their work as a legal investigation rather than the star chamber or kangaroo court that Nixon's men freely equated it with. July 24th was the date set for final deliberations on how to indict Nixon.

During this final week of the political grand jury proceeding, two other considerations were primary in the minds of the House Judiciary Committee's members: media coverage and court action. A Supreme Court ruling on the tapes was forthcoming; and during the week in which the House Judiciary Committee specified charges, rumors spread around Washington that the Court was going to decide very soon. The justices, as things turned out, met on the morning of July 24th to announce their judgement.

Once this date was definite, the House Democrats made two key decisions. On the 22nd, they voted to allow live television and radio coverage of the Judiciary Committee's final deliberations. The day afterward, these meetings, originally scheduled to begin on the morning that the Supreme Court was due to meet, were delayed until 8 P.M. that evening—prime TV viewing time.

A mixture of caution and calculated advantage, as so often before in Watergate, ruled here. The Supreme Court was widely perceived as politically neutral. If it ruled against Nixon *before* the political jurors of the House Judiciary Committee cast their votes to accuse or not accuse, the Democrats would look less biased. Timing like this would also make it easier for Republican and conservative Democrats on the Judiciary Committee to vote against the president. Further, televising the committee's proceedings would capitalize upon Nixon's ills in the most visible way. That House leaders took such actions testified to the now almost total coalescence of judicial and political efforts to resolve the Watergate case. With and without backdoor contracts, the courts and the Congress were now complementing each other to Nixon's disadvantage.

Nixon knew what was happening. A week after returning from his trip to the Soviet Union, the president flew to California for what was advertised as a two-week working vacation. There, in his San Clemente estate, Richard Nixon secluded himself from July 12th to July 28th.

Meanwhile, more strands of his presidency unravelled. On the 23rd, Lawrence Hogan, a Republican member of the Judiciary Committee then running for election for governor of Maryland, announced that he intended to vote against Nixon. For the first time, one of the House Judiciary Committee's 17 Republicans stated he believed the president guilty of crimes and misdeeds against the government and people of the United States. A conservative had decided that casting Nixon overboard was a politically advantageous thing to do. Other conservative politicians took note.[134]

At 11 A.M. the following day, it was the Supreme Court's turn to make political determinations. This it did by deciding by a vote of 8 to 0 (one justice excusing himself) that Nixon must obey the subpoenas obtained by the special prosecutor for more Watergate tapes. Both the judicial trial and the political trial of the Watergate case, the judges had decided, required the best evidence available. The justices made a political decision that removed most of the final executive privilege and national security barriers to the impeachment trial. The power circle ringing Richard Milhous Nixon had finally closed—a year after the existence of the White House tapes had first become known.

No one recognized this better than the men and women of the House Judiciary Committee. Once the Court ruled unanimously against a president who had appointed four of its members, including Chief Justice Warren Burger, Nixon had few political friends left. Within hours, southern Democrats and moderate Republicans on the committee met to determine strategies for the impeachment debates that began the same evening.

## The Judiciary Committee Decides

What followed focused the country's attention as nothing about Watergate had before. Not even the Senate Watergate Committee hearings of the summer of 1973 became an instantaneous folk event the way the week-long House Judiciary Committee debates and votes on five separate impeachment articles did. Via live television and radio, interested citizens were symbolically and actually admitted into the elite regions of their political order. In the process, it was easy—even natural—for tens of millions of people to think of themselves, too, as members of the political grand jury debating and deciding the issues before them.[135]

Realities were otherwise, and very much went on behind the scenes, but Watergate was visible as it had never been before. The fundamental question the House Judiciary Committee had to decide was whether Richard Nixon still deserved to lead. The audience knew that, whether they had ever read the Constitution or not, or whether they knew much about the nuances of the many different aspects of the case. Everyone—audience and participants—was a part of history now. This vote mattered.

Rarely before had members of Congress played to such a large, diverse, and involved national audience. The experience was heady and intimidating. Fundamental issues of political power and privilege were very clearly at issue. The thirty-eight committee members at the center of the national stage worried, therefore. They would not have been human—or politically successful—if they had not. Sandwiched between an opening speech by Democrat Committee Chair Peter Rodino of New Jersey and a closing speech by ranking committee Republican Edward Hutchinson of Michigan, all the members—Democrat and Republican alternating—were given fifteen minutes to make an opening statement of their views on the overall case for or against Richard M. Nixon.

Nine and one-half hours of speechifying by thirty-eight people could have induced yawns or worse, but it didn't. For, in giving each member a quarter-hour before the cameras, the Judiciary Committee made itself known to a national audience for the first time. The committee became less of an abstract whole and much more a collection of individuals arguing different views in differing ways. Moreover, the opening statements were, in effect, a poll of a political grand jury, and the tens of millions in the television and radio audiences, listening to the general arguments for and against, could more easily understand and identify with the process of judgement.

The audience was also a jury, of course, one which would soon deliver electoral judgements on all of the assembled members of Congress. So all the committee's members did their best to couch their opening statements in fashions which would best make their case and best reflect upon their motives in arguing as they did. They sought to involve their electorates on their behalf. The president's opponents provided long sequences of details about his involvement in the cover-up. The president's defenders countered that the committee's Democratic majority was mostly engaged in a partisan vendetta using a "grab bag of allegations."[136]

Three legal issues were basic to all the argument and counterargument. First, did the committee, to vote articles of impeachment, have to accuse Nixon of specific violations of criminal law, or was it sufficient for a majority of the House Judiciary Committee to determine that he had offended against public trust and right political behavior by a "pattern of misconduct" that invalidated his right to continue in office? Second, was smoking-gun proof required, or could the committee base its charges largely upon circumstantial evidence? Third, was the House Judiciary Committee bound by the rules of *grand juries*—who indict for trial on the basis of majority determinations that "probable cause" exists that suspects have committed criminal offenses—or should it function as a *trial jury*, which determines guilt only when defendants are unanimously deemed guilty "beyond a reasonable doubt?"[137]

For all the debate within the Judiciary Committee, many of the legal issues were irrelevant to the political realities of the Watergate case. The vast majority of the audience to the hearings were not lawyers. The differences between types of evidence, juries, and standards of proof were vague in their minds. All they knew was that Richard Nixon was on trial, and that the House Judiciary Committee was a jury trying to determine whether he was guilty or not. The lines between accusation and final judgement blurred.

The same was true of many members of Congress as well. Watergate was complicated, and few politicians had been assiduous in putting the pieces of it together. Fewer had read the reports and evidence the Senate Watergate Committee and the House Judiciary Committee had recently published. "Nobody really understands [this material]," a moderate Republican member of Congress told Elizabeth Drew two weeks before the Judiciary Committee's final debates began. "Nobody but the committee has taken the time to listen or read. Around here, it's the same old refrain: they want to wait until the committee makes its recommendations . . . We have given our proxies to the Judiciary Committee. The whole issue still seems kind of remote. It's strange and scandalous; it's sort of like we had parked our morals on some obscure shelf."[138]

Congress now had no choice but to decide, by proxy or otherwise. The courts had moved out of the way; the Supreme Court had denied the president's last legal argument for not turning over the tapes to Jaworski; and the House Judiciary Committee, nine months after the Saturday Night Massacre, had to begin the political trial by charging Nixon with something. The issue was not at all obscure now: it was a majority-Democrat Congress versus Nixon. The Judiciary Committee had to weigh what charges should be brought and how they should be brought. It had to shape the prosecution for the later benefit of Nixon's opponents in the Senate.

The process was full of last-minute fits and starts. After the nine-and-one-half hours of nationally televised opening statements were completed on the evening of July 25th, Nixon's defenders on the House Judiciary Committee knew they didn't have the votes to stop the committee from voting out some impeachment charges. Representative Charles Sandman of New Jersey said as much near the start of the proceedings, but by their conclusion, the numbers were clear. The twenty-one Democratic members all intended to charge Nixon with something and six of the seventeen Republicans were off the reservation. Three were leaning strongly toward indictment, and another three (Cohen of Maine, Hogan of Maryland, and Railsback of Illinois) were definitely going to vote to indict.

At long last, the Democrats had the bipartisan alliance they had been trying to create for more than six months. The eleven Republicans who intended to vote against any and all charges hadn't convinced a single Democrat that Nixon had done nothing wrong, but the president's defenders did not lack for political energy. They intensified their efforts to make whatever charges were brought as innocuous and narrowly drawn as possible. As so often before, Nixon's defenders were arguing that the president should enjoy every conceivable benefit of a criminal justice system he had repeatedly flouted. With the last act in the Watergate drama about to be played, Nixon's congressional supporters kept on defending him.[139]

They were not fools, these people. They mixed ideals with self-interest, just as their opponents did. Regarding interests, most feared that the Republican Party would be branded as the "party of Watergate" for as long as the Democrats could get away with it and that this political equation would cost the G.O.P. and themselves dearly.

Their ideals enabled them to rationalize and explain their concerns about their political interests and also to express some legitimate indignation. Hypocrisy and double standards were the charges the president's defenders hurled at his attackers, privately and publicly. Nixon was no saint and nobody was arguing that he was. But he hadn't done anything that every recent president before him hadn't also done, and most of these presidents had been Democrats. "Post-Watergate morality" was all very well, but all the Democrats were doing was obscuring their own domestic dirty tricks by blaming Nixon (and, through him, the Republicans) for everything, just as they had earlier done about sins committed in Vietnam.

These charges had substance, enough to make it clearer why Watergate took so long, and why a Democratic Congress was so very often hesitant to proceed quickly or expeditiously to resolve the case. Watergate had evolved out of the Vietnam War and the divisions and fears spawned by it. The politics of fear and discord that Nixon exploited was no peculiar creation of his. He was more its creation than its creator. So it appeared unfair to make Nixon what Democrat John Conyers of Michigan had called him at the start of the House Judiciary Committee's debates: "in a very real sense a casualty of the Vietnam war."[140]

Nixon's defenders also opposed making Nixon a casualty because of his various domestic sins. Lyndon Johnson had been a thief and worse, but the Democratic congressional leaders who had known that hadn't mounted any sort of coup against him. Instead, they had stonewalled Republican efforts to trace millions of dollars in kickbacks and favoritism and misuse of government property and corruption of favored subordinates like Bobby Baker in the White House inner sanctum. Now these same people, joined by journalists and bureaucrats and uppity lawyers and judges, were out to get Nixon. They were mounting a coup because they were "marinated in hatred" for Nixon and all he stood for.[141] So, thinking in this way, it was comparatively easy for some Republican members of Congress to keep fighting for Nixon. Watergate was, in this view, merely a skirmish in a much wider Cold War. If Nixon were denied office because he had mismanaged a skirmish, the nation might lose its war against foreign and domestic radicalism, and America could swiftly return to the bad old days of 1968.

Had Watergate not happened when and how it had, this hypocrisy and double-standard argument of the president's defenders might have had far more force. But popular fears about Vietnam, Black Power, and the New Left were passé in July 1974. Moreover, the White House had blundered far too many times in its efforts to squelch the case. The combination of these two factors removed just enough of the inhibitions within the House Judiciary Committee against charging Nixon with broadly defined political crimes. Defensive legalisms and logic chopping got nowhere.

The debate within the House Judiciary Committee then shifted from *how* to charge Nixon to *what,* precisely, to charge Richard Nixon *with.* A menu of alternatives presented themselves. Again, the president's defenders sought to decrease the potential damage as much as possible. Now the majority had to decide how many different kinds of misdeeds with which to charge Nixon.

More problems surfaced. Watergate offered no lack of varieties of misconduct, and the question was how many the committee should identify in its bill of particulars against the president. One aspect of the problem was identified by Representative Robert F. Drinan of Massachusetts in his opening remarks: "Can we impeach a President for unlawful wiretapping but not impeach a President for unlawful warmaking? Can we impeach a President for committing a burglary but not for concealing a massive bombing [of Cambodia in 1969 and 1970]?"[142] The nub of the issue was how broad to make the list of different *types* of offenses which would form the basis of his trial.

The televised debate heated up again, and for good reasons. The bipartisan alliance on the House Judiciary Committee opposed to charging Nixon narrowly was equally opposed to charging him as broadly as Representative Drinan preferred. Drinan and other liberal Democrats shared none of the conservative views that Richard Nixon was a martyr to changed political circumstances and moral codes. They thought of the Nixon administration as a Hydra, and of themselves as heroes engaged in a Herculean labor to destroy that evil. It wasn't enough for them merely to chop one or another of the heads off; new evils would only sprout from the roots of the old. All of the heads had to be burned away, roots and all. Then and only then would their labors be successful.

For this reason, the Democratic staff of the House Judiciary Committee apparently drafted no less than twenty-five different "grounds for impeachment" shortly before the panel's televised hearings began. Republicans and conservative Democrats, however, resisted this liberal approach, and the spectrum of misdeeds the president would be charged with shrank steadily. Even as committee members made their preliminary statements on July 24th and 25th, seesaw battling about the number and forms of the impeachment articles continued.

By the time the thirty-eight members of Congress began their public debate, the types of offenses had shrunk to five. These were: (1) obstruction of justice; (2) abuse of presidential power; (3) contempt of congress; (4) unconstitutional warmaking; and (5) tax evasion. The obstruction of justice was blazingly obvious, yet it required eighteen hours of debate on Friday, July 26th, and Saturday, July 27th for this charge to be voted on. Conservatives and liberals fought over an impeachment article redrafted at the last minute by liberal Paul Sarbanes of Maryland to include nine different counts of cover-up activity. Nixon's defenders fought hard to keep these manifest misdeeds from being assessed against him, on the logical assumption that if they could somehow defeat this, they could defeat everything else. The liberals, meanwhile, tried to tar Nixon with as many brushes as possible in one impeachment article. The resulting debates added little to the sum of constitutional knowledge, but they did lead betwixt-and-between member Hogan of Maryland to advise the committee that his wife was distinctly unimpressed with their work. She wondered, Hogan added, "if the deliberations would take as long if [House] Speaker [Carl] Albert had entertained sending it to a select committee made up of nonlawyers . . . She also then said that she understand full well why lawyers are barred from serving on grand juries.[143]

For all of Mrs. Hogan's understandable reactions to two days of legal acrobatics, the moment of truth finally came at 7 P.M. on the evening of July 27th. By a bipartisan majority, Nixon was charged with obstructing the administration of justice in the Watergate case. All twenty-one Democrats and six Republicans voted aye; eleven Republicans, nay.

The committee took the next day, a Sunday, off. The first and hardest step had been taken now. Nixon had finally been charged with something. But, as Elizabeth Drew noted, no feeling of triumph or jubilation was in the air. No one in Congress enthused that "the system worked." It hadn't worked yet. Richard Nixon was still in the White House, and no one yet knew whether Congress could force a president to relinquish office for the first time in American history. All that anyone knew for sure was that battle in the political trial of Watergate had been finally and irrevocably joined. "There is a feeling of sadness and exhaustion, at what everyone has been through," Drew wrote. "A feeling, too, of foreboding about those unimaginable next steps. It is a drained feeling. When history records events, it tends to leave out this kind of human emotion."[144]

History does indeed. It tends to forget how conditional actions are until the moment they are taken. Then it tends to assume that what was done was always planned that way. The truth of Watergate was otherwise. All Congress knew now was that its proxies on the House Judiciary Committee had voted out one impeachment article. Whether there would be others was anybody's guess. So, too, was the result of the eventual Senate trial.

When the thirty-eight House Judiciary Committee members returned to work before the TV cameras on Monday, July 29th, therefore, such unheroic thoughts were very much on their minds. Facing them were four remaining impeachment articles. Initially, the bipartisan alliance which had passed the obstruction of justice charge held together. Enough to pass a second impeachment article: one concerning abuses of power.

The result of this second debate was far more important than that which occurred two days previously. Congress, now, had to do more than point a finger at a president for covering up evidence, disobeying subpoenas, and firing a special prosecutor. Now it had to draw some lines in the sand, to set a standard for future presidents regarding what Democrat William C. Hungate of Missouri called "a consistent disregard of the law."[145]

The concept of "deniability" was basic to the debate—the ability of a president to operate through intermediaries to break laws and perform dirty tricks, and then walk away from these same operations—if and when discovered—while claiming to have taken no active part in them. The law tended to give one answer to this question, and politics another. So, as before, the president's allies argued that Nixon should be given every benefit of any doubt, while the president's opponents argued that Nixon's presidency was one long catalogue of abuses of power. The lawyers lost and the politicians won. In the end, the vote against Nixon on the abuse of power charge was 28 to 10, as Republican Robert McClory of Illinois joined the twenty-one Democrats and six Republicans who had also voted for the first impeachment indictment.

These twenty-seven however, stayed solid only long enough to cast this second vote late on the evening of July 29th. The very next day, the bipartisan alliance started falling apart. The Republicans and southern Democrats who charged Nixon with obstructing justice and abusing power were not willing to go further. This was evident during debate on the third impeachment article, contempt of Congress, on Tuesday morning, July 30th. At issue was whether Nixon's refusal to provide Watergate tapes to the House Judiciary Committee was an impeachable offense.

Although this third charge was sponsored by a Republican, McClory of Illinois, it speedily ran into trouble. Nixon's opponents therefore confined themselves to generalities and avoided the details of congressional actions and inaction. Given the particulars of the Watergate case, it ill-behooved the majority on the House Judiciary Committee to wax too eloquent about how the president held Congress in contempt, considering that the House of Representatives had been so careful about using the constitutional powers it possessed. It behooved most committee members, instead, to think about the practical politics of impeachment. And this they were forced to do by comments made throughout the abbreviated debates on the third impeachment charge.

"Political overkill" was the operative phrase, and it emanated from those Republicans and southern Democrats whose support for the preceding two impeachment articles had given a political indictment of Richard Nixon an unmurderous flavor. Now the same men were talking about how "fragile" bipartisanship was, and about how too much shouldn't be added into an already brimming pot. Two broadly written charges were enough for the House Judiciary Committee to vote out, for the full House to approve, and for the full Senate to pass judgement on.[146]

What followed proved the point. The third article, after only two hours, was voted in, but only two Republicans (sponsor McClory and Hogan of Maryland, who was leaving Congress to run for the Maryland governorship) voted for it, while all the other Republicans voted against. Joining the latter were several southern Democrats who had done much to achieve bipartisan compromises on articles one and two: Walter Flowers of Alabama and James Mann of South Carolina. Although the charge of contempt of Congress passed by 21 to 17, it looked bad for the two impeachment charges to come. Close observers like Elizabeth Drew knew what was involved. The day before the contempt of Congress vote was taken, Drew interviewed Representative Mann of South Carolina, who told her that a "lowest common denominator" finally had been found to enable Democrats to ally with one another, and then with a minority of Republicans, to pass the first two impeachment charges against the president. What remained, however, was up in the air. "Mann feels," Drew wrote, "that they [the Democratic and Republican swing voters like himself] have a 'semi-commitment' that [the last two] articles on Cambodia and taxes will not be passed—'so that there will be no dilution in the principles we are willing to support.' "Moreover," Mann added, he believed members like himself could probably enforce said "semi-commitment."[147]

Mann was right. The House Judiciary Committee's chair, Peter Rodino, and most Democrats were unwilling to press their luck. Article four, you see, reopened the Pandora's box of the Vietnam War by arguing that the secret bombing of neutral Cambodia in 1969 and 1970 was an impeachable offense because Congress had been denied its constitutional right to declare war. Much, however, as Watergate had been engendered by Vietnam, the war never, ironically, figured directly in the charges voted against Richard Nixon. Congress, the president's defenders argued, simply had no moral or other right to try to impeach Richard Nixon for a war which was not his alone. The prowar leadership of a Democratic Congress *had* known about the secret Cambodia bombings, and there hadn't been a peep out of any of them in opposition.[148]

Finally, the whole war powers issue had become moot. In November 1973, Congress had passed a War Powers Resolution over Nixon's veto to choke off Nixon's or any other president's ability to engage in unconstitutional warmaking in future. The resolution required presidents, "in every possible instance," to "consult with Congress" before placing U.S. armed forces "into hostilities or into situations where imminent involvement in hostilities is clearly indicated by the circumstances." Presidents now not only had to inform congressional leaders in writing when they did something, but they had to keep them informed thereafter. If Congress, moreover, did not grant "specific authorization for the operation through a declaration of war or otherwise within 60 days," presidents must remove all military forces within thirty days from that date. Presidents could not wage war in highly debatable circumstances for more than three months unless *both* houses of Congress specifically said they could. If both houses of Congress did not, the president must cease and desist. In other words, *one* house could passively exercise what is called a "legislative veto" over presidential war powers, a veto which could not be appealed. Thereby, the Judiciary Committee's members—including several liberals—argued, Congress's power to declare war could be preserved, and in ways which would not inhibit a president from using force in emergency situations such as hostage rescues.[149]

Against such bipartisan contentions, the liberal Democrats supporting article four had no chance, and knew it. This was crystal clear when the total time allowed for debate was limited to one-and-one-half hours, and when, shortly thereafter, the committee's chair, Rodino, exited the chamber for the entire discussion. Only eight members argued for the Cambodia article, and only twelve voted for it. Everyone else voted against—all seventeen Republicans, four of the seven southern Democrats, and five other Democrats, including chairman Rodino. Cambodia was overkill, and was, accordingly, dropped. The country also soon ceased to exist, and as many as two million Cambodians with it, victims of American, Vietnamese, and internal violence. The War Powers Resolution, meanwhile, remained but a fragile barrier—spotty in its application and more than probably legally unenforceable upon any president who disputed its legislative veto aspects forcibly enough. Congress basically decided, in Republican Caldwell Butler's words, "We can't impeach ourselves—yet."[150]

Early in the evening of July 30th, the third impeachment article to be voted on that day came before the Judiciary Committee. This article, too, was doomed to failure. But, as it concerned Nixon's financial frauds and tax cheating, liberal Democrats—and a few not-so-liberal ones—took their last opportunity to get some licks in before the largest television audience any of them had ever addressed in their lives.

When the final televised vote was taken, the logic of the House Judiciary Committee's proceedings was about as linear as the flight of a drunken quail. Nixon, most members said, had had enough, and so had they. The vote, again, was 26 to 12 against ratifying the article. All Republicans and most southern Democrats again opposed, and several liberals who had voted for previous charges let the president have the benefit of the doubt on this one. At 11:08 P.M. on Tuesday, July 30th, the show was over. The House Judiciary Committee had voted out three of a total of five possible indictments against Richard Nixon. For only the second time in American history, a president of these United States was about to be tried by Congress for his political life.

## Resignation and Aftermath

To many a politician the point now became to insure that an impeachment trial would never happen. Trent Lott, the thoroughly conservative Mississippi Republican whose district had given Richard Nixon the largest majority he'd won anywhere in 1972, illustrated the trend when he told reporters on July 29th: "Secretly, maybe all of us are hoping for resignation."[151] A loaded statement like this from one of Nixon's strongest initial supporters on the House Judiciary Committee spelled big trouble for the White House, for it demonstrated that the last firm foundations of presidential power on Capitol Hill had eroded.

But still Nixon would not resign, and thus spare his remaining allies the risk of defending him and save his opponents the risk of trying to convict him. The White House suspected, by now, that the House was a lost cause. The 239-to-192 majority that the Democrats enjoyed there was sufficient to vote out at least the obstruction of justice and abuse of power charges that the Judiciary Committee's Democrats were united upon and which about a third of its Republican members also backed.

Once the House sent its charges on to the Senate by a simple majority vote, however, a different sort of impeachment arithmetic came into play. The Senate, to convict Nixon, required a *two-thirds* vote, and the Democrats did not then have a two-thirds majority in the Senate. They held only 56 of 100 seats. A maximum of 74 percent of the House Judiciary Committee had voted against Nixon on the first two impeachment articles, but the committee was vastly more familiar with the details of Watergate than most of the Senate was. A chance still existed that just enough Senate conservatives would not vote to convict. The magic number was 34, one-third plus one.

While the White House made lists of senators and checked them twice, however, another political dynamic came into play: a jumble of political exhaustion, desire to avoid further risk, and media appeals to the president's pocketbook instincts. Exhaustion occurred because of a sense that Watergate might *never* be over. As the case entered its twenty-sixth month, only a small amount of the genuine best evidence in the case—seven White House tapes—had been obtained. It was not until July 30th, after the first two impeachment indictments had been voted against him by the House Judiciary Committee, that Nixon finally turned over additional installments of unedited tapes to Sirica and Jaworski as the Supreme Court had ordered him to on July 24th. Yet, even without this additional evidence, the House Judiciary Committee—as the Watergate grand jury had in February—had decided that the evidence against Nixon was convincing enough to warrant a trial. What would the new tapes now in Jaworski's hands show? What further unpleasant surprises were in store, particularly for Republicans running for reelection in November?

Thus risk-avoidance came into the picture in a new way. Before the Judiciary Committee's indictments of the president, it had often seemed more risky to depose Nixon than to avoid the struggle entirely. Most members of Congress gladly left the task to somebody else. After the House Judiciary Committee voted out its charges, however, it began to look riskier to keep Nixon in office than to remove him. The Judiciary Committee's members were hardly bomb throwers. They'd voted against the president on the basis of principle, but they had also acted because of political considerations. The fact that other politicians were able to see and hear the proceedings during which their peers came out in open opposition to Nixon made it easier for those others to take back their proxies from the Judiciary Committee, join a bipartisan coalition supporting the two carefully written and least-common-denominator charges of obstruction of justice and abuse of power, and plan on surviving the experience. Their careers wouldn't fall apart any more than the country would. Who knew, however, what might happen if Watergate dragged on and on? The fact that one of the first new tapes Nixon began delivering to Sirica on July 30th was announced to contain a five-minute gap in an important conversation on August 1st further eroded whatever faith remained that the president was going to tell anything like the truth when it came time for the impeachment trial.[152]

At precisely this point, the press reentered the picture. Important newspapers sent pointed messages to the White House, political messages that Nixon must resign, and do so because of pocketbook considerations. On July 31st, the *Washington Post* ran a lead story that if Nixon were convicted by the Senate he stood to lose more than honor. The $60,000-a-year pension paid to him as a former president would be voided. So would the $96,000 a year former presidents normally received for staff salaries. Perquisites like office space for himself and his staff and Secret Service protection would go. His wife Pat would lose her eligibility for a widow's pension of $20,000 a year. Nixon might also be disbarred and thus unable to practice law. By August 4th, the *New York Times* had picked up and elaborated the story. Unnamed "longtime financial backers" were said to be sending word that Nixon "should weigh his financial future carefully before reaching a final decision." And "some Republicans on Capitol Hill

. . . have discussed the idea of using his finances as a lever to persuade the President to quit."[153]

None of this was subtle. Nixon faced very nasty legal problems. He had no choice, now, but to turn the subpoenaed tapes over to the courts. These tapes could very likely convict him, by his own words, of criminal offenses. The courts, however, were not going to indict a serving president. Thus, so long as Richard Nixon *stayed* president, he was also protected from criminal punishment or the huge legal cost of trying to avoid it. Impeachment, however, would deny him the protection of his office *and* any post-retirement income from that office as well. Nixon would then face his judicial prosecutors a broken—and, more important, broke—man: a disbarred lawyer who could not even represent himself in court.

This was what the bottom-line messages in the elite press were all about: resign, and have money to fight to avoid jail. Don't resign, and be left financially naked.

This was powerful stuff. It also told Nixon that the Senate numbers weren't adding up the way he wanted them to. The one-third plus one vote needed to escape impeachment wasn't there. Estimates by Elizabeth Drew on August 1st ranged from twenty certain votes against impeachment to a maximum of thirty-six, which an unnamed Senate Republican leader added included all the "maybes." Nixon didn't need "maybes"; he needed a minimum of thirty-four definite no's. He didn't have them.[154]

Now, then, Nixon had to somehow seize back the waning political initiative once again. And, again, the question of how to do that came down in the end to the tapes.

On August 2nd, one day after the latest gap on one of the tapes given to Sirica was announced, Sirica ordered Nixon to get every tape the special prosecutor had demanded over to Sirica's office by Wednesday, August 7th. No exceptions. No more waiting. No more gaps or surprises. But there *were* more gaps and more surprises. Ten of the sixty-four subpoenaed tapes were eventually declared never to have existed. And, on August 6th, Nixon's lawyer, St. Clair, had to tell a by-now utterly unbelieving Judge Sirica that a nineteen-minute gap existed on yet another important tape.[155]

Had this been all, it would have been bad enough, but what remained on one surviving tape doomed Nixon's presidency. This recording covered a meeting Nixon had had with Haldeman on June 23rd, 1972, six days after the break-in. It was the earliest remaining Watergate conversation that the prosecutors knew about, owing to the fact that an earlier Nixon-Haldeman meeting had been replaced by the eighteen-minute gap. On June 23rd, the president and Haldeman had discussed how the FBI had almost traced the laundered money paid to the Watergate burglars back to a secret fund at the Committee to Re-Elect the President. The point then became to give the FBI's Acting Director Patrick Gray some excuse for not proceeding further. One proposal was to have CIA's deputy head Vernon Walters call Gray and say (in Haldeman's words) "stay to hell out of this—this is ah, [CIA-related "national security"] business here [and] we don't want you to go any further on it." Nixon agreed that this gambit should be attempted, not least because "Well, we protected [then-CIA Director Richard] Helms from a lot of things." At the same time, Nixon agreed that it was also important to cover up CREEP head John Mitchell's probable advance knowledge of the political sabotage of the Democratic National Committee offices.[156]

Here, finally, was the smoking gun that tied Nixon directly into the Watergate cover-up long before March 1973, when he had claimed he first became aware of it. Here was the end of all Nixon's efforts to paint John Dean as the lone cover-up mastermind. Here was evidence that Nixon's "national-security" orations had always been part of a cynical strategy to obstruct justice in a criminal case.

News of the existence of this June 23rd, 1972, tape apparently spread around the upper reaches of the White House from July 24th (the day the Supreme Court ruled that Nixon must turn over everything his judicial opponents were demanding) to July 28th (the day after the House Judiciary Committee voted its obstruction of justice charge and the day the president at last returned to Washington after spending sixteen days in California). Nixon started listening to tape recordings again in earnest.

Nixon's staff was also at great risk. Nixon could not defy the Supreme Court and survive, an impeachment trial loomed, and the June 23rd tape showed Nixon had been part of the cover-up from the beginning. No one knew what other time bombs might also be ticking away on tapes yet to be delivered or on others the courts or Congress might demand later. Were these White House staffers going to ruin *their* careers trying to get Nixon out of this? The answer was no. The odds were too bad and the danger too immediate. It paid, at this point, to act naïve, indignant, or confused, or to claim you would do more for Nixon when he could assure you evidence was forthcoming demonstrating that no presidential obstructions or abuses of power had taken place. It also paid to get lines out to cooperative reporters, including Woodward and Bernstein of the *Washington Post,* to make it clear that none of this had been *your* idea at all, and that *you* were doing everything in *your* power to resolve it for the greater good of the Republic. All this meant Nixon's resignation. Nixon had to leave before he was forced out and he had to leave in a way that damaged the reputation of his remaining political allies the least.

The politics of self-preservation accelerated after July 30th, when the House Judiciary Committee voted out its third and final impeachment article. Nixon's lawyers were especially fearful. Sirica would brook no more delaying tactics or destruction of evidence. The judge, in addition, pressured Nixon's chief attorney, St. Clair, into acquainting himself with the contents of key tapes (including the smoking-gun tape) on July 30th. St. Clair could no longer claim self-protective ignorance about anything that was on tape—or that the president might still be destroying. Further, St. Clair might conceivably be disbarred if he didn't at least advise Nixon to admit guilt once he'd discovered that Nixon had obstructed justice. If any more tapes went missing, finally, St. Clair might find himself charged with obstruction of justice too.

Now that Nixon's lawyers were being threatened with the possibility of criminal prosecution themselves, White House Chief of Staff Alexander Haig was drawn into the picture. General Haig had taken over from Haldeman fourteen months earlier and he helped engineer the Saturday Night Massacre, so he'd never been soft on any sort of opposition to Commander in Chief Richard Nixon. But Haig knew what the White House lawyers began telling him. He knew why they were fearful. He also understood, as they did, that the smoking-gun evidence affected a crucial technicality of impeachment. This technicality was—and is—that the Constitution mandates that "When the President of the United States is tried, the Chief Justice [of the Supreme Court] shall preside . . ." This meant that the political trial before the U.S. Senate would very likely be carried on upon firmer and more judicial rules of evidence than the House Judiciary Committee's proceedings had been. Impeachment would remain a political matter, but it might also be that the rafts of circumstantial evidence regarding abuse of power and obstruction of justice would not be allowed to form the basis of the Senate prosecution. If it was not, a third and more of the Senate might give Richard Nixon the benefit of the doubt. No matter how much smoke there was on the tapes, there might be insufficient fire to drive Nixon out of office. Nixon had only recently appointed Chief Justice Warren Burger—and Burger's Court, up to now, had had nothing to do with Watergate other than to order Nixon to produce evidence to a criminal proceeding. Radical the Court wasn't.

It was not, then, utopian to hope that Nixon could survive a Senate trial, before the smoking-gun evidence came along. After that, his defenders knew that Nixon was more directly implicated than ever before in obstruction of justice: the first indictment the House Judiciary Committee had voted out and the first charge the Senate would probably debate and decide upon. The smoking gun was crucial. It removed the last prop from under Nixon in the forthcoming political trial, the hope that the chief justice of the Supreme Court could somehow preside over the trial in such a narrow legal fashion that most of the most damning evidence against Nixon would never be allowed to be heard in court. Now there was no chance that Burger could manage evidentiary proceedings to save Nixon on the first impeachment charge, obstruction of justice. And conviction on one charge was all Congress required to drive Nixon from power.

Nixon was caught. He was dead if he kept the tapes, dead if he gutted them before releasing them, and caught dead to rights if he released complete versions. Guilt or innocence wasn't the question. Haig and other White House political operators knew that Nixon was guilty of obstruction of justice, and they had probably known that for a very long time. Now that victory was impossible, Haig, ever the good military man, began to concentrate on arranging a surrender on the best possible terms. And this meant resignation and pensioned political retirement. Nixon had to impeach himself before others did the job for him. It also meant that Haig had to try to get Nixon a postretirement pardon so he would not immediately become liable to indictments, trials, judgements, and punishment in the courts after he left office.

Nixon was the fly in the ointment. He didn't want to go and he told aides repeatedly he'd done nothing really wrong. He was sincere in what he said, and also sincerely wrong. His self-serving arguments were a mixture of wholesale forgetting and selective remembering. Many on Nixon's staff shared his "After me, the deluge" belief. But they still had to get him to leave office before he took them all with him and before the likelihood of hard times ahead for conservatives was replaced with certainties. Nixon was a goner.

The week from July 30th—when the House Judiciary Committee finished its work—to August 5th was primarily occupied with alerting the president to the unpalatable facts of life. Woodward and Bernstein's *The Final Days* is a lively treatment, though in the often very crafted recollections of the principals.[157] The overall nature of what was going on by this point was clear enough. Nixon was being deserted by his remaining allies, in order to save themselves and what they could of the conservatism he represented. By August 3rd, even supreme White House loyalist, gut fighter, and speechwriter Patrick Buchanan, after listening to the smoking-gun tape, said Nixon had to go. He'd been caught in the lie for the last time, and so badly that he could no longer lead effectively. Nixon could not even lead his own White House aides any more. This was demonstrated several days later, when Nixon released a transcript of the smoking-gun tape to the press. The same man who was still breathing defiance at efforts to arrange a quiet resignation held an evidentiary gun to his head and pulled the trigger in a supremely public way.

August 4th and 5th were the most important dates. By August 4th, Nixon's men were almost all telling him that he had run out of maneuvering room. His two chief lawyers, St. Clair and Buzhardt, and Chief of Staff Haig were threatening to resign. Haig and others, moreover, were burning up the telephone lines telling Congress what was coming in the June 23rd, 1972 tape. All ten of the Nixon loyalists on the House Judiciary Committee got advance warning so they could try to protect themselves. On the morning of the 5th, the process was essentially complete. Nixon had signed a statement stating that he had known about the "potential problems" on the June 23rd tape since May 1974, and that neither his White House staff nor his lawyers had been informed about any of this. Thus Nixon cleared his remaining palace guard of the risks of having perjury and other cover-up indictments thrown at them by Special Prosecutor Jaworski. Haig and St. Clair thereupon called Jaworski and told him that the smoking-gun tape was about to be publicly released because they had insisted upon it, and that the tape spelled a lot of trouble for Nixon.

Jaworski was skeptical. The press, it seemed, was going to get another transcript and another tape was going to go over to Sirica for vetting and later transmission to Jaworski as well. Haig and St. Clair were hardly Jaworski's candidates for Nature's Noblemen; they were part of the problem, not part of the solution. Here, however, Special Prosecutor Jaworski was wrong. After legally protecting themselves, Haig and St. Clair were finally stepping out of the way. When the June 23rd tape was made public early on the afternoon of Monday the 5th, precious little was expurgated. The obstruction of justice conversation was bad enough. But also included were declarations about international monetary issues ("I don't give a shit about the lira"), the art world ("The arts, you know, they're Jews, they're Jews, they're left wing—in other words, stay away"), and other matters, all of which made Nixon look far less than august. Presidential public-relations staffers were appalled, But public relations were not the primary concern of aides like Haig and St. Clair, not so far as Richard Nixon was concerned, anyway. Nixon was history, and the quicker he understood that, the better for all concerned.

Republican members of Congress were right behind Al Haig. All ten House Judiciary Committee members who had voted against indicting Nixon for anything quickly reversed themselves on the obstruction of justice charge. They'd been had too, all said. On August 6th, the Senate was heard from in a big way when Barry Goldwater, speaking for other Republicans, give it to Haig straight. "Al," Woodward and Bernstein quote Goldwater as saying, "the President has only twelve votes [against his impeachment] in the Senate. He has lied to me for the last time and he has lied to my colleagues for the last time." Republican Senator Milton R. Young of North Dakota put it in equally unvarnished style when he observed that "If the Senate holds a trial, then the Republican Party goes down with it."[158] Nixon was alone except for his family. With them, he tried to cope with the trauma and rage that marked his final days in office. Meanwhile, Haig and others organized a transfer of power to the first nonelected president in U.S. history.

The incoming president was no political innocent. As a twelve-term member of Congress from Michigan who had been House Minority Leader for eight years, Gerald R. Ford had sensed what was coming. Although he'd acted the complete loyalist from October 1973, when he'd succeeded Agnew, until May 1974, Ford subsequently began to put as much distance as possible between himself and the man who'd appointed him. Now, however, Gerald Ford had a big problem. What was *he* going to do about Nixon?

Gerald Ford quickly pardoned ex-president Nixon. But as we shall see, he did this at a time when official Washington was rife with evasion and when most major political and judicial actors believed that criminal prosecution of Richard Nixon was too dangerous to contemplate. The pardon evolved within that supremely cautious political matrix, and it was only after the pardon induced shudders of revulsion out in the country that criticism blossomed. During and immediately following the in-house rebellion that marked the final days of Nixon's presidency, however, questions of good or evil meant nowhere near as much as getting Nixon out of office without any more of a struggle.

The resignation came first. On the morning of August 8th, people learned that Nixon had finally given up. In a televised address to the country at 9 P.M. that evening, Nixon gave his explanation of what had happened.[159] "In all the decisions I have made in my political life," he began, "I have always tried to do what was best for the Nation." Regarding Watergate, Nixon had had a "duty to persevere" to "complete the term of office to which you elected me." But perseverance was no longer possible. Congressional support had eroded to such a point that there was no more point in fighting against what might be a "dangerously destabilizing precedent [impeachment] for the future," much as he "would have preferred to carry through to the finish." "I have never been a quitter . . . But, as

President, I must put the interests of America first. America needs a full-time President and a full-time Congress" to deal with pressing national and international problems. Vice president Ford would be president as of noon on August 9th. Ford should be supported because a "process of healing" was "desperately needed in America." Nixon had made wrong judgements and some of these had hurt people, but all he had done had been done for America, not for himself.

The accomplishments of his five-and-one-half years in office, he went on, should not be forgotten. The Nixon administration had "ended America's longest war," and the Ford administration would continue efforts to secure a lasting world peace. Nixon had improved relations with China and with Arab nations, signed important nuclear arms limitation agreements like the Anti-Ballistic Missile Treaty and the SALT I Treaty with the Soviet Union in 1972, and had tried to do something about "turning away from production for war and expanding production for peace" so that the earth's poor would benefit. Throughout his quarter-century in public life during the "turbulent history of this era," Nixon had succeeded and failed. But, throughout that career, he had always valued something President Theodore Roosevelt once said about the man in the arena [in responding to the Eastern Establishment gentlemen of his day who had criticized his politics]. The man in the political arena is always superior to his far more uninvolved critics, Roosevelt had said, because he "strives valiantly"; because he "errs and comes short again and again because there is no effort without error and shortcoming"; and because he tries his best regardless, and thus "knows the great enthusiasms, the great devotions" of someone who "spends himself in a worthy cause." Such a person thus knows the "triumphs of high achievements and . . . at the worst, if he fails, at least fails while daring greatly." Nixon would continue, he concluded, working for noble causes, especially peace. Above all, he asked his countrymen to remember that "the world is a safer place today" than it was when he had arrived at the White House in January 1969: safer for Americans and for people of all nations. "May God's grace be with you in all the days ahead," Nixon closed, and was gone.

It was vintage Nixon and it was effective. He did not overdo the self-justification, he avoided the nasty details of Watergate entirely, he tried to rally support for Ford, and he downplayed the snarls at his hated liberal-intellectual opponents by couching them in a historical idiom few could comprehend. In nothing that Nixon said, however, was there a sense of the man or of what Watergate meant to him personally.

Nixon's more revealing statements came later. At 9:30 A.M. on August 9th, Nixon gathered his Cabinet and staff around him for the last time as president. Here, before what remained of his administration, Nixon came as close as he ever did to explaining himself as a human being during the entire twenty-six months of the Watergate struggle. It wasn't a neat performance; such public intimacies rarely are. Nixon mixed gallant gestures, self-justification, hope, and anger in about equal proportions. Cameras were rolling as Nixon arrived in the East Room of the White House. This address, too, was being televised and shown nationwide. The "record should show," Nixon began, that what was happening was "one of those spontaneous things that we always arrange whenever the President comes in to speak . . ." The press might report that, or it might argue that Nixon had packed the room with what sympathetic audience he could find. But "on our part, believe me, it is spontaneous."

The event wasn't spontaneous, but much of what Nixon proceeded to say was. Emotionally, he discussed the devotion and dedication of those who had been presidents of the United States of America and of the many others who had loyally assisted them. Service to the nation had characterized the Nixon administration's five-and-a-half years. "Not one single man or woman" in all that time had feathered his or her own nest with public funds. "Mistakes, yes. But for personal gain, never." Government was a rugged business sometimes. But the cause of America's government was still the cause of all mankind. Without America's leadership, "the world will know nothing but war, possibly starvation or worse, in the years ahead. With our leadership it will know peace, it will know plenty." Having thus justified politics in general, and his administration in particular, by highlighting the issue of corruption, and by ignoring the obstruction of justice and abuses of power which had finally driven him from office, Nixon switched to himself.

His father, he began, was a person "they" would have called "a little man, a common man." But Nixon's father was no failure. He had been a streetcar motorman, lemon grower, and a grocer. He had not been a great success, perhaps, but he'd done every job as well as he could do it, regardless of what cards Fate dealt him. His mother had been "a saint." She had buried two children who had died of tuberculosis; and nursed four children of others, three of whom had also died. Strength like his mother had possessed was more than saintly, it was also necessary to survive the tragedy of the world.

That was why he had quoted Theodore Roosevelt about the man in the arena the preceding evening, Nixon erratically continued. Roosevelt, too, had suffered greatly. In his twenties, his first wife died, and a stricken Roosevelt wrote that "the light went from my life forever." But Roosevelt had recovered from his beloved's death [and the simultaneous death of his mother] and moved on—"tempestuous, strong, sometimes wrong, some-times right, but he was a man."

Nixon would do the same. It was not "good-bye" but "au revoir," until we meet again. Nixon was leaving the presidency, but not disappearing from political life. A defeat was not an end. "It is only a beginning, always." Only those who have "been in the deepest valley can . . . ever know how magnificent it is to be on the highest mountain." Every one in government should remember this. They also needed to realize something else, Nixon added as he closed: "Always give your best, never get dis-couraged, never get petty; always remember, others may hate you, but those who hate you don't win unless you hate them, and then you destroy yourself."[160]

There, finally, amidst tears and the more hard-eyed emotions, was the distilled personalized wisdom of the Watergate case. Nixon had hated well and excessively. That hate, in turn, had destroyed him. Minutes later, Richard Nixon and his family left the White House for a plane trip home to San Clemente, California, on a presidential aircraft named the Spirit of '76. In flight, shortly after noon on August 9th, 1974, Nixon's presidency ended.

## The Politics of the Pardon

The practical details of Nixon's departure from office concerned politi-cians far more than the media drama. To the politicians, none of it was history at all. Nixon was very much alive and he remained a threatening factor in ongoing power equations. A priority in solving such equations was minimizing the losses that could result from Nixon's resignation. The Republicans wanted Nixon to disappear immediately from the public mind, the Democrats were afraid to continue to pursue him alone, and the courts and the Special Prosecutor's Office were not willing to risk crimi-nally indicting Nixon after his resignation had brought an abrupt end to Congress's political trial.

The Republicans' motivations were the easiest to comprehend. Their interests decreed that Nixon be given immunity from further prosecution in return for as little as possible in the way of a guilty plea. This would inhibit Democrats from waving the bloody shirt of Watergate before the electorate in November. The Republicans did not want Nixon hauled into court repeatedly in connection with either the ongoing trials of many former White House aides or in connection with damage claims due to be filed against him because of dirty tricks he'd visited upon people during his presidency. The more the ex-president was in court, the likelier that prosecutors or defense lawyers might obtain testimony from him which could ruin politicians—including some Democrats who'd made private deals they'd never admitted publicly. The proofs on Nixon's White House tapes might cause similar damage if, as seemed likely, they were sub-poenaed for use in other criminal trials. So long as Nixon remained liable for criminal prosecution—so long, in fact, as he was liable to be involved in court cases at all—he and the tapes were time bombs waiting to go off. A pardon in return for some minimal guilty plea was one way to try and keep these bombs from ever exploding at others' expense. An uncontested pardon would send a clear message that the commanding heights of the political and judicial order thought Watergate had gone far enough.

The Democrats understood this logic. They knew that the privileges of presidential office no longer covered Richard Nixon in any way. They knew that a pardon was aimed at keeping Nixon out of court, period. But many Democrats also wanted to keep Watergate temporarily alive by publicly opposing a pardon for the moment. Younger liberals who hadn't been in Washington very long and who'd cut no private deals with Nixon tended to oppose a pardon because they wanted to change the balance of congressional-presidential power. Keeping Nixon and Watergate in the public eye for as long as possible might help accomplish that end. These same young liberals tended to see Watergate more as a systemic than a personal problem. A jungle of misdeeds had not occurred because of one man's moral failing, but because Nixon and others had occupied an office which had become too imperial. Too much power had accumulated in presidential hands, the checks and balances of the Constitution no longer checked or balanced, and power was therefore bound to be abused by whoever occupied the Oval Office. A key factor in reforming the system was to make sure that Nixon did not slip out of the legal net now that an impeachment trial had been avoided by his resignation.

If most Democrats in Congress had agreed with logic like this, a pardon would have been impossible. But the older and more power-acculturated members of the party, conservative and liberal alike, operated on different principles. Their concerns were a good deal more personal than systemic. Their opposition to a pardon was usually short-term rather than long-term. Younger liberals might think about cleaning the Augean stables; older Democrats thought about the next election.

It actually profited many older Democrats to downplay the institutional elements of Watergate and to understand the problem as personal moral failure on the part of Nixon and some of his closest associates. The Imperial Presidency, after all, was not a unique creation of Richard Nixon. The leadership of Congress had repeatedly gone along, and Congress had had Democratic leadership in both houses for all but four of the preceding forty years. Warmaking, during both the Johnson and Nixon presidencies, had only highlighted the war powers problem. Democratic leaders were not anxious to throw lots of light on what recent presidents had done with their war powers during the House Judiciary Committee's impeachment debates. Democrats, as well as Republicans, had made war without declaring it. Prowar Democratic congressional leaders had known about unsavory things like the secret bombing of Cambodia, kept quiet, and allowed it to go ahead by default. These, and other problems of checks and balances were not ones many Democrats who had been around in Washington for a long time wanted to publicize. Understandings had been arrived at, plentiful support had been given to now failed policies, and concern inevitably existed that the longer Watergate stayed in the limelight, the riskier leadership or survival might be in future. Did Senator John Stennis, who was chair of the Armed Services Committee throughout Nixon's presidency, and who had cooperated with the Stennis Compromise regarding the tapes Nixon had almost stage-managed before the Saturday Night Massacre, want lights shone into all nooks and crannies by lots of criminal court cases?

No, Stennis did not. He supported a pardon. But he and other longtime political survivors did not want to be the ones who initiated that pardon. They wanted somebody else to shoulder that burden, somebody Republican, somebody like President (nonelect) Gerald Ford.

Ford was in an unenviable situation. He knew what most Republicans wanted him to do and why they wanted him to do it. He also knew that a majority of congressional Democrats were more concerned to appear to be against a pardon than they were opposed to one in fact. Republicans were afraid of getting murdered in the upcoming congressional elections unless something was done to defuse Watergate, and most Democrats were thinking no further ahead than November.

This left the judiciary as the only remaining actor in the play so far as the insiders of Washington were concerned. The judiciary—including the Special Prosecutor's Office—had the action regarding all of the current prosecutions of Nixon's closest aides. If the Special Prosecutor's Office and the courts indicted or prosecuted Nixon—or forced him to testify in the many ongoing criminal trials—Ford's ability to pardon Nixon was going to be materially reduced. The judicial system, however, had no burning desire to go after Citizen Nixon. Within the Special Prosecutor's Office, the situation was cogently known as the "monkey problem," or "who should shoulder the responsibility and take the heat" of trying ex-President Nixon on criminal charges?[161]

Had Jaworski and his aides wished to proceed full speed ahead, the legal direction was clear. The Watergate grand jury, recall, had wanted *President* Nixon indicted on criminal charges months before. But the Special Prosecutor's Office was more cautious than the jury. It wanted Congress to impeach, or some "more representative" body to take the lead in Nixon's criminal prosecution. After the resignation, Jaworski still wanted Congress to take the lead in punishing Nixon. Congress might have, for instance, if it had proceeded with the impeachment trial despite Nixon's resignation, convicted him of crimes and misdeeds, and thus given a political imprimatur to further prosecutions. Special Prosecutor Jaworski, however, basically opposed prosecuting ex-President Nixon in the courts at all. So did Judge Sirica. Even the suggestion of pro forma indictments (Nixon was to be tried, but spared any jail term), which some of Jaworski's staff tried to get the Special Prosecutor's Office to initiate, got nowhere. No "monkey" went on Jaworski's or Sirica's back.

Public-opinion polls appeared to support the caution of such older and wiser men and their unwillingness to risk punishing Nixon with more than subsidized removal from office. Late in August 1974, a Gallup Poll reported that 55 percent of those queried thought Nixon should be "left alone rather than brought to trial" on criminal charges. The poll results were mercurial, but they measured what Gladys and Kurt Lang have aptly called the "pulling together" mood that characterized public opinion immediately after Nixon's resignation. This mood, the Langs explained, was "somewhat akin to what has often been observed among survivors of a disaster, when people are swept up in a sudden inexplicable wave of good feeling, a new-found comradeship accompanied by unusual displays of generosity and altruism."[162]

The press shared in the brief era of good feeling. The nation had survived because "the system had worked," was the Good News message. America could take pride in its political, judicial, (and journalistic) institutions. Watergate and all it represented was "history," part of a nightmare. The point now was to get on with life and to hope none of it ever happened again. This postresignation sense of relief, and the accompanying tendency to treat Nixon's departure as the key event in what Andrew Szasz has called "the political analogue of a medieval passion play—the Passion of St. Democracy," assisted elite efforts to let Nixon off the hook and allowed President Ford to take the next step in the procedure.[163] The procedure gave Nixon his political "golden parachute," largely so that many other power brokers would not lose any more of their status as a result of his misdeeds. It was the psychology of the political guild at its less than finest.

The damage control began almost immediately. No person-to-person deal between Nixon and Ford occurred, and it is unlikely that efforts to arrange a pardon before or after Nixon's resignation through deniable intermediaries like Alexander Haig ever got anywhere. But, though no explicit accord was ever made, it was also true that no such deal had to be made. Gerald Ford knew what was at stake, and had every reason for not wanting to know any more about the menagerie of evil that was Watergate. The men around Ford also wanted an end to Nixon and Watergate. During the month in which the pardon decision was made, Ford's White House staff was also largely Nixon's staff. Ford loyalists like Robert T. Hartmann fumed at Nixon's "Praetorian Guard," but Haig wasn't replaced as chief of staff until late September. And Haig and others had excellent reason for ending the Watergate-related revelations quickly and completely: it was their careers, potentially, on the line. Haig, even according to Hartmann, tried to take all of Nixon's records and tapes out of the White House in a military truck the very night after Ford became president. Ford's staff foiled that effort and told Haig to bring back some of the personal records he had spirited out of the White House as well.[164]

While the many Nixon holdovers feared prosecution, Ford's staffers—of which there were at first very few—wanted their boss to get himself free of the Nixon albatross as quickly as possible so he could start leading on his own account and save the institution of the presidency from those who would weaken it. The point was to bury the Nixon presidency, but to do so in ways that would not entangle Ford in the obstruction and abuse which had spelled Nixon's political doom.

Appearances were as important as realities in all of this. A congressional majority was glad Nixon was gone and was in no hurry whatsoever to go after him. The Special Prosecutor's Office, meanwhile, abdicated responsibility for charging Nixon in the courts and informed the White House, on September 4th, that it would be "a year or more" before Nixon could be brought to trial for anything. None of this meant that the Ford administration could afford more arrogant missteps like night-time removals of Nixon's official papers and tapes, however. Much as Nixon's political and judicial opponents were going nowhere fast, they could be counted upon to scream to the high heavens in tones of outraged virtue if Ford acted too precipitately.[165]

So Ford tested the waters. Five days after he took office, the White House announced that the Watergate tapes were now in the custody of the

Secret Service, and that lawyers for the Special Prosecutor's Office, the Justice Department, and the White House had agreed that these tapes were the *personal property* of Richard Nixon. That set the reporters baying. Up until that time, presidents' records had been assumed to be their personal property when they left office, but no president had ever departed the way Nixon had. And no president had tapes that had incriminated him and which might be used in a host of Watergate criminal trials.

Jaworski immediately told reporters that he had been "informed" about this White House statement, but denied that he'd been "consulted" about it. In plain English, the special prosecutor said that he hadn't agreed to any such idea. The press thereupon complained that Ford was trying to destroy proof by using a legal scam, instead of army trucks, to ship the tapes off to Nixon in his California home in San Clemente. That was the end of that particular political trial balloon.[166] A new legal dodge had to be devised to have Ford "safeguard" the tapes as evidence while, at the same time, giving Nixon de facto control over them. In the next several weeks, Nixon's and Ford's aides hashed out another plan. All the records of the Nixon presidency, including the Watergate tapes, were to be put in the institutional equivalent of a safe-deposit box. Two keys would be required to open the box. Nixon would have one key, and Ford the other key. Ford would give his key to the General Services Administration (GSA) the government body then responsible for all federal archives and records. The GSA would guard the tapes (for five years) and all other records of the Nixon administration (for three years). During that time, however, nobody could use the records or tapes but Richard Nixon. If a court came along and ordered Nixon to produce tapes, he could fight that subpoena. He could destroy any record he wanted after three years and "some or all" of the tapes after five years. In ten years, *all* the tapes would *automatically* be destroyed, whether Nixon ordered it or not.

All this was an involuted way to safeguard the tapes for Nixon without appearing to. Nobody expected Nixon to use his key to open anything up unless he was forced. Nixon could keep stonewalling in hopes the courts would continue to avoid prosecuting him on criminal grounds even after his resignation. The protection that Ford was being forced to provide for the tapes would be only temporary: during the first five years in which Nixon was to be the only one guaranteed access to all the records and tapes, in fact, the statute of limitations would actually run out on Watergate-related crimes. After 1979 nobody could charge Nixon with anything, much less convict him. All this was a lot different from Ford providing evidence to the courts or the Congress to send Nixon and others to jail.

But Gerald Ford no more thought of a free-access alternative to Nixon's tapes than he thought of swallowing cyanide. As things turned out, he committed political suicide in another way. This occurred because, during the same period that White House lawyers put the finishing touches on the "two keys" proposal, Ford was launching an effort to insure that Nixon would not be convicted by anybody for anything no matter what evidence might become available from any tapes or court testimony.

Ford possessed the pardoning power of the president, the right that any president has to give clemency to people convicted of crimes—and to do so independent of congressional review. Presidents are not unique in this power. Governors of states have it, too. But all exercise it only *after* a person has been tried and convicted of something. Ford, uniquely, chose to pardon Nixon *before* he had been charged with or tried for a criminal offense. Ford passed along word to Nixon that a pardon was a distinct possibility by September 4th. The majesty of the law was never going to apply to *him*.

To get this unique pardon, Nixon was supposed to do two things. First, he was supposed to agree to the "two keys" method of unlocking the tapes. Second, he was to make some admission that he was either guilty of something or sorry for something he had done. The two keys posed no major problem for Nixon, but about admitting guilt he was adamant. No mea culpa was forthcoming. Ford's lawyers then tried to finesse this sticking point by requesting "statement of contrition." Nixon eased his way around that by stating only that he had made "mistakes" and "misjudgements" and that he had been wrong only in "not acting more decisively and forthrightly in dealing with Watergate." Mea culpa this was not; Nixon admitted error, not guilt.

But Nixon did not hesitate to accept the pardon when Ford gave it to him anyway, for it was the blankest of blank checks. It pardoned him "for all offenses against the United States which he . . . has committed or may have committed or taken part in" during the entire period of his presidency. Nixon was pardoned for what he'd done, and for what he might have done, for what he'd assisted others to do, and for what he might have assisted others to do. He was pardoned for what was known and for what could only be guessed at. Everything was covered from Day One in the White House down to the last minute of Nixon's term of office. Such a universal exoneration had never before occurred in U.S. history.[167]

Ford had caved in, but he'd also miscalculated badly. He got his timing wrong. Had he simply floated his "two keys" trial balloon, he might have succeeded, and then he could have moved on to a less-all-encompassing pardon later. But in attempting to secure the tapes from the courts and in giving a "full, free, and absolute pardon unto Richard Nixon for all offenses" simultaneously, Ford went too far, too fast. When Ford announced his pardon to the nation on the morning of September 8th and had an intermediary announce the "two keys" proposal that same afternoon, he had only been in office for a month. His reasoning that Nixon and America had suffered enough from the "ugly passions" that the Watergate trials were engendering, that Nixon would be "cruelly and excessively penalized" if he were ever charged and brought to trial, and that the only way to protect good order and the credibility of national institutions was to "write 'The End' to it" so far as Nixon was concerned led to immediate speculations that Ford would use exactly the same logic to insure that pardons were eventually given to everyone charged with Watergate-related offenses, especially the higher-echelon defendants still before the courts that Watergate summer. The White House confirmed these rumors by stating that Ford was "studying the possibility" of pardoning all these men, plus those already convicted as well, just after he pardoned Nixon and announced the "two keys" solution.[168]

It was too much. Too many doors were slamming shut all at once. Tapes gone; Nixon with a universal pardon; the possibility of pardons for everybody else as well. Ford's efforts to put Watergate behind him forever backfired—not because Congress and the judiciary were rabid about convicting Richard Nixon but because Ford tried to do too much simultaneously. He sought to deny whatever opportunities existed either to find out more about Watergate or to punish any major offenders other than those, like Dean, Magruder, and Colson, who had already pled guilty and started serving prison terms. Blanket pardons and blanket protection and sanctioned destruction of the tapes was too much, especially as it threatened all of the work already undertaken by the courts, the Special Prosecutor's Office, Congress, and the press.

Normally cautious congressional leaders became immoderate, but they proceeded carefully. First they attacked the idea of blanket pardons for all Nixon's former aides. Then they moved on to attack the "two keys" approach to the tapes. And, last and least, they attacked Ford's unprecedented pardon of an unconvicted Richard Nixon. House Speaker Carl Albert and Assistant Senate Majority Leader Robert Byrd joined their G.O.P. counterparts like Senate Minority Leader Hugh Scott in immediately coming out against blanket pardons. The fate of the Republic, all argued, did not depend upon letting men like Haldeman and Ehrlichman go free.[169]

Haldeman and Ehrlichman and others had different ideas, but they availed them not. Ford speedily backed away from "studying" general pardons and said he was considering them on a "case by case" basis. Then he almost as quickly backed away from that as journalistic and public opinion was heard. The news was uniformly bad for Ford, including the news from the White House's own news-management office, where just-installed Presidential Press Secretary Gerald ter Horst resigned in protest. Ford's argument that ending Nixon's legal and personal agonies would also magically end the country's polarization and self-doubt went over just about as well as Nixon's earlier theory that his personal fate was identical with the fate of the presidential office. It didn't wash.

Ford and his aides had a right to seethe at some of this criticism. Ford was only doing what a lot of politicians in Washington wanted done but didn't want to take responsibility for doing themselves. The monkey was on Ford's back anyway.[170] By rights, Ford should have been crucified on his own account, but the politicians and lawyers who complained loud and long about what Ford had done were not about to follow up with deeds— especially if Ford protected only Nixon and dropped any effort at general pardons for everyone.

Ideals, again, proved less powerful than interests. The judges and most of the staff lawyers at the Special Prosecutor's Office knew that what Ford had done in regard to Nixon made for surreal precedent. They could have made it grist for their mill by fighting against the legality of exoneration in advance. But they did not. Ford was an appointed president with only a little over two years left to serve. Given the glacial pace of Watergate's legal proceedings and the Supreme Court's ability to evade political issues it felt like evading, it was an open question whether anything could be decided before the November 1976 presidential election. Waiting to see what happened to Ford in the presidential primary elections, at the Republican convention, or on Election Day was a convenient excuse for inactivity and for letting the politicians or the voters handle it.

The same sort of evasive logic, however, also characterized the politicians and the voters. The congressional elections of 1974 were now only two months away, and bevies of congressional Democrats believed that the Nixon pardon was a great club to beat Republicans with at the polls. Whether they were correct or not is debatable, but by the time the dust cleared on November 7th, the Republican membership in the House dropped from 192 to 144, and from 42 to 37 in the Senate. The Democrats enjoyed a two-to-one majority in the House and a three-to-two majority in the Senate. The election of 1974 was a disaster on the scale of 1964 for the G.O.P.

The voters were generally willing to express their discontent with their ballots. They threw Republicans out of Congress, rather than demanding the head of another Republican president. A mixture of fatigue, cynicism, skepticism, and concern governed. A majority of the population increasingly favored benign neglect so far as a too-complicated and too-prolonged Watergate was concerned. These citizens had not opposed the opening of doors that illuminated crimes and other offenses, but, after Nixon left office, these same people tended to believe that Watergate had gone far enough. Ford's head shouldn't now be put on a chopping block. Guilt was a personal, not an institutional, matter, and Nixon's head was enough.

This did not mean, however, that the majority who supported benign neglect also backed Ford's version of it. They did not want doors opened any further, perhaps. But that did not mean that they wanted doors slammed shut, either. The popular logic went basically as follows: those who had *already* pled guilty or been indicted should be punished. Nixon, meanwhile, had been punished enough by being forced from office. Continued wrangling about tapes, and lots more criminal trials, would be too much. More revelations about official wrongdoing would be counterproductive, particularly if they involved Ford or his pardon of Richard Nixon. Anything that might toss the first nonelected president in U.S. history onto the political scrap heap after one month in office would menace the peace and security of the nation and risk re-igniting tensions the like of which America had not seen since 1968. Ford's pardon of Nixon was stunningly stupid, but it wasn't criminal. Besides, Ford was *our* fool. Given such logic, Ford's pardon was ironic. It sought to bolt shut an open door whose existence most citizens were content to ignore and which Nixon's judicial and political opponents were far too cautious to attempt to walk through.

Weaving these different skeins of opinion and motive together, then, it is perhaps easier to see why outrage about the Nixon pardon was never followed up by action. In a Gallup poll taken on September 10th, 62 percent voiced opposition to what Ford had done, but this did not induce either the Congress or the Special Prosecutor's Office to push for a court test of the legality of the pardon.[171] The Langs summarized the atmospherics of the postpardon period well when they wrote that:

> Few people after the drawn-out battle of Watergate were in the mood to question the integrity and honor of yet another President—not most of the people, not most of the press, and certainly not most of Congress. There was no disposition to open old wounds. The authority of the Presidency had survived the "wrongdoing" of one President but would it have survived a second Watergate investigation? There was a tacit agreement not to pry too hard."[172]

In the end, all Congress did (through a subcommittee of the House Judiciary Committee) was to demand that Ford come before it to talk for two hours on October 17th about why he had given his unique pardon to Nixon. Ford thus became the first U.S. president to testify before a Congressional committee. He argued that no "deal" at all had been made between him and Nixon or Nixon's representatives. The Special Prosecutor's Office, meanwhile, sat on its hands. The pardon was allowed by default.

The other two key components of Ford's effort to write finish to Watergate fared less well. Nixon failed to get near-total control over his tapes and records, nor was Ford able to pardon Nixon associates already enmeshed in the courts. Resolving both issues took four more months. A relatively successful effort was made to void Ford's agreement with Nixon regarding the tapes, largely because these records were clearly useful in criminal trials. Once these trials began on October 1st, 1974, the House voted, the very next day, to quash the Ford-Nixon tape deal. The Senate followed suit on October 4th.

Then, for two more months, the House and Senate did little as the courtroom performances of Richard Nixon's former top aides—Ehrlichman, Haldeman, and Mitchell—got Watergate in the headlines again. The charges and countercharges from the Watergate defendants reminded lots of people about Nixon, and Nixon's tapes. Even Ford's postelection assurances that Watergate prosecutors could have access to all the Nixon tapes and records that they wanted was too little, too late. On December 9th, after last-minute efforts to reconcile differences in House and Senate bills, Democrats rushed through legislation ordering Ford to turn over all Nixon's presidential records to the General Services Administration and its bureaucratic subsidiary, the National Archives. The GSA and National Archives were ordered to destroy nothing without Congress's OK and to draw up regulations to govern public and legal access to the tapes and records in future. Ford stopped attempting to keep Nixon's historical records as unknown as possible, but years of litigation by Nixon and his aides followed. By 1983, twenty-nine former members of Nixon's staff got the GSA's regulations governing access to most tapes and records voided on a technicality. Written records of Nixon's administration slowly began being made public in 1986–87, but would-be researchers bemoaned the unavailability of almost everything, fifteen years after Nixon's resignation.[173]

Ford's inability to release all those on trial for Watergate crimes was also a defeat that was more apparent than real. Though unable to pardon Nixon's aides, Ford helped to insure that the number of those enmeshed in Watergate did not widen further and watched while the federal judiciary punished most of those who were convicted with light jail terms. The

Nixon pardon was the key element in this. Once Ford's pardon was allowed to stand, it sent a very clear message that neither leaders of Congress
nor Jaworski were going to take risks to insure that the Watergate prosecutions maintained momentum. Two members of the Special Prosecutor's
legal staff wrote that "The Nixon pardon guaranteed that many investigations would wither and die on the vine. In practical effect, our office was
emasculated the day Nixon was pardoned." Jaworski's unwillingness to
bring a court case contesting the pardon insured that his assistants were
left with the choice of trying for half a loaf or quitting entirely.[174]

What remained, however, wasn't very much. Immediately after a jury
was selected for the Haldeman-Ehrlichman-Mitchell trial on October 11th,
Special Prosecutor Leon Jaworski resigned, effective October 25th. Nobody closely involved in Watergate needed to be told what this resignation
meant. Not only was Ford's pardon of Nixon acceptable to Jaworski, but
he also believed that all those who could be tried were already in the
criminal net. All that was left, therefore, was cleaning up that could be left
to assistants.

Jaworski said that his resignation was unrelated to the pardon and the
consequent weakening of the Special Prosecutor's ability to legally
threaten present or former Nixon personnel to squeeze out more information about political sabotage and cover-up. But his actions spoke louder
than his words, particularly when the words of ex-President Nixon were
proving impossible for the judicial system to obtain.

Nixon's health became the publicly stated rationale for doing nothing.[175]
The courts had supremely good procedural reasons to expect Nixon to give
testimony in the trial of his former associates, and the prosecution had
obvious reasons to put Nixon on oath to try and strengthen their cases
against Haldeman, Ehrlichman, and Mitchell. The defendants, for their
part, particularly Ehrlichman, wanted Nixon put on the stand so that their
defense counsels could try to foist as much criminal responsibility as
possible on an already pardoned man who would avoid prison no matter
what he was forced into admitting: the more punishment Nixon took, the
less might be left over for others to take. Given all this, Jaworski asked the
court to issue a subpoena to Nixon on September 19th. However, he
apparently requested Nixon's presence at the trial reluctantly—preferring,
instead, that he be allowed to testify by deposition, a procedure that allows
a witness to answer written questions in writing instead of having to come
to the courtroom to testify. Depositions in criminal trials are relatively rare,
because it is assumed to be any defendant's right to confront and cross-
examine witnesses against him.

Defense lawyers in the Watergate case definitely wanted to confront

Nixon on behalf of their clients. It was they, not Jaworski, who pressed for Nixon's physical presence on the witness stand. If only one juror gave the defendants the benefit of the doubts Nixon might engender, their clients could yet go free. Richard Nixon, however, had no desire to be forced onto a witness stand. Testimony of any sort was a no-win situation for him. It might ignite further debate about the pardon, and it would certainly threaten what was left of his credibility. On the other hand, he could not refuse to testify. Executive privilege might cover presidents but it did not cover a man who had just returned to private life. Citizen Nixon could not stonewall the courts like President Nixon had done. So, instead, Nixon asked for sympathy. A man who had just accepted a full, complete, and universal pardon of a sort that would delight the heart of any good felon argued that he was being harried to death by merciless lawyers.

He did more than that: he had sympathy argued for him by others whose believability was not thoroughly suspect as a result of previous involvement in Watergate. On September 12th, only four days after Ford's pardon message, son-in-law David Eisenhower appeared on the popular TV news and entertainment show, the "Today" program, to say that Nixon was depressed and in worsening health. The next day, Nixon's personal physician reported that his phlebitis had resurfaced and that a blood clot had appeared in his left lung. Poor and worsening health, possible suicide, and feelings of being driven to death were all staples of medical reporting from Nixon's home in San Clemente in subsequent days. Nixon was described as a ravaged man who had lost the will to fight. so much so that he was refusing to go into the hospital because he believed that, if he did, he'd never come out alive. Starting September 17th, Nixon's lawyers began to use his health as an excuse for his failure to make court appearances.

The subpoena relating to testimony at the Haldeman-Ehrlichman-Mitchell trial issued two days later also helped get Nixon into the hospital on September 23rd. There doctors discovered another lung clot described as potentially dangerous but not yet critical. Anti-coagulants rather than surgery were prescribed, and were reported to be working on the 27th. By the 30th, at the end of his expected week in the hospital, Nixon's physician stated that his patient could not travel from California to Washington to obey the trial subpoena for from one to three months and could not even give a deposition for an absolute minimum of three weeks.

The timing was important. The very next day, October 1st, the Watergate trial began. Three days later, Nixon went home from the hospital. By October 14th, when the prosecution first began to present its case following a contentious two-week jury selection, Nixon's physician said that the phlebitis condition was improved but that Nixon still couldn't come to

Washington to testify. Presiding Judge Sirica thereupon got overtly suspicious. Maybe, he announced, he'd just have to send three court-appointed
doctors to California to see for themselves whether or not Nixon was in
any shape to testify at the Watergate trial. No need, allowed Nixon's
lawyer the very next day: the ex-president's health was improving rapidly,
and his client should be able to testify after all.

Nixon *was* ill, no.doubt about that. But let there also be no doubt that
the reported severity and extent of that illness came at an exceedingly
convenient time. Sirica had more than enough right to wonder whether
Nixon's maladies hadn't worsened in direct proportion to the likelihood of
being hauled into a court he had done everything in his power to stay out
of for two-and-one-half years. For a week, it looked like Nixon *was* finally
going to get his day in court, but only as a witness rather than a defendant.
But on October 24th, just as John Dean had almost finished eight full days
of testimony at the trial, Nixon was hospitalized again after more blood
clots showed up. An operation was said to be a real possibility; on the 29th,
vein surgery was performed to remove clots and Nixon was listed as in
critical condition. Improvements were noted by physicians in subsequent
days, but so were postoperative dangers. Not until November 3rd was
Nixon taken off the critical list, and not until November 14th was he
released from a California hospital a second time.

By November 14th, the Watergate trial was six weeks old, Ford had lost
on the tapes and records issue, the 1974 election had come and gone at the
expense of the Republicans, and Haldeman, Ehrlichman, and Mitchell
were all blaming each other for as much illegality as they dared.

Judge Sirica, therefore, remained interested in Mr. Nixon's testimony,
interested enough finally to appoint his panel of three doctors on November 13th, the day before Nixon left hospital for home. These physicians
were to report back to the judge by the 29th, just after the prosecution was
due to rest its case—and before defense lawyers were to present their cases
at the trial. Hardball with Nixon's lawyer followed, and, on November
18th, Nixon agreed to have Sirica's doctors examine him. They did so just
in time to meet their deadline, and reported that justice and the ex-president didn't mix. Nixon wasn't going to be able to testify for another two
months, minimum. Moreover, he should not even begin giving depositions
for five more weeks and, even then, for not more than one or two hours
a day.

This cut it. Given this medical imprimatur, it was a great deal easier for
Nixon to string out his efforts to avoid testifying for as long as might be
required to make Sirica and the Special Prosecutor's Office appear to be
inhumane in demanding it. Judge Sirica gave up: the prosecutors had

several score Watergate tapes, they had John Dean, and they would have to make do with that. Some of what Richard Nixon had recorded about himself would have to take the place of whatever else he might have been forced to offer in court, with threats of perjury charges dangling over his head. On December 5, 1974, Sirica ruled that Nixon need not testify either in person or via a deposition at the Watergate trial.

The prosecutors did not object to this, but defense lawyers screamed bloody murder. In the dog-eat-dog atmosphere of the Watergate trial, the whole point was to pin everything on somebody else. Dean, the CIA, Nixon, anybody. It *was* Nixon's cover-up, that was obvious. But it was also obvious that defendants Haldeman, Ehrlichman, and Mitchell had very few friends left in official Washington. So defense objections were overridden, and the trial moved on. Nixon had finally and completely eluded the judiciary. Lacking the tapes, the president for whom it had all been done wouldn't have been present in the courtroom at all.

But the tapes were enough to convict most of those under indictment—the tapes and the testimony of those already convicted for their part in what had transpired.[176] The Watergate defendants' weakness, like Nixon's, was that they claimed not to have known what they were doing and that they were pawns in others' games. But they were not sick, nor were they in California. They were right there, and right then.

On January 1st, 1975, they also became felons. On that date, the jury found four of the Watergate defendants—Ehrlichman, Haldeman, Mardian, and Mitchell—guilty as charged. The fifth, Parkinson, was acquitted. Sentencing followed almost three months later. Maximum John, belying his nickname, awarded Haldeman, Ehrlichman, and Mitchell not less than two-and-one-half or more than eight years apiece. Though these were stiff punishments for first offenders in white-collar crimes, they were also a lot less than the twenty-five-year maximums that Haldeman and Mitchell could have received, or the twenty years that might have been meted out to Ehrlichman. Robert Mardian, additionally, got only ten months to three years, instead of a maximum of five.

Appeals and reduced sentences promptly followed. Even before he sentenced Nixon's big three, Judge Sirica ordered the immediate release of those Nixon aides who had cooperated with prosecutors or testified at the Watergate trial. John Dean left prison on January 8th after serving four months of a one- to four-year sentence. Jeb Stuart Magruder served seven months of a ten-month to four-year sentence. Herbert Kalmbach, a Nixon lawyer who had raised millions in illegal campaign contributions from major corporations and distributed hush money to the Watergate burglars, ended up serving six months of a six- to eighteen-month term. Chuck,

"When you've got them by the balls," Colson stayed in jail for only one additional month, there to be more thoroughly Born Again.

Sirica justified his leniency toward Dean and others not only on the grounds that they had cooperated with the prosecution, but also because he should pardon them so that the prison terms all were serving would not "get mixed up in political considerations." Given that Watergate was rife with precisely such considerations from first to last, the judge protested too much.[177]

Meanwhile, the federal judiciary stayed busy, as the convicted appealed their sentences, and as other, less well known, Watergate actors faced their day in court at last. Thirty Nixon aides eventually pled guilty or were convicted of Watergate-related crimes while the big three utilized judicial delay after delay. Ehrlichman did not finally go to jail until December 1976, two years after being found guilty as charged. Haldeman and Mitchell were incarcerated later still: after deciding, as Ehrlichman had not, to exhaust *all* their appeal possibilities. Mitchell wasn't finally put behind bars until June 1977.

By this time, judicially mandated vengeance no longer smelled so sweet. Robert Mardian, for instance, never ended up in prison. His conviction was reversed on appeal. Former Attorney General Kleindienst got a minimum sentence of one month, which was promptly suspended by a judge. Others not involved in the earliest period of the Watergate cover-up (e.g., Alexander Haig) were never charged or tried. Deference and elitism, as James Doyle of the Special Prosecutor's Office later put it, ruled. Judges other than Sirica tended not to be maximum about anything in the crime-and-punishment departments.

In the end, even Sirica relented. In the fall of 1977, he reduced the sentences of Haldeman, Ehrlichman, and Mitchell to the four-year maximums he had earlier assessed against John Dean and Jeb Magruder even though the big three hadn't cooperated with the court in the slightest. The fact that their former boss Nixon had got off scot-free, so far as judicial punishments were concerned, was an operative principle here, as was the thought that all of the three men were sorrowful and regretful: a guaranteed norm for anybody behind bars.

Haldeman, ironically, ended up serving only six months, but sixty days more than Dean, the witness who had done the most to put him behind bars. Ehrlichman was imprisoned for three times as long as Haldeman; and John Mitchell wasn't released on parole until nineteen months after beginning his sentence. Mitchell, when he went free in January 1979, was the last convicted Watergate felon to be freed. There was no joy in any of this for Doyle of the Special Prosecutor's Office, who'd been paid to be a public affairs staffer and who explained the involutions of the judicial system to reporters trying to put pieces of legal jigsaw puzzles together without bending edges in the process. The criminal courts were "complicated, sprawling, and snarled," Doyle concluded. They tried few and imprisoned fewer. "There are miscarriages of justice all along the way, and many believe that the greatest miscarriage is leniency for certifiable criminals. Watergate seemed no different."[178] By these low standards, the political system had performed better than the courts, which preferred to assume they operated independently of politics and power. Congress's complexities, sprawl, and snarl at least had meted out some punishment to the one man whose interests all of Watergate had been designed to serve. In that, at least, the Congress could rest temporarily more content.

# EPILOGUE

## *LEARNING LESSONS,*

## *REPEATING MISTAKES*

THE END of the sprawling drama of Watergate closed, for the moment, the rip in time which opened with the terrible year of 1968 and the political disappointments and polarizations that accompanied it. For seven years, Americans received uncustomary lessons in humility: lessons which weren't pleasant even to try to learn. A nation which began the period inaccurately boasting that it had never lost a war and equating its fate with the fate of all mankind marvelled, toward the end of 1974, that its system had worked. Worked not in the sense of accomplishing greatness but, rather, in the sense of avoiding catastrophe.

There was vainglory and intellectual melodrama even in this. For the fact was that the system which worked was not the system that most Americans had started out the Anxious Years believing in. That earlier system was cast in a heroic mold. It was the America of John F. Kennedy and Camelot, the America of universal burdens and transcendent missions, the America of fulsome civics texts and grandeur-ridden campaign oratory, the America in which things like Vietnam and Watergate couldn't happen.

But Vietnam and Watergate *had* happened; and both events induced trauma and a sense of overwhelming crisis. This is why Watergate and Vietnam induced widespread popular mistrust of government. This is why national swagger was succeeded by national self-pity, and by an America often psychologically at war with itself.

Heroism remained desirable, for it also remained the antidote to ambiguities of American power at home and abroad. It was the antidote to a political culture in which basic contradictions had developed between the structure of American government and America's role as a world power. It was the antidote to fears about an Imperial Presidency which had developed to wage cold and hot wars abroad and contain communist and other menaces around the globe. Heroic expectations were a way of ignoring the fact that the Constitution under which America operated had never been designed for great-power politics. But it existed, rather, to preserve domestic liberties in a Continental Switzerland, where external dangers were few, and where the designs of political decisions could, accordingly, be relatively many. Congress was a key part of the resulting difficulty; it was part of the contradiction between structure and assumed role. So presidents had eased around Congress in foreign policy-making and war making, often with Congress's consent. Saviors of the Republic and of liberty and freedom around the world had proliferated within the executive branch and the inner circles of the White House.

So long as the presidents for whom these largely invisible men and women worked were larger than life, the ambiguities of American power did not have to be faced. Great leaders would do the job somehow, and the nation and its missions at home and abroad would be the better for it. Lyndon Baines Johnson would replicate the oft-romanticized experience of FDR, and Nixon could be a soldier of freedom like Dwight David Eisenhower.

But there was no shining solution to Vietnam. The screaming eagle did not perch on a crag in official Washington. Rhetoric was impressive, but actuality was not. Technocratic War Managers designed and implemented a limited war that ran amok. Bloodless equations, body counts, and kill-ratios were cooked up for a society few leaders ever bothered to learn anything significant about. Once the technocratic equations failed to work, the War Managers beat discrete retreats away from their creations, as if these equations had never been created by them in the first place. Or as if the equations would have worked, if only the American or Vietnamese peoples had been worthy of the equation-makers' visions.

When Richard Nixon and the Republicans took over the executive branch from the Democrats in the wake of Tet and the sordid events of 1968, they fought no messianic crusade in Southeast Asia. They sought to save what they could of a bipartisan limited-war policy; which eased around contradictions between structure and role. The United States was to be a policeman of the noncommunist world without undergoing full and complete mobilizations which risked nuclear holocaust or disconcerting "command economy" changes in the structure of domestic affairs. Nixon's resulting hi-tech "Men Out, Machines In" strategy was a clear result. Nor was it one that a Democrat-controlled Congress opposed. Congress and congressional leaders steadily voted the monies for the Electronic Battle-fields and for the seven-mile-high B-52 strikes that made parts of Laos, Cambodia, and Vietnam look like the far side of the moon. Meanwhile, the messy specifics of the ground war were increasingly left to the despised natives. Our technology replaced our blood, as it often had before in our American Way of War. The political leaders of both parties who believed that this hi-tech equation would not unsettle the grass roots back home with too many body bags or too many frustrated demands for unilateral withdrawals or "all-out" war supposed correctly. Gradual withdrawal back to the pre-1965 arms and money norms was OK with most of those opposed to the war, just as it gradually became acceptable to most of the middle grounders and most of the right. The general desire was not to have America lose in Vietnam; and to try and make sure that the Saigon and Phnom Penh regimes didn't lose either. By end of 1970, the New Left was intimidated into inactivity. Nixon went on to erode most remaining opposition to his strategy of continued high-technology and low-casualty war in the 1972 election. Vietnam had never really been about the Vietnamese. It was about an American vision of itself and of its place in the world. Vietnam was only a pawn in achieving a vision of America as a model for all humanity, and as a means of doing it easily enough that Americans need not worry whether the Cold War and checks and balances mixed well together.

Richard Nixon, like the Cold War presidents before him, rarely worried about such matters himself. To him, as to his predecessors, America's global role was all-important. Without it, America would surely lose all its freedoms held dear. Crisis was everywhere, and Nixon believed—to the very core of his being—that his domestic opponents had been unpardonably soft. They were giving away the global game in advance. They had overpromised and mismanaged and then retreated back into the commanding heights of the Establishment. They were blaming him for doing what they had done and would have done. In the process, they had undermined America's strength in crisis times. Worse, they had made it easier for communist enemies to test America's will on other frontiers of freedom in hopes they could get away with it, or in the belief that weak liberal spirits would sag when they realized how much the defense of freedom inevitably cost.

Nixon would show them all. The real war, after all, was all about determination and will in what Kennedy had called the "long twilight struggle." The Russians and Chinese would be treated as amoral international actors. They'd get advantages like long-delayed political recognition for their regime or long-deferred efforts to start putting caps on the levels of nuclear weapons in the world. But every time they sought to use other revolutionary proxies to make the United States look weak, those proxies would be pummelled into the ground via high technology just as the Hanoi regime's forces were during the Easter Offensive of 1972 or as Nixon tried to do to the Khmer Rouge and Vietnamese alike in Cambodia during and after the secret bombings of 1969–70. Twilight struggles were not for the constitutionally squeamish, nor could they be, in the view Nixon shared with his immediate predecessors in the presidential office.

The holier-than-thou liberals, too, were going to learn this lesson, and learn it well. Politics—foreign or domestic—was an amoral business, most especially when you were dealing with people who opposed you. The Democrats were weak and divided after Vietnam, and Nixon would divide them further. He would show those liberals who had always hated him that he knew how to play hardball. Abuses of power were inevitable. But when push came to shove, America's role as a great power was more important than the civil liberties that lots of liberals whined about. Lots of liberals were merely dupes of the enemy anyway, and nobody's liberty extended to being intentionally—or even unintentionally—treasonous. This hadn't been true of Alger Hiss of Pumpkin Papers renown; and by God, it wasn't going to be true of Daniel Ellsberg of the Pentagon Papers either.

So secret government it was, and widening circles of dirty tricks and cover-ups into the bargain. Political sabotage was a fact of life, after all. Nobody had any right to demand that Nixon be better than any of the Democrats. JFK and LBJ had used bad means to accomplish good ends, too. Civics texts were fine for those who didn't know what the nitty-gritty of politics was really all about. But the practical operators knew that you got back what you gave out, and liberal Democrats and "radicals," as Nixon defined them, were going to be on the receiving end.

Thus the war came home at last. Frustrations abroad were partly compensated for at home, and the price was to accentuate the problem within America itself: the problem that there was a basic contradiction between the structure of American government and its role as a great power in a world where success was very often considered as the ability to beat enemies at their own amoral game in a relentless and bipolar struggle.

Watergate, therefore, flowed from Vietnam. Guerilla war abroad became

Guerilla Government at home. This was the kernel of what happened in America during these Anxious Years.

Watergate, when it came, pitted strength against weakness more than good against evil. Nixon broke laws and violated constitutional limitations and lied about all of that repeatedly. All true. But Watergate justice was fearful, erratic, deferential, and very often self-interested. It worked only because of a series of fortunate coincidences, and an equally fortunate tendency by the president and his defenders to blunder repeatedly. The *Washington Post*'s political cartoonist, Herbert Block, caught the flavor of three years' worth of drama, melodrama, and comic opera well when he argued that "A few flashbacks of events . . . show that the system worked about the same way W. C. Fields captured a criminal in a movie: being unwittingly caught up in the chase, and finally winding up, by accident, sitting in a daze on the chest of the unconscious criminal."[1]

Herblock got it right. The criminals very largely caught themselves. They were simply no good at what they were doing. They sensed the growing contradictions between structure and role, not least because so many of the principals were lawyers. Had these would-be political sabo-teurs and cover-up artists been less aware of how illegal many of their actions were, they might simply have acted decisively instead of con-stantly kibitzing and attempting to protect themselves at others' expense. This might have allowed Nixon and his men to tough everything out. Instead, they hedged their bets in so many directions at once that they ended up ensnaring themselves further.

John Dean certainly thought so, and he'd had as much experience in the folkways of Guerilla Government as any other veteran of Watergate. To Dean, "The lesson was clear: Take your losses fast, and take them openly." If you get caught, come out super-tough at the start and dare anybody to do anything about it. Steal big, and don't apologize.

Dean gave a frank example of what he meant when he described a conversation he had during his 1974 prison term with a former Mafia hit man named Joey:

> "Let me ask you something, Deano," Joey began . . . "What would have happened if Nixon had told everybody to go fuck themselves, you know, that he wasn't turning over no damn tapes, nothing?"
>
> "He probably would have been impeached for obstructing justice by withholding vital evidence," I responded.
>
> "Bullshit, no way. You can't tell me that, 'cause it just wouldn't have happened. I aint no specialist in politics, but I've known guys in the

Congress, and I know that unless a case had been made against Nixon, there aint no way he would have been removed. And since he had all the [taped] evidence [that tied him into the cover-up in his own words], unless he gave it to them, there weren't no ['smoking gun'] case."

It wasn't the most articulate analysis, but, the more we debated the point, the more compelled I was to agree with Joey. . . . Joey's point cuts right to the core of the assumption that the system worked: it worked because Nixon let it work. It was never really tested.

"I'll tell you this, Deano, if me and my onetime former associates had been counselling Nixon, and giving him a little hand here and there, he would have been like a pig in shit—a little dirty and smelly, but nobody would have touched him."[2]

Maybe nobody would have. Maybe, if the tapes had gone up in smoke after their existence was made public in mid-July 1973, Nixon would have been able to preserve his all-important deniability in the cover-up. Or perhaps, had Nixon quickly admitted that some of his associates had planned and committed a burglary at Democratic National Committee headquarters in June 1972, then argued that politics is a dirty business, and then dared the Democrats to make something of that if they could, the Watergate political investigation might never have gotten off the ground— not in a way which could have harmed him or his topmost associates. For it was the constantly unravelling cover-up, far more than the initial break-in, that eventually spelled their doom.[3]

But Nixon and his men *were* stupid. They sensed contradictions without being able to resolve them, so they constantly hesitated. Writing in another context, and after an unsuccessful tour as Reagan's first secretary of state, Watergate veteran Alexander Haig spoke to what they proceeded to do when he observed that "It is difficult for politicians to do bold things, it is almost impossible for them to do nothing. Instead, they will take small, cautious steps." Haig, like Joey, preferred Imperial Presidents who acted the part.[4]

Nixon was an emperor who sat too tenuously on his throne until Haig helped engineer the Saturday Night Massacre of October 1973. And by then it was too late, too late because the cover-up had been unravelling for fifteen months. It was too late, also, because Nixon, like Lyndon Johnson and others before him, was paying the price for a political style that bred both a lack of loyalty and timid ministers.

Nixon needed all the guts and devotion he could get from his associates.

He was not mistaken at all that growing numbers of people wanted to get him and his staff as Watergate progressed—or even before Watergate started. But paranoia was easily bred, within Nixon's own ranks, by the fact that no one aide knew what the others were doing—or might be doing—at his expense in conjunction with the president. Just such corroding suspicion and fear characterized the steadily worsening relations between John Dean and John Ehrlichman vis-à-vis the cover-up, but the process was far more widespread and debilitating than that. Defense Secretary Melvin Laird, one of those who left Washington just before Watergate blew up in Nixon's face in the spring of 1973, is cited by Woodward and Bernstein as once telling White House lawyer Fred Buzhardt that "the President didn't want any one person to have the full picture. No one was ever to be given the entire story. With matters thus arranged, the President could counter any argument by hinting that only he had the necessary facts and background. Nixon's strange methodology made timid ministers, Laird had said."[5]

It also bred none too trusting ones, men who operated in what John Ehrlichman later called "watertight compartments"; aides were not sure of what Nixon was ordering other aides to do. His aides accordingly distrusted other aides and, given enough time and tension, even distrusted the president himself.[6] The "timid minister" problem Melvin Laird identified was worsened by the earlier-mentioned fact that Nixon had "made" all of the men most immediately around him. Thus he could easily afford to keep most of them balkanized, ill-informed, and operating in a twilight world of perpetual gossip and innuendo. Only Henry Kissinger who, during his tenure as national security adviser, secretly taped Nixon bested his boss in this regard.

The negative aspect of this organizational strategy was that Nixon couldn't easily play the game of many a politician who gets into the habit of sacrificing ideals for interest: he could not reap the benefit of bad acts and let others take the blame for them, for those others were his own creatures. Comparatively few believed that they ever acted on their own account, whether they be John Dean in the White House or John Mitchell and others at CREEP. Nixon lacked the advantages of deniability because he did things too directly, directly enough that too many lines of investigation converged on the president of the United States.

Once those lines converged, Nixon faced an unpalatable choice. He could either say he knew nothing whatsoever about break-ins and cover-ups arranged by his topmost aides—or he could admit that he was, in fact, involved in Watergate up to his eyebrows. He could choose between looking like a criminal—or a fool. It was the sort of no-win choice that

Lyndon Johnson had faced after the Tet offensive in Vietnam, and, like Johnson, Nixon hesitated and was lost. Nixon argued that there was no cover-up, just as Johnson argued that Tet had not handed U.S. military and political leadership the blackest of political black eyes. In this process of bland denial aimed at avoiding unpalatable choices, both men destroyed their credibility and lost the political initiative, never to regain it.

By the time Nixon counterattacked strongly, using national security and executive privilege as the two cornerstones of his political argument, Haldeman, Ehrlichman, Kleindienst, Dean, and Mitchell were gone, his own tape recordings were the issue, and he faced the gathering forces of judicial, political, and journalistic opposition without benefit of intermediaries. Again, his experience was like that of his Democratic predecessor. The major difference was that, while Johnson was abandoned by his aides, Nixon first abandoned his. The result, however, was the same—both men became ever more isolated and less and less trusted by their remaining associates.

The process of isolation and failure was gradual, however: this, above all, we have seen in our passage through the various tributaries that, in combination, composed Watergate. Johnson's experience in Vietnam was similar. Tet was his version of Nixon's Saturday Night Massacre. Both events testified to the spectacular rot of presidential policies, but neither president fell immediately. Johnson decided not to run for reelection, yet the mainstream of the Democratic Party would almost certainly have renominated him for another term. Nixon hung onto office like grim death, and the mainstream of his party, along with many conservative Democrats, hung onto him with equal determination until almost the last act of the Watergate drama.

Practical political actors had reasons for such caution. They rarely forgot that Vietnam and Watergate were very closely related and that one problem had flowed from the other. They realized that Nixon and his people had undertaken political and other sabotage against their Democratic opponents because they believed that it was almost as necessary to national security as the spying and dirty tricks earlier launched by Johnson against Marxists and non-Marxists within the loose antiwar alliance.

Nixon's opponents knew that a climate of Cold War crisis had empowered presidents. They also knew that Nixon could appeal to the frustration, anger, and polarization in America during Vietnam in ways that could allow him to beat their brains out. Thus the continual caution with which Congress approached Nixon's political trial, especially in the House of Representatives.

The timing of Watergate, however, helped Nixon's opponents, eased their caution, and gradually allowed them to stop splitting legal and other hairs and recognize the obvious. The president was bound firmly in a web of circumstantial and other evidence that made an impeachment trial necessary if constitutionally mandated checks and balances were not going to become irrelevant in a world of great-power politics and if judicial and legislative power and reputations were not going to suffer more than they already had.

Watergate hit national headlines at the right time for Nixon's opponents, and the wrong time for his defenders. It became high-profile, nationwide, during the spring of 1973—the period, loosely, from McCord's letter of March to Dean's and Butterfield's revelations in June and July. At precisely this time, the Vietnam War had faded into the deep background of popular concern. With the signing of the Vietnam peace treaty in Paris at the end of January and with the withdrawal of the final U.S. ground forces from South Vietnam at the end of March, America's Longest War became subject to widespread and thoroughgoing amnesia. The war was a failure that deserved sudden and immediate forgetting more than anything else—if heroic assumptions were to be maintained. So it was forgotten by a nation fortunate enough never to have had to learn from failure.

Such collective and individual amnesia vastly weakened Richard Nixon's ability to wrap himself up in the flag or to defend Watergate for what it was, in fact: a secret war against domestic opponents of the war. Thus there was no postwar red scare, as there had been after another limited war in Asia had gone wrong in Korea in 1950 and 1951. And careful congressional efforts to stop the ongoing air war in Cambodia and to pass the War Powers Act both finally proved successful. Congress, for instance, stopped the Cambodia and Laos bombings by August 1973, by the long overdue expedient of voting to cut off funding just after most members of Congress discovered that Nixon had started secretly bombing Cambodia back to the Stone Age four years earlier. The War Powers Act, for its part, became law immediately after Nixon ordered a worldwide alert of all American military forces during the latter stages of the October 1973 Arab-Israeli War. The Cambodia-Laos legislation finally brought an end to twelve years of American combat in Southeast Asia, and the War Powers Act finally attempted to do something about limiting presidential power to wage limited wars without some sort of legislative approval. None of this would have been possible but for the fact that Watergate was hemorrhaging the power and prestige of Nixon's presidency during precisely these same months via the discovery of the White House tapes, Agnew's resignation, the Saturday Night Massacre, and all the rest. Once again, therefore, Watergate and Vietnam were related. As the Nixon administration lost popular trust and internal cohesion over Watergate, it also lost credibility and clout regarding Vietnam, Laos, and Cambodia. The president was in no position to try to mobilize frustration engendered by the war to eviscerate his opponents and rationalize his actions by, for example, blaming military defeat on a New Left cabal which had sapped America's will and energy in an hour of maximum peril. Millions of Americans believed precisely this—Ronald Wilson Reagan of California, for one—but millions of others did not. The New Left organizations, such as they were, had self-destructed no later than 1971, and it was difficult for many to imagine them as a Trojan horse inside the gates in 1973 and 1974. Nixon's defenses of the whys of Watergate, therefore, rang hollow. The radicals did not seem to be on the verge of toppling the government or turning America into a pitiful, helpless giant divided against itself. Richard Nixon did. The contradictions between America's political structure and its great power role, therefore, destroyed Nixon—not his opponents.

Richard Nixon didn't like any of this one bit. He raged against his fate and branded his opponents hypocrites and worse. Hypocrisy there was; holier-than-thous, too. Congress, the judiciary, and the Special Prosecutor's Office were not staffed by naïve or romantic figures. They were—or speedily became—political operators as cold and calculating as any in the White House. (Leon Jaworski was only one example.) As Watergate stretched on, and as the struggle centered more and more on the possession of the Watergate tapes, Nixon's opponents—partisan, journalistic, judicial, and otherwise—found it easier and easier to argue that the Imperial Presidency was an abortion which had resulted from the character flaws of a single man, instead of being part of a much broader pattern of tension between great-power status and constitutional precept. Approaching Watergate as a result of personal failings, rather than institutional flaws, allowed men and women who had done little enough to challenge presidential pretensions at home or abroad to now conveniently assume that the ills that afflicted America existed because a single evil genius—or a few bad men—had lied to them. Thus many members of Congress who had had a great deal of opportunity to know better during their political careers could and did develop a perceived need to be naive about what had been going on in official Washington for many years and during more than a few presidencies. Many a journalist and lawyer and judge did the same; many a citizen, too.

Watergate, then, became a barometer of American innocence and historical exceptionalism. Richard Nixon fell not alone for his own sins but for those of his predecessors in office as well. These sins were cumulative.

They did not wrench the fabric of the body politic until the combined results of over a decade of failed war abroad and bipartisan political sabotage at home undermined the special and unique aura of honor, morality, and political fibre that surrounded America's president. An American public that did not generally believe that its great men even swore in private conversations with their aides eventually learned otherwise. And, when they did, they didn't like the knowledge one bit. It was all demeaning, somehow. It dirtied the nation and its ideals.

What most Americans forgot was that the procedural rules that legitimized their nation and its political culture had not been designed for heroes, but for people. The Constitution and all that it symbolized was the moral center of the nation, but that did not mean that the nation was uniquely moral. Presidents weren't heroes any more than members of Congress were, or any more than jurists or journalists. The checks and balances beloved of the civics texts were just that: efforts to institutionally balance power among human, all-too-human, people.

Americans, however, were not used to being human, all-too-human, in the period under discussion here. They liked to assume that they were very special and very powerful indeed—and so the banality of power and of the people who held it surprised and shocked them.

The Robert Strange McNamaras, William Westmorelands, Lyndon Johnsons, John Deans, Bob Haldemans, John Ehrlichmans, and Richard Nixons of the world, however, were very human. As all human beings are, they were creatures of their times, times delineated in gargantuan strokes of greatness. None was great. None lived up to the expectations all had for themselves in the service of their country or to the expectations that others had for them; none could. For the level of expectations—personal and popular—was so high as to defy achievement; and, in the end, even to defy belief. The sin of pride exacted its inevitable price in America during this period, as so often before in human affairs.

The Arrogance of American Power, then, set ill with assumptions of American innocence and historical exceptionalism. The war in Vietnam exposed this problem, but it did not create it. The nation which accounted itself the paragon of the noncommunist world and a beacon for all people everywhere yearning to be free found itself acting like any other nation fighting a limited war on the periphery of its power. This awareness was profoundly shocking to Americans, and it explains the political agonies and the hyperbole of the Anxious Years—whether that was the mindless melodrama of the Plumbers equating moderate-to-liberal Democrats with Vietcong, or whether it was sundry New Leftists frenetically equating democracy, as Americans know it, with a bloodsucking mutation of militaristic fascism. It also explains why widespread nostalgia for better (and, in particular, more uncomplicated and heroic) times was another enduring result of the Anxious Years that stretched from the Tet offensive to the Nixon pardon.

Outsiders, watching all of this, often wondered, Were Americans crazy? Did they really believe that they were so innocent and special, did they really assume that their ways of doing and thinking were so universal—or could be? Were they really so shocked and confused as millions seemed to be by domestic political spying and sabotage, the banalities of power, and the fact that high-technology wars are bloody and unselective businesses to which the ideals of chivalry very rarely apply?

The answer was yes to all of these questions. Americans had never had much practice equating their ideals with their interests in foreign policy. And foreign policy, and a foreign war which had flowed from it, had been what induced the friction and frustration in the first place. America's foreign policy had started out as a comparatively simple and idealistic phenomenon. The United States lectured and, more occasionally, castigated, but stayed clear of entangling military and political alliances and was in no sense a world power. Thus passed the first century of the national life.

In the second century, things began to change. America became the largest single economic power in the world; then it became a regional military and police power in the Americas and, to a much lesser extent, in the Pacific; finally, as a result of two world wars, it found itself both the dominant economic and military power on the planet.

The experience was a heady one indeed for many an American leader. But there was a problem. The problem we have outlined. The Constitution had not been designed for any of this. So what to do? How to be a largely passive Light unto the Nations and a far more active policeman of the world at the same time? The answer caused difficulties for American leaders because they had problems other leaders didn't. America was special. Its foreign policy could not be designed or perceived only as a matter of self-interest. Ideals were necessary as well, and America had lots of those. America's ideals, in fact, tended to become its interests, especially in non-European nations its leaders tended to know excruciatingly little about. American-style freedom would be forwarded (the ideal) and, thereby, communist military and political threats would be contained (the interest). Americans would take over and fight a war in a far-off land that few had even heard of and even fewer had any interest in. That land would be remodelled quickly on the American plan. Once the natives learned the American Way of government and war, their superiority over their opponents in that same land would be obvious, and Americans could go home knowing that they had done the right thing.

Things didn't turn out that way, of course, and consequently the debate over ideals and interests in Vietnam, and in Southeast Asia more generally, gathered force. Moreover, another debate began about the universality of American ideals in non-European and formerly European-controlled lands. Finally, the constitutional and other corners that had been cut in order to wage an increasingly frustrating and lengthy war in the first place caused domestic trial and tribulation back home, particularly after what should have been easy and obvious turned out to be difficult and far from obvious at all.

Perceptions of crisis, complexity, and of things being out of control flowered in such an environment. An America which started off boasting ended up moaning. Self-praise alternated with self-pity. Nobody looked particularly heroic after Vietnam, the New Left, and Watergate—politicians, academicians, and members of the legal system included. Journalists basked in a heroic light, true, but even that moment was comparatively brief. Honesty and integrity, many affirmed, was the key missing ingredient in American life. The nation's leaders might be intelligent, but they lacked character.

The political order bore the brunt of most of this criticism, for America, after all, was a political culture. It became normal, in the aftermath of Watergate, for America's leading politicians and intellectuals to bemoan a dangerous sense of skepticism and doubt among the citizenry, and it also became normal to blame the people for those opinions. Americans expected too much from government. Resolving political issues was a much more complex business than most citizens supposed. The limitations of what government could do to resolve outstanding economic, social, and diplomatic problems had to be recognized. Arguments like these became especially frequent after a "post-Watergate morality" set in and after higher moral and ethical requirements were enforced upon those who would account themselves to be leaders in all branches of the national life. Congress, for example, did not escape: sexual, pecuniary, and alcohol- and drug-related weaknesses of a series of members—liberal and conservative, highly placed and more modestly circumstanced—helped to fuel an ongoing series of reforms in legislative procedures throughout the 1970s that, combined, weakened the powers of senior members, forced the recording of votes on most bills and amendments, strengthened subcommittees at the expense of committees, opened up floor debates, hearings, and conference committee sessions to public inspection, and placed limits on the maximum amounts of monies that could be contributed to political campaigns by either individuals or political action committees (PACs). Reforms like this were important. And, much as Congress remained an imperfect place, its system of operation—actual, rather than idealized—could now be much better grasped by those willing or able to spend time in front of their television sets watching committees and subcommittees trying to hash out workable compromises on important issues of the day.

Congress, however, was not august enough for many, including many intellectuals who accounted themselves far more sophisticated than the norm. Congress was committees and subcommittees, but two generations of Americans had been nurtured—by their political and intellectual leadership not least—on "great men" who heroically and individually embodied the nation's greatest ideals while, as politicans-in-chief, they also kept a sharp eye out for its interests. Gerald R. Ford and James Earl Carter paid the price for failing to preside over national and international affairs in the grand style. Carter, in addition, was cordially despised for nattering away about a burgeoning "crisis" and about "national malaise" toward the end of his plagued term of office. Carter blamed the American people for their ills, and the American people disliked him intensely for it.

They had a point, these tens of millions of concerned Americans, for they too sensed the ambiguities of American power. They realized, whether dimly or articulately, that a Constitution drawn up for a Switzerland of 1789 had problems of relevance to the sprawling global political and military guardianship of two centuries later. They wanted a way out of this dilemma, and heroism was the easiest. It was the norm they knew, and one that their elite had repeatedly taught them.

Ronald Wilson Reagan knew this, too. It made him able to capitalize on opportunity several times deferred and take advantage of the ongoing civil war within a Democratic Party still split by its Vietnam-era foreign policy and further split by its domestic and economic policy under Carter. Reagan gave us the old time religion—avuncular likableness in the FDR mold, the public wit of a Theodore Roosevelt or a John F. Kennedy, the domestic politics of Dwight David Eisenhower, and the foreign policy of Eisenhower's secretary of state John Foster Dulles. Vietnam was a failed crusade, the Great Society had been an abortion, but America remained a great City upon a Hill spreading the light of liberty to all mankind.

Rhetoric like this worked well for a while, but it also exacted a price— the price being that the ambiguous relationship between traditional American rules of the game and the new realities of American power in the world were not resolved in a realistic fashion. In particular, the War Powers of presidents relative to those of Congress were not resolved. The War Powers Act of 1973 floated in limbo, a constitutional struggle waiting to happen; meanwhile, Reagan generally edged around the limitations that some in Congress still wanted to enforce by keeping direct U.S. military intervention as high-technology and short-term as possible. Had he any tendencies in another direction (and he did), the political reaction to his administration's failed intervention in Lebanon in 1982–83 speedily taught him otherwise. From there on out, he fought battles where quick resolutions were possible or where quick punishments could be meted out by American forces. The invasion of Grenada in October 1983 and the bombings of Libya in April 1986 were examples of the resulting military techniques, techniques which posed no danger to his political popularity at home. The moral was simple: keep American boys out of foxholes anywhere and fight quick battles where the United States could use its technological advantages, especially air and naval, to deliver quick punishment against small and isolated nations. When different sorts of struggles were required—lengthy and necessarily bloody ground wars, for example—do the job with such local allies as were available. *Contra* rebels fought the Sandinista regime in Nicaragua, Afghans of many types struggled to repel the Soviet military invasion of their homeland, tribal rebels fought other tribal and mulatto groups for control of the whole—or large-enough part— of the former Portuguese colony of Angola in southern Africa, and so on. If enough of direct American military intervention was kept short-term and high-technology, the spectre of another Vietnam might not arise. The Reagan Doctrine was to back local allies or allies-of-convenience with guns and money, but not, after the Lebanese fiasco, with men. Americans could stand tall once again, much as they had when Lyndon Johnson had simply bombed North Vietnam, instead of both doing that and sending more and more American troops to southern Vietnam, and much as they had when most had supported Nixon's Men Out, Machines In approach to withdrawing from Vietnam with honor, especially enough to keep badly frightened politicians in business.

The Reagan Doctrine worked well for a time. But a temptation constantly existed—just as it had in Kennedy, Johnson, and Nixon's time—for presidents to take over the management and operation of allied war efforts in the event that those efforts were faltering or in the event that Congress—in particular, anti-interventionist congressional Democrats—were getting restless about the duration, expense, or creeping Americanization of any war effort beyond limits that congressional majorities were trying to set.

Nicaragua, as matters turned out, finally provided the straw that broke the camel's back. A lackluster *contra* war was shored up by more and more U.S. money and effort, both overt and covert, while congressional anti-interventionists and others concerned about a too thoroughgoing Americanization of the conflict initially looked the other way or lacked sufficient daring and votes to challenge Reagan formally. The Central Intelligence Agency, accordingly, moved full steam into the bog, but once the illusion of easy victories evaporated, impatience took over. In early 1984, a series of ineptitudes scandalized official Washington—including CIA mines planted in Nicaraguan harbors, too-direct American involvement that lacked deniability. The standard excuse was that everything had occurred in military operations that were under the control of somebody else, that somebody else's fingers were on all the triggers.

Once the CIA's bureaucratic fingers were burned, however, congressional anti-interventionists were briefly able to mount a campaign to end all further direct involvement of the CIA in the day-to-day running of the war. The CIA, further, was constrained from using any of its funds to aid the *contras* in any way, and so was the executive branch of the federal government as a whole. Congress continued to vote relatively small amounts of "humanitarian" aid (money that was to be used, for example, to buy medical supplies, rather than bullets) to the *contras,* but other aid was cut off for a year beginning early in 1985. Congress also sent a message to the White House that no future aid for the *contras* should be paid for by creative financing, directly or indirectly supplied. Reagan was to wage his *contra* war with only such money, and only under such limitations, as Congress chose.

Reagan promptly got some *contra* funding restored, to begin in 1986. But Guerilla Government flowered in the White House once again. The president and his staff heartily disliked congressional efforts to get the CIA out of the *contra* war and they also disliked Congress's spotty efforts to limit the amount of money and the way it could be used. Saviors of the Republic were recruited to salvage another limited war gone wrong, a war not being waged well enough by proxy. The names were different this time. Marine Lieutenant Colonel Oliver North, Admiral John Poindexter, retired marine officer Robert C. McFarlane, and others replaced G. Gordon Liddy, John Dean, John Mitchell, and Bob Haldeman of yesteryear.[7]

The modus operandi, however, was the same. When in doubt, or when angered by the folkways of Congress, violate law and constitutional requirement by waging war without a license. Wage war, too, upon one's domestic enemies by an exceedingly suspicious series of about sixty break-ins and burglaries at the offices of groups opposed to the Reagan administration's support for the *contra* rebels, some later admitted to by the FBI. This time, have the White House's National Security Council take over from the banned CIA the work of funding and administering large segments of the *contra* war. Use the NSC's varied personnel (among whom

North and former NSC directors McFarlane and Poindexter were numbered) to "semi-privatize" U.S. foreign policy by raising money for the *contras* from private groups and even foreign governments. Have the NSC, in addition, creatively finance other *contra* funding by, for instance, secretly selling U.S. arms to Iran at inflated prices and then using part of the profits to protect freedom in Central America. Be sure, above all things, to protect the president's deniability in any and all of this. Hope that nobody would press the issue of crime or cover-up in a fashion that could make the administration look stupid.

It all might have worked, but for Iran. There the White House's picked men, doing what the president wanted done, strayed over an invisible line and ruined them all. Widespread hatred of secret palaver and bargaining and military support for mullahs in another far-off land that most Americans knew little about, but had convincing-enough reasons to despise, finally gave the president's political opponents the opportunity many had long been seeking. Now the *contra* war misdeeds could be tied in with an issue that involved and energized people and politicians alike in a fashion that the proxy war in Nicaragua alone never had. Now it was safe again to address the nagging questions consequent upon the basic contradiction between the structure of our government and our role as a great power.

The year 1987, therefore, was 1973 all over again. The Congress began televised hearings, the only major difference being that the Senate and the House cooperated to hold joint investigations this time. "What did the President know, and when did the President know, it?"—Senator Howard Baker's query of fourteen years earlier—was front-page news again, although Baker was plotting the White House strategy as Reagan's recently appointed chief of staff at the time. Another special prosecutor was well and duly appointed to conduct a by now badly faltering criminal investigation of what was becoming known as "Irangate" or the "Iran-Contra affair" for later submission to the courts. Calculatedly-arcane legal and political debates about "national security" were once again all the rage as government agencies refused to release needed documents. Again, a president who had recently gained an impressive reelection victory at the polls faced the choice between seeming a fool or a criminal that Nixon had faced, refused to make an unpalatable choice, and so lost massive public support in national-opinion polls.

Analysts many and various moaned and groaned. Would another Watergate wrench the nation again? Would Nicaragua become another Vietnam affecting U.S. power and stature in the world? Would Ronald Reagan's successor become another Nixon or another LBJ, another president who would lose the power to lead? The intensity of the questions was obvious, even though the answers to those questions were not. The very ways in which the questions were posed, however, testified to the uneasy ghosts in the national consciousness, spirits first glimpsed during the Anxious Years of 1968 to 1974. Whether a new rip in time would open was unclear. The fear that it would was undeniably there, in the infinite confabulations of official Washington and throughout the country.

A far more important question, however, remained unanswered, indeed, largely unasked. Was it time, finally, for a political culture to learn from political experience, to abandon efforts to resolve ambiguities with the inflated heroisms of great men, and start about the business of amending the Constitution to make it more relevant to the realities of a government composed of human beings rather than heroes? It was a risky question, this, the kind that risk-averse political actors dislike asking. But risk, it paid to remember near the end of the Constitution's two-year long bicentennial celebrations, had always been what that document was all about. Heroic glosses can be added on later. They generally are, in fact. But living documents, like living and growing societies and individuals, are based upon more quiet, modest, human, and even sometimes disinterested, helping. Let heroism be an assumption of many an academic analyst—past, present, or future—but let us remember that heroism is very rare in human affairs. People do the best they can, and occasionally the results are termed heroic, but heroism is usually no part of their intent. Truth, as Japanese filmmaker Akiro Kurosawa demonstrated in his classic *Rashomon,* is most likely to be found among those who are most likely to admit that their involvement in events is not valiant, gallant, courageous, or mighty—and that they, too, are as often erring and all-too-human as the opponents they have faced. Once people tell you a story about anything that makes them or those they honor look spotless or profound, they may very well be lying, not least to themselves.

So, good reader, we have come to the end of this long, and, I hope, informative, story. It is a story of our world and of formative events that have affected us all as historical actors within it. It is a story of failure, more than of success. But, as Lincoln Steffens, the ironic philosopher of American reform, once wrote, "[W]e need some great failures, especially we ever-successful Americans—conscious, intelligent, illuminating failures."[8] The alternative is myth, myth which fails to give the past the future it once had; illusion which replaces what analysts believe should have happened for reality itself and finally results in a self-defeating effort to justify our past for posterity—especially when that record be as rough or even sordid as that described here. We have to do better, if only to pay our debt to our own times in a fashion the future may find of some use as well.

# NOTES

No effort has been made to list every source consulted in the preparation of this book. Materials are cited only when they are directly drawn upon or when the author wishes to direct the reader's attention to particularly useful books or articles. Those interested in obtaining more complete bibliographies of specific interest may find them in, for example, Allen J. Matusow, *The Unravelling of America: A History of Liberalism in the 1960's* (New York: Harper & Row, 1984); Charles R. Morris, *A Time of Passion: America, 1960–1980* (New York: Harper & Row, 1984); William E. Leuchtenberg, *A Troubled Feast: American Society since 1945,* Updated ed. (Boston: Little, Brown, 1983); Stephen E. Ambrose, *Rise to Globalism: American Foreign Policy since 1938,* 4th rev. ed. (New York: Viking-Penguin, 1985); and in the outpouring of books about specific aspects of the 1960s which started making an appearance on bookstore shelves starting about 1987.

## PROLOGUE / *AMERICA THE FORTUNATE*

1. Henry Kissinger, *White House Years* (Boston: Little, Brown, 1981), p. 5.
2. Tacitus, *The Annals of Imperial Rome,* rev. ed., translated and with an introduction by Michael Grant (Harmondworth, England: Penguin Books, 1982), p. 16.

## PART ONE / *1968: THINGS FALL APART*

1. For recent journalistic versions of this approach, see "1968: The Year That Shaped a Generation," *Time,* 11 January 1988, pp. 16–27; and "The Legacy of Vietnam," *Newsweek,* special issue, 15 March 1985.
2. A good contemporary treatment is Don Oberdorfer, *Tet!* (Garden City, N.Y.: Doubleday, 1971).
3. For an argument that policy advisers and political leaders alike were "both realistic and pessimistic about the chances for success in Vietnam" before Tet (an opinion this author does not share), see Leslie H. Gelb with Richard K. Betts, *The Irony of Vietnam: The System Worked* (Washington, D.C.: Brookings Institution, 1979).
4. By far the best single source of the political texture of events in the United States in 1968, and one regularly used by the author, is Lewis Chester, Godfrey Hodgson, and Bruce Page, *An American Melodrama: The Presidential Campaign of 1968* (New York: Viking, 1969). William L. O'Neill, *Coming Apart: An Informal History of America in the 1960's* (New York: Quadrangle–New York Times Books, 1971) is also very readable.
5. See, for example, Walter Isaacson and Evan Thomas, *The Wise Men, Six Friends and the World They Made: Acheson, Bohlen, Harriman, Kennan, Lovett, McCloy* (New York: Simon & Schuster, 1986).
6. Richard J. Barnet, *The Roots of War* (Baltimore: Penguin, 1973), pp. 57–58. See also Louis Heren, *No Hail, No Farewell* (New York: Harper & Row, 1970), pp. 264–66.

7. As Walt W. Rostow put it in a speech to young corporation presidents in January 1968, "Since 1966, the war has not been about Vietnam, but about American politics. It's a race between Hanoi's rate of loss of manpower in South Vietnam and Lyndon Johnson's rate of loss of support in the United States." Quoted in Richard J. Whalen, *Catch the Falling Flag: A Republican's Challenge to His Party* (Boston: Houghton Mifflin, 1972), pp. 67–68.

8. The phrase "Crackpot Realism" is from C. Wright Mills. For a nice vignette of the Power Elite that Mills despised, see Peter Davis, "The High and the Mighty Crowd," *Esquire,* June 1985, esp. p. 225.

9. I. F. Stone was the best single critic of the willful blindness of policy elites throughout the Vietnam War. See especially his *Polemics and Prophecies, 1967–1970* (New York: Random House, 1970); and *In a Time of Torment* (New York: Random House, 1967), pp. 54–105, 178–261.

10. Oberdorfer, *Tet!,* pp. 115–235, 237–77.

11. Peter Braestrup, *Big Story: How the American Press and Television Reported and Interpreted the Crisis of Tet, 1968, in Vietnam and Washington,* abr. ed. (New Haven: Yale University Press, 1983), pp. 465–507.

12. Todd Gitlin, *The Sixties: Years of Hope, Days of Rage* (New York: Bantam Books, 1987), pp. 97–135; 177–83; 242–49; 261–74.

13. Braestrup, *Big Story,* p. 471.

14. Richard L. Schott and Dagmar S. Hamilton, *People, Positions, and Power: The Political Appointment of Lyndon Johnson* (Chicago: University of Chicago Press, 1983), pp. 96–102.

15. Eric F. Goldman, *The Tragedy of Lyndon Johnson* (New York: Knopf, 1969), pp. 394–531; Doris Kearns, *Lyndon Johnson and the American Dream* (New York: Harper & Row, 1976), pp. 295–301.

16. Kim McQuaid, *Big Business and Presidential Power: From F.D.R. to Reagan* (New York: Morrow, 1982), pp. 223–58; Vaughn D. Bornet, *The Presidency of Lyndon B. Johnson* (Lawrence: University Press of Kansas, 1983), pp. 233–45.

17. *Public Papers of the Presidents of the United States: Lyndon B. Johnson, 1968–69,* vol. 1 (Washington, D.C.: Government Printing Office, 1970), pp. 469–76.

18. Arthur Herzog, *McCarthy for President* (New York: Viking, 1969), pp. 3, 17, 45, 71. McCarthy's autobiographical version of events is *The Year of the People* (Garden City, N.Y.: Doubleday, 1969).

19. John Galloway's *The Gulf of Tonkin Resolution* (Rutherford, N.J.: Fairleigh Dickinson University Press, 1970) is the best single source.

20. Herzog, *McCarthy for President,* pp. 25–35, 70–71; Chester, Hodgson, and Page, *American Melodrama,* pp. 58–67.

21. Chester, Hodgson, and Page, *American Melodrama,* pp. 65–67.

22. Herzog, *McCarthy for President,* p. 35.

23. Braestrup, *Big Story,* p. 506; Whalen, *Catch the Falling Flag,* p. 90.

24. Herzog, *McCarthy for President,* pp. 105–106; McCarthy, *Year of the People,* pp. 88–95. The pro-RFK version of these events is given in Arthur Schlesinger, Jr., *Robert Kennedy and His Times* (Boston: Houghton Mifflin, 1978), pp. 822–71.

25. The details of the Kennedy-McCarthy meetings are all covered in Herzog, *McCarthy for President,* pp. 105–106; and Chester, Hodgson, and Page, *American Melodrama,* pp. 105–26.

26. Ibid., p. 125. See also Herzog, *McCarthy for President,* passim.

27. For the quandaries of the liberals see Chester, Hodgson, and Page, *American Melodrama,* pp. 56, 58. See also Norman Podhoretz, *Why We Were in Vietnam* (New York: Simon & Schuster, 1982), pp. 110, 194, 204–206; and Charles R. Morris, *A Time of Passion: America, 1960–1980* (New York: Harper & Row, 1984), pp. 100–101.

28. Bornet, *Presidency of Lyndon B. Johnson,* p. 272.

29. For an early and representative cross-section of liberal and other statements on Vietnam, see Marvin E. Gettleman, ed., *Vietnam: History, Documents, and Opinions on a Major World Crisis* (New York: Fawcett, 1965), esp. pp. 282–438.

30. Allen J. Matusow, *The Unravelling of America: A History of Liberalism in the 1960's* (New York: Harper & Row, 1984), pp. 378–79.

31. Karnow, *Vietnam: A History* (New York: Viking Penguin, 1983), pp. 375–76, 491. Senator Morse was defeated for re-election by Republican Robert Packwood in 1968. Criticism of Morse's votes against Vietnam war funding were an especial item in Packwood's campaign arsenal. Senator Gruening was also defeated in 1968.

32. William J. Fulbright, *The Arrogance of Power* (New York: Random House, 1966), pp. 5, 9, 15.

33. Ibid., p. 77.

34. Ibid., p. 17.

35. Ibid., p. 119.

36. Ibid., pp. 188–96. Fulbright also argued for the unification and eventual neutralization of Vietnam in a stronger fashion than either Kennedy or McCarthy in 1968.

37. For the effect of war on race relations, see Richard Polenberg, *One Nation Divisible: Class, Race, and Ethnicity in the United States since 1938* (New York: Viking Penguin, 1980), pp. 231–50.

38. William C. Westmoreland, *A Soldier Reports* (Garden City, N.Y.: Doubleday, 1976), p. 362.

39. For the Columbia events, see Jerry A. Avorn and the members of the staff of the *Columbia Daily Spectator, Up Against the Ivy Wall: A History of the Columbia Crisis,* edited by Robert Friedman (New York: Atheneum, 1969).

40. Chester, Hodgson, and Page, *American Melodrama,* p. 548. For the "charisma" point, see ibid., pp. 307–10.

41. James Simon Kunen, *The Strawberry Statement: Notes of a College Revolutionary* (New York: Avon reprint, 1970), pp. 66–67.

42. For a good survey, see Daniel Walker et al., *Rights in Conflict: Chicago's Seven Brutal Days, A Report Submitted by . . . the Chicago Study Team to the National Commission on the Causes and Prevention of Violence* (New York: Grosset & Dunlap, 1968).

43. Chester, Hodgson, and Page, *American Melodrama,* pp. 414–15.

44. Ibid., p. 145.

45. Ibid., pp. 566–67, 574–75.

46. For details about how the Daley, Johnson, and Humphrey forces rigged the convention itself, see Norman Mailer, *Miami and the Siege of Chicago: An Informal History of the Republican and Democratic Conventions of 1968* (New York: New American Library, 1968), pp. 104–105, 113–15, 160, 199, 206.

47. Chester, Hodgson, and Page, *American Melodrama,* pp. 593–604.

48. Ibid., pp. 585–86 et seq. Mailer's *Miami and the Siege of Chicago* is also required reading.

49. Joe McGinniss, *The Selling of the President, 1968* (New York: Pocket Books, 1969), p. 104.

50. Ibid., p. 25.

51. Ibid., pp. 19, 32–33.

52. Chester, Hodgson, and Page, *American Melodrama,* pp. 434–63, 178–207, 219; Lou Cannon, *Reagan* (New York: Putnam, 1982), pp. 157–65.

53. McGinniss, *Selling of the President,* pp. 78–80, 129.

54. For unhysterical views of the conservative shift of which the Wallace movement was such a high-profile part, see Kevin Phillips, *Post-Conservative America* (New York: Random House, 1982); Alan Crawford, *Thunder on the Right: The "New Right" and the Politics of Resentment* (New York: Pantheon, 1980); and Donald I. Warren, *The Radical Center: Middle Americans and the Politics of Alienation* (Notre Dame, Ind.: Notre Dame University Press), 1976.

55. Chester, Hodgson, and Page, *American Melodrama,* pp. 702, 706–10, 717, 764.

56. Ibid., 737 ff.

57. Ibid., pp. 699–700.

58. Ibid., pp. 700–56.

59. Ibid., pp. 628–29. For Agnew's rhetorical style, see Spiro T. Agnew, *Frankly Speaking: A Collection of Extraordinary Speeches* (Washington, D.C.: Public Affairs Press, 1970)

60. Chester, Hodgson, and Page, *American Melodrama,* pp. 647–49.

61. Godfrey Hodgson, *America in Our Time: From World War II to Nixon, What Happened and Why* (Garden City, N.Y.: Doubleday, 1976), p. 136.

62. Chester, Hodgson, and Page, *American Melodrama,* p. 747.

## PART TWO / *VIETNAM, INCORPORATED*

1. Three general histories are exceedingly helpful for anyone trying to understand the U.S. and Vietnamese background to the Vietnam War. These are Frances Fitzgerald, *Fire in the Lake:*

*The Vietnamese and the Americans in Vietnam* (Boston: Atlantic, Little Brown, 1972), George C. Herring, *America's Longest War: The United States and Vietnam, 1950–1975* (New York: Wiley, 1979); Stanley Karnow, *Vietnam: A History* (New York: Viking, 1983).

2. Quoted in Norman Podhoretz, *Why We Were in Vietnam* (New York: Simon & Schuster, 1982), pp. 49–55.

3. Loren Baritz, *Backfire: A History of How American Culture Led Us into Vietnam and Made Us Fight the Way We Did* (New York: Morrow, 1985), p. 42. Charles R. Morris, *A Time of Passion: America, 1960–1980* (New York: Harper & Row, 1984), p. 42.

4. David Halberstam, *The Best and the Brightest* (New York: Random House, 1972), p. 248.

5. "In the long history of the world, only a few generations have been granted the role of defending freedom in its hour of maximum danger. I do not shrink from that responsibility, I welcome it." So John F. Kennedy announced in his Inaugural Address on 20 January 1961. See John W. Gardner, ed., *To Turn the Tide* (New York: Harper & Row, 1962), esp. p. 10.

6. Morris, *Time of Passion,* p. 27; Louis Heren, *No Hail, No Farewell* (New York: Harper & Row, 1970), pp. 102–103.

7. Halberstam, *Best and Brightest,* pp. 213–14.

8. Henry Trewhitt, *McNamara: His Ordeal in the Pentagon* (New York: Harper & Row, 1971), pp. 86–88. See also Gregory Palmer, *The McNamara Strategy and the Vietnam War* (Westport, Conn.: Greenwood Press, 1978), p. 58.

9. Trewhitt, *McNamara,* pp. 201, 197.

10. Daniel Yankelovitch as quoted in *Atlantic Monthly,* September 1972, p. 54.

11. Halberstam, *Best and Brightest,* pp. 258–59.

12. Trewhitt, *McNamara,* p. 232.

13. Anthony R. Herbert with James Wooten, *Soldier* (New York: Dell, 1973), pp. 127–28, 211, 241, 268; Baritz, *Backfire,* pp. 292–302.

14. Ibid., pp. 292, 302; Herbert and Wooten, *Soldier,* pp. 127–28, 211, 241, 268.

15. William R. Corson, *The Betrayal* (New York: Norton, 1968), pp. 147–48.

16. Baritz, *Backfire,* pp. 307–309, 311. The tour of duty of the average civilian adviser in South Vietnam, who did not speak Vietnamese, was eighteen months to two years. See Don Luce and John Sommer, *Vietnam: The Unheard Voices* (Ithaca, N.Y.: Cornell University Press, 1969), pp. 203–206.

17. James Fallows, *National Defense* (New York: Random House, 1981), pp. 117–20; William C. Westmoreland, *A Soldier Reports* (Garden City, N.Y.: Doubleday, 1976), p. 229; Douglas Kinnard, *The War Managers* (Hanover, N.H.: University Presses of New England for the University of Vermont, 1977), pp. 11–112; Baritz, *Backfire,* pp. 307, 309.

18. Baritz, *Backfire,* pp. 287, 284.

19. Kinnard, *War Managers,* p. 110. See also James Fallows, *National Defense,* pp. 117–20; and Cincinnatus, *Self-Destruction: The Deterioration and Decay of the U.S. Army during the Vietnam Era* (New York: Norton, 1981), passim.

20. The phrase "Vietnam, Incorporated" is from Philip Jones Griffiths's fine photo-essay of the same name (New York: Macmillan, 1971).

21. Arnold R. Isaacs, *Without Honor: Defeat in Vietnam and Cambodia* (Baltimore: Johns Hopkins University Press, 1983), p. 161; Kinnard, *War Managers,* p. 46; Baritz, *Backfire,* pp. 110, 148–49.

22. Robert Pisor, *The End of the Line: The Siege of Khe Sanh* (New York: Ballantine, 1983), pp. 39, 6–7, 17.

23. "Dr. Strangelove," a character in a 1961 movie of the same name by filmmaker Stanley Kubrick, was a mad scientist character to whom high technology—and in particular, thermonuclear high technology—was the answer to every question.

24. Corson, *Betrayal,* p. 250.

25. Baritz, *Backfire,* p. 323.

26. Westmoreland, *A Soldier Reports,* p. 200. For the McNamara line, see Paul Dickson, *Electronic Battlefield* (Bloomington: Indiana University Press, 1976), pp. 21–49, 76; Pisor, *End of the Line,* pp. 86, 114, 230–32; Ernest B. Furgurson, *Westmoreland: The Inevitable General* (Boston: Little, Brown, 1968), pp. 320–31; Halberstam, *Best and Brightest,* p. 630; Trewhitt, *McNamara,* p. 162.

27. For all the quotes here, see Westmoreland, as quoted in Appendix A of Dickson's fine *Electronic Battlefield,* pp. 215–23, esp. pp. 220–21.

28. Pisor, *End of the Line,* p. 192. See also Baritz, *Backfire,* p. 110.

29. Peter Braestrup, *Big Story: How the American Press and Television Reported and Interpreted the Crisis*

*of Tet 1968 in Vietnam and Washington,* abr. ed. (New Haven: Yale University Press, 1982), p. 177; from Edward Gibbon, *The Decline and Fall of the Roman Empire* in *The Portable Edward Gibbon,* edited by Dero A. Saunders. (New York: Viking, 1980), p. 229.

30. Dickson, *Electronic Battlefield,* p. 196.
31. Ibid., pp. 201, 208–209.
32. Griffiths, *Vietnam, Incorporated,* p. 55.
33. Westmoreland, *A Soldier Reports,* pp. 164, 387; Pisor, *End of the Line,* p. 53.
34. Daniel Ellsberg, quoted in Podhoretz, *Why We Were in Vietnam,* pp. 46–47; Braestrup, *Big Story,* pp. 8–11, fn. p. 13, p. 531; Godfrey Hodgson, *America in Our Time: From World War II to Nixon, What Happened and Why* (Garden City, N.Y.: Doubleday, 1976), p. 127; Luce and Sommer, *Vietnam,* p. 206.
35. Luce and Sommer, *Vietnam,* p. 52.
36. The phrase "Political Chessmen" is from ibid., p. 22.
37. Ibid., pp. 34–35.
38. Ibid., p. xiii.
39. Charles A. Joiner, *The Politics of Massacre: Political Processes in South Vietnam* (Philadelphia: Temple University Press, 1974), p. 3.
40. Ibid., p. 23.
41. Nguyen Cao Ky, *Twenty Years and Twenty Days* (New York: Stein & Day, 1976), pp. 45–46; Isaacs, *Without Honor,* pp. 119–20.
42. Ibid., pp. 102–103.
43. For Chiang Kai-shek's effort to use weakness as a strength in his bargaining with American policymakers, see Sterling Seagrave, *The Soong Dynasty* (New York: Harper & Row, 1985), esp. pp. 394 ff.
44. Larry Berman, *Planning a Tragedy: The Americanization of the War in Vietnam* (New York: Norton, 1984), pp. 28–29; Joiner, *Politics of Massacre,* p. 192.
45. Luce and Sommer, *Vietnam,* p. 215.
46. Pham Van Dong, quoted in Baritz, *Backfire,* p. 100.
47. Ibid., p. 117; Isaacs, *Without Honor,* pp. 120–21; Luce and Sommer, *Vietnam,* p. 285; Ky, *Twenty Years,* pp. 124, 137.
48. Milovan Djilas, *Rise and Fall* (San Diego and New York: Harcourt Brace Jovanovich, 1985), pp. 142–78. Another relevant statement of Djilas's is that the American proconsuls in South Vietnam did not see "their task as being to understand" the Vietnamese—North or South—"but rather, to bring them to heel," just as Stalinist proconsuls did vis-à-vis postwar Yugoslavia (p. 142).
49. "Their Lions, Our Rabbits," *Newsweek,* 9 October 1967, p. 44. For General Westmoreland's critique of the approach, see *A Soldier Reports,* p. 251.
50. Isaacs, *Without Honor,* pp. 113–14.
51. Ibid., p, 129; Kinnard, *War Managers,* pp. 95 ff.
52. Garry Wills, *The Kennedy Imprisonment: A Meditation on Power* (New York: Pocket Books, 1982), pp. 294–95.
53. Isaacs, *Without Honor,* p. 126.
54. Ibid., pp. 126, 138–39.
55. Corson, *Betrayal,* pp. 278–79, 99, 109.
56. Ibid., pp. 101–102; 98–99, 180.
57. Anthony R. Herbert and James T. Wooten, *Soldier* (Englewood, Colo.: Cloverleaf Books reprint, 1979), p. 298.
58. Ibid., p. 205 ff.
59. Westmoreland, *A Soldier Reports,* pp. 251–54; Isaacs, *Without Honor,* pp. 102–103; Jonathan Schell, *The Village of Ben Suc* (New York: Random House, 1968), pp. 108–109; Corson, *Betrayal,* pp. 99–102.
60. Kinnard, *War Managers,* p. 98 fn.
61. Braestrup, *Big Story,* p. 337.
62. Pisor, *End of the Line,* p. 117. See also Tran Van Don, *Our Endless War Inside Vietnam* (San Rafael, Calif.: Presidio Press, 1978), chap. 9.
63. Ky, *Twenty Years,* pp. 172–73.
64. Stuart A. Herrington, *Silence Was a Weapon: The Vietnam War in the Villages* (Novato, Calif.: Presidio Press, 1982), pp. 31 ff; Corson, *Betrayal,* pp. 127–32; Joiner, *Politics of Massacre,* pp. 276, 286. Belated land reform began under the Thieu regime in 1970.

65. Luce and Sommer, *Vietnam*, pp. 160–61.

66. Kinnard, *War Managers*, pp. 56–57; Corson, *Betrayal*, pp. 104–105.

67. Ibid., pp. 262–90.

68. Robert F. Kennedy, *To Seek a Newer World* (London: Michael Joseph, 1968), p. 182.

69. Luce and Sommer, *Vietnam*, pp. 89 ff; Joiner, *Politics of Massacre*, pp. 228 ff.; Baritz, *Backfire*, pp. 24, 39. The monk's quote is from Luce and Sommer, *Vietnam*, pp. 267–68.

70. Ibid., pp. 267–78. See also Isaacs, *Without Honor*, pp. 89 ff.; Joiner, *Politics of Massacre*, pp. 229 ff; and Baritz, *Backfire*, pp. 24, 39.

71. The best single source for the effect of the uprooting of Vietnamese from their villages is Schell, *Village of Ben Suc.*

72. Braestrup, *Big Story*, p. 403.

73. Luce and Sommer, *Vietnam*, pp. 183–84; Ky, *Twenty Years*, pp. 140–50.

74. Schell, *Village of Ben Suc*, passim; Luce and Sommer, *Vietnam*, pp. 165–75, esp. p. 170; Joiner, *Politics of Massacre*, p. 285; Stephen A. Ambrose, *Rise to Globalism: American Foreign Policy since 1938*, 4th rev. ed. (New York: Viking Penguin paperback, 1985), p. 246; Westmoreland, *A Soldier Reports*, p. 332; Griffiths, *Vietnam, Incorporated*, p. 77.

75. Corson, *Betrayal*, pp. 213–14, 216–17, 232–33, 240; Luce and Sommer, *Vietnam*, pp. 275 ff; Kinnard, *War Managers*, pp. 100, 103–108, 143.

76. Ibid., pp. 107–108. See also Corson, *Betrayal*, pp. 232–34.

77. Kinnard, *War Managers*, p. 143.

78. Stanley Karnow, *Vietnam*, and Herring, *America's Longest War*, are best for an overview of diplomatic strategies during the war. For a useful compilation of official statements, see U.S. Senate, Foreign Relations Committee, 93d Cong., 2d sess., *Background Information Relating to Southeast Asia and Vietnam*, 7th rev. ed. (Washington, D.C.: Government Printing Office, 1975).

79. Herring, *America's Longest War*, pp. 235–37.

80. For a good summary of the Nixon-Kissinger approach, see Karnow, *Vietnam*, pp. 588–612.

81. Herring, *America's Longest War*, pp. 221–24.

82. Karnow, *Vietnam*, p. 491.

83. Baritz, *Backfire*, pp. 199–200.

84. See, for example, the discussion in Karnow, *Vietnam*, pp. 634–35.

85. Berman, *Planning a Tragedy*, pp. 8–9.

86. Jonathan Schell, *The Time of Illusion: An Historical and Reflective Account of the Nixon Era* (New York: Vintage paperback ed., 1977), pp. 362–63. See also Richard J. Whalen, *Catch the Falling Flag: A Republican's Challenge to His Party* (Boston: Houghton Mifflin, 1972), p. 137.

87. For the Huston Plan, see Theodore H. White, *Breach of Faith: The Fall of Richard Nixon* (New York: Atheneum–Reader's Digest, 1975), pp. 134–36.

88. Isaacs, *Without Honor*, p. 493.

89. Herring, *America's Longest War*, pp. 231–33.

90. For material on Cambodia, see William Shawcross, *Sideshow: Kissinger, Nixon, and the Destruction of Cambodia* (New York: Simon & Schuster, 1979); and Isaacs, *Without Honor*. Isaacs is the best single source for post–1971 developments regarding Vietnam.

91. Karnow, *Vietnam*, pp. 638–39.

92. Richard M. Nixon, *RN: The Memoirs of Richard Nixon* (New York: Grosset & Dunlap, 1978), pp. 544–624; Henry Kissinger, *White House Years* (Boston: Little, Brown, 1979), pp. 144–45, 160–61 ff.

93. Karnow, *Vietnam*, pp. 639–40; Ambrose, *Rise to Globalism*, pp. 238–40; Raymond L. Garthoff, *Détente and Confrontation: American-Soviet Relations from Nixon to Reagan* (Washington, D.C.: Brookings Institution, 1985), pp. 69–261.

94. Karnow, *Vietnam*, pp. 647–48; Isaacs, *Without Honor*, pp. 57–68.

95. Karnow, *Vietnam*, pp. 651–54; Isaacs, *Without Honor*, pp. 49–50; Herring, *America's Longest War*, p. 249; Seyom Brown, *The Faces of Power: Constancy and Change in U.S. Foreign Policy from Truman to Reagan* (New York: Columbia University Press, 1983), p. 379; Weldon A. Brown, *The Last Chopper: The Denouement of the American Role in Vietnam, 1963–1975* (Port Washington, N.Y.: Kennicot, 1976), pp. 312–13.

96. Joiner, *Politics of Massacre*, pp. 145, 166, 170–71.

97. Podhoretz, *Why We Were in Vietnam*, p. 141; Kissinger, *White House Years*, p. 1032.

Kissinger, in discussing the nuts and bolts of the peace accords later in his book, avoids reiterating this supremely obvious point.

98. Isaacs, *Without Honor,* pp. 61–68.

99. Nixon, *RN,* pp. 742–43.

100. See, for example, Garthoff, *Détente and Confrontation,* pp. 434–37; and Herring, *America's Longest War,* pp. 251, 255–56.

101. Nixon, *RN,* pp. 887–89.

102. Shawcross, *Sideshow,* pp. 287–88; *New York Times,* 17 July 1973, p. I, col. 1.

103. Isaacs, *Without Honor,* pp. 303–304, 313–14; Herring, *America's Longest War,* pp. 257–58; Karnow, *Vietnam,* p. 661. These figures, like much else about Vietnam, are very slippery.

104. Isaacs, *Without Honor,* pp. 299–300, 329; Karnow, *Vietnam,* pp. 660–61. For the view from the North Vietnamese side, see General Van Tien Dung, *Our Great Spring Victory: An Account of the Liberation of South Vietnam . . .* (New York: Monthly Review Press, 1977); and General Vo Nguyen Giap and Van Tien Dung, *How We Won the War* (Philadelphia: RECON Publications, 1980).

105. George H. Gallup, *The Gallup Poll: Public Opinion, 1972–1977,* vol. 1, *1972–1975* (Wilmington, Del.: Scholarly Resources, 1978), p. 456.


## PART THREE / *THE NEW LEFT AND AFTERWARD*

1. C. Wright Mills, "Letter to the New Left," (1962) in *The New Left: A Collection of Essays,* edited by Priscilla Long (Boston: Porter-Sargent, 1969), pp. 14–25.

2. Garry Wills, *The Kennedy Imprisonment: A Meditation on Power* (New York: Pocket Books, 1982), p. 283.

3. "Corporate liberal" analysis in America in this period was often based on the work of three historians: William Appleman Williams, especially *The Contours of American History* (Cleveland: World, 1961); Gabriel Kolko, especially *The Triumph of Conservatism: A Reinterpretation of American History, 1900–1916* (Glencoe, Ill.: Free Press, 1963); and James Weinstein, *The Corporate Ideal in the Liberal State* (Boston: Beacon, 1968).

For two early compilations of "corporate liberal" essays, see Barton J. Bernstein, ed., *Towards a New Past: Dissenting Essays in American History* (New York: Random House, 1968); and Ronald Radosh and Murray N. Rothbard, eds., *A New History of Leviathan: Essays on the Rise of the American Corporate State* (New York: Dutton, 1972).

4. Charles R. Morris, *A Time of Passion: America, 1960–1980* (New York: Harper & Row, 1984); Kim McQuaid, *Big Business and Presidential Power: From F.D.R. to Reagan* (New York: Morrow, 1982), pp. 236–37; Norman Moore, *The Neurotic Trillionaire* (New York: Harcourt Brace, 1970), pp. 20–30; Jonathan R. T. Hughes, *American Economic History,* 2d ed. (Glenview, Ill.: Scott, Foresman, 1987), p. 561.

5. Michael Harrington, Introduction to *A Prophetic Minority,* by Jack Newfield (New York: New American Library, paperback ed., 1966), p. 18.

6. Todd Gitlin, *The Whole World Is Watching: Mass Media in the Making and Un-Making of the New Left* (Berkeley: University of California Press, 1980), p. 186. See also idem, *The Sixties: Years of Hope, Days of Rage* (New York: Bantam, 1987); and Myra MacPherson, *Long Time Passing: Vietnam and the Haunted Generation* (Garden City, N.Y.: Doubleday, 1984), pp. 127, 149. Gitlin's two books are especially valuable for their discussion of New Left dynamics.

7. Gitlin, *The Sixties,* pp. 165–66, 225–26, 366; Gitlin, *The Whole World,* pp. 167–68, 203–204.

8. None of what I argue here ignores the fact that the Civil Rights movement in the South from 1961 to approximately the middle of 1965 was a key formative political experience for important New Left leaders, and particularly those connected with the student Non-Violent Coordinating Committee (SNCC) and the SDS. Between 1965 and 1967–68, however, separatism had become the norm within SNCC, and the SDS, the Trotskyist Young Socialist Alliance, and other New Left organizations had become almost completely lily white, to the frustration of many New Left leaders.

By the time, then, that the SDS's and other New Left groups' memberships really began to surge upward during 1966, 1967, and 1968, white college and university youth came to compose a very decided majority within New Left ranks and interracial cooperation (for civil rights or anything else) was at best a spotty proposition. Civil rights continued to provide important organizing principles and patterns of thought for New Left organizations and their leaders, however. These are dealt with later in the chapter, when the perils and possibilities of "participatory democracy" are discussed.

The author, then, is not arguing that civil rights were irrelevant. He is contending that younger (than twenty-two) New Leftists who composed the bulk of the membership of SDS and allied groups during and after the polarizing events of 1968 were relatively unacquainted with hands-on biracial cooperation. Such facts only decreased the ability of New Left organizations to move beyond the isolation of an elite collegiate base.

To be, for instance, a young man from Maine working as a psychiatric social worker in Harlem in New York City (and also living there) in early 1967 was to realize that New Left outreach into this largest single black ghetto in the United States was essentially nonexistent. Other important New Left demonstrations (like those based at the University of California, Berkeley, during the People's Park events of early 1969) benefitted little from interracial anything, even though the Black Panthers were headquartered, at that time, in immediately neighboring Oakland. The New Left, bluntly, signally failed to build upon the civil-rights experience as part of an interracial political organizing strategy. It was simply too afraid of Black Power separatism to try very hard.

9. Kenneth Kenniston, *Youth and Dissent: The Rise of a New Opposition* (New York: Harcourt Brace Jovanovich, 1971), pp. 143–72, 213, 229, 269–86, 318–38, 369–400. See also his *Young Radicals: Notes on Committed Youth* (New York: Harcourt Brace Jovanovich, 1968), esp. pp. 257–90.

10. Stephen Cohen, quoted in MacPherson, *Long Time Passing,* p. 127, puts the matter thus: "That [upper-class] guilt led to looking for an easy, quick catharsis."

11. The King = Communist equation also affected the FBI throughout the early 1960s. See, for example, David J. Garrow, *The F.B.I. and Martin Luther King, Jr.* (New York: Penguin, 1983), pp. 78–100 ff.; U.S. Senate, 94th Cong., 2d sess., *Final Report of the Select Committee to Study Governmental Operations with Respect to Intelligence Activities: Supplementary Detailed Staff Reports of Intelligence Activities and the Rights of Americans,* vol. 3 (Washington, D.C.: Government Printing Office, 1976), pp. 79–184.

12. Henry Fairlie, *The Kennedy Promise: The Politics of Expectation* (Garden City, N.Y.: Doubleday, 1973), p. 247; "Students: The Personalists," *Time,* 22 November 1963, pp. 44, 47.

13. Newfield, *Prophetic Minority,* p. 198.

14. Jonathan Schell, *The Time of Illusion: An Historical and Reflective Account of the Vietnam Era* (New York: Vintage paperback, 1977), remains the best single source for the dilemmas of cold war theology in this period.

15. Ibid., pp. 368–69. See also Robert Brustein, *Revolution as Theatre: Notes on the New Radical Style* (New York: Boni & Liverwright, 1971), passim; and Morris, *A Time of Passion,* pp. 123–24.

16. MacPherson, *Long Time Passing,* p. 33.

17. Godfrey Hodgson, *From World War II to Nixon: What Happened and Why* (Garden City, N.Y.: Doubleday, 1976), pp. 393–94.

18. Ibid., pp. 384–85, 387, 392.

19. Lewis Chester, Godfrey Hodgson, and Bruce Page, *An American Melodrama: The Presidential Campaign of 1968* (New York: Viking, 1969), pp. 62 ff.

20. Tom Wolfe, *Radical Chic and Mau-Mau-ing the Flak Catchers* (New York: Farrar, Straus, & Giroux, 1970).

21. Newfield, *Prophetic Minority,* p. 159.

22. Assar Lindbeck, *The Political Economy of the New Left: An Outsider's View* (New York: Harper & Row, 1971), pp. 36–37 and passim. See also James Simon Kunen, *The Strawberry Statement: Notes of a College Revolutionary* (New York: Avon reprint, 1970), pp. 77, 128; Raymond Mungo, *Famous Long Ago: My Life and Hard Times with Liberation News Service* (New York: Pocket Books, 1971), pp. 45, 118, 134.

23. The term "The Movement" was commonplace during the years after 1968. For a representative example of its use to string disparate groups together into a falsely unified whole, see Bruce Franklin, *From the Movement: Toward Revolution* (New York: Van Nostrand Reinhold, 1971). This book of readings and commentary, significantly, was designed as a text for college students trying to puzzle out what was happening on the left after Tet.

24. For Agnew's "radical liberal" and other statements, see Spiro T. Agnew, *Frankly Speaking: A Collection of Extraordinary Speeches* (Washington, D.C.: Public Affairs Press, 1970), esp. pp. 9–36, 44–51.

25. For examples of just how undiscriminating Johnson- and Nixon-era fears could be, see U.S. Senate, 94th Cong., 2d sess., *Final Report of the Select Committee*. The author's alma mater, Antioch College, was deemed to be the "vanguard of the New Left" by the FBI on page 5 of this report.

26. Agnew, *Frankly Speaking,* pp. 86–99.

27. Author's personal observations on the scene. The more obstreperous members of the fleeing crowd broke several windows at one of the museums at the Smithsonian Institution. Medical teams, to give credit where credit is due, performed ably, well, and without panic during these and other demonstrations.

28. U.S. Senate, *Final Report,* pp. 185–225. For a good collection of the Black Panthers' political and racist statements, see Phillip S. Foner, ed., *The Black Panthers Speak* (Philadelphia: Lippincott, 1970); and Gail Sheehy, *Panthermania: The Clash of Black against Black* (New York: Harper & Row, 1971), passim.

29. Gitlin, *Whole World Is Watching,* p. 279.

30. Lawrence M. Baskir and William A. Straus, *Change and Circumstance: The Draft, the War, and the Vietnam Generation* (New York: Knopf, 1978), passim; MacPherson, *Long Time Passing,* pp. 27, 94–99, 131, 354, 377–82, 461; Todd Gitlin, "Seizing History," *Mother Jones,* November 1983, pp. 35–36.

31. Charles Macomb Flandrau, *Harvard Episodes* (New York: Stokes, 1897), p. 15.

32. The best single contemporary source on the counterculture remains Nicholas von Hoffman, *We Are the People Our Parents Warned Us against* (Chicago: Quadrangle, 1968).

33. Allen J. Matusow, *The Unravelling of America: A History of Liberalism in the 1960s* (New York: Harper & Row, 1984), pp. 335–36.

34. Gitlin, *The Sixties,* pp. 377–408; idem, *The Whole World Is Watching,* pp. 1, 156, 176, 241, 285–86.

35. Isaac Asimov, *Foundation's Edge* (London: Granada, 1984), p. 369.

36. Schell, *Time of Illusion,* pp. 148–51. See also Ron Kovic, *Born on the Fourth of July* (New York: McGraw-Hill, 1976).

37. H. F. Harding, ed., *The Speeches of Thucydides* (Lawrence, Kan.: Coronado Press, 1973), p. 87.

38. See, for instance, *Newsweek's* special issue, "The Legacy of Vietnam," 15 March 1985, p. 37.

## PART FOUR / *WATERGATE*

1. La Rochefoucauld, *Maxims,* translated by L. W. Tancock (Baltimore: Penguin, 1959), p. 85.

2. For the personal factors in Nixon's career, see Stephen E. Ambrose, *Nixon: The Education of a Politician, 1913–1962* (New York: Simon & Schuster, 1987); and Fawn M. Brodie, *Richard Nixon: The Shaping of His Character* (New York: Norton, 1981).

3. Richard J. Whalen, *Catch the Falling Flag: A Republican's Challenge to His Party* (Boston: Houghton Mifflin, 1972), p. 362.

4. David Halberstam, *The Powers That Be* (New York: Knopf, 1979), p. 620.

5. *New York Times,* 16 May 1980, pt. 2, p. 4, col. 1; ibid, 9 August 1980, p. 43, col. 1. Rock star Alice Cooper, not to be outdone, reportedly asked the GSA to borrow five of the palace guard uniforms for a concert, but he was refused.

6. *Public Papers of the Presidents: Richard M. Nixon, 1973* (Washington, D.C.: Government Printing Office, 1975), pp. 12–15.

7. La Rochefoucauld, *Maxims,* p. 77.

8. Richard M. Nixon, *RN: The Memoirs of Richard Nixon* (New York: Grosset & Dunlap, 1978), pp. 351–52.

9. Theodore J. Lowi, *The End of Liberalism: The Second Republic of the United States,* 2d ed. (New York: Norton, 1979), chap. 3.

10. The best edition is Mike Gravel, ed., *The Pentagon Papers,* 5 vols. (Boston: Beacon Press, 1971).

11. Thomas Powers, *The Man Who Kept the Secrets: Richard Helms and the C.I.A.* (New York: Knopf, 1979), pp. 249–50.

12. Dan Rather and Gary Paul Gates, *The Palace Guard* (New York: Harper & Row, 1974), p. 286. This Green Beret slogan was one that Colson "proudly displayed over the bar in his den." Ibid.

13. Richard Ben-Veniste and George Frampton, Jr., *Stonewall: The Real Story of the Watergate Prosecution* (New York: Simon & Schuster, 1977), pp. 49–50.

14. For the plumbers' unit, see John J. Sirica with John F. Stacks, *To Set the Record Straight: The Break-in, the Tapes, the Conspirators, the Pardon* (New York: Norton, 1979), pp. 44–47; John Dean, *Blind Ambition: The White House Years* (New York: Simon & Schuster, 1976), pp. 26–88.

15. *Public Papers of the Presidents of the United States: Richard Nixon, 1971,* pp. 819–20.

16. For the details of the "freeze," see Arnold R. Weber, *In Pursuit of Price Stability: The Wage-Price Freeze of 1971* (Washington, D.C.: Brookings Institution, 1973), esp. pp. 1–9.

17. Good surveys of the political, diplomatic, and economic initiatives discussed here include Rowland Evans and Robert Novak, *Nixon in the White House: The Frustration of Power* (New York: Random House, 1971); A. James Reichley, *Conservatives in an Age of Change: The Nixon and Ford Administrations* (Washington, D.C.: Brookings Institution, 1981); Leonard Silk, *Nixonomics: How the Dismal Science of Free Enterprise Became the Black Art of Controls* (New York: Praeger, 1972); Richard M. Nixon, *RN: The Memoirs of Richard Nixon* (New York: Grosset & Dunlap, 1978), pp. 351–52 ff; Craufurd D. Goodwin, ed., *Exhortation and Controls* (Washington, D.C.: Brookings Institution, 1975), pp. 295–352; and Raymond L. Garthoff, *Détente and Confrontation: American-Soviet Relations from Nixon to Reagan* (Washington, D.C.: Brookings Institution, 1985).

18. C. P. Snow, quoted in Loren Baritz, *Backfire: A History of How American Culture Led Us into Vietnam and Made Us Fight the Way We Did* (New York: Morrow, 1985), p. 227.

19. G. Gordon Liddy, *Will: The Autobiography of G. Gordon Liddy* (New York: Dell, 1980), pp. 236–37, 273–77; Ben-Veniste and Frampton, *Stonewall,* pp. 45–46; Dean, *Blind Ambition,* pp. 79–87.

20. Carl Bernstein and Bob Woodward, *All the President's Men* (New York: Simon & Schuster, 1974) is the classic version of these events. The book covers events up to the beginning of the Senate Watergate Committee's hearings in May 1973. The title of the book comes from a statement of then-National Security Adviser Henry Kissinger during the Cambodian invasion of April 1970. When arguing against the decision of several key National Security Council aides to resign over the issue, Kissinger is reported to have said, "We are all the President's Men, and we've got to behave that way." Quoted in Bob Woodward and Carl Bernstein, *The Final Days* (New York: Simon & Schuster, 1976), p. 192.

21. Odell Shepard, ed., *The Heart of Thoreau's Journals* (Boston: Houghton Mifflin, 1927), p. 58.

22. For a good general treatment of all these events see Theodore H. White, *Breach of Faith: The Fall of Richard Nixon* (New York: Atheneum–Reader's Digest Press, 1975), pp. 161–68.

23. For the transcript of the essential segments of the Haldeman-Nixon meetings on 23 June 1972, at which this scheme was discussed, see Congressional Quarterly, *Watergate: Chronology of a Crisis* (Washington, D.C.: Congressional Quarterly, 1975), appendix, pp. 89A–91A.

24. Thomas Powers, *The Man Who Kept the Secrets: Richard Helms and the C.I.A.* (New York: Pocket Books reprint, 1981), pp. 325–45, 366–68, 378–90, 470–78, esp. pp. 334–35, for all the CIA–FBI bureaucratic gamesmanship discussed here.

25. Ibid., p. 336.

26. Ibid., pp. 131, 336 ff.

27. For the members of the "enemies list," see Congressional Quarterly, *Watergate,* p. 153. Dean was later surprised at the furor the list created when he released it to the Senate Watergate Committee, mostly because no revenge had been meted out to the twenty individuals on the list. Dean, *Blind Ambition,* pp. 316–17.

28. Sirica with Stacks, *To Set the Record Straight,* pp. 50–55.

29. Carl Bernstein and Bob Woodward, *All the President's Men* (New York: Simon & Schuster, 1974), pp. 113–14.

30. Ibid., pp. 126–28.

31. Ibid., p. 131.

32. Schell, *The Time of Illusion: An Historical and Reflective Account of the Vietnam Era* (New York:

Vintage paperback, 1977), pp. 287–89. An example of self-defeating Democratic smear rheto-ric was McGovern calling Nixon the "most deceitful president in history" and his administra-tion "the most corrupt in history" by October 1972. Ibid.

33. Sirica, quoted in Fred J. Cook, *The Crimes of Watergate* (New York: Franklin Watts, 1981), p. 94.

34. Sirica with Stacks, *To Set the Record Straight*, pp. 74–75.

35. Schell, *Time of Illusion*, pp. 305–306; Fred J. Cook, *The Crimes of Watergate* (New York: Franklin Watts, 1981) pp. 106–107.

36. Liddy, *Will*, pp. 350–53; Dean, *Blind Ambition*, pp. 98–99, 101, 287, 372. Liddy allows in *Will* that he always knew he would be convicted of Watergate crimes and that he told his lawyer well before the trial that he could not win his case; see pp. 338, 348.

By 1987, Liddy was a popular and well-paid speaker on the college and university lecture circuit, had enjoyed a cameo role on the popular TV law-and-order series "Miami Vice," and was providing "executive protection" services and training for healthy fees. Compared with evangelical prison reformer Chuck Colson or with Jeb Stuart Magruder, by then an ordained Presbyterian minister and the head of an Ohio State ethics commission, Liddy had benefitted greatly from his Watergate experience.

37. Bernstein and Woodward, *All the President's Men*, p. 241.

38. Ibid., p. 249.

39. David Halberstam, *The Powers That Be* (New York: Knopf, 1979), pp. 681–82.

40. Sirica, *To Set the Record Straight*, pp. 97, 106 ff. The climate of corroding suspicion that increasingly characterized the Watergate period is testified to by the fact that McCord gave his confession to Sirica, rather than to federal prosecutors or the FBI. He also secretly gave a copy of his confession to a reporter for the *Los Angeles Times*, with instructions to publish it if Sirica failed to make it public.

41. For the "Gray debacle," see Cook, *Crimes of Watergate*, pp. 99–104.

42. U.S. House of Representatives, *Hearings before the Committee on the Judiciary, 93d cong., 2d sess.: Transcripts of Eight Recorded Presidential Conversations"* (Washington, D.C.: Government Printing Office, 1974), p. 61.

43. Ibid., esp. pp. 101, 103.

44. Dean, *Blind Ambition*, p. 214.

45. Ben-Veniste and Frampton, *Stonewall*, p. 99.

46. Dean, in *Blind Ambition*, pp. 226–306, provides the best single source for the legal bargaining involved here.

47. *Public Papers of the Presidents, Richard Nixon, 1973*, p. 299; Cook, *Crimes of Watergate*, pp. 121–22.

48. Dean, *Blind Ambition*, pp. 273–74.

49. Ibid., pp. 328–33.

50. I take this key idea from Gladys Engel Lang and Kurt Lang, *The Battle for Public Opinion: The President, the Press, and the Polls during Watergate* (New York: Columbia University Press, 1983), p. 306.

51. The "national atmosphere" argument is well made in Schell, *Time of Illusion*, p. 317.

52. Lang and Lang, *Battle for Public Opinion*, p. 306; Schell, *Time of Illusion*, p. 317.

53. For a good discussion and tabular presentation of press coverage, see Lang and Lang, *Battle for Public Opinion*, pp. 49–59, esp. p. 50. For TV coverage in 1972, see ibid., p. 309.

54. The best sources for Dean's bargaining with the Senate Watergate Committee are Samuel Dash, *Chief Counsel: Inside the Ervin Committee, the Untold Story of Watergate* (New York: Random House, 1976), pp. 102–25; and Fred D. Thompson, *At That Point in Time: The Inside Story of the Senate Watergate Committee* (New York: Quadrangle–New York Times, 1975), pp. 60–70.

55. Dean, *Blind Ambition*, pp. 291–92.

56. The vivid ad hominem insult "bottom-dwelling slug" came from conservative Wash-ington columnist, Joseph Alsop. See, for instance, Dash, *Chief Counsel*, p. 145.

57. Charles R. Morris, *A Time of Passion: America, 1960–1980* (New York: Harper & Row, 1984), p. 102.

58. Dean, *Blind Ambition*, pp. 147–48.

59. A convenient source for the "impoundment" debate and its importance is James L. Sundquist, *The Decline and Resurgence of Congress* (Washington, D.C.: Brookings Institution, 1981), esp. pp. 1–4, 210–15.

60. Schell, *Time of Illusion*, pp. 309–11. Nixon publicly retreated from his absolutist approach toward executive privilege on 3 May 1973. See Congressional Quarterly, *Watergate*, p. 47.

61. Schell, *Time of Illusion*, p. 310.

62. Ibid., p. 313.

63. Ibid., pp. 295–97.

64. Ben-Veniste and Frampton, *Stonewall*, p. 363; James Doyle, *Not Above the Law: The Battles of Watergate Prosecutors Cox and Jaworski, a Behind-the-Scenes Account* (New York: Morrow, 1977), p. 95.

65. Dash, *Chief Counsel*, pp. 54–55, 67–69, 86–102, 112–14, 153–54, 169–74, 209–11; Dean, *Blind Ambition*, pp. 291, 302–303, 322–23; John Dean, *Lost Honor: The Rest of the Story* (Los Angeles: Stratford, 1982), pp. 228–29; Doyle, *Not Above the Law*, pp. 172–73. For a defense of Baker written by a longtime political associate, see Thompson, *At That Point in Time*, passim.

66. Congressional Quarterly, *Watergate*, p. 149.

67. Dean, *Blind Ambition*, p. 269.

68. Sam J. Ervin, Jr., *The Whole Truth: The Watergate Conspiracy* (New York: Random House, 1980), p. 187.

69. Dash, *Chief Counsel*, p. 180.

70. John Ehrlichman, *Witness to Power: The Nixon Years* (New York: Simon & Schuster, 1982), p. 393.

71. Congressional Quarterly, *Watergate*, pp. 104, 112, 176, 181, 218, 240, 242, 262, 264, 274, 296. According to Gallup polls, Nixon's approval ratings were at the lowest point of his presidency (44 percent) in mid-May. These figures stabilized in June. Then came Dean's and others' testimony to the Senate Watergate Committee. By mid-July, Nixon's approval rating had fallen to 40 percent, and by early August to 31 percent. During the same period, the percentage of Americans who believed Nixon should be impeached rose from 18 to 28 and the percentage of those who believed he should resign rose from 14 to 22.

72. Cox's defenders later argued that he attempted to postpone the Senate Watergate Committee's public hearings only to make a record to prevent any Watergate defendant's lawyer from arguing later that the special prosecutor had not tried to stop pretrial publicity from prejudicing his prosecution: see Dash, *Chief Counsel*, p. 145. I do not find this argument believable. For the legal principles involved, see Philip B. Kurland, *Watergate and the Constitution* (Chicago: University of Chicago Press, 1978), pp. 53–56.

73. Kurland, *Watergate and the Constitution*, p. 76; Ben-Veniste and Frampton, *Stonewall*, pp. 12, 15, 87; Doyle, *Not Above the Law*, pp. 33–45.

74. See Kurland, *Watergate and the Constitution*, p. 39, for the legal arguments for executive privilege.

75. Doyle, *Not Above the Law*, pp. 91–92, 94; Schell, *Time of Illusion*, pp. 285–86.

76. *Public Papers of the Presidents of the United States: Richard Nixon, 1973*, pp. 698–703.

77. Sirica with Stacks, *To Set the Record Straight*, pp. 180–81.

78. Ben Veniste and Frampton, *Stonewall*, is the best single source. See, for example, pp. 121–22, 158–66, 170–79, 181–86, 208–10, and 294–95.

79. Ibid., esp. pp. 122, 164–68, 174 ff, and 294–95. Who, precisely, edited and "lost" tapes is debatable. The fact that an eighteen-and-a-half minute gap and the "losing" of tapes did not occur by accident is not.

80. Ibid., pp. 126–29. Doyle, in *Not Above the Law*, discusses the various pressures Richardson operated under: pp. 108–10, 133–34, and 140–90.

81. Doyle, *Not Above the Law*, pp. 141–45; Morris, *A Time of Passion*, pp. 193 ff, and esp. pp. 246–49.

82. Sirica and Stacks sum up all the Machiavellian machinations preceding the Saturday Night Massacre when they write that: "Having constructed a [Stennis] compromise they knew Cox wouldn't accept, they [in the White House] decided that instead of having Cox fired after agreement upon the plan had been reached, they would get him fired now for not accepting the compromise." Sirica with Stacks, *To Set the Record Straight*, p. 165.

83. Ben-Veniste and Frampton, *Stonewall*, pp. 130–31; Dean, *Blind Ambition*, pp. 337–39. Dean's observation to his lawyer, when about to plead guilty, was: I think it's the right thing to do, but so did Custer." What he did took great courage, however much we may prefer to see him as a cardboard villain.

84. Doyle, *Not Above the Law*, pp. 138–71, is the best single source for the October events immediately preceding the firing of Archibald Cox.

85. Doyle, *Not Above the Law,* p. 204; Ben-Veniste and Frampton, *Stonewall,* pp. 141, 144.

86. Doyle, *Not Above the Law,* pp. 180–81.

87. Ibid., pp. 183–84.

88. Ibid., pp. 190–91; White, *Breach of Faith,* pp. 266–67.

89. Doyle, *Not Above the Law,* p. 194; Roger Morris, *Haig: The General's Progress* (Chicago: Playboy, 1982), p. 251.

90. One rule of thumb in American politics is that for every person who writes or phones or telegrams a Congressman personally on any issue, another ten-to-twenty equally concerned citizens do not. If half-a-million telegrams, letters, and phone calls reached Washington during the week after the Saturday Night Massacre, this means that as many as ten million voting adults vehemently opposed what Nixon had done. Ten million was approximately 13 percent of the 77.7 million people who had voted in the 1972 election. White, in *Breach of Faith,* p. 268, records the numbers of telegrams alone as totalling 450,000 at the end of ten days.

91. Edward Mezvinsky, *A Term to Remember* (New York: Coward, McCann, & Geohegan, 1977), p. 69.

92. Ibid., p. 66.

93. Tacitus, *The Annals of Imperial Rome,* translated and with an introduction by Michael Grant, rev. ed. (New York: Penguin, 1977), p. 174.

94. For the journalistic reaction, see, for example, White, *Breach of Faith,* pp. 268–69; Sirica with Stacks, *To Set the Record Straight,* p. 201; Gladys Ethel Lang and Kurt Lang, *The Battle for Public Opinion: The President, the Press, and the Polls during Watergate* (New York: Columbia University Press, 1982), pp. 99–105. *Time's* editorial appeared on 12 November 1973.

95. White, *Breach of Faith,* pp. 268–69.

96. Congressional Quarterly, *Watergate,* p. 433.

97. Ibid., pp. 353, 369.

98. Ibid., p. 360.

99. The best source for the trials and tribulations regarding the tapes is Ben-Veniste and Frampton, *Stonewall,* esp. pp. 187–205.

100. Congressional Quarterly, *Watergate,* p. 432; Elizabeth Drew, *Washington Journal: The Events of 1973–1974* (New York: Random House, 1976), p. 140.

101. For Sirica's and the first reactions of the attorneys of the Special Prosecutor's Office to hearing the Watergate tapes, see Sirica with Stacks, *To Set the Record Straight,* pp. 201–209; and Ben-Veniste and Frampton, *Stonewall,* pp. 199–203.

102. For a summary of the Teapot Dome episode and a comparison to Watergate, see ibid., p. 19.

103. Sirica with Stacks, *To Set the Record Straight,* pp. 212–13.

104. For the early tensions between Jaworski and his staff, see Leon Jaworski, *The Right and the Power: The Prosecution of Watergate* (New York: Reader's Digest Press, 1976), pp. 10–11, 22; and Ben-Veniste and Frampton, *Stonewall,* p. 187 ff.

105. Halberstam, *The Powers That Be,* pp. 693–94. *Time's* editors knew good fortune when they found it or it found them. Jaworsky was portrayed on *Time's* cover two weeks later, as one act of journalistic appreciation.

106. Congressional Quarterly, *Watergate,* pp. 512, 462–63.

107. For the story of the expert investigation of the eighteen-and-a-half-minute (and other) gaps, see Ben-Veniste and Frampton, *Stonewall,* pp. 172–76, 180–85, and esp. pp. 183–84.

108. Lang and Lang, *Battle for Public Opinion,* p. 304.

109. For the details, see Jaworski, *Right and Power,* pp. 87–108, esp. pp. 95–101; see also Doyle, *Not Above the Law,* pp. 280–81.

110. Ben-Veniste and Frampton, *Stonewall,* pp. 250–52; Doyle, *Not Above the Law,* p. 277.

111. Kim McQuaid, in *Big Business and Presidential Power: From F.D.R. to Reagan* (New York: Morrow, 1982), pp. 258–83, gives a brief overview of economic problems and policies during the Nixon years.

112. Mezvinsky, *A Term to Remember,* p. 57; James L. Sundquist, "Whither the American Party System—Revisited," *Political Science Quarterly* 98 (winter 1983–84): 575.

113. The often-understated Leon Jaworski, for example, later wrote that "It was torture to remain silent in the face of such duplicity" as Nixon himself often provided—*Right and Power,* p. 57. Mezvinsky, in *A Term to Remember,* describes the effect on Congress. His memoir, and

Senator Ervin's *The Whole Truth: The Watergate Conspiracy* (New York: Random House, 1980), are the only inside stories written by members of Congress. Drew's *Washington Journal* remains the best single source of congressional reactions as a whole.

114. William Shakespeare, *Julius Caesar* (New York: New American Library, 1963), p. 57.

115. Ibid., pp. 61–62. There were also those Democrats who, to borrow a line from Plutarch, were "seeking by persuasion to bring all things to such safety, as there should be no peril"— *The Lives of the Noble Greeks and Romans,* translated by Thomas North, ll. 1594–1595.

116. For Nixon's tax transgressions, see Congressional Quarterly, *Watergate,* pp. 581–84. The IRS's tax audit of Nixon had begun in November 1973.

117. Mezvinsky, *A Term to Remember,* p. 81.

118. *Public Papers of the Presidents: Richard Nixon, 1974,* pp. 389–97.

119. For examples of just how thorough the White House editing was, see U.S. House of Representatives, Committee on the Judiciary, 93rd Cong., 2d sess., "Comparison of White House and Judiciary Committee Transcripts of Eight Recorded Presidential Conversations" (Washington, D.C.: Government Printing Office, 1974), passim.

120. Elizabeth Drew, *Washington Journal,* pp. 353–61.

121. U.S. House of Representatives, *Transcripts,* p. 183.

122. Drew, *Washington Journal,* p. 256.

123. As one Democratic senator put it to Elizabeth Drew at the time, "Releasing those transcripts made him more human, one of the boys, . . . [but] making him more human makes him more likely to be impeached." Drew, *Washington Journal,* p. 265.

124. Ibid., pp. 271, 257.

125. Drew's *Washington Journal,* pp. 313 ff, is the best source for the Democratic desires for bipartisanship throughout the Judiciary Committee's impeachment investigation.

126. Ibid., p. 294.

127. Congressional Quarterly, *Watergate,* pp. 628, 650, 659.

128. Ibid., p. 657.

129. Drew, *Washington Journal,* p. 282.

130. Congressional Quarterly, *Watergate,* pp. 647 ff., esp. pp. 655–56.

131. Ben-Veniste and Frampton, *Stonewall,* pp. 294–95.

132. U.S. House of Representatives, *Transcripts,* p. 183.

133. Ibid., p. 705. The phrase is Senator Sam Ervin's.

134. Drew, *Washington Journal,* pp. 330–31; Congressional Quarterly, *Watergate,* p. 715.

135. The best discussion of the effect on public opinion of the Judiciary Committee's deliberations is in Lang and Lang, *Battle for Public Opinion,* pp. 137–80, esp. pp. 168–73.

136. U.S. House of Representatives, *Hearings before the Committee on the Judiciary, 93d Cong.: Debate on Articles of Impeachment* (Washington, D.C.: Government Printing Office, 1974), p. 134.

137. For details of these legal debates, see ibid., pp. 45, 77, 64, 181, 29–30, 13–14, 15, and 111.

138. Drew, *Washington Journal,* 316–17.

139. For the fundamental legal points at issue, see U.S. House of Representatives, *Debate on Articles of Impeachment,* p. 177.

140. Ibid., p. 37.

141. The "marinated in hatred" phrase I owe to the late Bryce N. Harlow, who was kind enough to write me his opinions on October 28, 1984, and to have several interviews with me shortly thereafter.

142. *Debate on Articles of Impeachment,* p. 98.

143. Ibid., p. 256.

144. Drew, *Washington Journal,* p. 363.

145. U.S. House of Representatives, *Debate on Articles of Impeachment,* pp. 339, 342.

146. Ibid., pp. 449 ff.

147. Drew, *Washington Journal,* p. 377.

148. U.S. House of Representatives, *Debate on Articles of Impeachment,* pp. 448–89, 495 ff.

149. Two good sources for the passage and implementation of the War Powers Act are the quadrennial *Congress and the Nation* volumes, published by Congressional Quarterly in Washington, D.C., and Sundquist, *Decline and Resurgence of Congress,* pp. 254–72.

150. A 1983 Supreme Court decision may well have invalidated the "legislative veto" foundation of the War Powers Act. For the basic legal effects, see *Summary and Preliminary*

*Analysis of* I.N.S. v. Chadha, *the Legislative Veto Case, extracted from House of Representatives, Decision concerning the Legislative Veto, Hearings, July 19–21, 1983, Foreign Affairs Committee, the U.S. Supreme Court* (Washington, D.C.: Congressional Research Service, 1983), pp. 231–70. For the story of the Chadha case itself, see Barbara Hinkson Craig, *Chadha: The Story of an Epic Constitutional Struggle* (New York: Oxford University Press, 1987). Anyone who still believes that Congress will move strongly to implement the War Powers Act in the wake of Chadha is operating under a delusion, as the Lebanon intervention of 1982–83, the Grenada invasion of 1983, and the Libyan bombing of 1986 all demonstrate.

151. Drew, *Washington Journal,* p. 366.
152. Drew, *Washington Journal,* p. 385. For other missing tapes, see Ben-Veniste and Frampton, *Stonewall,* pp. 158–59, 170–72, 180–85; and Congressional Quarterly, *Watergate,* pp. 404, 425, 460, 462, 485, and 2-A.
153. Ibid., pp. 383, 388. Also see the day-by-day record in Congressional Quarterly, *Watergate.*
154. Drew, *Washington Journal,* pp. 384–85.
155. Sirica with Stacks, *To Set the Record Straight,* p. 298; Congressional Quarterly, *Watergate,* pp. 761, 766.
156. The text of June 23rd, 1972, conversations is in Congressional Quarterly, *Watergate,* pp. 89-A–91-A.
157. Woodward and Bernstein, *The Final Days,* pp. 403–50.
158. Ibid., pp. 391–92.
159. *Public Papers of the Presidents: Richard Nixon, 1974,* pp. 626–30.
160. Ibid., pp. 630–33.
161. Ben-Veniste and Frampton, *Stonewall,* pp. 299–300.
162. Lang and Lang, *Battle for Public Opinion,* p. 255.
163. Andrew Szasz, "The Progress and Significance of Political Scandals: A Comparison of Watergate and the 'Sewergate' Episode at the Environmental Protection Agency," *Social Problems* 33 (February 1986): 213.
164. Robert T. Hartmann, *Palace Politics: An Inside Account of the Ford Years* (New York: McGraw-Hill, 1980), pp. 242–43.
165. Ibid., pp. 261 ff.
166. Ben-Veniste and Frampton, *Stonewall,* pp. 311–12.
167. Congressional Quarterly, *Watergate,* pp. 792, 790; Hartmann, *Palace Politics,* pp. 262 ff.
168. Congressional Quarterly, *Watergate,* pp. 792, 797–98.
169. Ibid., pp. 798.
170. Hartmann, *Palace Politics,* pp. 240–71, contains the best discussion to date.
171. Congressional Quarterly, *Watergate,* p. 798.
172. Lang and Lang, *Battle for Public Opinion,* p. 313. Also see Doyle, *Not Above the Law,* p. 235.
173. See, for instance, "And Battles Long Ago," *Economist,* 6 December 1986, p. 24.
174. Ben-Veniste and Frampton, *Stonewall,* p. 313; Doyle, *Not Above the Law,* pp. 363, 365.
175. See Congressional Quarterly, *Watergate,* pp. 799 ff., for all of the medical minuet regarding Nixon's health and his court testimony.
176. Ben-Veniste and Frampton, *Stonewall,* pp. 316–87, is the best single source for the Watergate trials.
177. Sirica with Stacks, *To Set the Record Straight,* p. 293.
178. Doyle, *Not Above the Law,* p. 404

## EPILOGUE / *LEARNING LESSONS, REPEATING MISTAKES*

1. Herbert Block, *Herblock Special Report* (New York: Norton, 1974), p. 250.
2. John Dean, *Lost Honor: The Rest of the Story* (Los Angeles: Stratford, 1982), p. 255. See also p. 139.
3. Gladys Ethel Lang and Kurt Lang, *The Battle for Public Opinion: The President, the Press, and the Polls during Watergate* (New York: Columbia University Press, 1982), pp. 307, 102 ff.
4. Alexander Haig, *Caveat: Realism, Reagan, and Foreign Policy* (New York: Macmillan, 1984), p. 128. When the Iran-*contra* affair surfaced in 1986, Haig publicly and privately advised

Reagan to fire a couple of National Security Council staffers and Cabinet officers, refuse to appoint a special prosecutor or allow Congress to hold hearings, and tell the American people, "And if you don't like it, impeach me!" General Haig was running for the Republican nomination for the presidency at the time. *Washington Post National Weekly Edition,* 8–14 February 1988, p. 13.

5. Bob Woodward and Carl Bernstein, *The Final Days* (New York: Simon & Schuster, 1976), p. 37. See also John Ehrlichman, *Witness to Power: The Nixon Years* (New York: Simon & Schuster, 1982), p. 342; and Dean, *Lost Honor,* p. 65.

6. Ehrlichman, *Witness to Power,* pp. 342, 337.

7. For the various aspects of the Iran-Contra affair, see *Report of the Congressional Committees Investigating the Iran-Contra Affair* (Washington, D.C.: Government Printing Office, 1987); and Bob Woodward, *Veil: The Secret Wars of the CIA, 1981–1987* (New York: Simon & Schuster, 1987).

8. Lincoln Steffens, *The Autobiography of Lincoln Steffens* (New York: Harcourt, Brace, 1973), p. 788.

# INDEX